AF600281

EXCAVATING NATIONS

Archaeology, Museums, and the German-Danish Borderlands

GERMAN AND EUROPEAN STUDIES

General editor: Rebecca Wittmann

Excavating Nations

Archaeology, Museums, and the German-Danish Borderlands

J. LAURENCE HARE

UNIVERSITY OF TORONTO PRESS
Toronto Buffalo London

Toronto Buffalo London
www.utppublishing.com

ISBN 978-1-4426-4843-2

Library and Archives Canada Cataloguing in Publication

Hare, J. Laurence, 1975–, author
Excavating nations : archaeology, museums, and the German-Danish borderlands / J. Laurence Hare.

(German and European studies)
Includes bibliographical references and index.
ISBN 978-1-4426-4843-2 (bound)

1. Archaeology – Political aspects – Germany – History. 2. Archaeology – Political aspects – Denmark – History. 3. Archaeology and state – Germany – History. 4. Archaeology and state – Denmark – History. 5. Borderlands – Germany – History. 6. Borderlands – Denmark – History. 7. National characteristics, German – History. 8. National characteristics, Danish – History. I. Title. II. Series: German and European studies

DD126.H37 2015 943′.01 C2014-906561-2

University of Toronto Press acknowledges the financial assistance to its publishing program of the Canada Council for the Arts and the Ontario Arts Council, an agency of the government of Ontario.

University of Toronto Press acknowledges the financial support of the Government of Canada through the Canada Book Fund for its publishing activities.

for Thomas, Anders, and Jack

Contents

Illustrations

Acknowledgments

The initial research for this project was supported by a German Chancellor Fellowship from the Alexander-von-Humboldt Foundation, which enabled me to spend a year working in the archives in Germany and Denmark. At the University of Kiel, I was fortunate to count the late Manfred Jessen-Klingenberg as a mentor, while in Schleswig, the staff at Schloss Gottorf went out of their way to welcome me and support my research. I would especially like to thank the museum's director, Claus von Carnap-Bornheim, who placed the museum's resources at my disposal, and Michael Gebühr and Volker Hilberg, who helped me navigate sections of the museum archive and patiently answered my many questions. For my time in Denmark, I would like to thank Lars Jørgensen and the staff at the National Museum.

Lynda Coon at the University of Arkansas helped me secure a generous pre-tenure leave to finish writing the book. Richard Ratzlaff and Kate Baltais at the University of Toronto Press cheerfully shepherded the manuscript through the publication process, while Nani Verzon in the Department of Geosciences at Arkansas worked with me over a summer to draft a map of the borderlands. I also owe a debt of gratitude to all those who read and critiqued the work at various stages, including Konrad Jarausch, Christopher Browning, Lloyd Kramer, Karen Hagemann, Jay Smith, Benjamin Pearson, Michael Andre, Thomas Goldstein, and Fabian Link. Finally, I would like to thank Nicholas Honerkamp at the University of Tennessee at Chattanooga, who twenty years ago first taught me to love archaeology and whose infectious teaching inspired me to ask the first questions that ultimately led to this project.

Portions of chapters 1 and 2 were previously published as "'When the Germans Ran Wild in Denmark': The Discovery of Prehistory and the German-Danish Wars, 1848–1864," in *From Weimar to Christiania: German and Scandinavian Studies in Context*, edited by Florence Feiereisen and Kyle Frackman (Newcastle: Cambridge

Scholars, 2006), 8–22. Portions of chapters 6 and 7 appeared as "Nazi Archaeology Abroad: German Prehistorians and the International Dynamics of International Collaboration," *Patterns of Prejudice* 48, no. 1 (Feb. 2014): 1–24. And a portion of chapter 7 appeared in a report to the Humboldt Foundation, available as "A Past beyond Reach: The Challenge of Meaning in German Archaeology," in *Ein Jahr wie ein Augenblick: Reflections by the 14th Group of German Chancellor Scholars 2003/2004* (Bonn: Alexander von Humboldt-Stiftung, 2005).

Abbreviations

AA	Alte Akten
Afd.	Afdeling
AFS	Akten zur Flensburger Sammlung
ALM	Schleswig-Holstein Archäologisches Landesmuseum Archiv
ANO	*Annaler for nordisk Oldkyndighed*
AOH	*Aarbøger for Oldkyndighed og Historie*
ASHL	*Archiv für Geschichte, Statistik, Kunde der Verwaltung und Landsrechte der Herzogthümer Schleswig, Holstein und Lauenburg*
BA	Bundesarchiv Berlin
BioA	Biographisches Archiv
BGSH	*Berichte der Gesellschaft für die Sammlung und Erhaltung vaterländischer Alterthümer*
FNN	*Flensburger Norddeutsche Zeitung*
HU	Humboldt Universitätsarchiv
IN	*Itzehoer Nachrichten*
KA	Correspondence Archive
KB	*Kieler Blätter*
KM	Kiel Museum Archives
KNN	*Kieler Neueste Nachrichten*
KZ	*Kieler Zeitung*
NM	Danish National Museum Archives
NS	National Socialism
NSM	*Neues Staatsbürgerliches Magazin*
MuG	Archiv für Museumsgeschichte
OA	Ortsakten
Reg. Akt.	Registratur Akten
SHLA	Schleswig-Holstein Landesarchiv

SHLB	Schleswig-Holstein Landesbibliothek
SJAB	*Sønderjydske Aarbøger*
SN	*Schleswiger Nachrichten*
SP	*Slesvigske Provindsialsforetninger*

THE GERMAN-DANISH BORDERLANDS

The Danish counties of Ribe, Vejle, Fyns Amt, and Sønderjylland are now part of the Region of Southern Denmark (Syddanmark). The former duchy of Holstein and the southern portion of the former duchy of Schleswig are now part of the German federal state of Schleswig-Holstein.

EXCAVATING NATIONS

Archaeology, Museums, and the German-Danish Borderlands

Introduction

The German-Danish borderlands bear the marks of deep roots in the ancient past. Across the southern half of the Jutland Peninsula, where the German federal state of Schleswig-Holstein touches the Danish county of Sønderjylland, thousands of sites, from Stone Age tombs to Iron Age towns, offer proof of a rich prehistoric legacy. Some lie unnoticed, encircled by hedges and roads and the trappings of modern life. Others lie unseen, hidden beneath layers of marshy peat. A few, however, are celebrated, like the Danevirke, the medieval walls that stretch across Schleswig to the Treene River, or Haithabu (Hedeby in Danish), the lost Viking village along the Schlei Inlet. Where the former once bristled with warriors gathering for battle, the latter bustled with the commerce of the Baltic Sea. Today, they are little more than dilapidated mounds and empty fields, with only the occasional pile of brick and stone to signal their dwindling presence.

Such is the prehistory of northern Europe. There were no circuses or colosseums here, no ancient cities of stone with markets and forums, and no temples with columns and friezes. Ubiquitous but unassuming, the remains of antiquity in this region suggest themselves only gingerly. Yet, their power over modern Europeans is unmistakable. For generations, the ancient sites and artefacts of this region enchanted both Germans and Danes, from nineteenth-century Romantics to twentieth-century Nazis and beyond. They evoked a mythical past while offering potent symbols for the present. Above all, they became part of an intellectual project that sought to appropriate the distant past for "national" histories, which brought modern identities into conflict.

The purpose of *Excavating Nations* is to assess the powerful relationships between archaeology and modern nationalism in the German-Danish borderlands. It is the first study to trace the connections between past and present over the course of the entire modern border dispute and the first to use these con-

The Danevirke. Photographed by J. Laurence Hare.

nections to reassess the region's broader importance in European history. The book begins with the emergence of popular antiquarianism and the founding of the first regional museums in the early nineteenth century, when German- and Danish-speakers shared a new vision of the ancient past. Later, it explores how regional antiquity became implicated in the conflicts over the border in the late nineteenth and early twentieth centuries and reveals the close ties between the growth of nationalism and the emergence of professional archaeology and modern museums. Finally, it considers the region's role in the Nazi use of Nordic antiquity and the impact of archaeology on the transformation of the borderlands in the period after the Second World War. At the centre of the study is a cross-border network of scholars, both antiquarian enthusiasts and professional archaeologists, who collaborated to discover and interpret the past and made antiquity available to the present for appropriation. It is thus essential to understand how these scholars claimed and contested common heritages for diverging nationalist ends and made the borderlands a focal point in the creation of German and Scandinavian identities.

Attempts to link the remote past to modern self-conceptions are by no means unique to Schleswig-Holstein, but, as I will argue, Schleswig-Holstein provides a unique way to study them. To understand how, we need simply look at the lessons that have emerged thus far from the growing literature on this topic. Historians have shown how the ancient past was used to create feelings of unity and authenticity within national communities. This has held true in a variety of contexts, as seen in Eric Hobsbawm and Terence Ranger's work on the "invention of tradition" in Britain, or in Susan Crane's history of collecting in nineteenth-century Germany.[1] Moreover, academic institutions and professional scholarly disciplines played especially important roles in the process of forming links between past and present. Such was the conclusion of Suzanne Marchand's study of German philhellenism, which underscored the role of universities and archaeological societies in mediating the cultural influence of classical antiquity,[2] or Yannis Hamilakis' research on antiquities in modern Greece, which highlighted the close ties between the history of archaeology and nationalism. "Archaeology developed," Hamilakis writes, "as an organized discipline at the time when the emerging nation-states were in need of proving their perceived antiquity with physical proofs. It thus developed as a response to the need to produce the national archaeological record."[3] Finally, a number of studies have recognized that claims to the past do not always occur evenly and have consequently emphasized areas where multiple groups contested ancient remains. Recent examples include the debate over the alleged tomb of Philip II in Greece and Macedonia or the bitter struggle over the site of the Babri Masjid mosque in Ayodhya, India.[4] These cases have shown the contested nature of the distant past and have demonstrated the vital role of scholars in shaping the ensuing conflicts.

The German-Danish borderlands experienced similar trends, but with some key differences. In most examples around the world, claims to ancient artefacts may be murky, but the dividing lines between the modern claimants are quite clear. Religious identities, for example, sharply demarcated the struggle at Ayodhya, while ethnicity distinguished the contours of the Macedonian controversy. The German-Danish borderlands are unique because they witnessed protracted attempts to delineate boundaries with no entrenched ethnic, religious, or racial criteria separating the groups. Culture featured prominently in the border debate, and both sides fretted about whether schoolchildren would be taught in the German or Danish languages. Yet, there was nothing essential about either. As we will see, advocates often switched languages to match their shifting political allegiances, and it was easy to elide the problem altogether by appealing to a common set of linguistic and cultural roots. With no seemingly immutable characteristics to divide them, both sides were torn between seeking, on the one hand, a distinctive kernel of German or Danish identity within a shared heritage and appealing, on the other, to a broader "Germanic" or "Nordic" community. In either case, those wishing to discover the prehistoric roots of Schleswig-Holstein depended on the cooperation of their neighbours across the border for access to material and for theoretical guidance. Even if claims to the past were mutually exclusive, all depended on the fruits of a common enterprise.

As in many other cases around the world, the relationship between modernity and antiquity in the German-Danish borderlands was mediated through institutions and disciplines. But here the process occurred most prominently within the museum rather than the university. Just as archaeologists honed their skills by reaching across the border, so too did the museums in which they worked develop through dialogue and exchange with sister institutions outside the particular country. These institutions, as Stine Wiell has shown, frequently became embroiled in the border struggle,[5] but they were also points of contact for moments of reconciliation. Tracing these connections among museums more fully is thus essential for understanding the process of appropriating the past, but it also promises to teach us much about the development of museums and disciplines themselves. It can enrich our understanding of the power dynamics and levels of institutional exchange while adding a layer of complexity to what Robin Ostow has described as the unifying role of museums within the national context.[6]

Exploring the links between the ancient past and the modern nation in this unique setting can also teach us something new about how visions of nations interacted across borders. Many comparative studies have emphasized moments of overlap and movement across boundaries in order to render familiar national categories unstable.[7] This book, by contrast, will not seek merely to undermine the integrity of German and Danish national identities. Instead, it will endeavour to throw into relief the process of their creation. On the one hand, by studying the rhetorical and symbolic use of regional antiquity, the book will show how antiquarians and archaeologists along the frontier sought finer distinctions between themselves and their neighbours across the border in order to integrate their own provincial self-images into new nation-states. On the other hand, it will also explain how nationalist ideologues outside the region drew on evolving notions of the borderlands and even looked across the border to shape their own conceptions of what it meant to be a German or a Dane.

The results of this study will show that the German-Danish borderlands offer much more than a simple case study; rather, they had a central role to play in both German and Danish history. The border dispute itself, of course, was a key engine of German unification in the 1860s, but we will also see how it inspired nationalist thinkers both before and after Otto von Bismarck's war against the Danes answered the so-called Schleswig-Holstein Question. Because they were home to sites and artefacts deemed so critical to discovering northern European origins, the borderlands served as a vital anchor in the construction of German and Scandinavian identities. Prominent German cultural figures such as Jacob Grimm and Richard Wagner saw Schleswig-Holstein as a window to a German past unadulterated by Christian or Mediterranean influences. For Danes, Sønderjylland remained a touchstone in the transformation of Danish nationalism long after the country ceded the region to Germany in 1864. Indeed, Knud Jespersen has described the loss of the duchies of Schleswig and Holstein as "the definitive national trauma" of modern Danish history.[8] At the same time, the region was no less important to the development of professional archaeology. Pioneering Scandinavian scholars such as Jens Jacob Asmussen Worsaae and Sophus Müller shaped conceptions of prehistory through engagement with regional sites and artefacts, while Germans like Gustaf Kossinna placed the region at the centre of sweeping national prehistories that narrated the distant origins of the German nation-state. Understanding how and why this happened warrants an account that not only adds to our understanding of the borderlands, but also makes important contributions to the histories of two nations, as well as the development of a scholarly discipline and its ties to academic institutions, the state, and the public.

Antiquity and Nation

The study of the ancient past began in northern Europe as an amateur affair among learned individuals whose careful and educated approach to sites and artefacts laid the foundations for the highly trained, well-organized, and systematic pursuits of professional archaeologists who came later in the nineteenth and twentieth centuries. This early form of antiquarian study included both investigations of material culture, which we now call archaeology, and research into ancient texts and linguistic artefacts, such as runes and cyphers. The two approaches, while valuable to the study of almost all ancient cultures, were particularly essential in northern Europe, where textual remains were scarce and where the boundaries between the historical and prehistorical eras were more indistinct. Indeed, our knowledge of the Danevirke, which was first built as late as the eighth century CE, is largely derived from archaeological excavation. To accommodate such hazy distinctions, German archaeologists today refer to the study of *Vor- und Frühgeschichte* to place together prehistory with early medieval history. This book will employ the term "prehistory" to refer to the northern European past lasting roughly into the Viking Age, a long period known to us almost entirely from either archaeological evidence or limited and indirect historical accounts. While not strictly true in all cases, the term not only simplifies matters, but also underscores how important material artefacts were to the discovery of the remote past in this region.

Across northern Europe, the popular fascination with prehistory first emerged at the beginning of the nineteenth century. As Germans and Danes grappled with the consequences of the French Revolution and Napoleonic Wars, they entertained questions about the shape and character of their respective nations. In search of answers, they looked to language and culture, but also they sought guidance from the distant past. With the prehistoric remains beneath their very feet, they envisioned not a lost civilization, but a lost period of their own histories. Their discoveries provided tangible links to their ancestors and heightened the mystery of the world in which they had lived. By themselves, the relics could not fully illuminate the darkness surrounding ancient times, but they could provide just enough of a glimpse to fire the imagination of Romantic and nationalist thinkers. After the 1830s, the establishment of regional museums in cities such as Kiel and Flensburg began to shape the practices of collectors and antiquarians into an organized discipline of archaeology dedicated to an objective understanding of the past. Though closely tied to such neighbouring disciplines as history, philology, and anthropology, archaeology eventually came to dominate the investigation of artefacts and inherited the controversies that eventually surrounded them. It was a discipline practised by middle-class professionals and experts who spent long days in the heat with spade in hand, carefully wresting the secrets of the past from the earth. These specialists played the roles of discoverers and preservers. They were teachers and storytellers. And, ultimately, they were agents in the creation of identities.

Such projections onto prehistory were inevitably fraught with difficulty, since ancient communities did not conform to modern political geographies. Indeed, it was in border regions like Schleswig-Holstein and Sønderjylland where the national or ethnic categories defining archaeology began to unravel, and where archaeologists were forced to make choices that altered the way the past informed the present. Moreover, the shifting border in the nineteenth and twentieth centuries challenged overt ascriptions of symbolic value for many ancient remains. The Danevirke, for example, changed hands three times in the nineteenth century, finally becoming German territory after 1864. Even so, it remained a potent symbol that underscored the larger dilemma facing scholars, which was how to reconcile a cooperative, academic pursuit of the past with participation in exclusive nationalist projects.

All nations, of course, have a history, but the idea of a distant past raises especially interesting questions. Are nations "organic" entities with deep roots in the past? Or are they artificial communities firmly grounded in the present?[9] In other words, can one recognize in the distant past an earlier form of a modern national community? While scholars such as Eric Hobsbawm and Benedict Anderson have argued for the artificial nature of so-called ancient traditions,[10] others, most notably John Armstrong and Anthony D. Smith, have maintained that national identities must necessarily rest on some form of pre-existing ethnic or cultural consciousness with a belief in a shared past as an indispensable dimension.[11] "A sense of common history," Smith explains, "unites successive generations, each with its set of experiences which are added to the common stock, and it also defines a population in terms of experienced temporal sequences, which conveys to later generations the historicity of their own experiences."[12] The problem is that the further one follows preceding generations into the past, the less clear they become. As one moves beyond the historical record, the search for a national past looks ever more like a process of creating one, which supports a constructivist interpretation and places the archaeologist in the role of creator. Yet, the process is not an arbitrary one wholly in the hands of a small group of agents. As Anderson has shown, there is an essential difference between a "constructed" community and an "imagined" one. "Much," he writes, "depended on the relationship between the masses and the missionaries of nationalism."[13] It is not enough to create criteria; formulations of identity succeed only when they resonate within the community. Smith, meanwhile, reminds us that there is a deep sense of attachment to nations greater than any strictly artificial construction can engender. Only through integration with pre-existing identities is it possible to legitimize communities on an emotional level. For this reason, histories of nations must align themselves with existing cultural memory structures. They must appeal to symbols and episodes to which individuals feel, or can be convinced to feel, some prior connection.

In linking past and present, antiquarians and the archaeologists who followed them found themselves, consciously or not, following a set of rules pertaining to the national culture in which they worked. Smith refers to this structure as the "ethnie," which constitutes an integrated, holistic system of values, symbols, and shared meanings.[14] Usually, however, the cultural system is never as closed as Smith's model might lead us to believe, and it becomes even more complex in border regions, where zones of hybridity exacerbate the challenges of affixing firm political frontiers. Indeed, this is what made defining the German and Danish nations so difficult, because internally they faced confessional, dynastic, regional, and linguistic cleavages, while externally they shared borders that cut across a number of cultural and historical affinities. Because these factors precluded a unified ethnic identity for both countries, it is important to study how national identities are shaped by neighbouring identities, where commonalities may be just as influential as key differences.

The quest to rediscover and reconstruct the past sought to provide such elusive distinction for Germany and Denmark. Archaeologists took part in a project to derive an authentic German or Danish history as the core of a national identity. They were important not only in appropriating and interpreting symbols and meanings, but also in transmitting or affirming historical narratives. They were thus involved in what John Hutchinson has called "cultural nationalism," which concerns the ways in which a nation's people define themselves in terms of a unique public culture distinguished not from other nation-states as much as from other "national" groups. Historians, Hutchinson explains, "are no mere scholars but rather 'myth-making' intellectuals who combine a 'romantic' search for meaning with a scientific zeal to establish this on authoritative foundations."[15] Archaeologists were especially privileged in this project because they investigated a subject whose firm contours had long since eroded, leaving gaps in the record that lent themselves to conjecture. At the same time, their scientific approach afforded their conclusions a special credibility. In this way, their work provided a sense of tangibility, which derived from the physicality of artefacts and possessed a potential for symbolic appropriation absent in textual history, as well as a degree of malleability, in which the lacunae of material evidence created space for crafting national narratives.

Mindful of these circumstances, archaeologists have investigated the connections between their discipline and the social and cultural contexts in which they operate. In the early 1980s, Bruce Trigger described the impact of such modern ideologies as nationalism and imperialism in the interpretation of archaeological material.[16] Subsequent studies recognized the existence of distinct archaeological traditions corresponding to group identities, which, according to Philip Kohl, "characteristically coincide with nation-states."[17] In subsequent writing, Kohl has shown that such practices can exist in more multicultural polities, such as the Soviet Union, where an ethnos rather than the nation is the primary guiding principle.[18] In either case, national or ethnocultural identities have been powerful lenses through which scholars have viewed and understood archaeology. Kohl has suggested that this may stem from the strong ties between institutionalized scholarship and the state, which can influence the final interpretations of archaeologists eager to please state patrons and secure continued support for research. These sorts of revelations have led scholars to identify and study a number of independent archaeological traditions.[19] In many instances, the nation is the essential unit of analysis. Too few studies, however, have considered instances in which nationalist visions overlap and conflict. Indeed, this is what makes the borderlands so important, since they bring to the fore the complex interactions among various forms of identity within nation-states, and, as Peter Sahlins has shown for the Franco-Spanish border, become sites of negotiation and conflict that ultimately shape the broader consciousness. As Sahlins explains, "States did not simply impose their values and boundaries on local society. Rather, local society was the motive force in the formation and consolidation of nationhood and the territorial state."[20]

Archaeological Networks and the Intellectual Field

In 1844, the Danish prehistorian J.J.A. Worsaae, one of the foremost archaeologists of his generation, made a plea for preserving ancient remains in Denmark. "I wish to make it absolutely clear," he wrote, "what significance the remains of both the prehistoric and historical periods have as national memorials."[21] He directed his message at a broad audience of local officials, teachers, private collectors, and interested clergy, who had a stake in recovering and preserving ancient remains. They listened to Worsaae because he was a recognized expert with unique authority to make judgments about prehistory. He may not have stood alone in rescuing the ancient past, but he and his professional colleagues were nevertheless significant in both systematizing and legitimizing its connections to the present. They were no less critical in making connections to other countries. Indeed, while nationalist thinking dominated emerging narratives of prehistory, cross-border interaction was becoming an increasingly important factor in shaping their contours. After 1830, a cohort emerged with shared interests in the prehistory of northern Europe. They visited one another's collections, participated in cooperative excavations, inducted foreign colleagues into their own national societies, and even shared their precious artefacts. From the earliest days of their work, they comprised an international scholarly community, and their exchanges enabled them to play a central role in linking past to present and in shaping their respective national identities.

To explore this set of relationships, it is helpful to draw on Pierre Bourdieu's concept of the intellectual field, which addresses the problems of creative autonomy that scholars, writers, and artists face as they navigate the pressures inherent in their work and in their surrounding environment. According to Bourdieu, the concept explains how intellectuals create ideas within a shifting constellation of other intellectuals and ideas, and are thus limited by their connections with others in the field. Though they may not be aware of them, intellectual and cultural producers are constrained by the value judgments that attach to their creations, whether they be artistic, literary, or scholarly works.[22] Bourdieu's model has been particularly attractive to intellectual historians like Fritz Ringer, who used it to situate individual thinkers in relation to one another and contextualize their writings and ideas, and to sociologists like Niel Fligstein and Doug McAdam, who have broadened the notion of field to include any sort of "circumscribed social arena" in which one can discern a coherent organizational system.[23]

This study argues that archaeologists in northern Germany and Denmark comprised such a field. Since artefacts were scattered on both sides of the border, archaeologists found it essential to collaborate in order to interpret prehistoric remains. This means that neither Germans nor Danes could directly seize elements of the past for their own nationalist ends because doing so would place them in opposition to the field and deny them the credibility that they enjoyed as professional scholars. In this case, the field in question, which we might variously label as a "network" or a "community," consisted of the personal relationships among individuals, professional associations and orders, and institutions such as universities, museums, and bureaucratic offices. Finally, on the liminal fringes of the field were scholars in neighbouring disciplines, amateur scholars, and interested laymen. Just as in sociology, this study will reconstruct the field through an analysis of both its formal products, including published texts or museum exhibitions, and the textual traces, such as correspondence, field reports, or newspaper articles, that reveal how the field functioned, who participated in it, and how it interacted within the broader social milieu. This book's approach will differ from that of sociologists in that it will treat a particular intellectual field as a historical entity. In other words, it will examine the ways in which the network of regional archaeologists in the borderlands formed and changed over time.[24] In so doing, it will show how engagement with nationalism and the practice of rational scholarship acted as two guiding practices, or what Bourdieu calls *habitus*, that directed the "spontaneous orchestration" of individual voices to contribute towards common goals.[25] As we will see, these two habitus were at times mutually exclusive, forcing scholars to balance their participation in nationalist projects with their commitments to an international academic community.

There are, of course, limits to this approach, not the least of which is the daunting task of defining the parameters of a particular intellectual field. The archaeological community was, after all, not confined merely to Germany and Denmark; Sweden, Norway, Finland, and Great Britain were also heavily involved in the task of reconstructing northern European prehistory. A simple review of the archives of any museum in the region reveals close ties among dozens of institutions in these countries as well as in other parts of Germany, the United States, Russia, Poland, and France. Yet, while it is exceedingly difficult to recreate completely the community of archaeologists engaging in cooperative research during this period, it is possible to draw on a useful cross-section. Fligstein and McAdam have confronted this very problem in Bourdieu's work, and they have suggested that scholars consider interactions among discrete fields with overlapping concerns.[26]

In this case, one critical delimiting factor is the border question, which concerned some but not all of the scholars investigating the prehistory of northern Europe. With that in mind, this study will centre itself on those archaeologists preoccupied with the prehistoric past in southern Denmark and northern Germany, particularly those working in the two key institutions in the region: the National Museum of Denmark in Copenhagen and the Museum for National Antiquities in Kiel. The museums were important not only for their impressive displays of ancient artefacts, but also for the active engagement of the archaeologists who worked there with excavation and preservation. Because of their efforts, the museums at Kiel and Copenhagen became centres of prehistoric research in the region, and after 1864 dominated rival institutions. Limiting the approach in this way, of course, does not preclude glimpses of broader trends, or of contacts between those in the circle of border scholars with those in other parts of Europe. As we will see, these sorts of interactions were an important part of the dynamics shifting the contours of the field. By focusing on a "discrete field" like this one, however, we will better understand how the border question and archaeology informed one another over time.

Cross-Border Scholarship and the Schleswig-Holstein Question

Situated at the base of the Jutland Peninsula between the Baltic Sea and the North Atlantic Ocean, the borderlands consist of the old duchy of Holstein, which lies between the Elbe and Eider rivers north of Hamburg, and the duchy of Schleswig, which stretches north from the Eider to the Kongeå River.[27] Written sources identify a Danish king with claims to lands stretching to the Eider River by the early ninth century CE, but it remains unclear how well organized the Kingdom of Denmark was in this period.[28] By the fifteenth century, however, Danish kings had won title to Schleswig and Holstein, with Schleswig in particular bound in personal union to the crown rather than to the country. Moreover, in the words of the 1460 Treaty of Ribe, they were to be "*up ewig ungedeelt*," or "forever undivided," which later became a central point in the border conflict. Where the Danes sought to incorporate Schleswig into Denmark proper, pro-German activists maintained that the duchies were inseparable. The dispute was worsened by the fact that the two developed along different lines linguistically and culturally. Large numbers of Danish-speakers called Schleswig home, while Holstein was mostly German-speaking, with groups of

Frisian and Low German–speakers inhabiting the western coastal areas. There was also a great deal of language hybridity, with German being the language of many elites along the border and Danish remaining more common among the rural population in the northern parts of the region.

At the beginning of the nineteenth century and until the year 1864, the entire region belonged to the so-called Danish Composite State (Helstat in Danish or Gesamtstaat in German), which included the Kingdom of Denmark, Norway, Iceland, and the duchies of Schleswig and Holstein. The region eventually included the tiny duchy of Lauenburg along the southwestern edge of Holstein, the nearby port city of Lübeck, and North Frisia, a small area encompassing the islands and coastline along western Schleswig. In the nineteenth century, Schleswig was also called Sønderjylland, which means "south Jutland." The name expressed Danish hopes of annexing the territory by semantically linking it to Denmark's Nørrejylland, or "North Jutland," region beyond the Kongeå. After the Second World War, the Danes gave the name to their southernmost county along the border. Finally, in 2007, Denmark reorganized Sønderjylland and the surrounding counties into a new administrative region of Southern Denmark (Syddanmark). Meanwhile, the remaining territories south of the border have been part of the German federal state (Bundesland) of Schleswig-Holstein since the end of the Second World War.

The Schleswig-Holstein region is ideal for finding ancient remains. It is riddled with unexplored bogs and marshes, where the chemical properties of the surrounding peat preserves organic material. The landscape, meanwhile, contains hundreds of grave barrows of earth and rock that have survived undisturbed amid centuries of agriculture and therefore represent nearly perfect time capsules from the periods in which they were first made. After the end of the Napoleonic Wars, the region became the scene of frenetic archaeological activity. In the 1830s, local amateurs founded an antiquities society with the blessing of the Danish government. From the beginning, the society and its museum in Kiel were products of cooperation between Germans and Danes. Their success depended on the expertise of scholars working in Copenhagen, who donated artefacts, and the hard work and determination of regional collectors, who provided a wealth of new information beyond the reach of scholars living in the capital.

By the 1830s, however, many Germans and Danes had become dissatisfied with the "Composite State" solution by which since 1773 the kings of Denmark had governed Schleswig and Holstein as an addition to their own lands.[29] Within the context of a common liberal nationalist movement, Danish-speakers worked to consolidate their cultural domination over northern Schleswig by demanding more widespread use of Danish in schools and government, while German-speakers sought to preserve their traditional language and culture by seeking autonomy for the two duchies. A growing German separatist movement led to civil war in 1848 and then war with Prussia in 1864, after which time the region became part of the German Empire (Kaiserreich). With the German defeat in the First World War, the two sides agreed to hold a plebiscite in 1920, in which a portion of North Schleswig voted to return to Denmark. Active agitation for changing the border persisted, however, until shortly after the end of the Second World War.

In a recent analysis of identity formation along the border, Peter Thaler has shown that the Schleswig-Holstein dispute always entailed both a political and cultural dimension.[30] Interest in the past was one of the most important points at which the two converged. Inge Adriansen has shown, for example, the many instances in which Germans and Danes in the late nineteenth and early twentieth centuries sought to alter perceptions of the border wars by building or destroying monuments commemorating national leaders, key battles, or fallen soldiers.[31] Thaler, meanwhile, has delineated the role of historical scholarship in using the alleged settlements of ancient tribes to naturalize claims to territory. Thus, where Adriansen suggests that the border conflict raged in the realm of cultural memory even in years of peace, Thaler tears down the tidy distinctions between history and memory. Just as John Hutchinson's work implicates historical scholarship in the crafting of national identity, so Thaler's points out how "history struggled to escape its political entanglements."[32]

In a similar way, this book will inquire into how archaeologists related their research to the cultural memory of the borderlands while preserving their academic orientation. Whether employed as symbolic imagery, used to justify territorial claims, or disputed as national property, ancient artefacts were part of each stage of the conflict, and archaeologists were often at the forefront of the debate. Along the way, they struggled to maintain contacts across the border and carry on cooperative research. Relations became increasingly strained in the early twentieth century, when nationalist and racialized perspectives overshadowed the archaeological discipline and coloured the fierce debates over the 1920 plebiscite. Finally, during the Nazi era, the cooperation between German archaeologists and the Third Reich, coupled with the German occupation of Denmark during the Second World War, threatened the viability of the archaeological community.

The involvement of archaeologists in both the "political" and "cultural" dimensions raises two key problems. The first concerns the role of borders and frontiers in national development, which since 1989 has grown in tandem with renewed interest in nationalism studies.[33] In approaching the issue, anthropologists like Thomas Wilson and Hastings Donnan have focused on generating overarching theories to understand borders as "domains of contested power, in which local, national, and international groups negotiate relations of subordination and control."[34] They complain, however, that anthropologists have neglected to problematize the concepts of state and nation. For this, we might turn to historians such as Peter Sahlins, who has emphasized the fluid nature of nation-states. "National identity," he explains, "is a socially constructed and continuous process of defining 'friend' and 'enemy,' a logical extension of the process of maintaining boundaries between 'us' and 'them' within more local communities."[35] Sahlins thus argues that this process plays out along frontiers, which makes them especially important in forming nation-states.

Other scholars have questioned these conclusions, which leads to a second problem dealing with the ways in which ordinary people in the borderlands responded to nationalist ideology. Studies on Central European borderlands from James Björk and from Tara Zahra have questioned the salience of nationalism in frontier regions, pointing to the surprising persistence of "national indifference" into the twentieth century.[36] In his study of language activists in the Austrian Empire, Peter Judson goes as far as to claim that "most inhabitants of such regions rarely viewed themselves specifically as 'frontier people' or their regions as frontiers between nations."[37] By emphasizing other forms of identity, these scholars have discouraged simple models that place borderlands in a strictly dialectical relationship with either states or national identities. In this study, a related concern will be to assess the ways in which antiquarians and archaeologists acted as agents of the nation as they worked within a complex constellation of identities and political pressures in the borderlands.

It is ultimately from this set of problems that the key questions of this book emerge. How and why, for example, did Germans and Danes look to the distant past as a criterion of modern identity? In what ways did they relate antiquity to the present? And finally, what were the consequences of using the past in this way? By emphasizing the relationships among the scholars working with ancient remains, this study will approach these questions by examining both the process of professionalization in archaeology and the relative power of archaeologists to employ their scholarship in a larger nationalist project. Above all, it will consider the ways in which archaeologists in the borderlands reconciled their scholarly obligations with their nationalist commitments, and how they thus affected the development of national identity in their respective countries. Such questions entreat us to explore the uses of the past, to find its limits, to gauge its implications, and, finally, to assess its impact on two bordering nation-states.

1 Antiquarians and Patriots

In the 1830s, a new passion for the past awakened in the Kingdom of Denmark. Across Jutland, the Danish islands, and the southern duchies of Schleswig and Holstein, a cohort of enthusiasts scoured the countryside for the relics of a lost heritage. They explored ancient structures: passage graves descending into deep vaults, rocky cairns crowning hillsides, and solemn barrows ringed with stone. They collected, bought, and sold the artefacts they found. They corresponded with fellow collectors, and they formed associations to advance common understanding. More than mere curiosity seekers, this band of antiquarians yearned to know the past and strove to become curators of cultural memory. Ultimately, they erected new structures: museums to share the fruits of discovery and to fashion an image of the past that would manifest its message for the present. As they toiled, another revolution was underway. But where the first looked to the distant past, the other cast its gaze to the future. Defined by tenets of liberalism and commitments to nationalism, a movement for political reform struggled against the bonds of the Restoration Era and promised to tear at the fabric of the Danish Helstat. It brought to the fore latent divisions among German- and Danish-speakers, raised questions about the fate of Schleswig-Holstein, and launched the borderlands into decades of conflict.

Perhaps nowhere were these developments more momentous than in Kiel, a seaside town on the west coast of Holstein. During the 1830s, Kiel was not only home to the chief figures of the revolutionary movement, but also it was central to the search for northern European prehistory. It was in Kiel where antiquarianism and nationalism first collided, but it was also here where rival leaders worked together to unlock the secrets of the past. The result was a remarkable collaboration that yielded the region's first antiquities association and museum. Among those who took part were Niels Nikolaus Falck (1784–1850), a renowned legal scholar who presided over the duchies' first representative assembly; Christian Paulsen (1798–1854) and Christian Flor (1792–1875), who launched the pro-Danish movement in Schleswig; and Christian Jürgensen Thomsen (1788–1865), a luminary of early archaeology and founder of the National Museum of Denmark in Copenhagen. Together, these men would help unlock the mysteries of regional prehistory, cultivate a science of prehistoric study, and foster a network of German- and Danish-speaking scholars.

In 1830, these twin developments implicated the distant past in a larger set of cultural and political metamorphoses. On the one hand, the antiquities society, formally called the Schleswig-Holstein-Lauenburg Society for the Collection and Preservation of National Antiquities (Schleswig-Holstein-Lauenburgische Gesellschaft für die Sammlung und Erhaltung vaterländischer Alterthümer), reflected an enlightened confidence in knowing the heretofore unknowable. By seeking to share that knowledge with the public, it conformed to the political ambitions of liberals mired in a lingering age of absolutism. In this era, the search for antiquity was an act of patriotism, and the care of the past was a claim upon its present. The antiquities society was the sort of organization that Jürgen Habermas has identified as important to bringing private pursuits into the "public sphere" and to creating an alternative arena for political participation.[1] On the other hand, the collecting institution, named the Kiel Museum for National Antiquities (Museum für vaterländische Alterthümer zu Kiel), resonated on an emotional level in keeping with Romantic sensibilities. For visitors, the collection effaced the millennial distance between all things modern and ancient and united the two within an organic community. But the connection was a tenuous one, and, as Susan Crane has pointed out in her study of historical consciousness, hinged as much on a sense of the past's absence as on its presence in the museum.[2] An appreciation for the artefacts on display thus demanded acts of imagination to fill in the missing pieces and uncover insights hidden within the objects. Taken together, these trends suggest that the rise of antiquarianism, which was also the birth moment of archaeology, stood on a fault line of modernity astride hopes for change and concerns about its inexorability.

At this early intersection of modernization and modernity, antiquarianism in Schleswig-Holstein connected with new forms of identity and facilitated multiple levels of belonging. It supported personal curiosities, but also operated within provincial space. For Germans, in particular, it informed conceptions of Heimat, a word denoting "homeland" that invoked a broad range of geographical and cultural attachments. Indeed, it is tempting to see the regional interest in antiquities as a Heimat phenomenon preceding the German nationalist movement of the later nineteenth century. But Peter Blickle has countered that Heimat was not "a mobile term in the progression from provincialism to nationalism."[3] In other words, it was not a milestone to larger constructions of identity. Nor was it a simple palliative to ease the transition into modernity. Rather, the example of Schleswig-Holstein shows us that Heimat was an idea that enveloped a complex matrix of legal, dynastic, linguistic, and cultural ties.[4] With the outbreak of revolution in 1848, the lines between the opposing sides may have seemed less ambiguous, but, for both Germans and Danes, the region remained a concoction of provincial self-conceptions, statist loyalties, and burgeoning national identities.

It was no coincidence that the popularity of antiquities collecting occurred alongside the rise of liberal nationalism in the region. The founders of the Kiel Museum were integral to the emerging "Schleswig-Holstein Question," and they made the past available for each side to claim as its own. But, as this chapter will argue, there was more to antiquarianism than the national issue. Even where the two were directly related, the overlapping loyalties at work in the founding days of antiquarian scholarship complicated the appropriation of prehistory for the border struggle. For this reason, understanding how the ancient past came to operate as a cultural resource in later years warrants an account of its "discovery" in the early nineteenth century. Specifically, it calls for us to examine how the founding of the Kiel Museum came to intersect with three overlapping trends: the emergence of a new historical consciousness, the shifting conceptions of identity, and the legal, political, and cultural debate over the borderlands.

Key to these early years was the *antiquarian*, a term used here to identify an explorer of the past who stood above the uninitiated collector and prefigured the professional archaeologist. Among antiquarians, of course, there were those with greater or lesser knowledge, and one could easily argue that a pioneering figure like Christian Jürgensen Thomsen was an archaeologist in the truest sense. In placing him among the antiquarians here, I am making a claim about his generation, whose interest in artefacts first engendered a scholarly orientation towards prehistory but lacked the methods, norms, and dispositions of professional archaeology. As this chapter will show, Thomsen's generation was distinct from those that followed both in terms of scholarly development and political commitment. But in founding the first collecting institutions and in establishing the first collegial networks, they were no less critical to the creation of the discipline.

The Origins of Antiquarianism in the Danish Helstat

The early nineteenth century, of course, was not the first time that antiquities had piqued interest in Denmark and the southern duchies. For two hundred years, private collectors maintained "curiosity cabinets" (variously known in

German as *Kunstkammern*, *Schatzkammern*, or *Wunderkammern*) filled with biological and mineralogical specimens, along with historical and prehistorical artefacts. The cabinets, which first appeared in Italy, manifested the Renaissance idea of the "universal man" (*uomo universale*) and reflected the diversity of the world and the breadth of learning of the collector. In this way, they marked the beginning of a collecting impulse that would inform the museums and libraries of later centuries.[5]

In Denmark, the most noted of the early collectors was Ole Worm (1588–1654), a university professor and personal physician to King Christian IV (r. 1588–1648). Worm had likely been inspired while studying in Italy during the early 1600s, and he filled his own cabinet with an impressive array of biological and fossil specimens.[6] But he was also interested in human artefacts, and helped turn northern European humanists to the remains of ancient Germanic cultures.[7] As a scholar of ancient languages, Worm focused his studies on Denmark's ancient runes, which he reproduced in his 1643 work, *Danish Monuments* (*Danicorum Monumentorum*). The *Monumentorum* was also noteworthy because it featured an early rendering of the first Golden Horn of Gallehus, one of the most celebrated artefacts in Denmark. In 1639, a young peasant girl named Kirsten Svendsdatter reportedly unearthed this stunning gilded artefact in northwestern Schleswig. It appeared to be a curved horn adorned with relief carvings of animals and humans and fantastic creatures. Christian IV claimed it for his royal Kunstkammer, where Worm studied it and declared it to be a war horn from the age of the legendary early medieval king Frode Fredegod.[8] Worm's analysis and illustration later became important in popularizing the horn, which, along with a second horn discovered in the same area in 1734, became national symbols of Denmark.

After Worm's death in 1654, his private collection joined the horn of Gallehus as the core of a new Kunstkammer owned by Christian's successor, King Frederik III (r. 1648–1670).[9] By this time, the cabinet had become an expression of rivalry with the dukes of Holstein-Gottorf to the south.[10] Ever since the Thirty Years War (1618–1648), the dukes had been at odds with the Danish crown, and through an alliance with Sweden had managed to carve out an autonomous territory in Schleswig. At the Gottorf Palace (Schloss Gottorf) in the town of Schleswig, Duke Frederick III (1597–1659) purchased a noted collection from the Dutch physician Bernhard Pauldanus (1550–1633), and later passed it on to his son, Duke Christian Albrecht (1641–1695).[11] Albrecht, who founded the university in Kiel that now bears his name, expanded the collection and placed emphasis on local finds. For this, he enlisted the help of Johann Daniel Major (1634–1693), a professor in Kiel who, like Worm, had studied medicine in Italy. Major's interests lay primarily with botany, but he was also an avid numismatist and was well placed to help the duke acquire curios from across the area.[12]

In 1692, Major published a book based on his research entitled *Populated Cimbria* (*Bevölckertes Cimbrien*). Inspired by Worm's *Monumentorum*, it drew on an eclectic mix of biblical genealogy, Classical histories, and artefact evidence to tell the story of the Cimbri tribe, which had allegedly come down from Schleswig to make war on the Romans in the second century BCE. Major traced the etymology of the Cimbri back to Gomer, the grandson of Noah, and relied on *Plutarch's Lives* for evidence that the Cimbri had ultimately settled around the Anglia region of eastern Schleswig. In the second half of the book, Major explored Cimbrian culture by cataloguing prominent artefacts from ancient burial sites in the region. He acknowledged distinctions among grave goods fashioned from stone, copper, and iron, and he recognized the likelihood that higher-quality artefacts, such as engraved swords and silver objects, marked the burials of higher-status individuals.[13]

By placing regional remains into a universal history, Major enhanced the status of the ducal collection. Indeed, its scholarly worth became an emblem of the dukes' aspirations in Europe, which later included designs on the Swedish and Russian thrones. Later, its prestige made the collection a key prize in the ongoing conflicts between the Gottorf dukes and the Danish monarchy. During the Great Northern War (1700–1721), the Danish King Frederik IV (r. 1699–1730) defeated Christian Albrecht's grandson, Charles Frederick (1700–1739) and seized both the collection and the ducal lands. The artefacts became a part of the royal Kunstkammer, while the duchy of Schleswig came into personal union with the monarchy, setting the stage for the border conflicts of the nineteenth century.[14]

The founders of the later museums in Copenhagen and Kiel were in many ways the heirs of collectors like Worm and Major. The early collectors had not only sought to classify and interpret the pieces in their collections, but also they had been conscious of their political ramifications. Worm's *Danicorum Monumentorum* was a product of its author's broad interests, but limited its horizons to the sovereign realm of the Danish king. In a similar way, Major's genuine curiosity about ancient peoples highlighted the domain of the dukes in Schleswig. Later, the cabinets themselves became important, particularly after the emphasis began to shift to acquiring local pieces. By the time of the Great Northern War, ownership of a collection had begun to imply dominion over its provenance.

Similar trends re-emerged as features of nineteenth-century antiquarianism, but there were also marked differences between the patriotic antiquarian and the humanist collector of the late northern Renaissance. First among these was a new sense of the value of artefacts. Where Worm had been primarily concerned with rune stones because they represented sources of text, later collectors followed Major's lead in considering the meanings of the objects themselves. This was a departure from previous centuries, when the ancient monuments dotting the countryside were dismissed as dimly understood "heathen altars" for pagan worship.[15] Even Major, who used artefacts in his history, perpetuated myths about massive burial mounds as the work of giants, which was a common belief based on Protestant readings of scripture.[16] Indeed, this interpretation lived on in German terms such as *Hünengrab* or *Riesenbett*, invoking variants of the word "giant" to describe massive mounds and long passage graves.

By contrast, the new antiquarians, who emerged from an Enlightenment tradition of biblical criticism, were not compelled to see remains through a scriptural lens. They did not necessarily reject Christian themes, but adopted instead a more ambiguous perspective on northern European prehistory as both foreign and familiar. As Rosemary Sweet has argued in her study of English antiquaries, such a lingering impression of strangeness mattered because, as she explained, "The recognition of the past as qualitatively different from the present is obviously fundamental to being able to conceive of the desirability of actively preserving a building or an object simply on account of its age."[17] At the same time, a sense of familiarity was equally critical because it offered the potential of forging, or reforging, a relationship with the past using the artefacts as guides and as tangible links.

For this reason, the desire to collect was joined by the imperative to preserve. And this, in turn, drove collectors to form the early associations, the first of which was the Royal Commission for the Preservation of Antiquities (Kongelige Commission til Oldsagers Opbevaring). Among its most important members was C.J. Thomsen, whose contributions to archaeology became possible only through his dedication to saving the country's prized artefacts. When Thomsen joined the Commission in 1816, the royal collection had fallen into deep peril. During the Napoleonic Wars, the artefacts had been endangered by the two British bombardments of Copenhagen, in 1801 and 1807. In between, an unscrupulous goldsmith named Niels Heidenreich had stolen and smelted a number of pieces, including the Golden Horns of Gallehus.[18]

The wartime disasters informed a second key trend of the new antiquarianism, which was its concern with overlapping conceptions of modern identity. One was a national identity inspired by the struggle for and against Napoleon. In Denmark, the Golden Horns of Gallehus embodied the nation's great potential and its tragic loss, particularly after they were celebrated in the 1803 poem "Guldhornene," by Adam Gottlob Oehlenschläger (1779–1850). Oehlenschläger, who had family roots in the region where the horns were recovered, was already a well-regarded poet when he met Henrik Steffens (1773–1845), a student of the German natural philosopher Friedrich Schelling. After an intense conversation with Steffens, Oehlenschläger became enchanted with the ideas of German Romanticism, which he connected with the story of the Golden Horns. Unaware that they had been stolen only a year earlier, he allegedly halted his ongoing work and at a feverish pace penned an ode using the horns to unite a fallen present with a glorious mythical past.[19] In the poem, this theme is clear from the moment of the first horn's appearance, "When the North was uplighted / And with earth heav'n united." Oehlenschläger interprets the discovery as an act of providence, and describes ghostly heralds entrusting the horn into the care of its finders: "To hold in devotion / Our gift, is your duty!" The poem later strikes a tragic note as modern eyes fail to see the relics as they were intended, but view them instead as mere trinkets. The price for this failure is the loss of the horns: "Back is taken what is given / Vanished is the relic holy."[20]

The piece resonated with Danes because it mirrored so closely the real fate of the horns. It also evoked the recent history of Denmark, which was also seen as a treasure with a storied past demanding the love and care of all Danes. At the same time, the poem relied on a critical fusion of pagan and Christian elements that later became a leitmotif of Denmark's fascination with antiquity. It inspired a so-called Nordic Renaissance, in which Danes sought to extol the uniqueness of their country by appealing to prehistory but without sacrificing the Christian roots of modern Danish culture. In other words, they sought to elide the tension between longing for the particular and remaining embedded in the universal. In 1807, the Danish philosopher Nikolaj Frederik Severin Grundtvig (1783–1872) published perhaps the most crucial work of this new ethos, *The Mythology of the North*, in which he wrote, "The scholars of the North cannot and must never forget that the North also has a heroic age of its own to which they have a double relationship, both a closer one and a deeper one."[21] Echoing the sentiments in Oehlenschläger's poem, Grundtvig maintained that Denmark's special place in Europe stemmed from its fusion of Christian and Nordic themes, and he argued that understanding this mixed cultural legacy was important both for advancing the nation and reforming the Danish Church. As Leni Yahil has explained, "His striving for religious freedom merged with his patriotism. He stated that, unlike the Latin peoples who had adopted Roman culture along with Christianity, the Norse peoples had become Christian without abandoning their folk characteristics."[22]

The themes of the Nordic Renaissance became especially important after the end of the Napoloenic Wars. Denmark, the former ally of France, ceded its claim to Norway and Pomerania and surrendered its trading fleet, which eroded the country's economy and international standing.[23] Many Danes responded to their declining fortunes by rejecting grandiose visions of Denmark as a European power in favour of a fresh emphasis on the uniqueness of Danish national character. What followed was a period of intense introspection that fostered the advent of Romanticism and fuelled interest in Nordic mythology and antiquity.[24] Oehlenschläger's poem, which was intended as a critique of the missed opportunities of its past discoverers, took on a new meaning as an allegory of Denmark's own lost glory and desires for a more authentic renewal.

In the German-speaking lands, a similar mix of wartime humilitation and pride sparked a fresh look at prehistory. As Grundtvig was writing his *Mythology of the North*, Napoleon was defeating Prussia and dismantling the vestiges of the Holy Roman Empire. In response, German writers also fostered unity by appealing to the particularities of German character, which often led them to draw on historical examples. Most notably, Johann Gottlieb Fichte's 1808 *Address to the German Nation* looked to the Middle Ages for the source of the Germans' "spirit of piety, of honor, of modesty, and of the sense of community." Fichte also lionized the "good and honest" Germans of the pre-Christian era, but dismissed them as "semi-barbarians."[25] But others were eager to look to the ancient Germanic tribes for inspiration. The most popular subject by far was the Germanic chieftain Arminius (Hermann), who had defeated a Roman army at the Battle of Teutoburg Forest in the year 9 CE. Germans celebrated Arminius' victory in a variey of literary works during the later eighteenth century, most notably in a dramatic trilogy written by Friedrich Klopstock (1724–1803). Six years after Klopstock's death and only three after the Prussian defeats, Heinrich von Kleist (1777–1811) penned an updated drama, *Die Hermannsschlacht*, that drew parallels with the Napoleonic era by emphasizing the nobility of German resistance to a greater power and lauding the example of self-sacrifice to a larger cause.[26]

In terms of "seeing" the ancient past in a new patriotic light, perhaps none surpassed the vision of the artist Caspar David Friedrich (1774–1840). During the darkest moments of the wars, Friedrich painted a series of landscapes incorporating ancient monuments from his homeland in Pomerania. Years before, he had honed his gifts with landscapes at the Royal Academy of Arts in Copenhagen under the tutelage of Jens Juel (1745–1802), a cornerstone artist of Denmark's "golden age" of painting (1800–1850). After settling in Dresden in the 1790s, Friedrich became an active proponent of German unification. When Saxony allied with France in 1806, Friedrich left in protest and reportedly stayed on the Pomeranian island of Rügen with the poet Ludwig Gotthard Kosegarten (1758–1818). The two may have visited some of the island's ancient burial mounds, which had inspired Kosegarten's 1778 poem, "Das Hünengrab."[27] Kosegarten's poem was in part an ode to the mysterious sites:

> Chilling memory whispers around me.
> Between the moss-covered stones
> Among the three rustling oaks I sit
> Here.[28]

And it was also a critique of the present:

> Where are the commonplace morals?
> Where are the chastity of maidens and youthful shame
> Buried under the thousand-year-old stone.[29]

Inspired by Kosegarten's vision, Friedrich rendered similar sentiments in a visual medium. That year, he painted the burial mounds of Rügen to capture the spirit of his own distressed age. As Tina Grütter has argued, "Friedrich had found in the Hünengrab a form for the romanticization of patriotism: this was a generally understood emblem for a common past of the German nation."[30]

The parallels between Oehlenschläger and Grundtvig are striking. One image, *Cairn in the Snow*, recalls Kosegarten by depicting a stone-topped cairn and three oaks, but the greenery and cacophony of nature in the latter's work is replaced by a darkened and cold landscape, evoking loss. And, in Wieland Schmied's interpretation, the barren trees stand as "sentinels" around the snow-covered cairn as a reminder to safeguard the past. The work's emphasis on man's place in nature and its meditation on death thus corresponded to the sense of melancholy popular among early nineteenth-century Romantics. But Friedrich, much like Oehlenschläger and Grundtivg, was also concerned with Christian notions of resurrection and rebirth. *Cairn in the Snow* thus contrasts the coldness of winter with the hint of spring and renewal. Schmied explains, "The trees have not died; they will be green again and bear leaves ... [S]now was for Friedrich the great white cloth, the symbol of highest purity, beneath which nature makes ready for new life."[31] Such a portrayal stands in contrast to Friedrich's 1830 piece, *The Temple of Juno at Agrigentum*, which Helmut Börsch-Supan has interpreted as a critique of German classicism. Where the sterile background around the Greco-Roman temple was meant to "emphasize the desolation of the pagan world," the scenes on Rügen allowed Friedrich to blend his Christian and German sensibilities and to portray the defeats of his time as a temporary trial preceding a triumphant return.[32]

The antiquarians of the early nineteenth century similarly wedded their collecting and preserving activities to a desire for self-definition. It was not the case, however, that they were solely responding to patriotic fervour; rather, they were also cultivating the individual self. Of course, the nineteenth-century Renaissance historian Jacob Burckhardt recognized long ago that notions of selfhood were not unique to the modern era, but were prevalent at least as early as the fifteenth century. And as he explained, the "many-sided men" of the Renaissance based their individualism on the model of antiquity. Burckhardt believed that at the root of the process lay the objectification of the wider world, which freed the "spiritual individual" from its material moorings. "In the same way," Burckhardt noted, "the Greek had once distinguished himself from the barbarian."[33] Worm and Major belonged to this trend, and even if they sought their own distinction in the very remains of the barbarian, they nevertheless aspired to bring the whole world into the confines of their cabinet so that they might situate themselves within it.

How, then, was the nineteenth-century collector unique? At first glance, the difference merely seems to be one of degree. The preceding century had witnessed an increasing awareness of the self, culminating in what Charles Taylor has called a "radical reflexivity," defined as a "turn to the self as a self."[34] As Taylor has argued, this pervasive subjectivity, which manifested itself in contemporary novels and law codes based on personal rights, valorized the particularities of the individual. But the upshot was a disconcerting sense of alienation. Building on this point, Jerrold Seigel has explained that alienation was not merely a separation of the "material" and the "reflective" selves. Rather, what was missing was a sense of divine purpose to fill the space between the two. Enlightenment secularism had divorced individuals from the "cosmic architecture" that had imposed harmony from on high. Thus, the real distinction in the modern era was the need to fashion a new bridge between forms of selfhood, whether expressed in Cartesian terms as "mind" and "body" or in the vernacular of German Idealism as "subject" and "object."[35]

With this dilemma in mind, I would argue that antiquarians turned to the ancient past as part of a larger search for the means to overcome the pangs of modern alienation. To understand how, it is helpful to return to landscape art and to two pieces from Germany and Denmark: Caspar David Friedrich's *A Walk at Dusk*, painted around 1830, and *Autumn Lanscape: Hankehøj near Vallekilde*, painted in 1847 by Johan Thomas Lundbye (1818–1848). Each of these works depicts a single, anonymous figure contemplating an ancient burial monument. Friedrich shows a cloaked man huddled before a stone cairn. The monument rests in a small field ringed by trees and illuminated in the deepening dusk by a sliver of moon. Lundbye's image is a sunny pastoral setting in which a young boy, his back to the viewer, has paused to contemplate a barrow on the island of Sjælland.

Both paintings express nationalist sentiments. Friedrich had already marked cairns as key symbols of Germany, and Lundbye's work was typical of a "national Romantic" style and one that he painted only a few months before rushing off to die in the First German-Danish War.[36] But beyond their patriotism was a deeply personal element. As he painted *A Walk at Dusk*, Friedrich had become increasingly preoccupied with the end of his life, and this work represented a symbolic encounter with death and renewal.[37] Lundbye, meanwhile, painted *Hankehøj* in part because it lay close to his uncle's farm and would have been as much a feature of his own memory as of a larger national consciousness. Moreover, each painting undertakes a more general meditation on selfhood, in which the viewer considers not the monuments themselves, but the moment of connection between the modern figures and the ancient ruins. In this way, the paintings recall the line in Kosegarten's poem, "Among the three rustling oaks I sit / Here," which shifts from a description of the surroundings to an emplacement of the subject. The anonymous figures, with a cloaked face or back turned, invite the viewer to participate in an encounter with the past. And that experience involves a reintegration between the modern self and the ancient other buried beneath the earth. Indeed, the natural setting was critical to the relationship between descendant and ancestor. The artists deliberately emphasized or even manipulated the setting to embed the monuments within a landscape of grass, moss, and trees. The connection between modern and ancient evinces the alienation of the former while highlighting the possibility of reconciliation posed by the latter. The ancestors entombed within the monuments have, in other words, achieved the very rootedness in nature so greatly desired by the nineteenth-century Romantic.

Taken together, such yearnings afforded the monuments a utopian quality that not only idealized the ancient past's harmony with nature, but also epitomized qualities lost in the present: humility, morality, etc. The sites could thus easily speak to an abstract patriotism while retaining an intimate and provincial character. The monument celebrated as an archetype in art was, after all, almost always a named site recognizable to those who lived nearby. It could therefore hold appeal as both an expression of nation and regional homeland. Making these links, however, did not require the vicarious eye of the artist or poet. Rather, the Renaissance men of Worm's and Major's day had already offered collecting as an alternative. Though antiquarians may have lived within a town miles from ancient monuments, they could bring the experience closer by collecting its artefacts. As long as a record of provenance was preserved, the artefact could evoke for the collector both the rooted monument and the ancestry it represented. It could, in short, grant its owner a tangible means of becoming the figure in the painting.

The cabinet of curiosities served as a point of departure for the new ethos of the nineteenth-century collector. Its original purpose as a marker of status and erudition remained as a palimpsest of an earlier era. The time and money required for collecting meant that it remained an elite activity, even if it was one that now testified more broadly to membership in the emerging middle class. But it was more than a status symbol. It had become a portal for communion with a deeper past. This is what was new about the new antiquarianism. Even if the ways of interpreting the past would change in the ensuing decades, the potential for objective knowledge was nevertheless present in the earliest collections. Rather, the new antiquarianism distinguished itself, above all, in its emotional response to northern European antiquity. It afforded new purpose to the search for artefacts, and gave fresh relevance to finds. The result was a fusion of Enlightenment and Romantic impulses that would drive the study of European prehistory while assuring it a place in the social and political turmoil to come.

Collecting and Community in the Duchies

Nineteenth-century antiquarianism was a public pursuit. Where the collectors of old had laboured for royal or ducal houses or maintained their own private holdings, the enthusiasts of the 1830s were keen to share their work with their countrymen. In Schleswig-Holstein, collectors published reports of their finds, urged their peers to join cooperative networks, and longed for a museum of their own. In the duchies, this enterprise found a friend in Christian Jürgensen Thomsen. Shortly after joining the Royal Antiquities Commission, Thomsen's priority had been to protect the treasures in the Kunstkammer. Since the theft of the Golden Horns in 1802 had been a simple matter of an unsecured door,[38] Thomsen knew that he needed a safer facility for the collection. At the same time, there were already calls among leading Danish scholars for the establishment of a national museum in Copenhagen. Fortunately, ongoing restoration of the Christiansborg Palace, which had burned over twenty years earlier, offered an opportunity for Thomsen to move the collection to an elegant and safe space in the heart of the capital.

Once he had safely ensconced the artefacts in their new home, Thomsen set about creating a more orderly system for storing the finds. At first, his goal was more aesthetic than scientific. He simply sought a means of organizing finds to make them more presentable for display to the public. In part, this reflected a shift in the practice of collecting. Where sixteenth-century cabinets had celebrated the unity of diverse objects, the displays of the eighteenth emphasized difference and taxonomy. This change stemmed from the encyclopedic regimes of knowledge found in Enlightenment thought, and yielded a process by which the collector sought to deduce a natural order by uncovering patterns in the arrangement of material objects.[39]

By 1818, Thomsen had created a classification scheme based on the material composition of artefacts, whether they were made of stone, bronze, or iron. In accordance with Danish law, Thomsen had been paying individuals to hand over artefact finds, and his plan allowed him both to organize the existing collection and to anticipate new acquisitions.[40] But the process soon suggested a means of understanding the temporal progression of the distant past. The result was Thomsen's so-called Three Age system, which followed careful comparative analyses of style, manufacture, and associated artefacts to establish ages of prehistoric development, ranging from the earliest "Stone Age," through an intermediary "Bronze Age," and ending with an "Iron Age."[41] The system helped Thomsen understand the sequence of cultural evolution while cultivating public interest in prehistory. It infused individual pieces with a larger meaning and granted the uninitiated a chance to see how the collection could tell the story of the Danish past. From the assorted boxes of dusty remains, Thomsen managed to create a coherent exhibition, and in 1819, he established in the Christiansborg Palace a Museum for Nordic Antiquities, where he personally offered weekly tours for the public.[42] To promote the museum's work outside the capital, Thomsen joined the historian Carl Christian Rafn (1795–1864) in 1825 to establish the Royal Nordic Antiquarian Society (Kongelige Nordiske Oldskriftselskab), which went a step beyond the preservation commission in its expanded emphasis on antiquarian scholarship, runic studies, and saga research.[43]

Together, Thomsen's collection and the Royal Society became part of the same Danish golden age that oversaw the revival of a vibrant middle-class lifestyle in Copenhagen and the flowering of a national artistic and literary tradition. Both embodied the spirit of the Nordic Renaissance and provided patriotic Danes with a tangible link to the past celebrated by Oehlsenschläger and Grundtvig. But, unlike many of his contemporaries in Copenhagen, Thomsen adhered to a broader vision of Danish identity, and remained a committed Helstat patriot. He rejected the more nationalistic rhetoric of N.F.S. Grundtvig and was strongly influenced by political liberals such as the historian Rasmus Nyerup (1759–1829), who had founded the Antiquities Commission, and Frederik Münter (1761–1830), who had encouraged Thomsen's early interests in numismatics.[44] Their influence reinforced Thomsen's belief that the artefacts under his care spoke to all citizens and revealed a prehistory with as much relevance for Schleswig and Holstein as for Jutland or Sjælland. In the later

1820s, such sentiments motivated Thomsen to reach out to like-minded collectors across the country.

At first, Thomsen's gestures met with little success in Schleswig-Holstein. The political climate between Copenhagen and the duchies had grown tense after the end of the Napoleonic Wars. Holstein, which had had been occupied by Russian troops and later granted membership into the German Confederation (Bund), felt the stirrings of both revolutionary opposition to absolutism and nascent German nationalism. The University of Kiel had become a prominent centre of agitation. In the summer of 1815, the historian Friedrich Christoph Dahlmann (1785–1860), celebrated the defeat of Napoleon with his "Waterloo Address," in which he exhorted a crowd of students to seize the day and establish a new German nation-state. The speech angered both the Prussian and Danish governments, and led to Dahlmann's dismissal from the university.[45] But his words made him famous across the German states because they expressed a lasting desire for national unity, while at home they corresponded with a sense that Holstein, with its predominantly German-speaking population, should be a part of a future Germany. At the same time, they raised fears that Denmark might annex Schleswig, which did not belong to the Bund.

Thus, by the time Thomsen began his work to find partners in the duchies, the basic questions underlying the looming border dispute had emerged. First, to which nation-state did the duchies rightfully belong? Second, were the duchies truly inseparable, or was it possible to divide them between Germany and Denmark? This explains why Thomsen's first overtures met with such little success. In the 1820s, he contacted Friedrich von Warnstedt (1785–1836), a regional official and noted collector in Plön who belonged to the Patriotic Society (Patriotische Gesellschaft) of Altona. Thomsen asked that Warnstedt donate some of his holdings as the core of a prospective Schleswig-Holstein collection. Warnstedt was initially receptive to the idea of promoting his homeland, but at last rejected the offer because he worried the collection might end up in Copenhagen. In fact, he had already expressed disappointment over the dominance of Thomsen's museum. "I cannot deny," Warnstedt wrote in 1826, "that from time to time it concerns me when I learn that these antiquities are going to the honorable Copenhagen Museum." He argued that they depreciated "in scientific worth, when they are carried so far from their site of origin."[46]

A few years later, the revolutions of 1830 swept across the continent and touched the Danish Helstat. In Kiel, a Schleswig official named Uwe Jens Lornsen (1793–1838) published a landmark pamphlet entitled *On the Creation of a Constitution in Schleswigholstein* (*Über das Verfassungswerk in Schleswigholstein*). Lornsen declared that the duchies deserved their own constitution in accordance with the laws of the German Confederation, that to consider separating the duchies "is plainly unthinkable for every Schleswig-Holsteiner," and that the duchies deserved autonomy within the Danish Helstat.[47] Lornsen soon went into exile in South America, but his work became a rallying cry for a growing pro-German movement and further dimmed Thomsen's hopes of cooperation with his fellow antiquarians. As he gloomily reported the next year, "All attempts to found a meaningful collection in Kiel have come to an impasse."[48] In response, Thomsen convinced the Royal Antiquities Commission to support an institution in the duchies that would send only especially rare finds to Copenhagen.

In 1831, Thomsen approached Niels Nikolaus Falck, a professor of law at the University of Kiel, with a new proposal. This time, he offered to donate a part of the Copenhagen collection to ensure its success.[49] Falck and Thomsen proved to be kindred spirits. Falck had grown up in Emmerleff in predominantly Danish-speaking north Schleswig. He was fluent in both languages and studied law in both Kiel and Copenhagen. He thus maintained cultural affinities for Denmark and, like Thomsen, remained a political moderate. Moreover, he viewed himself first as a Schleswig-Holsteiner.[50] He held a steadfast belief in the unity of the two duchies but was ambivalent about the region's political future.[51] Since he was as uncertain about Schleswig-Holstein's connections to Germany as he was aware of its alienation from Denmark, he embraced the Helstat as the most viable political arrangement.[52] His liberal orientation led him to see antiquarianism as a means to preserve the integrity of Schleswig-Holstein and to empower its people through the care of its land and culture. He had long advocated for the protection of antiquities, publishing notices on finds in his journal, *New Citizen's Magazin* (*Neues Staatsbürgerliches Magazin*), and since 1828 had called for an official regional body to oversee the protection of ancient relics.

Falck and Thomsen agreed that politics was not the only issue driving the need for preservation. Even more pressing was the threat posed by the rapid pace of modernization, which had long been a concern of the Royal Antiquities Commission.[53] In the Helstat, the sweeping agricultural reforms of the previous century meant that more than half of Danish farmers now owned their own land and had numerous legal incentives to improve their property.[54] Consequently, the grave mounds and earthworks resting for hundreds of years undisturbed on empty fields suddenly found themselves at the mercy of industrious farmers enjoying a growing productivity. The fields soon became marked with fences and stones, and thousands of plows churned the earth and cut deeply into buried prehistoric remains. Even famous monuments were not immune from the inevitable processes of development. By 1840, for example, the walls of the Danevirke were in danger of disappearing forever. "It is hard to believe," wrote one impassioned observer, "how [the Danevirke] has in the last five or six years diminished, as it seems to be a true mania among the farmers to lay a hand everywhere upon all parts of the wall."[55]

Rural improvements also provided the capital necessary for industrialization, which only worsened an already desperate situation for antiquarians. By 1830, their proximity to Hamburg and Lübeck helped transform the duchies into the most industrialized sector of the Helstat.[56] They also became the scene of tremendous road and railway projects linking the principal cities of Altona, Kiel, and Flensburg. Transportation networks and related urban development took their toll, as the stones and earth of ancestral sites were pushed aside or pressed into service as building material.[57] Concerned antiquarians raised the alarm on the pages of Falck's journals. Time and again, they charted the course of progress and lamented the lack of regard for regional heritage. One local teacher, for example, even reported to Falck his astonishment at discovering a rune stone in Schleswig. Its inscriptions, which for centuries testified to a lost epoch, now served to cover a gutter in the street.[58]

The dramatic changes to the landscape created a need for archaeology, and encouraged its growth as a discipline. As builders and farmers burrowed into moors, flattened hills, and drained bogs, they uncovered a previously unimagined wealth of artefacts. Sites that had spent thousands of years fading from the living world suddenly re-emerged to become once again objects of wonder. Susan Crane has described these inadvertent discoveries as the key to a "culture of somnolence," in which contemporaries depicted their dawning awareness of antiquity's presence as a process of awakening. The metaphorical language of sleeping and waking, she argues, defined historical consciousness in the nineteenth century.[59] As they "awoke," Central Europeans seeking to nurture their awareness of the past looked to Denmark and to Thomsen's museum for inspiration. In 1833, a Prussian visitor to Copenhagen exclaimed, "The surprising success of the [the Danish Museum] has proved that it only takes a central institution to awaken the sleeping treasures within."[60] Yet, even without such museums, the precarious condition of ancient remains in the borderlands filled collectors with a sense of imperative urgency. Modernization thus made rediscovering the past possible even as it promised to erase it forever, and the new generation of antiquarians quickly realized that they had but a short time to save it.

Organized antiquarianism in the borderlands ultimately owed its existence not only to the will of local enthusiasts, but also to the limited reach of Danish institutions. In faraway Copenhagen, the members of the Royal Commission readily acknowledged their inability to protect remains in Schleswig-Holstein. Thomsen's collection of artefacts from the duchies was woefully insignificant, comprising at best 5 per cent of the entire holdings of the Copenhagen

Museum, with few prospects for acquiring more pieces.[61] Moreover, the Commission readily acknowledged the degradation of the Danevirke, but their meagre resources and distance from the site left them unable to assist in its rescue.[62] "Based on its own experience," they wrote to Falck in 1831, "the Commission believes it is capable of saying that it is by far not simply a matter of money that would resolve the issue, but rather that it is of much greater importance to find men who are willing and able to take on the care and preservation of antiquities."[63] The Commission's goal was to help Falck found a museum for the duchies, but Falck responded that such an institution would need the support of regional antiquarians, and he soon received an endorsement from the Commission to establish a collecting society with a steering committee to oversee the preservation of artefacts in Schleswig and Holstein.[64]

Falck's antiquities society was in every sense a regional enterprise, while the membership reflected his broader Helstat outlook.[65] It included both German- and Danish-speakers, and sometimes both, such as the legal scholar Christian Paulsen, who was among Falck's first choices for the steering committee. Like Falck, Paulsen hailed from a German-speaking family in Flensburg, but unlike his colleague found himself much more under the spell of Danish culture. While studying in Copenhagen in 1820, he suddenly switched from German to Danish in his diaries. He also became interested in Nordic antiquity and made a point to visit every notable collection in the capital city. Inevitably, he met and befriended Thomsen and was proud to be among the first to visit Thomsen's collection.[66] Before joining the antiquities society, Paulsen toured Schleswig-Holstein and acquainted himself with prominent antiquarians. He had even raised the possibility of making prehistory an area of responsibility for the Schleswig-Holstein Historical Society, which he had co-founded in 1833.[67]

Paulsen first met Falck while studying at the University of Kiel and again in 1824 after he joined the faculty as a law professor.[68] In these years, the focus of the debate over Schleswig-Holstein had been the legal relationship between Denmark and the duchies. The two men had thus bonded over their shared disdain for legal arguments calling for an independent status for Schleswig-Holstein. Paulsen, who previously had a reputation as a moderate,[69] made his presence known in the debate with his 1832 book, *On Popular Character and State Law in the Duchy of Schleswig* (*Ueber Volksthümlichkeit und Staatsrecht des Herzogthums Schleswig*), which argued against Uwe Jens Lornsen's proposal for a dual state, since it neglected the close ties between Schleswig and Denmark. The resulting debate pushed Paulsen in a more radical direction, and his personal fascination with antiquities collecting gradually shifted to match his interest in promoting the shared cultural ties between the duchies and Denmark.

The antiquities society also included outsiders, first and foremost Christian Flor, who later became the first director of the Kiel Museum. Flor was a native of Copenhagen who had moved to Kiel in 1826 to teach Danish language and literature at the university. He had been inspired after reading the essays of E.C. Wertauff (1781–1871) and Nicolaus Outzen (1752–1826) to travel to the region to safeguard the Danish language and way of life there.[70] His was a crusading mission to check the growing German influence that he saw eroding the Danish presence. For his work, he was later hailed as a Danish nationalist hero who "made the push to awaken the Danish people from more than six hundred years of slumber."[71] Flor was painfully aware of the German nationalist sentiment growing at the university and repeatedly disappointed by the poor Danish proficiency among his students. In fact, his entry into the political debate began with his arguments for increased Danish training for school pupils, which angered German-speakers in the area and made Flor a controversial figure.[72]

Flor may have learned of the new antiquities society through his friendship with Paulsen (he was godfather to Paulsen's daughter Sophie).[73] But his interest in antiquities had emerged earlier after a meeting with N.F.S. Grundtvig in Kiel in 1829.[74] One conversation had been enough to make Flor an unwavering Grundtvig disciple and a devotee of the "Nordic Renaissance," which led him to adopt his friend Paulsen's fascination with his country's ancient heritage. He proved a valuable member for the collecting society, but his politics added a touch of volatility to the project. There were, after all, leading pro-German partisans involved as well, including the historian Andreas Jacob Michelsen (1801–1881) and the lawyer and later mayor of Kiel Georg Ludwig Balemann (1787–1866), both of whom had studied under Dahlmann.[75] Each was a proponent of Lornsen's call for a separate constitution for the duchies, which put them inherently at odds with Paulsen and Flor. Although they had relatively little engagement with the museum in the first few years, they expressed outlooks on the goals of prehistoric research that were significantly different from those of their colleagues. Michelsen in particular sought to tie the antiquities society to the Schleswig-Holstein Historical Society, which was more openly engaged in challenging the links between Schleswig-Holstein and Denmark.[76]

Despite their differences, the steering committee managed to work in harmony throughout the 1830s. There were two key reasons for this success. The first was the presence of a cooperative spirit and an arrangement largely pleasing to all participants. Regardless of their pro-German or pro-Danish preferences, each of the leading members shared a similarly liberal orientation and could see the antiquities society as part of a shared goal of political emancipation. The statutes of their new organization mandated that they as Schleswig-Holsteiners would retain custody of most significant finds, and that it would be their duty to communicate with the regional populace through correspondence and a yearly journal.[77] In short, the society was taking an active role not only in fostering the study of prehistory, but also in broadening and enriching public life. The second ingredient was the absence of direct political pressure. Although the parameters of the Schleswig-Holstein dispute were forming in the 1830s, there was as yet no salient issue to test the loyalties of the members. The language question remained hypothetical, since King Frederik VI (r. 1808–1839) was loathe to alter the status quo, and he let the most controversial proposals to mandate language usage go unanswered. Even Lornsen's agitation did not produce an irreparable break between the camps.[78]

Among the only remaining obstacles to the antiquities society was the concession of Frederik VI, who withheld his approval pending affirmation of the Jutland Code (Jyske Lov), a law stating that recovered gold and silver objects first go to the royal Kunstkammer.[79] Falck and Warnstedt, meanwhile, were also eager to secure 160 objects from Schleswig-Holstein in the Copenhagen Museum.[80] After more than two years of negotiations, however, they were forced both to accede to the King's demands and to accept the refusal of the Royal Commission to relinquish the Schleswig-Holstein artefacts.[81] The Commission argued that they could not view the artefacts as the inherent property of a Schleswig-Holstein antiquities society, which was a logical extension of Thomsen's view that all relics belonged to the Helstat as a whole and not to individual communities.[82]

The final breakthrough came on 27 May 1834, when the Danish monarch officially chartered the Schleswig-Holstein-Lauenburg Society for the Collection and Preservation of National Antiquities (Schleswig-Holstein-Lauenburgische Gesellschaft für die Sammlung und Erhaltung vaterländische Alterthümer).[83] The directors of the society met in November and sent invitations to hundreds of potential members in every significant city and town in the duchies.[84] By the following year, the society had grown to 366 paying members, over two-thirds of whom were either middle-class professionals, especially lawyers, clergymen, and teachers, or members of the lower nobility.[85]

The Kiel Museum

The first task of the antiquities society was to establish an institution for preserving and displaying regional finds. To fulfil their dream, however, the leaders of the society faced a number of fresh challenges. The first was to acquire an initial collection with enough size and credibility to promote public interest and encourage future donations. Fortunately, the steering committee had guarantees from Copenhagen by 1833 on the delivery of two hundred rare coins.[86]

The coins were not, however, from Schleswig-Holstein. The second challenge was therefore to obtain local artefacts for the museum. Since the Copenhagen collection included very few pieces from the duchies,[87] Falck wrote to Warnstedt to ask for his mediation in acquiring part of the collection of the Patriotic Society in Altona, which contained several pieces from Holstein. Warnstedt went a step further and pledged his personal collection, which immediately made the Kiel Museum the largest collection in the region.[88] At the beginning of 1835, Falck proudly declared to the readers of his journal, "The first steps have been taken to establish in Kiel a Museum for National Antiquities ... Upon opening, the museum will be able to begin with no fewer than 1,000 artefacts."[89]

Flor, meanwhile, worked to find an appropriate location in which to house the collection. All agreed that the museum should stand in Kiel. Although it was not the largest city in the duchies, with fewer than ten thousand residents in the 1830s, it was the home of the Christian-Albrechts-University and of the members of the steering committee. The Royal Commission also favoured Kiel and in their letter of endorsement suggested that it would be most suitable for the middle-class visitors likely to patronize the museum. "One can always find men in this university town," they wrote, "who have historical knowledge and an interest in prehistory, and the university's library would offer the literary references for the interpretation of artefacts."[90] They clearly wanted the museum to be both a repository and scholarly institution, and included provision for the museum to be administered as an extension of the university library and for the chief librarian, Henning Ratjen, to sit on the board of directors.[91] Ratjen later recalled that the royal government afforded space in a building adjacent to the appellate courthouse for the collection's first home.[92]

In the summer of 1835, the Museum for National Antiquities (Museum für vaterländische Alterthümer) opened its doors to the public, offering tours every Saturday at noon and special tours for visiting scholars and dignitaries.[93] In the opening days, there was little discussion of the artefacts in the collection; rather, the excitement rested with the success of establishing a semi-autonomous regional institution. The collection was nevertheless noteworthy. It held an assortment of flint axe-heads, ceramic urns, bronze rings, a few historical items such as escutcheons and items found in churches, and the coins sent from Copenhagen. To mark the occasion, Warnstedt, whose gift to the museum and noble status made him the most recognizable member of the steering committee, delivered a public address in which he declared the museum an invaluable institution for the "research of our history, geography, and statistics," referring specifically to Schleswig-Holstein.

Warnstedt's address was also intended to calm the fears of private collectors. He assured them that the museum would not work to undermine their holdings, but desired only information and friendly exchanges.[94] The gesture was important, because cooperation with collectors made it possible for the museum to work towards its goal of safeguarding local sites. In response to ongoing requests for assistance at the Danevirke, the directors of the museum worked with the provincial administration of Schleswig-Holstein to intercede with farmers in the area. They spent years wrangling over private property rights and made dozens of impassioned pleas to the Danish government. In 1840, they persuaded King Christian VIII (r. 1839–1848) to make a personal visit, where he authorized a massive project to measure and record the remaining fragments of the walls in order "to acquire and preserve if at all possible the especially important and interesting pieces of the earthworks in the possession of private persons."[95] The directors also worked with railway workers to preserve finds as they were uncovered.[96] Private collectors aided these efforts through direct excavation of endangered sites and through regular reporting of results, which appeared in the society's annual journal. Correspondence with collectors also helped the museum identify new sites and objects. In 1836, the directors issued a circular asking the society's members throughout the duchies to report on objects "worthy of antiquarian attention."[97] They also requested voluntary inventories of collections, which they promised would be the only intrusion into the realm of privately owned relics. With the information they received, Falck and Flor quietly used membership dues to purchase key pieces while also encouraging collectors to donate or bequeath their relics to the museum.

Gradually, the antiquities society began transforming the world of the independent collector. The seemingly innocuous tactic of soliciting information was critical to the increasing control that the founders of the Museum for National Antiquities were exercising over the study of prehistory. They invited collectors to join the society, and they published activities in yearly reports and in Falck's new biannual almanac, *Falcks Archiv*. Collectors benefited from participation in a broader enterprise and in the local celebrity that came with announcing their finds. The price, however, was the uniqueness and independence they had previously enjoyed. Once collectors shared their work, their artefacts were measured against those of other antiquarians, and their authority to interpret their finds was likewise subordinated to the collective expertise of the new community.

The society's success raised awareness of its potential to yield broader views of prehistory and of its importance in the increasingly polarized politics of the region. Indeed, the growth of the museum paralleled rising tensions in the duchies, and as the middle ground disappeared politically, the increasingly irreconcilable views of the German and Danish camps mirrored growing disparities in the interpretations of the museum founders. In his address, Warnstedt argued that the museum needed to impose order on its exhibition, as Thomsen had done, but he looked not to Copenhagen but to the Oberlausitz region of southeastern Prussia, where the local antiquities society classified finds as "Heathen," "Christian," or "Indeterminate."[98] Flor, by contrast, was inclined towards the Danish three-age model, and he and Thomsen discussed the "distressful shape" and "confusion" of German museology, which ignored the markers of prehistoric development and instead classified objects based on their relationship to the historical era.[99] As an adherent of the Nordic Renaissance, Flor did not object to Christian interpretations of the past, but he did oppose a system that would relegate ancient cultures to a pejorative "heathen" category.[100]

Looking back on these events, Georg Kossak has hinted that the debate over the proper arrangement of the exhibition, and particularly Flor's intransigence in this matter, caused the founding cohort to dissolve in 1845. He has argued that while Flor focused almost exclusively on the custodianship of the objects, Falck and Michelsen wanted to apply interpretations of the artefacts directly to their historical narratives.[101] In fact, the debate was short-lived, since the sudden passing of Warnstedt in 1836 left Flor in control of the collection. Moreover, the museum continued to receive support from Copenhagen. Later donations included "two spiral finger rings" sent in 1836, and two additional gold rings in 1845 as a token acknowledgment of the museum's "good progress."[102] In truth, the break-up of the steering committee related to the ways in which the founders had politicized their work as antiquarians. And this followed a more general shift in the Schleswig-Holstein debate from an emphasis on legal arguments to disputes about language and culture.

In 1836, King Frederick VI made an important concession to liberals both in the capital and in the provinces by establishing advisory Estate Assemblies to represent Jutland, the Danish Isles, and the duchies. Although the assemblies had a strictly advisory role, the opportunity for some form of elected representation nevertheless met essential liberal demands for greater participation in politics. Moreover, they held the potential to placate those in Schleswig-Holstein who were demanding greater autonomy. But they were not a perfect solution, and they failed above all to answer the question of whether the duchies represented an indivisible entity. The Danish government made a feeble effort to placate all sides by creating a separate assembly for each duchy, but this gesture only further polarized the debate. Many German-speakers saw it as an attempt to separate the duchies, while pro-Danish advocates felt emboldened to demand that Denmark formally annex Schleswig and establish a new border at the Eider River.

Moderates, meanwhile, found themselves pushed to side either with the so-called Eiderdanes or with pro-German Schleswig-Holsteiners.

It is not surprising that antiquarianism should have become an important fault line in the shifting dispute, as the political and legal questions fused with notions of cultural identity. In Kiel, the cooperation that had characterized the work of the antiquities society began to falter after 1836. Extant correspondence reveals a tendency among members of the steering committee to communicate solely with colleagues who supported their respective pro-German or pro-Danish positions. The exchanges between Falck and Thomsen ended, and were carried on only by Paulsen and Flor. In that same year, the members began to express interest in questions of prehistoric origins. As Falck explained:

> If the former regional divisions [of Schleswig-Holstein] have lost their public meaning in the present, and if at the same time some names for these districts (for example, Southern Jutland and the region between the Eider and the Schlei) are long since out of use, these ancient regional divisions nevertheless remain important for the prehistorian … According to the foundations laid out in this text, we will direct our efforts with the goal of seeking, through the collection and examination of artefacts, an answer to the question of the degree to which these [regional divisions] coincide with the various tribes of Saxons, Sorbs, Frisians, and Danes in our duchies in ancient times.[103]

Such questions, of course, were nothing new, and Thomsen had also been interested in tracing the prehistoric roots of the Danes. Nor was there much initial controversy over the argument that the Germans and the Danes had common ancestries in prehistory. "With the highest degree of certainty," wrote the antiquarian D.F. Eschricht in 1837, "it is clear that the Germanic or Gothic tribes, which wandered into Sweden, Norway, and Denmark more than ten centuries ago ... were the fathers of the present-day Swedes, Normans, and Danes."[104] The difference now was a shift in tone. Before the turmoil of the 1840s, musings on the ancient kinship between Germans and Danes had a benign quality and made sense in light of the absence of a unified German state. While Danes could come to terms with their shrinking borders by looking to an unbroken dynastic legacy and centuries of unity, Germans had no such models, and therefore had little upon which to base their self-conceptions. At the same time, an emphasis on common origins only reinforced local identity. Danes and Germans could transcend the linguistic divide and define themselves through a common culture in the past.

As the political situation grew more divisive, however, the search for origins betrayed a latent potential for facilitating nationalist appropriations. It was simply too tempting to apply ancient clues to contemporary debates about the inherent unity of Schleswig-Holstein, to its place within Germany, or, conversely, to the relationship between Schleswig and Denmark. Already in 1835, Warnstedt's address included an assertion that northern Europe had been a point of origin for Germanic tribes. Most likely, Warnstedt intended for this statement to reinforce the value of Schleswig-Holstein for German history, but his broad ascription of Germanic origins inherently gave modern Germans a claim to the cultural legacy – the sagas, myths, and symbols – of Scandinavian countries like Denmark.[105] As such, this represented a challenge to Danish nationalist thinking, which was still defined by the promotion of supposedly unique aspects of Danish prehistory. Moreover, his claim added a geographical dimension to national origins that brought modern borders into question.

Advocates for Schleswig-Holstein's Danes also used prehistory to make their case. Christian Flor, for instance, did not publish on the artefacts in his care, but his letters to Thomsen reflected his thinking about their importance. He consistently referred to the museum as a collection of "Nordic Antiquity," and avoided the adjective "national" (*vaterländisch*), which his German colleagues used to indicate the museum's significance to their home region. In 1838, Flor and Paulsen joined the Haderslev printer P.C. Koch in publishing the journal *Dannevirke*, whose cover depicted a stylized image of the ancient walls complete with a fluttering Danish flag (Dannebrog), rune stones, and stone towers. Its purpose was to project strength and to announce a willingness to defend Danish culture in Schleswig. Flor and Koch used the journal to criticize the Estate Assemblies and to make appeals to the Nordic spirit of their countrymen. Even Paulsen, who remained committed to a bond with both Schleswig and Holstein, authored pieces in the journal attacking radical German nationalists.[106]

Shortly after the first issue of *Dannevirke* appeared, questions about the status of the duchies and language rights ruptured the coalition between Danish- and German-speaking liberal groups. Falck's election as president of the Schleswig assembly led to an irreparable rift in his relationship with Flor, who worked feverishly behind the scenes to ensure equal rights for Danish-speakers. In 1842, Flor helped force the language issue when he convinced assembly member Peter Hiort Lorenzen (1791–1845) to speak Danish in the assembly hall (despite the fact that Lorenzen spoke very little Danish). The moderate Falck, who had failed to mitigate the conflict or limit Flor's influence, was simply not up to the task of controlling the harsh reaction from the pro-German camp.[107]

By 1845, the leadership of the antiquities society began to break up along national lines. Flor left the city to found a Grundtvigian folk high school in Rødding. Paulsen departed soon after at the start of the 1848 Revolution. Falck, having failed to please either side, lost his position in the assembly in

1846 and began to write on the legal justification for Schleswig's entry into the German Bund, indicating that he, too, had radicalized to some extent. Two years later, Andreas Michelsen took a seat in the Frankfurt Parliament, as the region became engulfed in revolution and then in an unsuccessful war for independence against Denmark. The directorship of the museum passed to Karl Müllenhoff (1818–1884), a young philologist at the University of Kiel whose primary interest lay in the myths and legends of Schleswig-Holstein. As we will see in the next two chapters, Müllenhoff's tenure, which spanned the German-Danish Wars, preserved the local character of the antiquarian enterprise but marked a temporary end to the German-Danish cooperation that had sustained its earlier years.

Conclusion

As the crisis over his homeland reached its peak in the 1840s, Nikolaus Falck paused to reflect on the contents of the museum that he had helped create. "If one were to compare the Germanic and Nordic collection with the museums in which Greek and Roman monuments are preserved," he mused, "then our collection would fall far short."[108] There were, he acknowledged, no breathtaking marble sculptures in Kiel, but only a small assortment of notched swords and rusted rings, broken stone tools, and faded ceramic vessels. Yet, Falck's modesty was an implicit rebuttal to the old claim about the barbarian origins of northern Europe. What he did not need to say to his fellow antiquarians was that this attitude was changing. What had once been an overlooked epoch of the European heritage was quickly becoming a valuable object of study and would soon become embroiled in a test of arms across the German-Danish borderlands.

As we will see in the next chapter, antiquarians on both sides made northern European prehistory a central feature in the wars of the mid-nineteenth century. But no less remarkable was the cooperation that prevailed on the eve of the conflict. Indeed, it was in these years between 1830 and 1848 that the first modern antiquarians set the stage for the emergence of archaeology in the region. There were, to be sure, few notable scholarly achievements in these early years, but the development of an organized antiquarianism was itself a pathbreaking innovation. Just as Thomsen's Three Age system laid the groundwork for museums to become indispensable institutions for archaeology, so too did the formation of collecting societies set nineteenth-century antiquarianism apart as distinctly modern. Above all, they allowed the collector to place that intimate yearning for the past into a larger context and to understand the self as both an individual and as part of a community. They thus represented a monumental shift from satisfying the needs of a subjective *I* to a subjective *we*.

The shifting frame of collecting helps explain why pro-Danish and pro-German patriots were willing to work together to sustain a common association. It was what compelled the leaders of the Royal Antiquities Commission and the Schleswig-Holstein Antiquities Society to perservere in the turmoil of the Schleswig-Holstein debate. Thomsen may have been magnanimous in his partnerships in Kiel, but he had little choice otherwise. If he wished to safeguard relics across the Helstat, he had to bow to the wishes of his peers in Kiel. By the same token, Falck's pleas for a chartered organization fell on deaf ears until Thomsen convinced the Danish government to support a regional association. And, finally, the growth of the museum might have been impossible without Flor's and Paulsen's work to maintain ties with Copenhagen. Even if their motives gradually became intertwined with their respective political causes, they had laid a cornerstone free from partisanship that would colour later cross-border exchanges.

Organized antiquarianism succeeded in the borderlands for two reasons. First, it hinged on the quality of the relationships among the collectors. The antiquities society in Schleswig-Holstein was more than a network of casual acquaintances and intellectual exchanges. It was formed through close friendships that elided the debate over the duchies, brought collectors together, and helped spread enthusiasm for prehistory. Second, the project was dedicated to a common vision of the past. It began with the notion that the past was distinct from the present. Although antiquarians in this period made few claims about prehistoric culture, they seemed to understand that it was becoming increasingly remote from modern experience. Relatedly, each collector recognized that the past lay under threat from the present. Whether through war or agriculture or urban development, the encompassing changes of the nineteenth century promised to wipe out the vestiges of what had come before. Falck and his colleagues saw themselves as stewards rather than owners of the past. They based their sense of elite status as scholars not on the basis of their interpretations, but on the belief that they better than anyone else appreciated the need to preserve. Finally, each antiquarian shared a fundamental belief that the past was relevant to the present. Nineteenth-century collectors were driven less by pure curiosity and more by an urgency to uncover the secrets that artefacts held for their own day.

This was the world of the antiquarian in 1830, on the eve of a titanic shift in the fate of the borderlands. Even as the field was laying its institutional roots, the terms of the debate were shifting from law to culture and making partisans of all. There remained, of course, points of consensus that facilitated cooperation. All could see value in antiquarianism beyond the debate even as they recognized cultural scholarship as a subtle expression of political ambition. And all could envision prehistory as a symbol for their liberal and patriotic causes. The latent flaw lay with the diversity of symbolic language. Once the revolutionary movement began to yield the potential for success, it splintered along the lines of linguistic and cultural identity. Diverging visions of the future quickly harnessed the once-common utility of the past. Thus, where Falck continued to see his imagined Schleswig-Holstein embedded and whole in the ruins of foregoing epochs, his colleague Paulsen perceived a legacy of division between north and south, while Christian Flor, the outsider, placed the collection under his care into the broader realm of the Nordic lands.

Within a few short years of the founding of the Kiel Museum, the contours of the debate about prehistory began to appear. There were already disputes over taxonomy, arguments over the origins of national communities, and a concern first with how to relate the historic to the prehistoric and second with deciding on whose scholarly traditions, German or Danish, to appeal to in the search for answers. From this point, it was but a short journey to a final dimension of the antiquarian vision. With the outbreak of revolution and war, the question would no longer be whether the past mattered to the people of the present, but to whom should the past rightfully belong. This burden, however, fell to a second generation that came of age in the 1840s in the shadow of the first antiquarians. It was these scholars who inherited the scientific mission of early archaeology and who brought it into the wars to come.

2 National Prehistories in the German-Danish Wars

The Nydam Boat has long been a centrepiece of Schleswig-Holstein archaeology. Currently nestled in an exhibition hall at the Schleswig-Holstein State Archaeology Museum in Schleswig, this funerary craft bears witness to the cultural sophistication of prehistoric northern Europe. Measuring 23 metres in length, the vessel conveys to thousands of visitors each year the shipbuilding skills of the European Iron Age. Yet, the modern saga of its discovery often eclipses interest in its ancient history. The Nydam Boat, after all, was uncovered in 1863 in the midst of an open rivalry between German and Danish antiquarians. Its discoverer, the Danish schoolteacher Conrad Engelhardt (1825–1881), reassembled the boat and added it to his impressive Flensburg Museum, which had begun to challenge the dominance of the Kiel Museum with an array of impressive new finds, including bronze plates, hoards of Roman coins, and the swords and shields of forgotten wars rescued from the region's fens and bogs.[1]

Such animosities among regional museum curators soon collided with a looming war over the border. Questions about ancient heritage stood at the nexus of a new conflict, as the fate of Schleswig-Holstein became once again intertwined with nationalist movements in Denmark and the German states. As they had done over a decade earlier, expert prehistorians marshalled their scholarship for their respective causes, and both sides looked to archaeological artefacts as symbols and markers of their territorial claims. Ultimately, both sides came to see the Nydam Boat and the treasures of the Flensburg Collection among the greatest prizes of the war. When the Prussians captured Flensburg in 1864 with hopes of seizing Engelhardt's collection, they were dismayed to find that the Danes had already spirited it into hiding. After two years of threats and intrigue, the Germans managed to locate the finds, but the episode launched a protracted contest over ownership of the past that coloured border relations well into the twentieth century.

The drama surrounding the fate of the Nydam Boat and the Flensburg Collection was the highlight of what Stine Wiell has called a great "struggle for prehistory" that unfolded during the Second German-Danish War of 1864. German Schleswig-Holsteiners, such as the Flensburg archivist Fritz Graef, remembered the disappearance of the Flensburg Collection as an act of criminal theft.[2] More recently, Wiell has sought a more moderate position with two books charting the effects of the 1864 war on local archaeology. Though her writing retains a partisan flavour, referring to the Prussians as "the enemy" and lamenting that the collection has been "lost to Denmark forever," it nevertheless recognizes the ambiguous nature of prehistory's relationship to the present, reminding readers, "Prehistoric archaeology apparently knows no boundaries."[3]

Wiell rightly places the Nydam Boat at the heart of nationalist appropriations of the ancient past during the war of 1864, but her work only provides a partial picture of the convergence of archaeology and nationalism during the border conflicts of the mid-nineteenth century. A more complete account must also take into consideration the events between the First German-Danish War of 1848–1851 and the Austro-Prussian seizure of Schleswig-Holstein in 1864. Seen within this longer perspective, the real-life drama surrounding the Nydam Boat signifies not only changing attitudes towards antiquity, but also a transformation within antiquarian study. Its discovery was the work of a new generation of scholars, including Conrad Engelhardt and Jens Worsaae (1821–1885), who brought the study of northern European prehistory out of the museum and into the field, and whose years of toil coaxed true wonders from beneath earth and mud. They made hundreds of new artefacts available for symbolic appropriation just as the duchies were becoming the epicentre of a contest between an aspiring nation to the south and a nation in transformation to the north. As the example of the Nydam Boat shows, it was the gradual professionalization of archaeology in this period that helped bring antiquity to the forefront of two border wars and placed regional identity at the centre of an intense and bloody metamorphosis.

Jens Worsaae and the Practice of Fieldwork

On his way to London in the summer of 1846, Jens Worsaae, a student of C.J. Thomsen, became seasick on the Baltic. Fearing the resumption of his storm-tossed crossing, he spent six days in Kiel, where he was introduced one evening to Nikolaus Falck. He described the encounter in a letter to his mother, mentioning Falck not as a fellow antiquarian but as a respected leader of the Schleswig-Holstein Party. Despite his pro-Danish position, Worsaae seemed to appreciate Falck's company. The two even discussed the controversy surrounding Peter Hiort Lorenzen's outbursts in Danish in the Estate Assembly. "He sought quite earnestly to deflect the accusation that he had dismissed P.H. Lorenzen from the Estate Assembly because he had spoken Danish," Worsaae wrote, apparently accepting Falck's explanation that "he had only done it because [Lorenzen] did not wish to obey him as Assembly President." Falck confided that he expected future assembly meetings to be "very stormy," and he seemed anxious to stress to his Danish colleagues his waning ability to control the momentum of the looming conflict.[4]

In the acrimonious atmosphere of the late 1840s, Worsaae's meeting with Falck represented an increasingly rare moment of cordiality between German and Danish antiquarians. Christian Flor had by this time left Kiel for Rødding, Christian Paulsen would leave two years later, and Worsaae was on the cusp of becoming a leading voice against German claims to local prehistory. Indeed, even on this occasion, he did not spare his German colleague from some personal criticism, writing, "I found him to be neither an especially distinguished nor dynamic man."[5]

Worsaae seemed to harbour a similar attitude for his mentor, C.J. Thomsen, which suggested that he was part of a broader generational rift. Worsaae, born after the Napoleonic Wars with little attachment to the spirit of Helstat patriotism, was generally dissatisfied with the practices of the older generation. Both his political views and professional life intersected at a moment of conflict, pitting his own passion, ambition, and vision for archaeology against the more compromising attitudes of his elders. "As conservative as I was in politics," he wrote, "I was almost radical in my scholarship."[6] Above all, Worsaae felt it was important that the study of prehistory move away from a singular focus on museums and collecting. While he admired Thomsen's museum and valued its world status, he nevertheless wanted to promote the study of antiquities as a more independent discipline. It should, he believed, divest itself of its heavy dependence on textual and historical sources and engage in a comprehensive study of all types of prehistoric remains, including both artefacts and archaeological sites such as barrows and stone circles.

Worsaae's interest in sites may have been a product of his upbringing in Vejle, in the shadow of the magnificent barrows at Jelling in eastern Jutland.[7] He had been a collector of antiquities since childhood, and his enchantment with the past likely grew from these enigmatic landmarks on the horizon and later informed his approach to archaeology. This experience served him well at the beginning of his career, when he struggled to find a position in the Copenhagen Museum. His mentor Thomsen had supported his hopes and likewise expressed a desire to promote site excavations. Unfortunately, the Royal Nordic

Antiquarian Society had less interest in fieldwork, since so many of the group's members remained fixated on literary scholarship, especially translations of Norse sagas.[8] Moreover, Thomsen's resources were inadequate for hiring an assistant. But Worsaae, though displeased by the failure, remained undaunted, and looked elsewhere for the funds to pursue his interests. As it turned out, Worsaae's father, who had been a chief treasury clerk in Vejle, had connections to the crown prince and future King Frederik VII. Frederik was also a lover of antiquities, and soon became a patron of Worsaae's work.[9] With such assistance at hand, Worsaae undertook a study tour of Denmark during the 1830s and early 1840s, which included digs at sites across the country, including barrows near Vejby and Nyrup on Sjælland, and at Jelling in Jutland.[10]

Based on these investigations, Worsaae wrote *Danmarks Oldtid oplyst ved Oldsager og Gravhøie*, which was translated in 1844 as *The Primeval Antiquities of Denmark*. Here he laid out his reflections on archaeology, and made an argument for the importance of examining not only ancient artefacts, but also the sites in which they were discovered. "To obtain correct ideas on … the most ancient relations of our native country, it is … indispensably necessary to examine and compare with care the places in which antiquities are usually found; otherwise many most important collateral points can either not be explained at all, or at least in a very unsatisfactory manner."[11] Worsaae's approach was important for two reasons. First, it provided a new way to test Thomsen's hypothesis about the existence of distinct archaeological periods. He explained, "Thus, we should scarcely have been able to refer, as we have done in the previous pages, to three successive periods, if experience had not taught us that objects which belong to different periods are usually found by themselves."[12] Second, it suggested that there were features unique to sites associated with specific periods, and that these could reveal much about the culture of ancient Denmark. To make his case, Worsaae delineated a site typology based on an analysis of associated artefacts. For instance, he was able to align finds of flint axes with two particular burial structures: round stone cromlechs (*Steendysser*) and passage graves (*Jættestuer*). Doing so allowed him to show that these structures were built during the Stone Age. Similar comparisons led him to place earth-covered barrows, which contained caches of bronze rings and swords, within the Bronze Age. Taken together, these assessments reinforced the idea that the different "ages" indeed represented distinct periods of cultural development.

In 1847, Worsaae's work led King Christian VIII (r. 1839–1848) to appoint him inspector for the preservation of antiquarian monuments. Support from the royal government allowed him to continue his fieldwork and to travel abroad for wider comparative studies. His efforts won him a gold medal in Sweden and drew invitations from the Royal Geographical Society in London.[13] This was a significant step, since Worsaae was not only able to argue for the validity of the Three Age system for prehistoric remains outside Denmark, but also to strengthen the overseas ties of the Danish antiquarian community. Furthermore, C. Stephen Briggs has even argued that Worsaae's travels were part of a broader push to promote Denmark's international profile through cultural diplomacy. He claims that Worsaae carefully portrayed his travel itinerary as an attempt to explore sites of ancient Danish contact so as to pique the interest of the Danish government.[14]

In this way, Worsaae succeeded in revolutionizing antiquarian study even as he struggled to find his place within it. His systematic approach and careful reporting created credibility for site exploration that, in the words of Peter Rowley-Conwy, "served to place archaeology on the front line, as the branch of learning that now spoke for the ancient past."[15] His theories not only reinforced Thomsen's work, but also established a fundamental paradigm for the practice of archaeology in the field. His elaboration of the three-age typology provided excavators with a set of empirical guidelines for future digs. With each discovery, archaeologists could test Thomsen's theory and enter sites with a set of expectations about how to interpret finds. This, in turn, promised to unify the discipline of archaeology while transforming Thomsen's ideas about the order of artefacts in the museum into a potential point of orthodoxy across an emerging intellectual field.

The Brothers Grimm and the Roots of the Volk

The nature of Worsaae's work brought him into frequent contact with scholars in Germany and Schleswig-Holstein. While working as a museum volunteer in Copenhagen, he maintained a correspondence with Christian Flor regarding archaeological reports, which was one of the few remaining links between Kiel and Copenhagen in the 1840s.[16] A few years later, A.J. Michelsen wrote to Worsaae and convinced him to publish a German edition of *Primeval Antiquities*.[17] During the summer of 1845, the book's success in Germany afforded Worsaae a chance to tour the German states and to visit collections in Prussia, Saxony, Bavaria, and Hannover. Although he admired the German fascination with the past, he was singularly unimpressed by its representation in the museums he visited. With the exception of the northern German collections in Schwerin and Kiel, which had been influenced by Danish practice, Worsaae maintained that none of the assemblages had a notable scholarly value. In an article published the following year, he complained, "To a stunning degree, the antiquities from different periods and peoples are blended with one another … Chinese, Indian, Persian, and Turkish objects are displayed in the midst of pieces from the fifteenth, seventeenth, or eighteenth centuries and from various European countries."[18] In the same article, Worsaae took aim at the philologists Jacob (1785–1863) and Wilhelm Grimm (1786–1859), whom he accused of misinterpreting Nordic myths and symbols and claiming them as elements of German heritage. "In the Grimms' *German Mythology* (*Deutsche Mythologie*)," he wrote, "the Scandinavian element is so overwhelming, that when it is taken away, most of the substance disappears and only the names of gods remain behind."[19]

Worsaae's encounter with the Grimms introduced him to a long-running debate about the origins of Germanic and Nordic peoples, in which philologists on both sides of the border had been engaged since the end of the Napoleonic Wars. Before 1848, the dialogue was a collegial one among German and Scandinavian scholars, and Worsaae later recalled in his memoirs his feeling of surprise at the absence of tensions between Germans and Scandinavians outside the disputed border region.[20] Yet, within a few years of his visit, the consequences of this debate would bring Worsaae's research into conflict with various German and Scandinavian ideas about the connections between their past heritages and their present-day national communities.

Stepping back for a moment to the early nineteenth century, we see the Grimms as leading advocates on the German side of linking northern and Central European mythic traditions. They shared an attitude at the heart of what Jost Hermand has called a "Teutonic revival," which had appeared in the late eighteenth century. Reacting against a "Frenchified German aristocracy," this movement emerged from the thinking of such intellectuals as Johann Gottfried Herder (1744–1803), whose concept of a unified "national spirit " (*Volksgeist*) had led him to see ancient myths as carriers of an older and more egalitarian tradition that elided the class cleavages of modern civilization.[21] Herder and his cohort embraced the possibility of reclaiming a more democratic society, and, as Hermand has explained, "stopped placing their hopes in ... the disintegrating 'Holy Roman Empire.' Rather, they began to dream of a state, a nation, a community founded on the idea of simplicity, which all citizens could call their own."[22] Similar attitudes had shaped nationalist thinking in Denmark, where the philosophical worldview of N.F.S. Grundtvig stressed the value of community. Like Grundtvig, the Grimms studied Nordic myth as part of a hunt for the essence of their people, or *Volk*, which in Germany was often conflated with the idea of an integral national community. This placed the brothers on common ground with Danish scholars, who believed that the key to defining national character was to understand the intrinsic nature of a people. While there were notable differences between German and Danish conceptions, both essentially embraced the concept of a nation composed of an integral community with a collective spirit.

The search for Volk implied a search for origins, and, for the Grimms, the linguistic artefacts of myths and sagas were the surest means of finding the root of German culture, since as Jacob Grimm wrote, "The body of the spiritual functions of a people is its language."[23] By locating linguistic similarities in the body of Nordic and Germanic myths, they believed that they would find evidence of collective authorship shaped through generations and across communities. In order to verify their hypothesis, the Grimms needed access to a vast array of linguistic artefacts, but the scarcity and uncertainty of textual resources were as much a problem for their work in Germany as they were for Worsaae's archaeology in Denmark. Moreover, much of the available material bore the imprint of Christian influences, which attenuated their value as "pure" sources. The Grimms recognized, for example, that classic Germanic myths like the *Nibelungenlied* had been corrupted by Latin and Christian sources and no longer represented an unspoiled or original work.[24] By contrast, they saw the Nordic myths and sagas as relatively untouched by the passage of time, and argued that studying them would best reveal the spirit of the ancient Germans. As Jacob Grimm later noted in *German Mythology*, these myths bore clear linguistic affinities, similar nomenclatures, and several shared religious elements.[25] For the Grimms, there was thus virtually no difference between "German mythology" and "Nordic mythology."

It was the possibility of finding unadulterated sources that drew the Grimms to the North, but it was the Danes who made the first contact. In 1809, the historian Rasmus Nyerup (1750–1829) wrote to Wilhelm Grimm to commend him on his work on the *Nibelungenlied*. "I am amazed," he wrote, "by the exact and efficient knowledge of our language that you possess." Nyerup warmly greeted Wilhelm's early hypothesis that "the German folk poetry stood in close contact with the Danish in earlier times."[26] The two maintained a steady correspondence, even during the Napoleonic Wars, when Nyerup re-established contact through the help of a student, who was none other than a young C.J. Thomsen, then travelling through Heidelberg and Kassel.[27] Nyerup and his colleagues made it possible for both Wilhelm and Jacob Grimm to acquire many of the texts and scholarship they needed to carry out their research.[28] In return, they were pleased to see their national heritage promoted abroad by such noted scholars. "You are right when you note the enthusiasm with which the old Norse literature is now pursued [in Germany]," Wilhelm wrote to his friend, "You can rest assured that we take great joy in it here."[29]

In the early nineteenth century, there was nothing inherently threatening about this joint enterprise. Like the antiquarians in Schleswig-Holstein during the Restoration Era, the philologists studying Nordic and Germanic myths were able to work together in a common pursuit of the past. If this collegial exchange was the result of complementary national interest, it also came partly from the limits of national sentiment in the years preceding the Revolution of 1848. Nyerup was fascinated by the connections not only between German and Danish traditions, but also by the links among Scandinavian countries, and his intense interest in the work of the Grimms reflected ambivalence about Danish and Scandinavian identity. Although the Scandinavianist movement did not fully appear until the 1840s, Nyerup, who wrote in the context of a disintegrating Helstat and rising Grundtvigianism, already presaged sentiments familiar to later Scandinavianists. The implicit linkages among Nordic peoples that he perceived in the Grimms' work intrigued him, and he was open to the prospect of German participation in what was essentially a Scandinavian intellectual project.

During the 1830s and 1840s, the Grimms also maintained ties with Carl Christian Rafn, Thomsen's partner in the Royal Nordic Antiquarian Society. While he would later become one of their most vociferous critics, Rafn at first shared the Grimms' faith in the originality of Nordic sagas, and joined them in studies of the ancient literature of Iceland, which he called "the motherland of Nordic history."[30] Rafn, however, seems to have been much more conscious of his Scandinavianist leanings, and his collaborative work with Jacob Grimm on the Icelandic Eddas reflected a growing trend in the Scandinavianist movement to seek cultural anchors in order to cultivate a sense of unity and to downplay previous tensions among Nordic countries.[31] Inger Jensen and Jørgen Steen Jensen have maintained that this stemmed from Rafn's pro-Danish politics, and that one of Rafn's goals was to compensate for Denmark's losses in the Napoleonic Wars by strengthening the country's ties to its Scandinavian neighbours and cultivating friendly ties with nearby powers like Britain and Prussia.[32] Perhaps for this reason, Rafn encouraged Jacob Grimm to become a member of the Royal Society, writing, "Because [antiquities] are a national property of all of northern Europe, so the [Royal Nordic Antiquarian Society] is to be seen as a European foundation."[33]

The relationship between the Grimms and the Danes thus thrived in the spaces between national and pan-national ambitions. With the outbreak of revolution in 1848, however, the looming war in Schleswig-Holstein strained academic ties. Jens Worsaae's archaeology matured just at the moment when scholars on both sides were grappling with the political implications of their research. Like the Grimms, Worsaae soon brought his discipline to bear not only on questions of prehistory, but also on the shape and character of modern Denmark and Germany.

Archaeology and Politics in the First German-Danish War, 1848–1851

The 1848 revolutions, which began in Paris and then swept eastward, came to Schleswig-Holstein on 18 March. That evening, a hastily arranged meeting of assembly members took place in Rendsburg. King Frederik VII (r. 1848–1863), who had succeeded Christian VIII in January, was prepared to accede to the demands of revolutionaries and allow Denmark to become a constitutional monarchy. On this point liberals in the borderlands and in Copenhagen could agree. What remained undecided was the question of whether Denmark would get one constitution including Schleswig or two creating an independent and unified Schleswig-Holstein within the Danish state. At their meeting, the pro-German Schleswig-Holstein faction feared that the royal government would favour the pro-Danish "Eiderdanes," who sought the annexation of Schleswig and a new Danish border at the Eider River. At the same time, they took heart from the promises of the Prussian King Friedrich Wilhelm IV to take a leading role in uniting Germany.[34] Rather than wait for the outcome of events in Copenhagen, the participants at the Rendsburg meeting pre-emptively voted to form a provisional government and seek independence.[35] Once news of the secession bid arrived in Copenhagen, Eiderdane liberals led by Orla Lehmann (1810–1870) responded by organizing demonstrations aimed at pressuring the King to preserve the Helstat.[36] Within days, the stage was set for what became the First German-Danish War.

In the three-year war that followed, both sides felt they were fighting against the oppression of the other. While the Schleswig-Holsteiners viewed their struggle as an independence movement against the Danish crown, Danes saw in the conflict a broader German threat to the Danish kingdom. As N.F.S. Grundtvig explained: "My whole quarrel with the Germans is really concerned with the fact that they are determined either to make me a German or to regard me as a fool; and I give as good as I get and do not wish to be either. Instead I assert that Denmark is no more the tail of Germany than the Norse spirit is a sprite serving the imperial German reason."[37] It was this concern that led pro-Danish groups to portray the present battle against German encroachment as akin to struggles in the late prehistoric and early medieval periods. As early as 1839, Grundvig's poem, "Niels Ebbesen" evoked the heroic story of the fourteenth-century Jutlander to recall a similar time:

> The Danes were outlawed in forest and strath,
> Rulers we had from heaven's wrath,
> When the Germans ran wild in Denmark.[38]

Grundvig's allusions to the barbaric Germans fuelled a spirit of militant defensiveness, which Christian Flor later adopted in 1844, when he used the Danevirke fortress imagery in his *Dannevirke* journal to call for the preservation of Danish Schleswig. Clearly, by 1848 the elements of the distant past were already a symbolic presence in the conflict for Danes.

At the same time, antiquarians across the border had become equally aware of the potential value of the past for the present crisis. For the Germans, the past was an affirmation of the existence of the German nation, and a guidepost for its modern incarnation. In a letter to the Schleswig-Holstein Antiquities Society in 1848, the Henneberg Antiquities Association announced its sixteenth anniversary celebration, noting: "The various historical or archaeological associations must all the more wish for the prudent realization of the present state of affairs in and for Germany, not only because it coincides with our practices and conclusions, but also because the future existence [of Germany] itself depends on it."[39] Even if their counterparts in Kiel agreed, their shared enthusiasm could do little to halt the decline of the Schleswig-Holstein Antiquities Society during this period. With the region engulfed in revolution and war, correspondence among members declined, acquisitions became rare, and the leading members of the society largely withdrew from their scholarly pursuits. Local scholars consequently played little role in the conflict, as the impetus shifted to the national and international stages.

One former member, A.J. Michelsen, whose revolutionary politics had also forced him to leave Kiel, was elected to the new German Parliament meeting in Frankfurt. There he took part in fashioning a constitution for a prospective German nation-state, which invited a public discussion over the shape and character of the German national community. In particular, Michelsen joined the historian Friedrich Christoph Dahlmann and legal scholar and fellow expatriate Georg Beseler (1809–1888) in advocating for Schleswig-Holstein to become part of Germany. During a series of debates in the summer and fall of 1848, they argued that the two duchies were bound historically and legally, and that if Holstein was a member of the German Bund, then Schleswig had an equal claim. Michelsen also stressed the prominent role of German language and culture even in North Schleswig, where it was the emblem of the educated elite. Though he did not explicitly support a popular plebiscite, he maintained that a majority of Schleswigers supported inclusion. These positions adhered to a familiar emphasis on the political history and legal status of the duchies and elided the thorny questions of cultural and linguistic overlap. Moreover, as Brian Vick has argued in his study of the "patterns of thought" informing the work of the Parliament, the position was not incompatible with German notions of the Volk. By showing that the borderlands had shared historical elements and a legal tradition compatible with the southern German states, the Schleswig-Holstein faction in Frankfurt had proved that the region was culturally German, even if not all of their countrymen spoke German. As Vick has explained, "The Frankfurt Deputies only had to be satisfied that its administrative superstructure, high culture, and general will were sufficiently German-oriented to bestow upon it an overall German national character."[40]

Embedded within such arguments was more than a hint of chauvinism. Michelsen's point about German language clearly reflected a belief in the superiority of German culture, but by holding out the hope of incorporating Danish-speakers into the Volk, he stopped short of drawing sharp distinctions between the two peoples. A similar tension coloured uses of the distant past in the argument. Though Michelsen had been a committed antiquarian, he stayed away from archaeology in his claims. It was rather his fellow deputy, Jacob Grimm, who framed the German nation-state around notions of ancient heritage. His arguments carried a similar tension between embracing points of commonality between Germans and certain non-Germans and upholding a distinctively lofty view of the German nation. But where Michelsen looked to his expertise in law and politics, Grimm drew on his knowledge of language, folk culture, and history. In 1848, he published *History of the German Language* (*Geschichte der Deutschen Sprache*), which placed Dutch and Danish under a Germanic rubric and called for the inclusion of Switzerland, Holland, Flanders, and Alsace into a future German Reich. Turning to records of ancient settlement, he even suggested that Germany should incorporate Denmark's Jutland Peninsula and reduce Denmark to its islands. He based this proposal on the claim that Jutland's original inhabitants had been Germanic rather than Nordic peoples, and that the area had been occupied by the Danes relatively recently in history. In a letter to C.C. Rafn in December 1848, he explained, "Originally the peninsula was totally Germanic or German (whichever expression you like), and the ancestors of the Jutes were of one [German] blood with the Cimbrians and Saxons."[41]

Grimm's view was somewhat at odds with Brian Vick's characterization of German liberal thought. While his assertions about the affinity of language groups were not unusual, his claims to Jutland had little to do with shared history, which was an important prerequisite for many German liberals. But, then again, Grimm was hardly a typical liberal. He was hostile to parliamentary democracy and disdained constitutionalism. He was instead more concerned with defining and cultivating the Volk as an authentic, organic entity.[42] For these reasons, he maintained the same tenuous balance between national inclusiveness and cultural hierarchy that informed Michelsen's views, but he separated himself from his peers by relying on ancient heritage as a principal answer for the contemporary national question.

Grimm's colleagues in Denmark soon found themselves scrambling to counter his claims.[43] In December 1848, C.C. Rafn appealed to Grimm as a fellow scholar, sending him a copy of Caspar Frederik Wegener's *On Schleswig's Inseparable Bond with Denmark in Respect to Law* (*Über die unzertrennliche Verbindung Schleswigs mit Dänemark in staatsrechtlicher Beziehung*). "I do not doubt," he wrote, "that you as a truth-loving man will gain enlightenment and instruction with consideration of the circumstances that have previously been unknown to you, and it is therefore a pleasure for me to send you the manuscript."[44] He also pointed to statistics showing that Schleswig in 1848 had over 200,000 Danish-speakers, arguing that these numbers were more relevant than the traces of prehistoric peoples.[45] Unmoved, Grimm replied, "I am supposed to be enlightened and converted by Wegener's passionate pamphlet? I have discovered nothing in it that would tip the balance. The fate of the so-called duchies must be decided by completely different means."[46]

Grimm's means, of course, implied war, and, as he debated with Rafn, the conflict raged. When the war opened in April, the Danes had quickly overwhelmed the Schleswig-Holstein militias and scored a series of early victories. Within weeks, they pushed south to capture the city of Schleswig and seize the Danevirke. The Schleswig-Holsteiners were saved only by the intervention of 25,000 troops from Prussia and the German Bund. In late April 1848, they swept into the region and began pushing the Danish army out of Jutland. By the time the Truce of Malmö went into effect, in July, the Germans faced the tantalizing possibility of seizing the entire peninsula.

It is not clear how much these opportunities may have encouraged Grimm's proposals, but they certainly seemed to influence Jens Worsaae's response to the border question. Worsaae's first public comments came shortly after the Danes captured the Danevirke, a symbolic victory that had prompted an outpouring of patriotism.[47] He marked the occasion with a short book on the prehistory of the area. In it he proclaimed, "At this time, all eyes in Scandinavia are turned to the Danevirke, to the Danish nation's southern border. When thinking of the hard fight between Germans and Scandinavians, it is natural to think back to bygone times, … which bind themselves to the older struggles on Denmark's border."[48] He went on to express sympathy for the Eiderdane position, and argued that his archaeological research proved the special connection between Schleswig and the people of the Danish islands. "By contrast," he wrote, "Holstein, with its environment bound more closely to the German mainland, was also settled mostly by Germans from the mainland."[49] Finally, he rejected the popular conception that both the Angles and Saxons in the region were Germanic, and that the Danes had only come later. Instead, he cited the writings of Saxo Grammaticus, who believed that "Angles and Danes were brothers."[50]

Later that year, as the war turned against Denmark, Worsaae lashed out against Jacob Grimm's use of the past as a "playground for political fantasy."[51] In early 1849, he published *On a Prehistoric, So-called "German" Population in Denmark* (*Om en forhistorisk, saakaldet "tydsk" Befolkning i Danmark*) in which he attacked the Germans for linking past and present without taking into consideration the intervening history. At the same time, he countered Grimm's claims directly with interpretation based on his own field research. Using his digs in southern Jutland, Worsaae concluded that there was, in fact, no distinct Germanic society living alongside a Nordic neighbour, but rather a single culture inhabiting all of Denmark as far south as the Eider River.[52] To advance his argument, he pointed to the research of Peter Andreas Munch (1810–1863), a Norwegian philologist who concluded that the peoples of ancient Denmark and Sweden had actually been culturally closer to the Scandinavians than to the Germans. Munch, whose interest in Nordic origins was a product of his own Norwegian nationalism, had drawn on the work of the Grimms in the years before the war to seek evidence from linguistic artefacts such as rune stones and objects with runic inscriptions. In 1847, he had used Wilhelm Grimm's 1821 essay, "On the Study of Runes," to provide a new translation for the Golden Horns of Gallehus found in Schleswig. Although Munch agreed with Grimm that the runes were Gothic in character, he declared that the translation indicated an origin in southern Sweden. He suggested that they had been intended as a gift for guests in Holstein. Such evidence seemed to show that Jutland and Schleswig had borne a distinctively Nordic character for over a thousand years.[53]

Munch bolstered Worsaae's argument by providing an ostensibly "nonpartisan" assessment, but he did not share Worsaae's views on the close ties between Danes and Goths, who he felt did not enter Denmark until the end of the eight century CE. He continued to stress the Nordic character of the borderlands, but located its linguistic point of origin in Norway rather than Denmark.[54] Because Norwegian languages carried more primeval elements, Munch reasoned that they must be an original source. With this claim, Munch reversed Grimm's mental map of ancient Jutland, but in so doing undermined Worsaae's position and left him to refute two contrasting alternatives.

What was missing was archaeological proof, which led Worsaae to use his own research into regional sites and artefacts to disprove Munch's theory. He argued that, because Munch and Grimm had relied on linguistic evidence, they had not gone back far enough in time to get an accurate picture of ancient settlement.[55] Worsaae countered that finds across Denmark suggested a pattern of continuous settlement, and that its contours demonstrated earlier signs of cultural development during the Stone and Bronze Ages than elsewhere in Scandinavia. Moreover, the Iron Age, which many antiquarians believed to be quite old in

Scandinavia, had, according to Worsaae, not appeared until around the eighth century CE, and then only in Denmark.[56] This was a direct challenge to Munch because it revealed a northward trajectory of cultural diffusion. Finally, the characteristics of the artefacts did not differ widely enough within Denmark to support either Munch's claim of a local multi-ethnic mix of different Nordic and Germanic groups or Grimm's assertion of "an older Gothic origin with a sharply stamped German nationality."[57] In effect, where Munch and Grimm had used their philological research to trace large cultural groups, whether Germanic or Nordic, Worsaae had defended a notion of cultural uniqueness within the Danish realm.

By the spring of 1849, the Danes ended the Malmö Armistice and began an offensive. Although their forces suffered a number of military setbacks, the waning power of the revolution in Germany and growing international pressure led first to the Berlin Peace of 1850, which signalled the end of Prussian involvement, and later to the First London Protocol guaranteeing the integrity of the Helstat. These developments effectively dashed the hopes of the Schleswig-Holstein Provisional Government. On 2 July 1850, Schleswig-Holsteiners, without allies or experienced officers, met a crushing defeat at the Battle of Idstedt. While the battle decided the outcome of the war, it by no means settled the underlying dispute. The German Schleswig-Holsteiners only grudgingly admitted defeat in January 1851, and scores of soldiers and statesmen fled the country. Meanwhile, the London Protocol prevented Denmark from seeking to separate Schleswig from Holstein and incorporate it into the Danish Kingdom. The result was a return during the 1850s to an awkward status quo ante, with old tensions seething beneath new attempts at normalcy.[58]

Rival Museums and the Second German-Danish War, 1852–1864

Many Danes greeted the end of the war as a victory and a relief from the perceived German threat. Looking past the obvious tensions that lingered, they extolled their national character and mythologized their success. Along the way, Danish interest in national heritage grew, and, in the years between the German-Danish Wars, C.J. Thomsen and the Royal Antiquities Commission in Copenhagen responded by authorizing eight new collecting institutions across Denmark, the duchies, and in Iceland between 1852 and 1863. These regional museums were modelled on the example of Kiel, holding a collection of local finds, promoting the patronage of local citizens, and, at Thomsen's insistence, enjoying the support of the Museum for Nordic Antiquities in Copenhagen.[59]

The first of these branches was founded in 1852 in Flensburg, which guaranteed a separate institution for Schleswig and Holstein. The decision followed a souring of relations between Kiel and Copenhagen after 1848. Falck passed away in 1850, and the original museum curators and antiquarians were no longer involved in the project. In the 1920s, Fritz Graef accused Thomsen of intentionally creating a rival institution, but it is worth recalling the weakness of German antiquarianism during this period. The war had undermined the Kiel Museum, while German thinking about archaeology remained mired in historical and philological thinking in line with Andreas Michelsen and Jacob Grimm. It proved unable to embrace the changes that were shaping the budding discipline of archaeology in Denmark.

Following the departure of Christian Flor in 1845, the museum passed to the control of Karl Müllenhoff, who had studied history with Andreas Michelsen in the 1830s before turning his sights to philology. The trajectory of his career was rather remarkable, as he ascended the ranks of scholarship from a minor position as a volunteer school assistant in the small town of Meldorf on the west coast of Holstein. A devotee of the Grimms, Müllenhoff took a similar interest in exploring the connections between Nordic and Germanic myths and sagas. Moreover, he felt that Schleswig-Holstein, which stood at the crossroads of Germanic and Nordic traditions, deserved a more noteworthy status in literary scholarship. Through his writings on regional mythology, Müllenhoff earned a reputation as a formidable scholar that helped him secure first a position working with Henning Ratjen at the university library and later in 1846 a professorship in German language, literature, and antiquity.[60] The fact that he was appointed to direct the Kiel Museum in the same year suggests that the Schleswig-Holstein Antiquities Society continued to view material relics as an auxiliary responsibility of textual scholarship. Müllenhoff's lectures on Danish and German literature and his ongoing translation of *Germania*, written by the ancient Roman writer Tacitus, left him little time for museum work. Consequently, the institution grew very little at the beginning of his tenure, and with the outbreak of revolution soon came to a standstill.

The outcome of the war was a further devastating blow. The defeat forced many members of the antiquities society to emigrate from Schleswig-Holstein, so that by 1858, the rolls had dropped from 366 members to only 31.[61] The loss in revenue meant that the museum was unable to pay for new acquisitions or improve its display. The University of Kiel offered some assistance, granting, for example, a small sum for a new cabinet in March 1851,[62] but the decline meant that from 1850 to 1860 the society was only able to print four volumes of its annual report.[63] The shortfall also prevented the society from obtaining one of the most notable collections in the region. In 1847, the wealthy antiquities collector Claus Jaspersen died in the town of Schleswig, and in accordance with his will his wife Sophie put the collection up for sale after the war.[64] Christian

Flor had cultivated a relationship with Jaspersen during the early 1840s, but after Flor's departure, Jaspersen expressed a concern that the collection "might come into German hands."[65] After his death, the Kiel Museum requested financial support from the Antiquities Commission to purchase the collection, but Thomsen and Rafn could not agree whether to send the collection to Kiel or to Copenhagen. Worsaae made a case for sending them to Rødding, where Christian Flor could tend them at his new Grundtvigian school. The government ultimately sided with Thomsen and planned to meet the Kiel request, but the outbreak of war suspended negotiations with Sophie Jaspersen.[66]

After the war, the Antiquities Commission decided to send the artefacts to Flensburg in the Duchy of Schleswig. This satisfied Worsaae because it kept the artefacts near Jaspersen's home, and because the construction of the new secondary school (*Gymnasium*) meant that there would be ample space to house the collection. Thomsen was also amenable to the compromise because Flensburg had become home to one of his former students, Conrad Engelhardt (1825–1881). Like Worsaae, Engelhardt had been unable to secure a post with Thomsen's museum, but had found a respectable position in the Flensburg Gymnasium made vacant by departing pro-German Schleswig-Holsteiners.[67] On 22 September 1852, Jaspersen's artefacts joined an assortment of donations from Copenhagen to form a new Schleswig Collection of Nordic Antiquites (Slesvigske Samling af nordiske Oldsager). When it opened, it occupied two rooms with nine cabinets. Six contained local Stone Age artefacts and featured some remarkable axe-heads, another two housed a set of Bronze Age blades, and a final cabinet mixed Iron Age and historical artefacts, including a number of Roman and medieval swords.[68]

At first, only a few families and vacationing students patronized the exhibit each week, and Engelhardt complained to Thomsen that his collection was unable to grow because so many locals had pledged to support the Kiel Museum.[69] His remarks suggested that the Danish government, though at times supportive of the Flensburg Collection, was not trying to use it to diminish the nearby Kiel Museum. Rather, it was Engelhardt himself who began shaping his collection as a rival to Kiel. His strategy involved appealing not to Danish sympathy, but to the loyalties of local Schleswigers. He began a writing campaign to those members of the Schleswig-Holstein Antiquities Society residing in the Duchy of Schleswig, and he gave private tours to local collectors. His goal was to cultivate an interest in a more localized collection "for the benefit of Schleswig."[70] Engelhardt expected such sentiments to resonate with Danish Schleswigers who had just experienced a three-year war over the status of the duchies, but he found that his strategy also attracted a number of German-speakers in Schleswig. This came at a time when the Kiel Museum was already in marked decline, and when its remaining patrons were displeased by its apparent inertia. One antiquarian, W.H. Kolster, responded to a rare update from Müllenhoff, "With pleasure I see from your letter that the activities of the Society have not entirely silenced, as I had begun to fear."[71] Engelhardt took advantage of this unrequited enthusiasm to draw support away from Kiel and acquire other noted collections in Schleswig, including that of the German-speaking Heinrich Piepgras, which included an array of coins and Stone Age relics. He also succeeded in establishing a network with small-town antiquarians such as the apothecaries M.R. Mechlenburg and L. Henningsen, who were well-placed to stay abreast of new discoveries across the region.[72]

By the late 1850s, Engelhardt used his growing resources and newly found connections to launch a series of excavations in eastern Schleswig. In 1856, he learned from M.R. Mechlenburg of a potentially rich site discovered during reclamation work in the Thorsberg Bog near the village of Süderbrarup. Engelhardt spent two years pinpointing the best location to dig.[73] Although he had previously welcomed artefacts recovered by farmers on their own land, he recognized in this case that he would have to become personally involved, first because the land belonged to several farmers and second because it would be an expensive operation to drain and excavate the bogs. Moreover, Engelhardt had become aware through his exchanges with private collectors that archaeological remains demanded a higher level of care (Piepgras, for example, had once sent him a spearhead broken into pieces by his children).[74] Finally, he was unwilling to let Worsaae conduct the dig, fearing that he would send the choicest pieces to Copenhagen.[75]

With this in mind, Engelhardt announced in June of 1858 that he was planning to use a recent raise at the school to finance an excavation in bogs on the properties belonging to farmers Gosch Hansen and Peter Callsen.[76] He identified three key depressions in the bog, and within a few weeks had already uncovered some promising finds, including a number of Roman coins from the period of the Principate (including three Trajans, one Hadrian, one Antonius Pius, and one Marcus Aurelius), which helped date the site to around the third century CE.[77] Like Worsaae, Engelhardt took careful notes of his progress, preserving evidence in order to answer questions both about the contents of the site and about the processes of deposition.[78] By September, he and his hired labourers had, by digging in the soft earth with their fingers, recovered more than a thousand pieces, including an assortment of Roman breastplates, swords, shields, and helmets with curving bronze snakes. There were also a number of local artefacts: necklaces, spiral rings, and fragments of gold ring whose equal size and weight suggested they were once used as money. Among the other key finds were a number of iron implements and shield buckles inscribed with runes. Finally, Engelhardt was also delighted to find wood, cloth, and leather artefacts preserved within the marsh, which promised an unprecedented glimpse into the lives of the area's ancient inhabitants. In analysing his discoveries, Engelhardt was able to enter into Worsaae's emerging paradigm and make comparisons with other bog finds. He concluded that his site was significant not only because it provided evidence of links with Roman civilization, but also because it reinforced Worsaae's earlier argument that the Iron Age and the use of runic writing were much older in the region than previously believed.[79]

The discoveries at Süderbrarup dramatically increased both the reputation and credibility of the Flensburg Collection, and this early success soon led to other excavations, including one at a second bog site at Thorsberg and at a number of grave barrows in southern Schleswig. Yet, the greatest of these was the excavation of the Nydam Bog. In July 1859, Niels Kuntz, a schoolteacher in the small hamlet of Østersottrup, delivered to Engelhardt an iron spear fragment recovered from the narrow bog, which sat behind the local school.[80] Englehardt was immediately interested, since C.J. Thomsen had already relayed local suspicions about the potential for rich prehistoric finds in the area, and he was also eager to begin making comparisons with his Thorsberg discoveries. He therefore began excavations in the summer of 1859 and then again in 1862 and 1863.

From the beginning, the site generated a great deal of interest and speculation, and even brought two visits from King Frederik VII, but it was not until August 1863 that the most spectacular finds began to emerge. As Stine Wiell has since recounted, it was 7 August when Engelhardt and his team, with a visiting C.J. Thomsen anxiously observing, uncovered the first recognizable pieces of oak from a large, oar-driven boat buried within the earth.[81] After several more days, the excavators found more pieces, and then uncovered the bulk of the craft on 18 August. A number of other artefacts lay nearby, including jewellery, coins, and over 106 iron swords, which dated the site to the third century CE. Engelhardt surmised that the items had been carried in the boat via the nearby Alssund Strait and buried in a manner very similar to that seen at Thorsberg.[82] Eventually, Engelhardt's crew managed to transport the pieces of the craft to Flensburg, where they began the process of preserving and reassembling it. The discovery marked a high point in the growth of the Flensburg Collection just as the rumours of war began to place it under threat.

In 1857, Engelhardt wrote to Thomsen that, while he missed Copenhagen, his collection had become such a passion that he felt it bound him to Flensburg. He was not alone in his admiration. In the late 1850s and early 1860s, attitudes about the Flensburg Collection and about archaeology changed as old political tensions began to rise once again. Where Engelhardt had struggled for funding in the first few years, his early successes brought him the financial support from the Danish state that he needed to conduct his digs. In 1858, the Ministry for the Duchies awarded him an initial 700 Rigstaler for his Süderbrarup project, and later funded his digs at the Thorsberger Moor and at Nydam. Engelhardt desperately needed the money, since the property owners were demanding payment for artefacts removed from their land,[83] and Engelhardt also needed to finance a rather large operation to drain the bogs in order to carry out a controlled dig.[84]

The growth of the Flensburg Collection created tensions with the Kiel Museum. In 1858, the Plattdeutsch poet Klaus Groth (1819–1899) succeeded Karl Müllenhoff as director of the Schleswig-Holstein Antiquities Society after Müllenhoff received a chair in Germanic languages at the University of Berlin. Like Müllenhoff, Groth did little to advance the scholarship of the society, but it seems that he was more eager to challenge the pace of Engelhardt's advances. Correspondence from Engelhardt to Copenhagen suggests that in 1858 Groth sought clarification of the charter of the antiquities society, which stated that the Kiel Museum had the responsibility for overseeing finds in both duchies. He also allegedly expressed concerns that Engelhardt would take his finds to Copenhagen. That same year, he joined the rector of the University of Kiel in unsuccessfully attempting to purchase some of the property on which Engelhardt was excavating. The government responded in December that it was inappropriate for a non-political institution to represent both duchies, a decision that the society members protested in the Estate Assembly in Itzehoe.[85] That same year, Engelhardt seems to have known that the government would side with him, as he predicted that the antiquarians in Kiel would be reorganizing as a "Holstein-Lauenburg Antiquities Society."[86]

The sudden upswing in state support coincided with a growing desire on the part of Orla Lehmann and the powerful Eiderdane faction in the Danish government to effect the legal separation of the two duchies in spite of the London Protocol. As Engelhardt toiled at the Thorsberger Moor in 1858, a new debate began in Copenhagen on a prospective constitution for the Kingdom of Denmark, and the status of Schleswig and Holstein became a central question once again. Work on the constitution had progressed since 1852, but Eiderdanes demanded that any Danish constitution must guarantee the connections with Schleswig.[87] At the same time, the government altered its administrative structure in the duchies, which, as Peter Thaler has explained, "tied Sleswig more closely to the Danish economic sphere and temporarily divided the duchies through a customs border."[88] In this context, it is likely that the government's decisions on cultural matters matched its political and economic manoeuvres.

The prohibition against the Kiel Museum's involvement in Schleswig was effectively a limit on the links the Germans could make between the two duchies, and a de facto segregation of regional institutions. Moreover, it limited the degree to which Germans could make claims to Schleswig based on archaeological evidence.

The latent political tensions in the region finally erupted after the sudden death of King Frederik VII on 15 November 1863, which occurred two days before the signing of the new constitution. Because Frederik had no direct heir, a succession dispute presented an opportunity to alter the outcome of the 1848 war. While Frederik's distant male relative, Christian von Glücksburg, was legally entitled to the throne under Denmark's somewhat modified Salic Law, the succession of the duchies depended on a direct male heir. German Schleswig-Holsteiners rejected Christian's right to rule their territory, and instead looked to local nobleman Friedrich von Augustenburg (1829–1880).[89]

On the international scene, popular opinion in Prussia fumed against Danish obstinance and aggression. The novelist Theodor Fontane (1819–1898) roundly denounced the Eiderdane faction and praised the Prussians for their defence of the London Protocol.[90] Chancellor Otto von Bismarck (1815–1898), meanwhile, saw an opportunity to exploit the "Schleswig-Holstein Question" and secure Prussian hegemony in northern Germany.[91] He made official protests against Denmark's violation of the London Protocol and, after the newly installed Christian IX (r. 1863–1906) signed the so-called November Constitution, issued an ultimatum for the restoration of the status quo. During the debate, C.C. Rafn and Jens Worsaae made urgent appeals to their contacts abroad to help build international support for Denmark. Rafn in particular used his runic research to justify Danish claims to Schleswig and explain the logic of annexation.[92] This time, there was little time for a prolonged discussion, as Bismarck correctly assessed that Denmark was diplomatically isolated. When the Danes refused to accede to his demands, the Prussians joined the Austrians in invading the duchies in February 1864, thereby launching the Second German-Danish War.

Just as in 1848, the Prussians and Austrians used prehistory to support their claims to the region. Groups of scholars and military officers with antiquarian interests accompanied the invading armies, who saw the recovery of artefacts in Schleswig-Holstein as legitimate explorations of a collective German past. Wiell has documented a number of incidents during the conflict in which Prussian and Austrian forces orchestrated impromptu digs and transported artefacts to museums in Berlin and Vienna. Among the leading scholars involved was Leopold von Ledebur (1799–1877), director of the Royal Kunstkammer in Berlin, who Wiell claims came with the army to obtain finds directly from the

Flensburg Collection. In some cases, like the Austrian digs at the grave barrow at Hohøj in Mariager, the digs were merely opportunities to go treasure hunting and bring home gold and silver. Some officers made agreements to divide found artefacts among their men as spoils of war.[93] Others were drawn by Engelhardt's celebrity to find new rich sites in the region.[94] In the summer of 1864, an Austrian excavation at the Nydam site uncovered a metal anchor associated with the boat.[95] Within a few days of the outbreak of the war, the Prussian and Austrian forces stood before the Danevirke, where the Danish general Christian Julius de Meza (1792–1865) had strengthened the old fortifications to prevent a German advance into Jutland and the Danish Isles. On the night of 5 February, however, de Meza realized that the ancient walls would be no match for the modern armies of the Germans, and he withdrew to prepared positions at Dybbøl, across the Alssund Strait from Sønderborg and only a short distance from the Nydam Bog. On 18 April, the Prussians and Austrians attacked and forced the Danish army to abandon the duchies.

The possibility of Prussian forces arriving at his doorstep forced Conrad Engelhardt to make a difficult choice about the fate of his collection. On the one hand, he remained committed to the local dimension of his enterprise and felt personally connected to Flensburg, and he recognized the potential harm that could come to the delicate pieces should they be moved without a great deal of care. On the other hand, he was under no illusions about the intentions of the invading forces. He was also strongly encouraged by his colleague and fellow Thomsen student C.F. Herbst (1818–1911) to remove the artefacts from possible Prussian control. Worsaae also recommended that they be moved, and on his advice, Engelhardt decided that it would be far better to see his collection go to Copenhagen than Berlin. According to Graef, he packed up the contents of his collection in thirty-two crates with the help of colleagues from the Flensburg school, loaded them onto the steamship *Jylland*, and sent them to the city of Nordborg. When Nordborg also became threatened in the war, he transferred the collection a second time to Korsør on the island of Sjælland.[96]

The Prussians thus arrived to empty exhibition halls in Flensburg. Both sides quickly began a very public debate over the collection's disappearance. In Berlin, Leopold von Ledebur condemned Engelhardt's act in the *Neue Preußische Zeitung* newspaper,[97] while editorials in Copenhagen stressed the country's right to retain Engelhardt's artefacts.[98] In the *Berlingske Tidende* newspaper, for example, one commentator blasted the "shameless boldness" of the German claim, writing that it was all the more surprising, "when one thinks of how the German border dwellers, in all the years that they have dominated Schleswig (until 1850), never intended to lay a useful foundation for a scientifically ordered collection of Schleswig antiquities, because they have been constantly alienated from the Scandinavian past," or, the writer continued, "when one furthermore knows that the Kiel collection has nothing that can be compared in any way with Flensburg precisely because Holstein has an entirely different past than ancient Schleswig."[99] Once again, the emphasis for Danes lay with the distinctions between a presumably "Danish" Schleswig and a "German" Holstein, which were allegedly evident in the Flensburg artefacts. Indeed, they had become so important that Worsaae begged the Danish Foreign Ministry to offer the Germans a respectable collection of Nordic relics from Copenhagen in exchange for the right to retain the Flensburg Collection.[100] For ordinary Danes, the surest proof of their opinions was their silence. As the two sides assembled for peace negotiations in the late summer of 1864, there was no word about the location of the collection. In contemporary reports, journalists noted that dozens and perhaps hundreds must have helped pack the artefacts or transport them northward or must have otherwise witnessed their removal.[101]

The Germans were no less determined, and the Prussians in particular ensured that the artefacts remained at the centre of peace negotiations.[102] In October 1864, the belligerent nations signed the Treaty of Vienna, which brought an end to the war, granted the Prussians and Austrians administrative control over Schleswig and Holstein, and set a new border running west from Hejlsminde along the Little Belt Strait to the mouth of the Kongeå River on the North Sea. Within the text of the treaty, Article XIV specifically spelled out the fate of Engelhardt's artefacts: "The antiquities collection at Flensburg, which stands in connection with the history of Schleswig, and was in large part scattered during recent events, shall be restored to that place again with the help of the Danish government."[103] The Prussians brushed aside Worsaae's offer of exchange, and worked with Danish police investigators to recover the finds.[104] Yet, as 1865 drew to a close, their whereabouts remained unknown.

Conclusion

The Flensburg Collection remained a mystery for two years after the guns fell silent in the last German-Danish War. Even in their absence, the remarkable artefacts unearthed between the war years remained focal points not only of an emerging discipline, but also of two emerging nations. The story of their discovery reflected the decades-long process that yielded systematic field practices. Their incorporation into the museum in Flensburg was but one example of the wider popularization and institutionalization of antiquarian study. Finally, the controversy surrounding their disappearance mirrored the collision between new practices and lingering questions about the borderlands. In the ensuing decades, these artefacts would become more than curiosity pieces or the currency of private collecting societies. They would become symbols for conflicting causes and tangible markers of national frontiers. For this reason, the disposition of the Nydam Boat and the Flensburg Collection would re-emerge as a central issue of border relations over the next seventy years.

The dispute denoted a pendulum swing from a sense of stewardship to one of ownership of antiquities that went hand-in-hand with changes in the study of the past during the mid-nineteenth century. In these years, Worsaae built upon the work C.J. Thomsen to fashion an edifice that would transform antiquarianism into the discipline of archaeology, complete with its own far-reaching questions and theories to guide future discoveries. Engelhardt later expanded on Worsaae's promise, taking his fieldwork into the bogs and fens where few excavators dared go. Together, they transcended the antiquarianism of past decades and cast the prehistoric researcher not only as a collector and exhibitor, but also an explorer and interpreter. Above all, they laid a cornerstone for an emerging intellectual field that rested upon shared institutions and practices and on a common belief in their potential to tell the story of the past.

As we have seen, this field was from the beginning deeply infused with politics. Nationalist interpretations formed its most extreme edges, but also cut across constellations of orthodoxy. Worsaae's debate with Jacob Grimm and P.A. Munch in the First German-Danish War showed both the irresistible pull of the national question on prehistoric study and the ways in which antiquarian scholarship dramatically changed the discussion over international borders. As a criterion of national identity, ancient heritage proved more concrete than language, history, or custom. Any group could adopt new practices or learn a new language, but ancient cultures made their geography known through sites rooted in the earth and through artefacts with fixed provenance. They thus warranted firm boundaries and in this way helped transform the complex "Schleswig-Holstein Question" into a simple border dispute that delineated Germany and Denmark either at the Eider or the Kongeå. At the same time, however, prehistory made possible much more ambitious claims than those based on other criteria. When Jacob Grimm named Jutland a Germanic territory, he did so primarily on the basis of ancient lineage. He thus elided all modern markers of belonging and pushed beyond even Michelsen's questionable notions about North Schleswig's compatibility with the German Volk. He made a claim that, not for the last time, would convert mutable interpretations into immutable ownership.

In a similar way, nationalist visions had a hand in shaping the institutions in Kiel and Flensburg and placing them at odds with one another. Yet, when the unspoken goal of archaeology was to excavate nations, and when the nation was accepted as an a priori entity, then political engagement was inevitable.

Indeed, only at the border were the distinctions between scholarship and patriotism thrown into question. Only here did the ambiguities of identity demand a deeper search and a more rigorous scholarship. Regional archaeologists from Worsaae's generation seemed to have recognized to differing degrees the fine line between objective truth and political context. If they at times made choices that seemingly threw them off course, or if they failed to embrace a more rigid objectivity, it was at least partly because they experienced pressure from Frankfurt, Berlin, and Copenhagen. With so much at stake for both nations, it is little wonder that scholars in Schleswig and Holstein later found it challenging to find a moderate position and maintain commitments to the regional enterprise.

What was perhaps most remarkable under these circumstances was the resilience of the scholarly community, whose bonds unmistakably ruptured, but (as we will see) were never fully sundered. Even the most bitter debates did not put an end to correspondence, and institutional journals carried on the academic conversation even when nationalist passions rendered other forms of dialogue impossible. Indeed, the waning years in the Kiel Museum and the loss of the Flensburg Collection revealed just how important the cross-border community was to the discovery of the past. The archaeology that was forming in these years was not merely a matter of sites and artefacts, but of contacts and personal relationships. These years were thus a warning that the hunger for antiquity could only be satiated through cooperation, even as their consequences left the next generation struggling to find a centre in a polarized and politicized intellectual field.

3 Discovery and Rediscovery at Haithabu

In the years after the German-Danish Wars, the search for the ancient past in Schleswig-Holstein began anew on the shores of the Schlei Inlet across from the town of Schleswig. This bucolic setting of tilled fields and grazing cattle marks the eastern end of the Danevirke, whose linear works give way in its final metres to a curious semicircular ring of earth and rock. Long known as the Oldenburg, this feature reaches to the wind-swept inlet waters and shelters a grassy meadow. Here, at the turn of the century, archaeologists from Kiel and Copenhagen came together to discover the remains of Haithabu, a lost town from the Viking Age. Once the heart of a vast trading network, Haithabu had mysteriously vanished from medieval chronicles around the eleventh century and had since fallen into the realm of legend. Nearly nine hundred years later, Haithabu emerged again to join the Nydam Boat as a testament to the rich heritage buried within the borderlands. And where the latter marked the expansion of antiquarian study and became a prize in the border conflict, the former denoted the possibilities of a professionalized archaeology that matured during the late nineteenth century and served as a powerful reminder of the fruits of cooperation.

Haithabu was thus the culmination of the dramatic changes that took place between the end of the Second German-Danish War in 1864 and the outbreak of the First World War in 1914. The next two chapters will address these developments, first by dealing with the process of reconciliation in the borderlands and then by tracing the growth of "scientific" archaeology and its alignment with nationalist and *völkisch* thought at the turn of the century. As we will see, the connections between regional archaeology in Schleswig-Holstein and national identity in Germany and Denmark only deepened during these years, even as the distance widened between amateur antiquarianism and professional archaeology. In part, this was the natural result of ongoing modernization. For

The Haithabu site. Photograph courtesy Stiftung Schleswig-Holsteinische Landesmuseen Schloss Gottorf.

Danes adjusting to their country's truncated borders and Germans experiencing the rapid industrialization of their new nation-state, the changes of the late nineteenth century produced a sharp sense of dislocation that led both sides to invoke archaeology as a means of soothing the transition to modernity. For German-speaking Schleswig-Holsteiners living in the expansive German Empire (Kaiserreich), these same changes reinforced conceptions of Heimat, which, as Alon Confino and Celia Applegate have argued, drew on local understandings of the past to integrate regions into evolving nation-states.[1] As Confino has explained, "Heimat … connected the abstract nation with the personal local existence by making national history as tangible as local history; Heimat nationalized local history by, in fact, localizing national history."[2]

A yearning for the past and a desire for a "tangible" regional history brought fresh relevance to the study of northern antiquity, but archaeology was also distinctly modern. Indeed, methodological innovations, including more systematic and comparative approaches, made it possible to fit discoveries of the borderlands within larger narratives. But the growth of the discipline also created new challenges. The tendency for networks and institutions to orient themselves around national lines was at odds with the increasing need for artefacts, resources, and expertise that could only be found in neighbouring countries. As Germans and Danes learned during this crucial period, national frameworks for academic archaeology were untenable without assistance from beyond the border.

Schleswig-Holstein archaeology consequently remained at the nexus of regional, national, and transnational forces in the late nineteenth and early twentieth centuries. But the outcome of the wars and the establishment of a German nation-state meant that boundaries were becoming less fluid, cross-border exchanges less common, and scholarly networks more limited. How, then, was reconciliation ultimately possible? As this chapter will show, the professionalization of archaeology depended heavily on individuals who could transcend the increasingly rigid pedigree of those who enjoyed access and status within academia. Among those who proved most significant in crossing these figurative borders was Johanna Mestorf (1828–1909), who became director of the Kiel Museum at the turn of the century. While her gender and non-traditional education placed her at odds with the norms of scholarship, her experience abroad proved essential not only to building her own professional identity, but also to rebuilding old academic ties to the Nordic lands.

Behind the history of the discovery at the Oldenburg and the rediscovery of Haithabu is a much more complex story about the recovery of regional institutions, the revitalization of prehistoric study, and the re-emergence of cooperation between Germans and Danes. And below is an account that tells us much about the practice of "normal" scholarship as it chronicles the extension and metamorphosis of the intellectual field.

Regional Antiquities and State Institutions

In many ways, the German victory in the German-Danish War of 1864 should have been a windfall for the Schleswig-Holstein Antiquities Society and the Kiel Mueum. The Danish defeat in the war meant the end of Conrad Engelhardt's rival institution in Flensburg. As early as March 1864, the Prussians and Austrians had lifted the prohibition against the society's rights to collect antiquities in the northern duchy.[3] After more than a decade of neglect and competition, the members of the society found themselves once again overseeing the primary collecting institution in Schleswig-Holstein. They also asserted their claims to the Flensburg Collection. Two professors at the University of

Kiel, the art historian Gustav Ferdinand Thaulow (1817–1883) and the historian Heinrich Handelmann (1827–1891), pressured the Prussians to locate Engelhardt's artefacts and return them to Schleswig-Holstein. Another supporter, Christian Jessen, who was headmaster at the Latin School in Haderslev, responded in the press to writers from Copenhagen who claimed the artefacts as Danish. These outspoken members did more than simply identify the relics as German. They offered a third perspective that stressed the provenance of artefacts from an indivisible Schleswig-Holstein. Moreover, Jessen thwarted the partisanship of national claims through the language of objectivity, appealing to the need for "enlightening our ancient past in an unbiased manner." He went on to implore "his countrymen" in Schleswig to look to their (regional) homeland and join the society.[4]

It was November 1866 when Prussian authorities at last learned the whereabouts of the hidden artefacts. An informant, lured by the promise of a reward, entered the Prussian embassy in Copenhagen and provided the location. After a short period of diplomatic wrangling, the Danes finally handed over the collection in January 1868.[5] Their return was a final victory in the conflict for the Germans, and no less a victory for the members of the antiquities society, but the moment also underscored their lingering weakness. During the second conflict, regional collectors found themselves at the mercy of Prussian and Austrian antiquarians who moved across the countryside with their respective armies and removed an untold number of artefacts with little regard for regional authorities.

One of the most telling examples of the tense relations between Schleswig-Holsteiners and Prussians after the war was a scandal concerning the famed novelist Gustav Freytag (1816–1895). As an ardent national liberal and Prussian patriot, Freytag had commented often on Schleswig-Holstein affairs in his literary journal, *Die Grenzboten*, where he expressed his support for Prussian intervention in the duchies. Shortly after Prussia wrested control of Schleswig from Austria and incorporated the duchies in 1867, he toured the western coast of the new province. As a national liberal, Freytag was curious about the potential for Schleswig-Holstein to serve the needs of a German navy, but as an avid student of German history, he was also interested in visiting the stone passage graves that dotted the western island of Sylt. Shortly after his stay, a commentator in the *Itzehoer Nachrichten* newspaper publicly accused Freytag of being among a group of foreigners who had pilfered artefacts. As Freytag reported, "I for my part stand under suspicion of having made off with a kettle from one of the graves."[6] Freytag did not deny the charges, but pointed instead to the apathy he observed among locals for the care of antiquities. With such lack of concern in the region, he argued, it should scarcely matter whether he picked up a few odd pieces. He complained that if artefacts were at risk, then the true fault lay with Schleswig-Holsteiners and above all with the Museum of Antiquities in Kiel, whose pitiful state of disrepair reflected a general indifference about the past. He cited examples of untended artefacts and unopened boxes and noted, "One can often hear patriotic Prussian scholars express the opinion that it would be better for scholarship if the antiquities were to remain useful and well-ordered in Copenhagen instead of now being packed in a storeroom left to the humidity and rust."[7]

Freytag's justification hinted at his view on the finds. On the one hand, he clearly perceived a right to investigate the sites on Sylt because they were inherently German. On the other hand, his notorious Prussian patriotism was unmistakable in the disdain with which he regarded regional officials. His comments were bound to instil resentment in the many Schleswig-Holsteiners who had hoped in vain to retain autonomy under Duke Frederick VIII (1829–1880). More specifically, his critique of local collectors not only mischaracterized their sense of the value of prehistory, but also ignored the degree to which the museum itself had been a casualty of the wars. Indeed, concerns over such casual looting lent urgency to efforts to revive the museum in order to prevent the loss or destruction of other high-value artefacts. The fact that the perpetrators were often outsiders like Freytag also connected to long-standing anxiety about more systematic depredations at the hands of the Prussian and Danish governments. As one local observer noted, "It would be painful to complain if these valuable finds should be split up, but hopefully due care will be exercised in Schleswig, to save what can be saved, to reclaim what should be stolen by Danes and Prussians."[8] These were not entirely imagined fears, especially after word reached Kiel that J.J.A. Worsaae had convinced Georg Lisch (1801–1883), a well-known antiquarian in Schwerin, to help divide important finds between the antiquities museums in Berlin and Copenhagen.[9] Although the idea ultimately failed to win over the Prussians, it highlighted the potential of surrendering regional control of antiquarian scholarship.

In the first years after the wars, the biggest challenges facing the Kiel Museum were limited funding and inadequate expertise, particularly after the departure of Karl Müllenhoff. When Worsaae and Lisch argued that the scholars in Kiel did not have the capacity to treat and interpret the objects in their care, they appear to have been referring to Klaus Groth, who had succeeded Müllenhoff as director.[10] Groth was a well-regarded Plattdeutsch poet who taught Germanic languages and literatures at the University of Kiel, but had limited training in museum work. In fact, many Schleswig-Holstein antiquarians were critical of his tenure, as when Johanna Mestorf, the daughter of one of the society's founding members, wrote in 1868, "Mention Kiel and people laugh; the educated speak with contempt for [Klaus Groth], who has laid aside the most interesting [antiquarian] information without further inquiry, etc."[11] A year earlier, the Hamburg city librarian Christian Petersen (d. 1872), had written to report that many locals had lost faith in the Schleswig-Holstein Antiquities Society and had begun sending correspondence about antiquarian finds to him rather than to Groth in Kiel.[12]

In response to this pressure, the directors of the antiquities society turned to the Prussian state to grant their enterprise new legitimacy. In September 1866, they wrote to the provincial administration requesting a new state charter, which they received in November of the same year. The charter increased the authority of the museum director's position by adding to it the title of "Conservator of National Antiquities."[13] In 1866, this dual title went to Heinrich Handelmann, who was then a lecturer at the university and since 1861 a member of the steering committee of the antiquities society. Handelmann was a long-time Schleswig-Holstein patriot who had fought on the German side during the uprising of 1848. After the war, he studied in Berlin and Göttingen before earning his doctorate in history in Kiel in 1854.[14] He cultivated an interest in antiquities and numismatics while working with Groth in the Kiel Museum,[15] Once Groth received a professorship in Germanic languages in 1866, Handelmann became the obvious choice to replace him.

Upon receiving his new position, Handelmann quickly moved to restore the museum's regional standing. First, he petitioned the Prussian government to bring the Flensburg artefacts to Kiel. Along with Gustav Thaulow, Handelmann struggled not only against the claims of Conrad Engelhardt and the Danes, but also against leading citizens of Flensburg, who wished to see the collection exhibited once again in the Flensburg Gymnasium. Initially, the school's rector was able to win support from the provincial assembly, but the administration had second thoughts after finding the school's facilities unsuitable for housing the artefacts. The Prussian administration then gave Handelmann's claim another hearing.[16] To bolster his argument, Handelmann used the potential acquisition of the Flensburg Collection to convince the University of Kiel to include his museum in its budget.[17] With persistent lobbying and firm financial footing, Handelmann prevailed, and in July 1869, the Prussian administration awarded the collection to Kiel.[18]

Second, Handelmann built on his success by expanding the museum's collection through fieldwork during the early 1870s. Not surprisingly, his first digs took place on the island of Sylt, where Freytag's visit had been such a *cause célèbre*. The excavations afforded Handelmann a chance to establish his institution's authority over regional fieldwork, but from the beginning they depended on the largesse of the central government, which by this time was part of the new German Kaiserreich. To preserve state funding, Handelmann remained gracious in his reports. He acknowledged the plunder and damage that the sites had suffered during the war, which included the use of grave barrows as signal stations, but he refrained from criticizing the Prussian military or outside antiquarians. Rather, he made a point to thank all those who had conducted earlier digs. Moreover, Handelmann was careful to cultivate goodwill in Berlin by situating his own work within earlier German investigations of sites on the island. As a result, the German government provided support for a series of digs that lasted through much of the 1870s and included excavations of more than thirty prominent gravesites.[19]

Handelmann's cooperation with authorities in Berlin on both the Flensburg artefacts and excavations on Sylt signalled the Kiel Museum's institutional integration with the new German nation-state. By 1873, the Flensburg and Kiel collections were merged to form a new Schleswig-Holstein Museum of National Antiquities (Schleswig-Holstein Museum vaterländischer Alterthümer). The antiquities society dissolved itself, and the museum became an official branch of the University of Kiel under the authority of the Prussian Ministry of Religious, Instructional, and Medical Affairs (Preußisches Ministerium für geistliche, Unterrichts- und Medizinalangelegenheiten).[20] The transition assured that the museum would have the resources it would need to conduct archaeological research in Schleswig-Holstein once again. It also laid the foundation for renewed efforts to preserve the past by bringing government resources and the state legal apparatus into the business of collection and conservation. A decade later, Wilhelm Seelig, a professor of economics at Kiel, stressed the impact of the region's connection with the national state, writing, "With the security of our inalienable bond with the collective Fatherland began at the same time once again a renewed enthusiasm for this part of the Fatherland's history."[21]

In another sense, however, the museum's integration into the nation-state dimmed prospects for resuming Schleswig-Holstein archaeology as a cross-border enterprise. Handelmann had saved the reputation of the Kiel Museum, but he had done so by turning away from collaboration with Scandinavians and by converting regional archaeology into a strictly German enterprise. At the same time, the death of C.J. Thomsen in 1865 marked the passing of one of the last remaining ties to the liberal, regional origins of early antiquarian pursuits in the mid-nineteenth century. After Thomsen's death, the directorship of the Copenhagen Museum fell to Jens Worsaae. The dominant figures in the field were thus men who had participated on opposite sides of the two wars, and who had become fully invested in exclusive nationalist projects. But the growth of archaeology in both Denmark and Schleswig-Holstein led Worsaae and Handelmann to seek help from a younger generation, from whose ranks would come the key agents of change in this polarized environment.

Johanna Mestorf and Professionalization in the Museum

In 1873, Heinrich Handelmann's search for a custodial assistant ended when he hired Johanna Mestorf, who had moved to Kiel from Hamburg and had previously worked in the museum as a volunteer. Little is known of Mestorf beyond Schleswig-Holstein, but she was notable for becoming the first woman to be named a university professor and museum director in Germany.[22] She enjoyed a spectacular career as an archaeologist in an era when women struggled to gain acceptance in higher education.[23] Mestorf was instrumental in restoring the reputation of the Kiel Museum and in transforming it into a key site for the professionalization of archaeology. From the diary that she kept of her early years in the museum, we get a glimpse of her struggles with both her colleague Heinrich Handelmann and with the norms of the field in which she worked. Ultimately, her success in shaping her discipline stemmed both from her gender and from her experience across the border.

Mestorf grew up in a middle-class household in Bad Bramstedt in Holstein, but the 1837 death of her father, the physician Jacob Heinrich Mestorf, placed the family in difficult financial circumstances. During the 1840s, Mestorf was able to attend school in Itzehoe before going to work to support her mother and brother. Her first job brought her to Sweden as a governess for the noble Piper-Engsö family at Lake Mälaren. During her stay, Mestorf mastered the Swedish language and cultivated a deep love for the country and culture. Ultimately, her health forced her to return to her mother's home in Hamburg, but in 1858 her newfound language skills earned her a position first as a secretary and then as a translator for the C. Adler publishing house.[24]

Even during this early period, Mestorf harboured a deep fascination with prehistory. Her father had been an antiquities collector and had bequeathed his collection to the Kiel Museum.[25] It is likely that her own passion for the past had grown from her father's, and her pursuits may even have helped her reconcile his early death. In her early museum work, Mestorf paused in her diary to note the pieces that had belonged to her father. "The large urn 1303 is from my father's collection," she wrote in 1874. "Was it instinct, that the old vessel was of such concern to me?"[26] Yet, Mestorf's interests were also academic. She eagerly read the archaeological texts that came to her publisher from Scandinavia and later asked first the Swedish archaeologist Sven Nilsson and later Jens Worsaae to allow her to translate their work into German.[27] Recognizing that she lacked scholarly credentials, she made her case by emphasizing

Johanna Mestorf (1828–1909). Photograph courtesy Stiftung Schleswig-Holsteinische Landesmuseen Schloss Gottorf.

her earnest desire to promote their research in Germany. This argument was significant, because although Sweden and Denmark tended to be somewhat less conservative than Germany when it came to permitting females into professional fields, there remained strong limits on women's participation.[28] As Ida Blom has argued, many of the most successful women in the Scandinavian countries tended to characterize their advancement within the prevalent patriarchal discourse.[29] Mestorf seems to have used this very tactic when she justified her role as translator in a letter to Nilsson. "The pursuit of fame and recognition befits the man," she wrote, "while the women should rather strive to make themselves useful in some capacity, and whenever possible should do so in silence, without ostentation."[30]

Ultimately, her arguments convinced her male colleagues, and she succeeded in producing over a dozen translations and short articles on Scandinavian archaeology. By the end of the 1860s, her reputation had grown sufficiently to earn her invitations to international conferences, including one in Copenhagen in 1869 and a second in Bologna in 1871. Although she did not present at either conference, her correspondence suggests that she observed the proceedings closely, made dozens of contacts, familiarized herself with the current interests of antiquarians outside Germany, and published reports of the results.[31] Mestorf thus made an unconventional entrance into the profession, using her skills as a networker and circumventing the limitations of her sex by emphasizing the fit between her contributions and her place as a woman.

The advances in archaeology that she encountered only underscored the decline of scholarship in Schleswig-Holstein and led her to advocate a revival of interest in regional antiquarianism. She began by writing pieces on local prehistory in her hometown newspaper, *Itzehoer Nachrichten*. She was also an enthusiastic supporter of rechartering the Schleswig-Holstein Antiquities Society and of Handelmann's promotion in late 1866. The following February she wrote to congratulate him, exclaiming, "I celebrated your promotion to conservator of our fatherland's antiquities as if it were a Christmas party. I greet this act as the first ray of sunshine of a better time, which livens the general interest in archaeology and awakens it to a new life."[32] A year later, it was Mestorf who warned Handelmann of the need to respond through the press to calls from J.J.A. Worsaae and Georg Lisch to expropriate the museum's artefacts.[33] On the basis of this correspondence, Handelmann invited Mestorf to assist with the daunting tasks of reorganizing the museum.

Mestorf's years of work on the fringes of the discipline had finally won her a place within an antiquarian institution. In her search for a more permanent position, however, Mestorf encountered a great deal of resistance. In 1869, the museum's state of crisis convinced its new patron, the University of Kiel, to create a paid position for a custodian of the collection, but it was four years before Mestorf was finally offered the post. Writing to the Swedish archaeologist Emil Hildebrand (1806–1884), she complained that Handelmann was proving reluctant to speak on her behalf, and that the ministry was ambivalent about the appointment, "because I am a lady."[34] Ultimately, her reputation proved too great to ignore, as she used her connections to convince not only Hildebrand, but also a number of German archaeologists, including Georg Lisch in Schwerin, to write in support of her application, and her notice of appointment came on 1 October 1873.[35]

Very soon after she began her work at the museum, Mestorf suggested in her diary that her relationship with Handelmann had grown increasingly antagonistic. The rivalry between the two stemmed both from Handelmann's rigid adherence to gender and academic hierarchy and Mestorf's sense of her superior expertise in archaeology. Handelmann appears to have been a stern traditionalist who perceived his working relationship with Mestorf as a reproduction of a middle-class home. Her role, as he often reminded her, was to serve as a "technical assistant" and tour guide, and especially to maintain and clean the collection, while his was to maintain correspondence and handle all activities related to scholarship.[36] In other words, he saw himself as the public face of the museum. Mestorf, meanwhile, could not ignore the fact that Handelmann had never trained as an archaeologist, but was a historian with an expertise in numismatics. While he was an appropriate choice for maintaining the museum's coins, he was, in her mind, wholly unsuited to the task of tending and displaying the thousands of other artefacts in the collection.

The two repeatedly argued over arrangements and cataloguing. "I understand my boss less and less." she complained, "He is good, he is honest … but I cannot understand his work methods, nor tolerate them."[37] In part, the problem was one of aesthetics. With alarm, she watched Handelmann arrange spears in a display of finds from the Nydam Bog, musing, "How grand, how beautiful these cabinets could become."[38] A more important issue concerned methodology. The museum display was not merely a matter of appearance, but was crucial to presenting a more complete picture of the past. For this reason, Mestorf was committed to bringing Scandinavian methods of organization to Kiel, and in particular she wanted the collection to follow new conceptions of the Danish Three Age system. Such an approach, she argued, would create a narrative of cultural evolution in Schleswig-Holstein, complement the history of its people, and better serve to educate the public.[39]

Handelmann did not completely reject the Three Age system, and he used a similar three-tiered system (Stone and Bronze, Iron, and Christian Ages) to organize the museum.[40] But he remained sceptical of the potential to refine the categories of periodization and obtain a more certain chronology from artefact type.[41] Once again, Handelmann's preference was to follow the lead of his German colleagues, especially Ludwig Lindenschmit of the Central Roman Germanic Museum in Mainz. Lindenschmit was hostile to the Three Age system in part because he had not observed the same collections of artefact materials (stone, bronze, and iron) in the same patterns as Thomsen and Worsaae had seen in northern Europe.[42] In an 1874 letter to Handelmann, Lindenschmit questioned the tenacity of Scandinavian belief in using bronze and iron artefacts to date sites.[43] As a result, Handelmann's museum displays tended to lump together bronze and stone artefacts. Handelmann's views, no doubt, were also informed by his wartime experiences. If he was unwilling to consider Danish theories, he did so in part because of his reluctance to treat with Scandinavian colleagues after the war. At one point, he even forbade Mestorf from using Worsaae's notes to organize items from the Flensburg Collection that were incorporated into the Kiel Museum.[44]

Rather than wither in the face of such opposition, Mestorf took advantage of her nominally subordinate status and her position as an outsider to advance her own professional agenda. She began by rebuilding ties between German and Danish archaeologists. This was certainly no easy task, since Worsaae, Engelhardt, and their colleagues proved equally intractable in dealing with Handelmann.[45] It appears that Engelhardt's bitterness extended even to Mestorf. Upon learning of his death in 1881, she recalled, "I know, that he had no sympathy for me, but then again why should he have? I have never without melancholy been able to think on his prematurely white hair [or] his bittter, caustic character."[46] To bridge this chasm, Mestorf relied on her friendship with Worsaae. In 1875, she enlisted his help in preventing the sale of the Thorsberg bog site to English antiquarians by appealing to his concern for the artefacts and by reminding him that it would be preferable to see the relics stay in the region in Kiel rather than to have them disappear in London. "I know in the interest of scholarship that you will not withhold from me your advice and admonition," she wrote.[47] She stressed that Handelmann had no knowledge of her proposal and asked Worsaae to keep it in the strictest confidence, which placed their transaction outside the bounds of normal scholarly networks. In exchange for his help, Mestorf supported Worsaae by translating his responses to attacks against the Three Age system in the journal *Archiv für Anthropologie*, where Lindenschmit and his colleague Christian Hostmann had called into question the notion of a discernible Bronze Age.[48]

Mestorf also worked behind the scenes to promote the work of the museum to the broader public at home. Handelmann, like his predecessors in the antiquities society, had emphasized the collection's importance only for well-to-do educated antiquarians. By contrast, Mestorf, whose entrance in the society would normally have been impossible, took a much more populist view of the museum's current mission in the province. In a letter to the Education Ministry requesting support for promoting prehistoric study in provincial schools, she explained, "To the highest degree it is the case in Schleswig-Holstein that in the last three decades next to nothing has been done to awaken the general understanding and interest for the legacy of [our] forefathers."[49] In another letter to Handelmann, she argued that her articles in *Itzehoer Nachrichten* "proved that the interest of the people in the prehistory of our country is waiting to germinate, and comes to life with but little encouragement."[50] From the first year of her appointment, Mestorf urged Handelmann to educate the public as the best means of preserving finds, but his inaction left her frustrated, and, by the late 1870s, she responded by acting independently on her own recommendations. She began to publish a biannual report of the museum's activities in the press and petitioned the Ministry of Education to finance a pamphlet for schoolteachers, arguing, "Through the children the fathers are won to the cause."[51]

Such efforts, though comparatively modest, began to transform the relationship between archaeology and identity in Schleswig-Holstein. What had once been a liberal nationalist project to promote the participation of the educated middle class was suddenly cast as a duty for everyone in the province, including women and children. Mestorf held up Danish archaeology as a model, pointing out that it had made breathtaking advances in archaeological scholarship while placing priority on educating the public. She argued that Schleswig-Holstein was far behind in comparison, even though it possessed just as many rich prehistoric sites. Protecting the past and promoting scholarship was thus the responsibility of every individual, and she begged labourers and farmers to note remains while working outside and asked teachers to fill their students with a passion for the past.[52] In effect, her arguments made all Schleswig-Holsteiners participants in the search for prehistory and rendered the simplest acts of preservation into patriotic deeds.

Mestorf's enthusiasm for public involvement was, paradoxically, limited only by her zealous desire to prevent the rise of other collecting institutions in the province. On numerous occasions, she wrote to the Prussian government to discourage support for smaller district museums (*Kreismuseen*), and instead asked collectors to think regionally by supporting the museum in Kiel.[53] To prevent collectors from circumventing her institution, she was even willing to travel to Hamburg to trace artefacts sold from private digs.[54] Her views on local collections were not always well received. She was heavily criticized, for example, after voicing opposition to an antiquities association in the region of Dithmarschen in western Holstein. "What would they say in

Kiel," asked an 1882 article in the *Kieler Zeitung*, "if the great state museum in Berlin wanted to claim everything for itself?"[55] Upon learning of the public attacks, Mestorf replied: "The prehistorian does not use a small number of urns with their contents to understand an entire cemetery, nor the uncovering of one graveyard to determine the cultural relations of the region in the period which it reveals. For this purpose it requires all the materials one can get, and this is the reason why we are opposed to the splitting up of the artefacts in small community and private collections."[56]

There was also a concern about the competence of new collectors. In 1889, Mestorf argued against founding an antiquities club in Eutin, fearing that the group's local directors were ill-prepared for such an undertaking.[57] In effect, it was her goal to ensure that the interpretation of ancient remains would fall solely to specialists, who would base their assessments on large bodies of artefact evidence. This was indeed a revolutionary change in the relationship between past and present, and placed Mestorf at the heart of an emerging profession that jealously guarded its authority to interpret prehistory, even as it hoped to cultivate the interests of a broader audience.

The quality of this controlled discourse remained strongly pro-German in its orientation. In a speech to the local anthropology society, Mestorf took on Scandinavian theories of prehistory still naturalizing the divide between Holstein and Schleswig. Specifically, she attacked Ingvald Undset's thesis that the absence of passage graves south of the Eider indicated two distinct ancient cultures in the two former duchies. In her response, Mestorf maintained that negative evidence alone could not support such conclusions, and she advocated instead a research agenda seeking just such links between ancient peoples in Schleswig and Holstein as a means of reinforcing the inherent unity of the province.[58]

Although her public activities heightened Mestorf's celebrity across the region, they also led to increasing strife with Heinrich Handelmann. Publicly, Mestorf refrained from criticizing her boss, but in her diary she wrote: "I have worked quietly, I have used the local press, striven with tongue and pen to waken interest, to promote; the professor, [of] quieter temperament, has disdained this. I have corresponded with colleagues, visited congresses at length, am more well known. Is it then a wonder, when I am named, when I am written about, when letters are directed to me?"[59] Handelmann was clearly perturbed by Mestorf's independent activities, particularly in 1877, when she began making public appearances at excavation sites on behalf of the museum, which he deemed a direct attack on his authority.[60] That summer, the tension between the two erupted during the museum's planned transfer to a larger building near the Kiel Palace.[61] Handelmann saw the move as a chance to reassert his authority, and he made an effort to limit her involvement. Mestorf was forced to learn through the newspaper that artefacts had already been packed and moved. Distraught that she had not been told, she resumed her work, but in her state of anger became careless and was nearly injured when a display cabinet came crashing down on top of her. She reflected, "Perhaps it would be best for me, if I were to die today."[62] Within a few weeks, she recovered her nerve and took her case to the university rector, demanding a clarification of her position and declaring that she could not take responsibility for the transfer of so many delicate artefacts without being notified. Handelmann later explained to the rector that he wanted to relegate her to a lower position, but suddenly Mestorf threatened to tender her resignation, and he was forced to retreat.[63]

The ultimatum was a risky gamble for a woman in her position, but she judged correctly that she had developed real power in her field. In the subsequent years, she continued to draw hostility from Handelmann: "When he speaks to me, his eyes are horrible, glowering with brutish hatred."[64] But the crisis assured Mestorf's rise as the dominant figure in the museum and in regional archaeology. For Handelmann, the next decade was marked first by involvement in a new anthropology society (which we will discuss in the next chapter) and second by chronic illness. Mestorf's diary indicates that Handelmann came less frequently to the museum during the 1880s, and that most business correspondence was addressed to her. On occasion, he was obliged to ask her to see to the daily administrative business of the museum as he looked to his health.[65] In April 1891, Handelmann died, and by June, Johanna Mestorf was named his successor.[66]

Cross-Border Archaeology and the Discovery of Haithabu

Mestorf's promotion placed her in a position to foster more direct collaboration with Scandinavian scholars. As early as the 1870s, she worked to strengthen the standing of the museum internationally by inviting colleagues from abroad to examine the growing collection. Given her avowed goal of "making it possible to introduce Scandinavian methods of research," it was important that her organizational scheme met with the approval of her Nordic colleagues.[67] The visits were perhaps equally significant for Danes, since they created opportunities to work once again with materials from the borderlands. Among the early Danish visitors during this period was Sophus Müller (1846–1934), a student of Jens Worsaae who first visited Kiel in 1875 to conduct research on Bronze Age artefacts.[68] In the following years, Müller and Mestorf developed a close professional relationship that ultimately became a focal point of reconciliation efforts after Mestorf became the director at Kiel in 1891 and Müller a director of the prehistory section of the Danish National Museum a year later.[69] Müller, who shared Worsaae's strong anti-German feelings, later recalled Mestorf as the only German on whose support he could rely as he sought to refine and expand Worsaae's work on Bronze Age chronology.[70]

The scholarship that emerged from Müller's visit, in particular his 1878 work, *The Northern Bronze Age and Its Periodical Division* (which Mestorf translated into German as *Die nordische Bronzezeit und deren Periodentheilung*), marked the beginning of changes in Danish archaeological thought. Müller remained at first fairly close to Worsaae's understanding of the Bronze Age, arguing only that the period exhibited a much more complex pattern of cultural evolution than previously believed. Above all, he attempted to explain the wide stylistic differentiation in bronze artefacts, which had previously raised doubts about whether archaeologists could rightly identify a distinct Bronze Age. In his comparisons, he observed at least two forms of bronze artefact manufacture that had earlier been viewed as chronologically distinct. He did not, however, locate a corresponding transitional style, and thus concluded that they were not representative of successive styles, but instead signalled independent cultural incursions into Denmark. By comparing a variety of artefact types, including lance heads, swords, and ceramics, with finds from across continental Europe, Müller identified two major currents of migration and artefact introduction from the southwest and southeast.[71] As a result, he felt confident in overturning previous models of unitary cultural evolution, which in turn explained a number of discrepancies with Bronze Age chronology and thus placed the period on firmer scientific ground. This work was instrumental in bringing the last debates over the Three Age system to a close in Central Europe and underscored the benefits of resuming cooperation with Germans in Schleswig-Holstein.

Like Worsaae, however, Müller also held to the underlying premise that peoples in Denmark had created distinct Bronze Age styles that highlighted their cultural sophistication and uniqueness.[72] He implicitly linked this to the modern Danish nation, although his work lacked the political subtext that had characterized Worsaae's writing. Moreoever, Müller's later work in the 1890s departed from his mentor's view even further by de-emphasizing exclusive linkages between modern Danes and their prehistoric forbears and by extending the relevance of Danish prehistory to neighbouring regions – including Schleswig-Holstein. "And this history [of Denmark]," he wrote, "is in the larger sense the same as the history of Europe north of the Alps and especially northern Germany."[73]

Such a cooperative gesture reflected Müller's broad comparative approach and a commitment to scientific objectivity, but it did not represent a full departure from the nationalism embedded in Danish scholarship. In fact, Müller at times worked against German interests in Schleswig, as when he secretly conspired in 1894 to outbid Kiel for the rich Nydam II site near Flensburg.[74] Müller nevertheless walked a fine line between nationalism and transnational scholarship, since he knew that gaining access to sites and artefacts in Germany required a more open and collaborative approach. Indeed, this was a quandary for many contemporary Danish intellectuals seeking to preserve cultural ties with Schleswig. The solution for most, including Müller, was to soften their militant stance over the loss of the southern duchies and adopt what Povl Bagge has called an "anti-nationalist" attitude, which led them to accept the status of the border.[75] Even if Bagge's term elides the nationalism at the root of Danish overtures, it nevertheless helps explain how Müller and his colleagues managed to balance their national concerns with their academic pursuits.

An "anti-nationalist" approach was especially helpful for rekindling interest in sites with a strong symbolic resonance. It is thus little surprise that Müller became intensely interested in new German efforts to preserve the remains of the famous Danevirke, which had been the focus of early German-Danish cooperation in the 1840s. After the wars, the Danevirke had seen a steady stream of Danish visitors making pilgrimages to commemorate Denmark's historical presence in Schleswig. The Schleswig-Holstein Museum had undertaken a survey in 1877,[76] but a few years later Mestorf learned that farmers and brick-makers were uncovering a number of artefacts from the eastern end of the Danevirke at the Oldenburg, which had long been considered a simple peripheral fortification.[77] Mestorf had already charged her new assistant, the former schoolteacher Wilhelm Splieth (1862–1901), with the task of surveying the Danevirke's condition,[78] and in 1897 he reported that the Oldenburg site was in danger of disappearing because much of it rested on private property beyond the museum's reach.[79] Moreover, he expressed concern over the military's interest in building a cavalry training site nearby.[80] Alarmed, Mestorf wrote to the provincial administration asking officials to bring the site under government protection. In her letter, she stressed the national significance of the site for both sides:

> After it came to our attention that the Danevirke is visited throughout the year by numerous Danes … and that on the German side the complaint is raised that the old border wall is surrendered … to thoughtless destruction, the management of the [Kiel] Museum for National Antiquities felt itself obliged to take a closer look. The welcome fact that the German Empire has placed the Roman Limes under its protection and lent it its financial support has led us to hope that it might turn the same interest to the younger but no less historically significant Northern Limes.[81]

For Müller, the renewed activities at the Danevirke and Oldenburg offered a rare opportunity to revisit a site that had captivated Danish archaeologists for decades.[82] By the mid-1890s, he began to argue that the Oldenburg's poor tactical position and shallow inlet made it an unlikely military installation. Based on Splieth's survey reports, he began to suspect that the site was more comparable to other late prehistoric residence centres such as the Birka site in Sweden, which was also surrounded by a semi-circular earthwork. In 1897, he surmised that the site at the Oldenburg might be another such fortified trading town.[83]

Müller's interpretation was a dramatic breakthrough, because it suggested that the site might be none other than the mysterious town of Haithabu, which had been mentioned in early medieval and Arab chronicles.[84] The previous scholarly consensus held that Haithabu had been an earlier name used for an existing site that had fallen out of use. Indeed, in the late 1880s, Splieth and Handelmann had investigated a rune stone associated with a burial at Busdorf very close to the Oldenburg that contained the inscription, "KING SUIN ERECTED THIS STONE FOR SKARTHI HIS FOLLOWER WHO HAD JOURNEYED WESTWARD BUT NOW FELL AT HAITHABU," but, on the basis of other historical evidence,[85] had interpreted "Haithabu" as the Old Danish name for the nearby town of Schleswig.[86] Müller's analysis, however, transformed the work at the Danevirke from a preservation project to one of active discovery, and it encouraged Splieth to conduct fresh digs at the Oldenburg in 1900 that yielded ceramics from tribes hailing from present-day Sweden historically associated with the city.[87] The tantalizing finds helped Mestorf raise funds for a more extensive round of excavations.[88] In recognition of Müller's contributions, she made plans to invite him to observe the digging season in 1901.[89]

Before the excavation could begin, however, Splieth, who had long suffered from a lung disease, suddenly took a turn for the worse and died in February 1901 while convalescing in Italy.[90] His death left Mestorf without an experienced field assistant, and she turned to her Danish colleagues to help train a new custodian, Friedrich Knorr (1872–1936).[91] The result was a digging season in 1902 that produced hundreds of finds, including the skeletal remains of women and children. In early 1903, Mestorf finally felt confident enough to report, "Through the excavations of the last years is the hypothesis now considered fully certain, that the area of the present-day Oldenburg is identical with the famous residential trading city of Haithabu."[92] The announcement secured more permanent funding and launched decades of work at the site, which even today represents the largest ongoing archaeological project in the Federal Republic of Germany.[93]

Conclusion

In September 1903, the *Kieler Zeitung* announced the visit of sixteen leading Danish archaeologists, including Sophus Müller, to the Haithabu excavations.[94] A few years later, a German journalist referred to the site as a "rediscovered city."[95] Yet, it was not merely the physical community of Haithabu that these archaeologists had rediscovered. The search had also restored their own sense of community as scholars. The decline of scholarship and preservation during the 1860s had already highlighted the need for such a return to cooperation, but achieving rapprochement would have been impossible without dramatic ruptures in the traditional underpinnings of the intellectual field. This tells us much about how such fields operate, and is especially suggestive of the levels of agency possible within their boundaries. Johanna Mestorf's leadership of the museum and the broadening contacts with the public worked against prevailing arrangements of gender and class and proved the fluidity of the social order among specialists. As a young discipline, archaeology remained open to the non-traditional academic, but what also made such individuals successful were their unique backgrounds, from Mestorf's time in Sweden to Splieth and Knorr's training in Denmark to Sophus Müller's research in Kiel. It was these sorts of international experiences that allowed Mestorf to revitalize the Kiel Museum and Müller to recognize the significance of the digs at the Oldenburg. The discovery of Haithabu was thus a tribute to the success of the professional discipline of archaeology emerging from cross-border exchanges.

But what kind of success did it prove to be? After all, renewed cooperation did not lead archaeologists to abandon their nationalist orientations. In fact, the example of Haithabu suggests that in many ways transnational experiences helped make it possible for archaeologists to resume nationalist agendas. In this period of relative political calm, it is at times difficult to see manifestations of nationalism in scholarship as clearly as during periods of upheaval. Furthermore, there is no question that objectivity was becoming increasingly important in the late nineteenth century. Yet, the reason regional scholars made a priority of certain projects, including those at the Danevirke, stemmed from their potential to reconnect scholars to national symbols and to uncover deeper narratives of the history of two national communities.

There thus remained deeply embedded in the practices of the first professional archaeologists a set of underlying conceptions of identity, which informed the development of the Kiel Museum. As Eilean Hooper-Greenhill has argued, museums carried out multiple functions. They were both centres of scholarly research and educators of the broader public. Borrowing from Foucault, she maintains that both goals had a "disciplining" effect, first by using the museum space to arrange and classify objects of study and thereby place them under the "curatorial gaze" of the specialist, and second by conveying that sense of order to the public through exhibitions. The result was the articulation of a "modern episteme" that affirmed the totality of knowledge and placed individual objects in relation to a larger whole.[96] This was certainly the case for the museum in Kiel, but the "whole" to which Johanna Mestorf related her artefacts was not as universal as Hooper-Greenhill's theory would have us believe. Rather, it fluctuated at different moments among various provincial, regional, and national forms and depended in part on the viewer, whether he or she was a member of the public, a foreign visitor, or a professional colleague. In many instances, the distinct "wholes" were not incompatible and, in fact, reveal for us an important mechanism by which archaeologists in the borderlands incorporated their local communities into the nation. We must remember that the Kiel Museum did not operate in a vacuum, but coexisted with other provincial institutions. Regional archaeologists could collect relics from their own environs, rely on their neighbours to do the same, and count on delivering the national past through collective effort.

In the next chapter, we will return to this same period and examine more closely two further forces integrating the borderlands into the German and Danish nations. We will consider the relationship between Schleswig-Holstein archaeology and the norms of contemporary science, and assess the ways in which regional scholars responded to attempts to place the borderlands into larger, "national" narratives of history and prehistory. In so doing, we must carry along the lessons from the cross-border experience of the period. Even if the layers of identity at work in archaeology during this period proved compatible with one another, the contours of each remained uncertain. The grey areas were especially evident in these formative years of the archaeological discipline, and reveal the power that scholars like Mestorf exercised in managing competing permutations of both scientific and social order. In the shaping of her museum, in appeals to the public, in attacks on rival institutions, and in her research agenda, Mestorf oriented the discipline towards a specific image of Schleswig-Holstein as indivisible and resting comfortably within a German cultural tradition.

Such power did not completely mitigate conflict. It remains to be seen in the next chapter how much influence Kiel archaeologists could exert over scholarship at the national level, but it is clear that there remained gaps at home. The German-Danish Wars had firmly established political borders, but archaeologists struggled to align them with the boundaries of their discipline. Therefore, even if their motives for reaching out to colleagues on the other side were partly nationalist, that nationalism was a product of compromises. Above all, the archaeologists working in the borderlands recognized that it was no longer possible to pursue research positing immutable differences between their national community and the "other." Thus, Johanna Mestorf mediated the German nation through provincial appeals, while Sophus Müller reconnected Danes to Schleswig by casting a broader relevance for regional prehistory. The results were, if not attenuated, then at least moderated visions of the nation that created limits on the uses of the past and made Schleswig-Holstein an important fault line in the national struggles of the early twentieth century.

4 Nationalism, Science, and the Search for Origins

The summer of 1878 was an exciting time for supporters of the Kiel Museum. In August, Kiel hosted the Ninth General Convention of the German Society for Anthropology, Ethnology, and Prehistory (Deutsche Gesellschaft für Anthropologie, Ethnologie und Urgeschichte). When it opened, the convention welcomed members from across the nation and abroad, including such respected scholars of German anthropology as Rudolf Virchow (1821–1902) and Hermann Schaafhausen (1816–1893).[1] Much was at stake in this gathering. For Virchow and Schaafhausen, the convention served as a chance to reach out to the provinces and fulfil the Gesellschaft's mission of promoting the human sciences within Germany.[2] For Handelmann and Mestorf, the event promised to raise the profile of regional scholarship on the national stage. As Handelmann had announced the previous year, "We may expect a large number of visitors from Schleswig-Holstein for this event and hope that the convention will be received in the farthest reaches of our home region as inspiring and successful for anthropological and archaeological research."[3]

Neither side came away disappointed. Over 143 members travelled to Kiel that August, among them such luminaries as Oscar Montelius (1843–1921) of Sweden and Ingvald Undset (1853–1893) of Norway. Their participation affirmed Johanna Mestorf's efforts to renew cooperation with Scandinavian prehistorians. At the same time, the meeting helped launch a branch society (Zweigverein) for Schleswig-Holstein, which would allow locals to keep abreast of the latest advances in anthropology and archaeology. More than eighty individuals joined, including doctors, teachers, lawyers, and pharmacists, who found in the new organization an enthusiasm for prehistory not seen since the early days of the antiquities society. The 1878 convention thus signified a second critical dimension in the professionalization of archaeology in Schleswig-Holstein. For fledgling disciplines like archaeology, the path to scholarly recognition in Germany ran through the country's associational life, and the affiliation with the Gesellschaft für Anthropologie brought Schleswig-Holstein archaeology into a burgeoning German academic community even as it retained a distinctly international character.

Three key trends emerged as a result. The first was a growing perception of archaeological scholarship as an objective science. Through collaboration with natural science disciplines, archaeologists gradually embraced the power of empirical study to unlock the mysteries of ancient societies. They began asking new questions while recognizing fresh potential for analysing the vast amounts of artefact evidence recovered in the preceding decades. Similar changes were underway in northern Europe, where Oscar Montelius and Sophus Müller employed comparative methodologies to refine the understanding of the European Bronze Age. A second, and related, trend was a heightened interest in uncovering human origins. Since the early nineteenth century, German and Scandinavian philologists had traced linguistic threads in search of their cultural roots. But, as they exhausted their sources, they gave way to archaeologists, who offered the hope of using material remains to extend national histories into the remote past. While Danish and Swedish scholars debated whether artefact styles were truly the signatures of their cultural forebears, the Berlin archaeologist Gustaf Kossinna (1858–1931) created a new interpretative theory positing northern Europe, and especially Schleswig-Holstein, as the centre of the Germans' original homeland (*Urheimat*). Such theories exemplified a third trend, which was the convergence of the new "scientific" archaeology with the völkisch nationalism of the late nineteenth and early twentieth centuries. In the eyes of a new generation inspired by the fairy tales of the brothers Grimm and the operas of Richard Wagner, archaeology became an indispensable means of reconnecting the modern nation with the values and the spirit of Germanic ancestors. Across the border, the discipline became involved in a similar push to preserve Danish culture in the borderlands and to redefine Danish national identity after the loss of Schleswig-Holstein. In both cases, these resurgent nationalist movements preserved the ties between professional archaeology and its popular roots in antiquarian study, and shaped public interest in archaeological research.

The upshot was a set of deep internal contradictions that raise the question of how and why archaeologists incorporated völkisch ideology into scientific prehistoric research. At first glance, this appears as a surprising turn of events, when we consider how the anti-modern bent of contemporary völkisch movements stood at odds with the ostensibly universalist and humanist values of nineteenth-century science. To understand how it was possible for prehistorians to enlist scientific approaches to affirm nationalist assumptions, we can point first to the convergence between science and Romanticism in the nineteenth century. According to Richard Holmes, the so-called second scientific revolution of the late eighteenth and early nineteenth centuries blended Enlightenment and Romantic traditions. "It was," he writes, "a movement that grew out of eighteenth-century Enlightenment rationalism, but largely transformed it, by bringing a new imaginative intensity and excitement to scientific work."[4] Seen from this perspective, it is easy to agree with Woodruff Smith that there was a similarly close relationship between science and politics. Smith argues in particular that the German cultural sciences experienced a sort of scientific *Sonderweg*, finding their origins in liberal ideology as elsewhere in Europe but turning in a more right-wing direction following the failure of the liberal project in the German Empire.[5] In a similar way, these disciplines were affected by the process of institutionalization in Germany. They benefited from the rapid expansion of institutions, but as Konrad Jarausch has shown, the professors and students working in universities retreated into national-conservatism in response to the pressures of modernization.[6] For anthropology, archaeology, and other fields nominally outside the university, historians have noted the disciplines' encounters with imperialism and close ties to Social Darwinism.[7] Most recently, Andrew Zimmerman has cast the emergence of German anthropology, along with its interest in ancient cultures (*Urgeschichte*), as a challenge to older forms of humanism. According to Zimmerman, the rise of positivist thinking and the expansion of European imperialism allowed anthropologists to posit their natural science methodologies and more comprehensive interest in global humanity as a form of "counterhumanism" opposed to the text-centred and Eurocentric perspectives of German historicism. Yet, as Zimmerman argues, scientific approaches aimed at classification lent themselves to hierarchical thinking that in turn shaped racist and chauvinistic nationalist orientations.[8]

To provide a more complete explanation, this chapter argues that we must also look to the archaeologists themselves, both the national scholars like Kossinna and the provincial scholars, who were confronted with völkisch and racialized views of prehistoric origins. This was especially the case for those in the borderlands, whose work was so essential to the Nordic origin theory. Their engagement with scientific methods, on the one hand, and with two national academic milieus, on the other, placed them in a unique position to shape theories of Germanic origins and thereby address broader national discursive trends at the turn of the century. Thus, we may ask, when overtly nationalist scholars such as Gustaf Kossinna cast the German-Danish borderland at the centre of their theories, how would these scholars respond?

Archaeology as Science

The Gesellschaft came to Kiel in part because of the fascinating discoveries being made in Schleswig-Holstein at the beginning of the decade. Foremost among these was the so-called Rendswühren Man recovered in 1871. In June of that year, a peat farmer unearthed the remains of an adult male buried beneath the Rendswühren Marsh in southeastern Holstein. The body was found face down, and on the left side of its head was a gaping, violent wound. The surrounding peat had preserved much of the corpse's skin and clothing, including a cloak, woollen coat, and a single leather foot binding. It was so well preserved that authorities initially believed they had uncovered a recent murder, which led a local physician to write to Heinrich Handelmann, "Your presence is urgently desired before the state prosecutor appears."[9] Handelmann rushed to the scene, accompanied by a Kiel physician named Adolf Pansch (1841–1887), but by then the body had already become something of a sideshow, lying on display on a farmer's cart with local curiosity seekers plucking pieces of clothing as macabre souvenirs.[10] Handelmann and Pansch brought the find back to the museum, where its reputation grew and even "reminded" local farmers to report at least two other bog bodies in the province.[11]

There were a number of reasons for Germans to be excited about Rendswühren Man. First of all, as Johanna Mestorf later pointed out, there was a historical connection between the fate of the deceased and the practices of the ancient Germanic tribes mentioned by Tacitus in *Germania*.[12] His manner of death corroborated Tacitus' report that the ancient Germans had placed individuals in bogs as punishment for their crimes. Moreover, his state of preservation was fascinating to antiquarians whose only contact with their ancestors had come through pieces of ceramic, metal, or bone. The opportunity to come face to face with the intact remains of an ancestor even led Handelmann and Pansch to include a photographic "portrait" of the find in their published report that depicted the corpse in a near-standing position against a draped backdrop.[13]

Finally, Rendswühren Man was a celebrated discovery because he appeared at just the right moment. Bog bodies, after all, were not uncommon. The expansion of agriculture had produced a number of remains from bogs in northwestern Europe during the eighteenth and early nineteenth centuries, but these finds had rarely attracted the interest of antiquarian experts.[14] In her discussion of the Haraldskjær bog body in Denmark, Karin Sanders points out that it was Jens Worsaae, in a debate with the philologist Niels Matthias Petersen (1791–1862) during the 1840s, who first raised the possibility of studying these remains in their own right.[15] But even if a few scholars expressed fascination with bog finds, inspections of remains before the 1870s were usually cursory affairs conducted by pastors or local officials.[16] By contrast, the sense of urgency and thoroughness with which Handelmann and Pansch investigated this set of remains was new. Handelmann even referred to the Haraldskjær body in his report, citing the similarities between the two finds as proof that Rendswühren Man was of scholarly significance.[17] The result was a dual view of the bog body as both a vestige of an ancestor and an object of science.

As a specimen, Rendswühren Man was important because he held clues to the cultural practices and lifestyles of prehistoric peoples. Johanna Mestorf urged a larger excavation at the discovery site, hoping to recover additional items of clothing. She explained, "We still know absolutely nothing about the age of our Danish, Schleswig-Holstein, and Frisian bog people. Clothing and chemical analysis appear to me the only supporting points for some clues where other materials are lacking."[18] Mestorf's comments affirmed that the priorities of her institution had changed to include not only the collection and preservation of finds, but also their exploitation in the pursuit of new knowledge. They heralded the emergence of a scientific model of archaeology in the 1870s, which, as Karel Sklenar has shown, was shaped by positivist and materialist thinking.[19] Within this new intellectual framework, the past no longer seemed so mysterious, but rather appeared as a new frontier to be conquered.

The development of scientific archaeology was made possible through a series of collaborations between prehistoric study and natural science disciplines across Europe. As Mestorf had indicated for bog bodies, chemistry played an important role, but a number of other disciplines were also involved, including geology, zoology, anatomy, and anthropology. For instance, Charles Lyell's theory of uniformitarianism, which explained geological processes as unfolding evenly over long periods of time, led scholars to recognize the true antiquity of human beings and revolutionized the study of the Stone Age. In France, Edouard Lartet (1801–1871) and Gabriel de Mortillet (1821–1898) identified distinct periods of development within the Paleolithic, Mesolithic, and Neolithic periods.[20] In Denmark, the zoologist Johannes Steenstrup (1813–1897) used his studies of the Mejlgaard kitchen-middens (*Kjøkkenmøddinger*) to change contemporary thinking about the Mesolithic Period. His analyses showed that pigs were being consumed throughout the year, which proved that certain cultures had transitioned from nomadic to sedentary lifestyles well before the development of agriculture in the Neolithic Period.[21] The typical boundaries of the Three Age system thus shifted and splintered, as cross-disciplinary approaches revealed a human prehistory that was far older and more varied than previously imagined.

Partnerships with natural science also promoted empirical methods. Here the Scandinavians took the lead. Both Thomsen and Worsaae had long advocated a comparative approach, but it took decades of work by collecting societies across Europe to provide enough material to attempt far-reaching interpretations of the past. Ultimately, such work uncovered evidence of region-specific chronologies and potential traces of the diffusion of specific artefact types, manufacturing techniques, and creative styles. They raised new questions about the introduction of bronze and iron technology in northern Europe. In 1881, Ingvald Undset compared artefacts associated with iron finds and concluded that many predated Roman contact in northern Europe. He suggested that the Iron Age had been ushered into Scandinavia not by the Romans, as was the prevailing assumption at the time, but earlier by the so-called La Tené culture a few centuries before the Common Era.[22] Johanna Mestorf, who translated Undset's work into German, made an important contribution to this discussion a few years later, when she examined urn cemeteries in Schleswig-Holstein in 1886.[23] She confirmed Undset's hypothesis that the northern Iron Age predated Roman contact, but her studies failed to find corresponding evidence of the brooches that were emblematic of La Tené culture. She thus concluded that iron had been introduced even earlier, which further heightened the mystery of the origins of civilization in northern Europe.[24]

Similar questions guided Oscar Montelius, whose pioneering work in relative dating techniques sparked a heated debate with Sophus Müller over the periodization of the Bronze Age. While both recognized that northern Europe, which lacked significant metal resources, stood in a "dependent and receptive relationship" to the south in terms of technology,[25] they disagreed over the method of bronze introduction or its relationship to the indigenous populations. On the one hand, Müller viewed stylistic differences among bronze objects as evidence of multiple cultural migrations, and looked for similarities in various geographical regions to the south to determine points of origin. Montelius, on the other hand, focused not on the objects themselves, but on associated finds and noted striking similarities in burial practices in both Stone and Bronze Age sites. He thus began to see the Bronze Age as a period of unbroken settlement characterized by at least one cultural group, whose cultural evolution produced the stylistic variances described by Müller. Yet, Müller remained sceptical, writing, "No Stone Age people suddenly makes the jump to metalworking, not to mention the complete transition to a difficult technique, and certainly not to the degree that it [not only] copies as well as possible introduced objects, but also produces them themselves in a beautiful, indeed complete form and in their own refined artistic style."[26]

To settle the debate, Montelius and Müller turned to German anthropology. As Müller confronted mounting evidence of settlement continuity,[27] he finally allowed himself to be persuaded by the work of Rudolf Virchow, who used craniometric techniques to show the similarity between skulls found in late Stone Age burials in Denmark and those of modern Danes.[28] Indeed, the relationship between archaeology and anthropology was becoming an important final component in the creation of a scientific framework for archaeology. In Germany, the connection had begun with the discovery of Neanderthal remains in western Germany. In 1856, Johann Carl Fuhlrott (1803–1877) recovered a skull fragment from a construction site in the Neander Valley near Düsseldorf. The following year, Fuhlrott joined Hermann Schaafhausen at the University of Bonn in announcing the find as a new human species, *homo neandertalensis*. Although the find remained controversial for decades, it nevertheless sparked an interest in the physical remains of prehistoric peoples that would inform such later discoveries as the Rendswühren Man.[29]

Adolf Pansch deserves much of the credit for bringing anthropology to Schleswig-Holstein. His connection to the field stemmed both from his background as a physician and from his experiences as an Arctic explorer. Pansch had earned a measure of local celebrity when he served as ship's doctor on the steamer *Germania* as it undertook its first expedition to the North Pole in 1868.[30] Although the ship eventually turned back to Germany, it succeeded in exploring much of eastern Greenland, where Cape Pansch now bears witness to the journey.[31] Regrettably, Pansch's unexpected death in a boating accident in 1887 meant that he left no known memoirs, but it is tempting to surmise that he, like other German travellers of his day, saw in the native cultures he encountered a sense of European society in its ancient, primordial stage of development.[32] Upon his return, Pansch went to work promoting anthropology in the borderlands, working with bog bodies in 1871 and later writing in support of the Gesellschaft für Anthropologie. In 1878, he penned a column in the *Flensburger Norddeuetsche Zeitung* arguing that Schleswig-Holstein possessed unique potential to advance the study of mankind. As he explained, "Each year, Schleswig-Holstein sees a great number of her sons set out as sailors; from the Kiel Harbour the German navy sails out to the farthest, in part still scarcely known regions. There a broad and grateful field offers itself for ethnographic endeavours, be they collections or descriptions of cultural relationships, customs, etc."[33] Pansch's anthropology also had much to offer the province. Along with the installation of a new exhibition facility and a high-profile visit by Crown Prince Frederick in 1877,[34] the creation of the Schleswig-Holstein Anthropology Society in 1878 did much to restore the credibility of regional archaeology and mark the Kiel Museum as a respected institution within German academia. It placed local archaeology in the national spotlight and integrated regional institutions into an emerging German archaeological tradition.

Anthropology was in many respects an ideal partner for prehistoric European archaeology. First of all, both fields had grown up relatively recently from roots in popular culture, and both retained important links to the public through exhibitions, collections, and museums. Second, anthropologists were primarily interested in studying static cultures. As Andrew Zimmerman has shown, this translated into a preference for non-European societies living in an ahistorical, uncivilized state as so-called *Naturvölker*, a concept that stood in opposition to the historical *Kulturvölker* of Europe. Prehistoric sites in northern Europe were ostensibly compatible with the anthropological focus, because they belonged to cultures supposedly removed from classical civilizations that could be studied synchronically as a sort of ancient Naturvolk. Zimmerman's work also shows how both fields evinced a disdain for textual and linguistic resources, whether out of necessity, as in the case of prehistoric archaeology, or from a preference for artefacts as material objects of study.[35] Finally, the two increasingly shared a view that the surest way to understand human societies was scientifically. Such a model allowed scholars in Kiel to move beyond their erstwhile mission of collecting and preserving and to participate in a greater task of interpreting finds through rigid adherence to empirical principles.

There were, of course, limits to this vision. Zimmerman argues that anthropology began in Germany as a distinctly humanist alternative to historicism. By placing human cultures into a static scientific framework, anthropologists believed they could achieve a more comprehensive understanding of humankind. The problem was that as the research progressed, so too did the tendency to follow scientific models of taxonomy and place human groups into racial categories. The more distinct the categories, the more anthropologists undermined their humanist outlook. In his writings, Pansch casually explained away the paradox, describing anthropology's mission as one of uncovering "the totality of mankind in its emergence into different peoples."[36] Categorization fit well with archaeology, which had long wrestled with its own classification theories, but the two did not overlap completely. Archaeologists, after all, had long debated classification systems primarily to periodize finds and ascertain their geographical distribution. Only in the later nineteenth century did they begin to ask more questions about what artefacts might tell researchers about distinct human groups in ancient times. To aid their inquiries, many turned to anthropologists to seek clues in human remains. Only a few short months before the discovery of the Rendswühren Man, Mestorf sent a human skull found in an ancient mass burial in Dithmarschen to Hermann Schaafhausen in Bonn. Schaafhausen's response indicated the inherent difficulty in making firm determinations: "In northern Germany there are two very different forms of old skulls, long, which are called Germanic and more rounded, which could be

Roman or also Slavic or also Lappish. … Yet this skull does not show so much the Lappish form, and it could be a middle form, emerging from the mixing of both races."[37]

Such collaborations reflected the inherent tensions of the new scientific approaches. On the one hand, the essential questions about what archaeological finds could reveal about humanity were in line with what Benoit Massin has called a liberal, universalist perspective that many archaeologists and anthropologists seemed to share.[38] On the other hand, the outcomes of scientific inquiry give credence to Zimmerman's argument about the "antihumanism" embedded within the disciplines. Contemporary notions of science were at least partly to blame, but the relationship between anthropology and archaeology also depended on common understandings of diversity. In the borderlands, archaeology had already established a tradition of aligning past cultures with present-day nations. It was no mean feat to translate perceived cultural differences into biological terms. Yet, it remained a challenge, as Schaafhausen's advice to Mestorf suggested, to reconcile the lure of firm scientific pronouncements with the ambiguities inherent in archaeological discoveries.

Another problem related to the structural organization of scholarship. The broad outlook and sweeping approach of the Gesellschaft für Anthropologie ostensibly offered a firm foundation for archaeology to become part of a national scientific field. But its provincial outreach and affiliated Zweigvereine made it possible for local prehistorians to carve out scholarly fiefdoms and preserve a distinctly provincial orientation. This was certainly the case for Johanna Mestorf, who endorsed her museum's collaboration with the Gesellschaft,[39] but at the same time jealously guarded her institution's authority in the province against all potential challengers. Such was the case for the Hamburg Ethnological Museum (Hamburger Museum für Völkerkunde), which she criticized in a 1906 letter: "There you will find self-important gentlemen, but no prehistorians. They encroach into every foreign region, be it Hannover, Schleswig-Holstein, all the way into Jutland; always surreptitiously, never openly or in good faith."[40] This sort of obstinacy created challenges for crafting a common approach to scientific study. Mestorf's letter was an explicit rejection of institutional centralization, but it also implied differences of opinion on professional matters among scholars working in regional contexts.

By the turn of the century, the shifting orientation and structural reorganization of archaeological research had generated research questions that transcended the parochial horizons of older antiquarianism. These inquiries led inevitably to more far-reaching interpretations of the European past. But, as we will see, they did little to resolve the underlying tensions within the discipline. Even as German and Scandinavian archaeology formed itself in the image of the natural and social sciences, it retained its deep roots in early nineteenth-century antiquarianism and preserved its partisan allegiances from the revolutionary and war years. In fact, the very methods that archaeologists shared with their colleagues in the natural and social sciences made it possible for the first time to craft grand narratives that would once again render prehistory into a plane for projecting identities on both the local and national stages.

A Nordic Theory of Origins

The bridge between the scientific archaeology of the late nineteenth century and the Romantic antiquarianism of the 1830s was the rise of völkisch nationalist thought, which took place in the wake of German unification in 1871. The concept of the *Volk* was, of course, older than the German Empire, but its renewed popularity after 1871 was in many ways a commentary on the German nation-state. Put simply, the Prussian-centred Kaiserreich failed to measure up to the long-held Romantic visions of a united Germany. In some ways, it could never hope to do so. In George Mosse's words, "Idealized and transcendent, the Volk symbolized the desired unity beyond contemporary reality. It was lifted out of the actual conditions in Europe where both individuality and the larger unity of belonging were given scope."[41] Consequently, as Jost Hermand has shown, the Prussian unification of Germany shifted the völkisch movement to the periphery, where dreams of nation continued unabated, and where the dreamers invariably returned to an interest in Germanic antiquity.[42]

Similar trends touched Denmark during this period, albeit for different reasons. For the Danes, the founding of the Kaiserreich entailed not the possibilities of rebirth, but the realities of loss, as the Wars of Unification had deprived it of Schleswig and Holstein, including the areas north of Flensburg with large Danish-speaking populations. Bismarck's machinations thus sparked a movement in Denmark in which the popular fascination with the past soon became not a matter of fulfilling long-awaited expectations, but of searching for new sources of unity. The death of Nikolaj Frederik Severin Grundtvig in 1872 sparked a *folkelig* resurgence that stressed the spiritual and intellectual influences that had coloured Grundtvig's life and blended in particular a fresh interest in the ancient past with a renewed sense of "Christian awakening."[43] The late nineteenth century witnessed the sharp growth of Christian-oriented Grundtvigian Folk High Schools (*folkehøjskole*) and a new artistic interest in the symbolism of the Old Norse pantheon. The movement inspired a number of new monuments in Copenhagen, including a statue of the Norse fertility goddess Gelfion, erected by Anders Bundgaard in 1908, and another of a Valkyrie from Stephan Sindring the same year in the city's central square.[44]

The folkelig ethos also appeared in the border region after the 1880s, when the promises of a plebiscite and generous concessions to the Danish minority after 1864 gave way to overt policies of Germanization in North Schleswig.[45] The removal of pro-Danish officials and religious leaders and the imposition of limits on Danish language instruction in the province led advocates to form such groups as the Association for the Preservation of the Danish Language in North Schleswig (Foreningen til det danske Sprogs Bevarelse i Nordslesvig) and the North Schleswig School Association (Den nordslesvigske Skoleforeningen). Vocal protests from these groups and criticism from pro-Danish newspapers such as *Flensborg Avis* eventually drew a harsh response from the German government, particularly during the tenure of Schleswig-Holstein provincial administrator Ernst Mattias von Köller (1897–1901).[46]

In the face of pressure from the German side, many Danes abandoned the idea of bringing all of Schleswig back into Denmark and focused, instead, on regaining the northern part of the region (Nordslesvig), which was home to most of the Danish minority population. The idea of Danish nationhood consequently became less bound to the territories lost than to the ties forged with citizens who remained culturally Danish, a view that hearkened back to the inner nationalism of the early nineteenth century and to Grundtvig's notion of a popular spirit (*folkelig ånd*) as the core of Danish national identity. Danes began to speak not of the former duchy of Slesvig, but of Sønderjylland, a term that evoked the connections with northern Schleswig. For the historian Peter Lauridsen (1846–1923), accepting the loss of southern Schleswig was an important conciliatory gesture to German Schleswig-Holsteiners,[47] many of whom shared the Danish distaste for the local Prussian administration. Povl Bagge has interpreted such rhetoric as a sign of "anti-nationalism" in Denmark, but in this case there was no doubt that such sentiments remained tied to Danish national identity. By encouraging Danes to let go of southern Schleswig, activists like Peter Lauridsen, who recounted the region's struggles in his much-lauded eight-volume work, *When Sønderjylland Awakened* (*Da Sønderjylland vaagnede*) (1909–1922), found themselves in a better position to preserve Danish cultural life in the northern part of the province.

The turn of the century witnessed new Danish attempts to appropriate the past as a means of crafting unifying symbols for the sundered region. In addition to pilgrimages to the Danevirke in the 1890s,[48] borderland Danes revisited the memory of the Golden Horns of Gallehus, which had vanished from Copenhagen nearly a century earlier. In the first decade of the twentieth century, Sophus Müller and the National Museum supported a project to determine the precise area in North Schleswig where the peasants Kirsten Svensdatter and Erik Lauritzen had stumbled upon the horns in the seventeenth and eighteenth centuries. Leading the research was Peter Lauridsen, whose expertise in cartographic and agrarian history made him suited for the task but whose involvement signalled the nationalist undertones of the project. The Golden Horn project might have been a delicate affair, given the tense relations between the German government and local Danes, but by 1906 Müller's cooperative work at the Haithabu site had restored a spirit of cross-national cooperation in regional research. Moreover, his own studies of the Golden Horns had tempered their national worth with the claim that their engraved symbols were not, as Worsaae had earlier argued, affiliated with the Norse pantheon, but rather had been fashioned earlier during the Migration Period.[49] Lauridsen's research ultimately placed the original sites near the western city of Tønder on a patch of farmland, where the owner permitted the Danes to erect a memorial stone in December 1907.[50] The monument, though small, signalled the ties between Sønderjylland and the Kingdom of Denmark by assuring its place in the modern mythology of the Golden Horns, one of the nation's most potent symbols.

Creating similar links between antiquity and the state in Germany proved more difficult. While the Danish relationship with the distant past remained largely a private affair before the First World War, in Germany the national government frequently used the past as a means of enhancing its own legitimacy, often with mixed results. State visits to local museums, such as that of the crown prince in Kiel in 1877, proved very successful, since they highlighted the Prussian-centred government's investment in provincial institutions. Attempts to appropriate the symbolic value of the past, however, usually fell short, because the idea of Germanic antiquity was so closely tied to a völkisch conception of the German nation that was both inconsistent and incompatible with political reality. Consequently, while Prussian historians succeeded in portraying the unification of Germany as an inevitable denouement of a new "master narrative" of German history,[51] attempts to seek deeper roots only highlighted the shortcomings of Bismarck's Germany. In 1875, for example, Kaiser Wilhelm I attempted to associate his reign with ancient German heroes by attending the unveiling of the Hermannsdenkmal, a memorial to Arminius, the now legendary Germanic chieftain. However, as Andreas Dörner has explained, Arminius proved to be anything but an unambiguous symbol. Critics quickly blasted the Kaiser for aligning himself with what they considered a blatant bourgeois agenda, while Catholics decried the anti-Roman bias, and socialists portrayed Arminius as the usurper of the power of the German people.[52] Seen in this light, völkisch nationalists were reminded that the Kaiserreich omitted vast German-speaking areas; was rife with internal ethnic, religious, and class cleavages; remained dominated by the Prussian Hohenzollerns; and failed to inaugurate what many ideologues saw as the revolution needed to bring about the rebirth of the German spirit.[53]

Even as they criticized, völkisch thinkers entertained their own grandiose visions in the artistic sphere. Many looked above all to the work of Richard Wagner, whose famed operatic tetralogy, *The Ring of the Nibelungs* (*Der Ring des Nibeungen*) purported to fill the need for a national mythology by blending Nordic and Germanic elements and recasting them as an organic whole. An amateur student of Germanistik, Wagner preserved the philologists' attachment to Scandinavia. He shared the Grimms' interest in presenting Germanic mythology in its most unadulterated form in order to highlight his work's significance to the nation.[54] And, like the Grimms, Wagner believed that the Scandinavian myths represented the most authentic relics of the Germanic spirit (*Volksgeist*).[55] The Ring Cycle thus portrayed an eclectic mix of Scandinavian religious symbolism and German legend. The tragic tale of Siegfried mirrored elements from the medieval German epic poem, the *Nibelungenlied*, but Wagner placed it within a fantastic world of valkyries and dragons, with a narrative driven by the machinations of Norse gods in Valhalla. Wagner's art blurred the lines between the two traditions and brought them together under the same rubric of Germandom.[56] The *Ring*, of course, generated wide-ranging responses, but some commentators questioned in particular Wagner's amalgamation of cultural elements. In *Beyond Good and Evil* (*Jenseits von Gut und Böse*), for example, Friedrich Nietzsche remarked, "Let the German friends of Wagner ponder whether there is in Wagner's art anything outright German, or whether it is not just its distinction that it derives from supra-German sources and impulses."[57]

While the finer points of Wagner's attachment to myth reach beyond the bounds of this study, it is important to note that he further popularized a familiar vision of national identity linking elements typically associated with both Germany and the Scandinavian lands. And his work coincided with a renewed interest among German philologists in tracing the roots of Norse myths and legends. In the 1870s, Karl Müllenhoff, who now held a professorship in Germanistik at the University of Berlin, picked up the Grimms' search for literary traces of the German spirit, which culminated in his five-volume work, *German Antiquity Studies* (*Deutsche Altertumskunde*). In the fifth volume, Müllenhoff defended the originality of the Icelandic Eddas and hailed them as evidence that the German myths had survived in their purest form in northern Europe. Müllenhoff interpreted these myths as a sign of a cultural unity that existed at some point in the distant past, and he suggested that variations in Germanic and Nordic myths stemmed from the Migration Period (*Völkerwanderungszeit*), when massive population shifts interrupted the cultural continuity of Germanic tribal groups. The cultural core of Germandom remained, however, in the surviving mythic representations.[58] Müllenhoff died in 1883 before finishing his final volume, but he managed to transcend the parochial pursuits of his home region to seek the origins of the German nation, the remains of an irreducible German Volk, and clues to its original geographical homeland. His writing bolstered the links among tribal groups and illustrated their common cultural roots, but ultimately his methodology exhausted itself in the more distant prehistoric past, where the threads of myth grew too faint, and the earliest writings and oral traditions faded into silence.

It was Müllenhoff's student, Gustaf Kossinna who continued the pursuit by turning to archaeology. For Kossinna, the question of German origins became nothing short of a grail quest in which he equated the original Germanic homeland (*Urheimat*) with the source of a core "Indoeuropean" group, which German scholars since 1810 had referred to as "Indogerman."[59] Like Müllenhoff, Kossinna entered the field from a strongly national-conservative background that shaped his research agenda.[60] His works are peppered with stirring quotes from his ideological forebears. At the end of his 1911 work, *German Prehistory* (*Die deutsche Vorgeschichte*), he ended with the words, "Because I learned that its language, its law, and its past had been placed far too low, I wanted to lift up my Fatherland."[61] Here he was quoting none other than Jacob Grimm. From his mentor, Kossinna had become convinced that it was not only possible, but necessary to investigate the distant past and find a way to link it to the known history of the nation. While visiting Kiel in 1900, he scribbled a quote from Müllenhoff in the corner of his diary, "Without the awareness and establishment of the oldest living conditions of our people, a vital and proper treatment of its later history is absolutely impossible."[62]

Kossinna began his research in the philological tradition, using Greek and Roman sources, including Tacitus' *Germania*, writings from Pliny, and maps from Ptolemy, as points of departure for tracing the physical location of various Germanic tribes.[63] Where Müllenhoff and Kossinna parted ways, however, was in the priority of language and texts as research tools.[64] As Kossinna explained, "I soon recognized that classical and linguistic studies based on history and geography would not alone suffice, rather that domestic archaeology ... must be used as a founding method."[65] While he was musing on this question in the late 1880s and 1890s, Kossinna supported himself as a librarian in Halle, Bonn, and Berlin, which gave him access to dozens of catalogues and volumes of archaeological scholarship.[66] In his studies, he found himself drawn to the methods emerging from Scandinavian scholarship, in particular those stemming from the Müller-Montelius debate. He became convinced of Montelius' notions about continuities in the northern European archaeological record, which seemed to confirm what philologists had long believed about the settlement patterns of

Germanic cultural groups. Just as Montelius traced the continuities into the early Bronze Age, so Kossinna became interested in finding links between the Germanic tribes of Tacitus' day and the much older Indogermanic culture, whose presence might be revealed by discoveries of bronze artefacts. Indeed, when Kossinna compared the geographical distribution of Germanic tribes drawn from literary sources to known artefact distribution patterns throughout Germany, he concluded, "The result is the surprising similarity of both depictions, only with the difference that the map of the settlement patterns accomplished through archaeological means is much more exact in the indication of the borders of cultural areas of larger tribal groups."[67] Kossinna thus began to embrace archaeology both as an affirmation of extant texts and as a more certain means of establishing the whereabouts of historically known groups.

Unlike his peers in archaeology, Kossinna never conducted excavations or worked under the tutelage of an established prehistorian. Instead, he relied almost exclusively on the work of local societies. Beyond his library work, he conducted extensive tours of collections and museums in Germany and Scandinavia. He travelled to Kiel in 1900 and 1913 and to Copenhagen in 1900, 1904, and 1912.[68] Kossinna's observations, which he recorded in a series of private journals, reveal an ambitious approach that contrasted sharply with the more narrow focus of scholars such as Johanna Mestorf and Sophus Müller. Rather than mastering the discipline through micro- or regional studies, Kossinna seems even in his earlier journals to have looked at the various collections as pieces of a much larger puzzle that promised to illuminate grander patterns. He took notes on a variety of artefact types: ceramics, brooches, stone implements, jewellery, and weapons, and then reassembled them to find that they affirmed preconceived notions about Germanic origins.

Kossinna made his formal entrance into archaeology in 1895, when he delivered an address at the annual meeting of the Gesellschaft für Anthropologie in Kassel entitled, "The Prehistoric Diffusion of the Germanic Peoples in Germany" ("Die vorgeschictliche Ausbreitung der Germanen in Deutschland"). In the lecture, he stressed the long-standing continuity among Germanic tribal cultures stretching back into the Bronze Age, which he claimed led directly to Indogermanic peoples who had inhabited an Urheimat located within northern and Western Europe. It was here, he argued, that the Germanic civilization began. The claim itself was nothing new. Müllenhoff had already made a case for a German Urheimat in "the area of the Oder and the Elbe,"[69] a view supported by anthropologists such as Otto Georg Ammon (1842–1916) and Ludwig Wilser (1850–1923).[70] But Kossinna distinguished his findings by proposing that archaeological evidence could provide a more "exact" empirical basis for proving this theory.[71]

Kossinna later refined his theory. His affiliation with the Gesellschaft für Anthropologie drew him into the cultural-historical turn underway in anthropological circles at the turn of the century. Based on the work of the geographer Friedrich Ratzel (1844–1904), anthropologists discussed ways to account for changes within cultural groups over time and to track the movements of specific peoples. Such discussions ultimately led Ratzel's students to articulate the Culture Circle Theory (*Kulturkreislehre*), which posited that civilizations had diffused in all directions from a select number of origin points. Kossinna quickly adapted this theory for his own research and established the tenets of what he referred to as the Settlement Method of Archaeology (*Siedlungsarchäologie*). The approach was based on three premises. The first was that distinct prehistoric groups originated from a defined point of origin. Second, archaeologists could identify these groups with specific types and styles of sites and artefacts. Third, the settlement areas of these groups over time could be determined by the distribution of these artefacts. As he explained, "Sharply defined archaeological cultural provinces correspond continuously with completely distinct peoples (*Völker*) or tribes (*Volksstämme*)."[72]

In 1911, Kossinna published *The Origins of the Germanic People* (*Die Herkunft der Germanen*), in which he explained that Siedlungsarchäologie held the promise of identifying the origin point of the German Volk. The archaeologist merely had to begin by identifying the "cultural province" of the Germans in more recent times and then work backwards, tracing recognizable artefact and site patterns to their indivisible centre. Using this approach, Kossinna pushed the temporal borders of Germanic culture beyond the Bronze Age by noting continuities in a series of Neolithic grave structures found in northern Germany, Denmark, and southern Sweden. He interpreted these structures as the borders of an area in which the earliest Indogermans emerged with Neolithic technology and sedentary farming around 4000 BCE. Kossinna thus clearly intended to lump modern Scandinavians and Germans into the same core historical group, writing, "Here we fully have the right to speak of Germans in Scandinavia."[73]

By examining surrounding sites, Kossinna determined that Indogermanic peoples spread in all directions over the course of a few millennia. These migratory periods occurred in distinct waves correlating to specific artefact types. To explain changes in artefact style, Kossinna surmised that Indogermanic peoples intermingled with other groups as they expanded and thereby formed new cultures. In this manner, he recast the relationship between Indogermans and the civilizations of the Greeks and Romans and challenged conventional notions of archaeology. After pointing out the connections between the Classical Greeks and their Mycenaean ancestors, Kossinna attempted to show how Mycenaean grave finds indicated an Indogermanic influence. He claimed, for example,

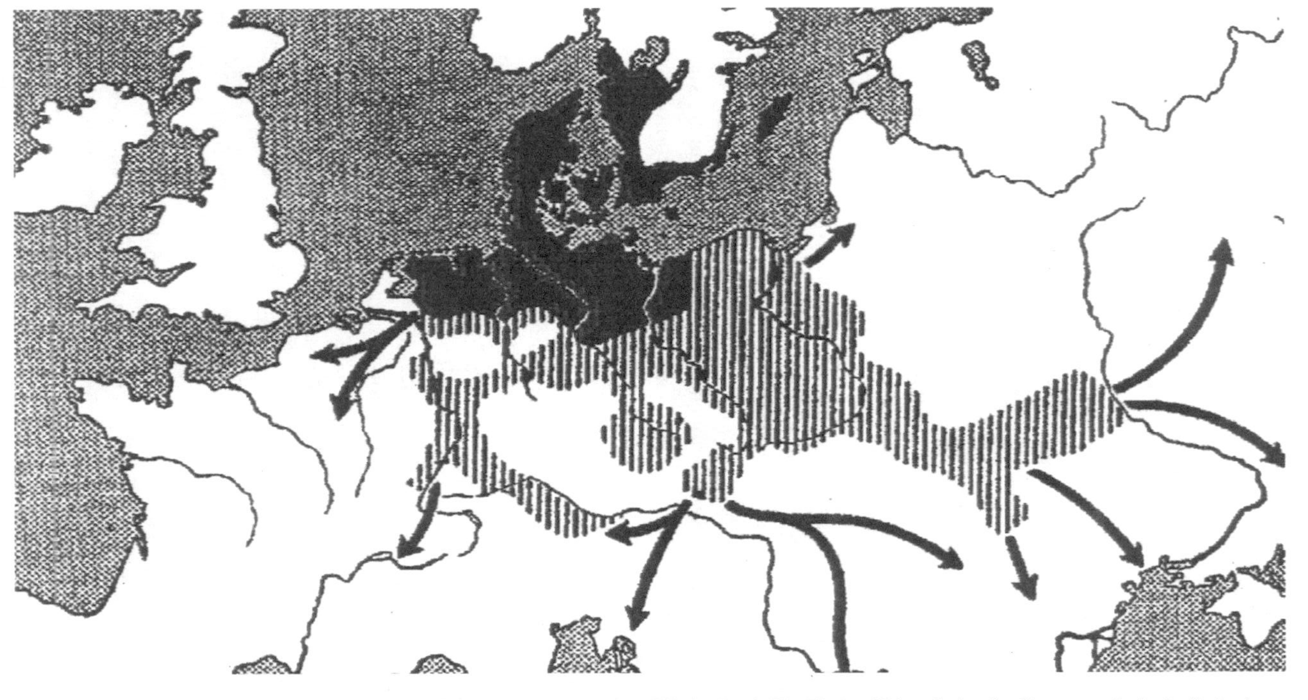

Map of the Urheimat of the Indogermans. Gustaf Kossinna, *Das Weichselland: Ein Uralter Heimatboden der Germanen*, 3rd ed. (Leipzig: Kabitzsch, 1940), 17.

that so-called hanging spiral decorative motifs found on recovered jewellery and ceramics were clearly of northern origin, and stemmed from the "eleventh Indogermanic migratory period" around 1500 BCE.[74] In another instance, he argued for a similar Germanic material influence in northern Italy during the Bronze Age, when he sought to prove through an analysis of brooches that these objects were copies of an earlier type found in northern and Central Europe. Kossinna extrapolated from such finds that the Indogermans had provided some of the cultural underpinnings of the later Classical world.[75] Here he directly refuted Montelius' previous research on brooches, arguing that his colleague had misinterpreted the dates of the finds under study.[76] While he was not suggesting that all Greco-Roman culture developed entirely from northern Europe, he was claiming that the Germanic regions, far from being merely grateful recipients of Mediterranean civilization, had in fact made valuable contributions to high cultural development.

With Siedlungsarchäologie, Kossinna established what amounted to an entirely new theory for interpreting archaeological evidence. It was a way of thinking about the past that corresponded well to the völkisch national ideal, since it diminished the role of external influences on early Germanic cultural development and stressed instead the independence and uniqueness of the Volk. Its claims of influence over the Classical world overturned notions of a "barbaric" Germanic heritage and served to distance German national culture from Mediterranean influence while affording it a comparable mantle of civilization. Moreover, it left space for Kossinna to link the notion of a biologically distinct German ethnic group to the cultural continuities evident in the artefact record.[77] In this way, his method strengthened the collaboration between archaeology and anthropology, which was also beginning to experience a conservative and racialized orientation after Rudolf Virchow's death in 1902.[78] The result was an affirmation of German national identity in the distant past and a renewed vision of the northern boundaries of a Germanic homeland. Yet, at the same time, it cast an image of the German Volk that ostensibly included Scandinavian peoples, which stood in contrast to the sharper distinctions made by German nationalist thinkers during the mid-nineteenth century.

***Siedlungsarchäologie* and Its Discontents**

Given the increasingly illiberal German academic climate in which Kossinna's theories emerged, it is perhaps not too surprising that he should have quickly found success in the university. Indeed, in 1902, the same year as Rudolf Virchow's death, Kossinna received the first chair in prehistoric studies at the University of Berlin. Yet, his meteoric rise in the discipline was not without controversy. Many professional archaeologists were bewildered by Kossinna's professional success. As one correspondent commented to Friedrich Knorr in Kiel, "Kossinna has yet never excavated, he always only watches, because he is himself too impatient, it is certainly better that he doesn't. It only occurs to one as strange that he occupies a university chair."[79] Moreover, many professional archaeologists in northern Europe wrestled with both Kossinna's methods and his conclusions. In 1903, Sophus Müller wrote to Kossinna and described his work as "attractive," but otherwise simply commented: "I have followed you in these studies with genuine interest. I would have much to note to you; but it is not possible to touch upon scholarly questions of such a delicate nature in a letter. I hope to meet you again here or there well prepared, if you want to have a thorough discussion."[80] Müller could see in Kossinna's work affirmations of his own connections between artefact types and ethnological characteristics.[81] Oscar Montelius, meanwhile, expressed gratitude for Kossinna's promotion of his views on continuities as the fundamental means of periodizing northern European archaeology.[82] But many Scandinavian scholars were more ambivalent when confronted with Kossinna's interpetations. In a 1921 collection of essays on the Swedish nation, the Swedish philologist Otto von Friesen (1870–1942) used uncritically Kossinna's scholarship on the migration of Germanic peoples along the Vistula River, noting, "His view seems to be accepted by a number of authorities."[83] Montelius, writing in the same volume, rejected Kossinna's notions of Indogermanic origins. "All that I know of the remote ages," he concluded, "when the Indo-Europeans left their native land to spread over the earth, has convinced me that we cannot take upon ourselves the honour of our country being the cradle of the Indo-European race." Yet, even with this assessment, Montelius shared Kossinna's assumptions about race and archaeology. He continued, "It is honour enough that the Teutons became Teutons in our country: a race that has inscribed its name on many pages of the history of civilization."[84] Accompanying Montelius' text was a map of "The Country of the Teutons," which appeared strikingly similar to Kossinna's chart of the Indogerman Urheimat.

As it turned out, Kossinna's most prominent critic was a German, Carl Schuchhardt (1858–1943), who in 1908 became the director of the prehistory section of the Berlin Museum of Ethnology (Museum für Völkerkunde). Like Kossinna, Schuchhardt had entered archaeology from a background in classical philology and in his later career engaged in broad, overarching surveys of European prehistory, but unlike his rival he had cultivated his expertise through extensive fieldwork in both Europe and the Near East.[85] Consequently, Schuchhardt approached the Indogerman problem from a perspective rooted in the Oriental paradigm of classical scholarship, which posited a Near Eastern origin for European civilization. He objected to Kossinna's work first on the grounds that it established no empirical link between cultural and ethnic continuities, and second because its depiction of Indogermanic diffusion was overly simplistic. He explained: "Archaeological observation ultimately teaches us that diffusion does not follow a course in this or that direction, that no distinct people (*Volk*) wanders from the North Sea to Troy or Mycenae, that the development much more often pauses, collects its strength, and constitutes a new cultural source (*Kulturherd*), whose impact is once again felt in different directions."[86]

The debate quickly carried into the structure of the discipline. In 1906, Schuchhardt endorsed the creation of a Union of Prehistory Museums (Verband vorgeschichtlicher Museen) attached to the Gesellschaft für Anthropologie, which was intended to bring provincial museums into a closer relationship with the Royal Museums (Königliche Museen) in Berlin.[87] Schuchhardt's plan also called for a new journal for prehistoric research entitled *Prähistorische Zeitschrift*, in which he intended to preserve the liberal scientific orientation of professional archaeology.[88] Initially, Schuchhardt wanted to include Kossinna in these endeavours, but by 1908 he became discouraged by the nature of Kossinna's vitriolic criticism. In a letter to Kossinna, Schuchhardt complained about his false sense of collegiality, writing, "In contrast to this collegial [sentiment], however, is the overbearing sentiment, which he takes who views everyone of a dissenting opinion as an adversarial intrusion into his field, which he believes must be beaten back with all means."[89]

The personal nature of this rivalry hastened the disciplinary split. That same year, Kossinna formed his own archaeological society, the German Society for Prehistory (Die Deutsche Gesellschaft für Vorgeschichte), and created his own journal, *Mannus*, which featured articles dedicated to ethnic, racial, and even antisemitic perspectives on European prehistory. In the first issue, the young philologist Hermann Schneider (1886–1961) published an article contrasting the prehistoric Germanic and Semitic races, writing, "Where the Germans arise, a glittering chivalry develops, an art full of innocent subjectivity, a world view full of deep mysticism; where Semites appear, arrogant clerics and callous money grubbers reign, art dies off, the world view preaches despotic, hard-hearted gods."[90] For his part, Kossinna seems to have avoided such blatantly antisemitic rhetoric, and his own acceptance of race theories did not fully mature until after 1918, but he nevertheless managed a journal that fostered a wide range of national-conservative perspectives. He even used it as a means of rewriting the history of the discipline, rejecting, for example, the Scandinavian foundations of the famous Three Age system and arguing instead for a new recognition of the German contribution to its theoretical development.[91]

The increasingly polarizing nature of the Kossinna-Schuchhardt dispute forced young archaeologists across Germany to make choices as to which theories they would subscribe. Among these was a young schoolteacher-turned-archaeologist named Gustav Schwantes (1881–1960), who conducted his first excavations in 1899 and eventually became director of the Kiel Museum in 1929. According to Michael Gebühr, Schwantes, who was born in Blankenese just west of Hamburg, grew up in a "rural middle-class" family with national-conservative political leanings.[92] In this respect, he shared a similar background to Kossinna, but his interest in prehistory stemmed from a love of the outdoors and a sense of Heimat patriotism.[93] Moreover, his scholarly development occurred under the tutelage of Johanna Mestorf, with whom Schwantes maintained a ten-year correspondence. When they began working together, Schwantes, then eighteen, was already making important contributions to the study of burial urns and advancing the understanding of early Iron Age culture in northern Europe.[94]

Schwantes was thus coming of age professionally just as the rupture in German archaeology was developing. His first involvement in the dispute came while writing a textbook for schoolchildren on European prehistory. As he neared completion of the text in 1907, he sent a letter to Mestorf that year seeking her guidance on how to evaluate Kossinna's theories:

> What do you think ... of the new ethnological direction of prehistory? When I read the works of a type like Kossinna … I have the feeling, as if our discipline will become a shipwreck under the leadership of these men as earlier under the influence of the first enthusiastic and uncritically won results of philology ... The cool and objectively thinking researcher of the Scandinavian North placed prehistory on scientifically incontrovertible ground of factual observation and freed it from the direction of historical scholarship. It seems to me that we Germans allow ourselves to be bedazzled more easily through creative speculations.[95]

In response, Mestorf wrote: "The struggles of these scholars, whose theories are based not on well-founded factual material but on literary documents as well as visits to collections that they do not fundamentally understand, must expend themselves ... All of these authors, including Sophus Müller and Montelius, must be read critically, although the latter have a great familiarity with the material and broad perspective. The products of our objectively, not subjectively coloured research are to be in a position justifiably to reject old theories or to accept them as correct."[96] Mestorf and Schwantes clearly had misgivings about the type of research espoused by archaeologists such as Gustaf Kossinna. Yet, this letter, which was not published during her lifetime, was the only strong statement Mestorf made against the Nordic origins theory.

Schwantes' text, which was published in 1908 as *From Germany's Prehistory* (*Aus Deutschlands Urgeschichte*), took a balanced view of the Kossinna-Schuchhardt debate, which has since led to controversy about his position on ethnological archaeology. While Allan A. Lund and Wiebke Künnemann have labelled him a "Germanophile racist,"[97] a more intensive reading of Schwantes' writings by Michael Gebühr purports to show that Schwantes was at times ambivalent about racial thinking in his research. In analysing Schwantes' publications before 1933, Gebühr points to Schwantes' rejection of a northern Indogermanic origin and his agreement with the Jewish philologist Sigmund Feist (1865–1943) that the Germans and Indogermans were not directly related as evidence that he was not in line with the Kossinna camp. In fact, Schwantes did not directly reject the northern origin of the Indogermans in northern Europe, but reported it as a possible theory advanced by other prehistorians. In the second edition of *Aus Deutschlands Urgeschichte* (1913), he added, "Some researchers, however, are not satisfied with this and narrow down the borders of the [Indogermanic] region by viewing Scandinavia or northern Germany as the point of origin." A few sentences later, Schwantes seemed to side more closely with Schuchhardt when he argued first that the Indogermans must have received their knowledge of metals from Near Eastern cultures and second that the so-called Danube Culture of southeastern Europe might also have been good candidates as the original Indogermans. "What then," he asked, "is the difference between Danube Culture and North German-Scandinavian Culture?"[98] In this way, Schwantes sidestepped the issue. He never mentioned Kossinna in his texts, but he also never took a strong stand against Kossinna's conclusions.[99] Schwantes, like so many of his colleagues, remained ambivalent, accommodating the models and theories that had emerged at the turn of the century and wrestling with the question that had come to drive his field, and that he himself posed in 1926: "How far back does the German Volk allow itself to be traced beyond written history into primitive times?"[100]

Conclusion

Along with the restoration of cross-border scholarly ties, the advent of scientific archaeology had profound implications for the study of the past in the borderlands. It dramatically expanded the field of inquiry and integrated regional scholars into a national framework. But, as Schwantes' questions suggested, the trends also implicated Schleswig-Holstein in the tensions between scientific norms and the yearning for a national past. Even as the trappings of empiricism lent credence to the search for national origins, the seeming incongruities between science and nationalism were hard to ignore, and it is little wonder that the myriad musings about the shape of Germany and Denmark should produce such strident differences among specialists.

As it turned out, the problem rested with the contemporary impression of science. In his 2002 book, *The Landscape of History*, John Lewis Gaddis writes that science and history are actually more intimately connected than they appear. Scientists may have once rejected historicism's fetishization of the specific, offering instead a means of measuring more objectively and of identifying more precisely the order beneath the chaos. But Gaddis explains that natural scientists in the period also found themselves grappling with uncertainty, peculiarity, and change. Recounting the writings of the historians E.H. Carr and Marc Bloch from the early twentieth century, Gaddis observes, "They both saw science as a model for historians, but not because they thought historians were becoming, or ought to become, more scientific. It was rather because *they saw scientists as becoming more historical*."[101] Andrew Zimmerman's study of German anthropology echoes this sentiment, noting that the discipline's commitment to observing humanity in controlled, static terms gave way to an interest in change over time through the influence of diffusionism and Darwinism.[102]

Prehistoric archaeology worked in much the same fashion. Indeed, it distinguished itself from other social sciences by its deeper roots in the humanities. Where anthropology appeared as the scientific alternative to traditional humanism, archaeology matured astride the two. Scholars like Kossinna and Schuchhardt or Montelius and Müller claimed the mantle of scientific authority, but their work was invariably informed by backgrounds in history and philology. Therefore, the differences in method belied long-standing continuities in the search for the ancient past. There remained the drive to know ancient humans as foreigners, but also a need to overcome that sense of strangeness by linking them to the present.

Nothing demonstrates the differences better than the case of the Rendswühren Man. In many ways, the interest in bog bodies was emblematic of archaeology's turn to anthropology. Zimmerman explains that anthropologists were eager to recover human remains, and especially skulls, which "meant for anthropologists a human body without the subjective history of tissue."[103] Skulls could be measured and classified, and could speak to the diversity of humankind. Certainly, the archaeologists in Schleswig-Holstein were curious about Rendswühren Man's "type," but they were ultimately drawn to him not because he was devoid of flesh, but because he retained it.

Though decayed, he still looked human. He was prized not merely for the data he yielded, but for the glimpse he offered upon the face of an ancestor. In other words, it was not enough to see him as a specimen, but also to recognize him as a man.

In a similar way, archaeology on the national stage offered a tempting alternative to older textual studies. When scholars like Gustaf Kossinna travelled across northern Europe to record finds, they did so to capitalize on the taxonomic potential of thousands of artefacts and to piece together the elusive image of ancient societies. Yet, just as Handelmann and Pansch strained to see themselves in the withered visage of the bog body, so Kossinna searched the archaeological record for the image of his country. Along the way, he crafted a grand narrative of prehistoric societies that evolved and expanded before blending seamlessly into the histories of modern nations. And he was not alone. The turn to a more conservative and racialized scholarship was by no means solely a German phenomenon. Montelius' contributions on race testify to the ways in which Scandinavian scholars were also intrigued by race and curious about the deeper legacies of their homelands. Germans and Scandinavians both believed they had answered the questions that had bedevilled the antiquarians of past decades: Who were our ancestors? Where did they come from? Now they asked a new question: How did they become us? At that moment, archaeology "became historical."

At the heart of these narratives was Schleswig-Holstein. The centre of an imagined Urheimat, the borderlands stood as a linchpin around which the surrounding nations formed in the ensuing centuries. As we will see in the next chapter, the discovery of Haithabu in these same years would heighten the interest in the region as a crossroads of the German and Scandinavian traditions. This should have placed the scholars in the region, whose research spoke directly to the assumptions underlying a conception of Nordic origins, in a powerful position to validate or challenge contemporary theories. Yet, even as Mestorf and Schwantes harboured misgivings about the work of colleagues in Berlin, they generally remained silent, in part because the regional feudalization of archaeological scholarship narrowed the focus of provincial scholars and created limits for those who might have opposed the new methodologies. At the same time, the silence marked a different set of research concerns. We have seen that Mestorf remained deeply concerned with articulating the connections between modern and ancient groups, but her questions were much more focused on the boundaries between ancient German and Danish tribes. For this reason, Mestorf was critical of outside scholars and sceptical about the very possibility of creating a broad prehistoric narrative.

Seen from this perspective, Schleswig-Holstein and Sønderjylland appear as another sort of crossroads, in this case between two visions of nation. Where the one looked to the past to reinforce the finer differences between modern peoples, the other placed all under a broader rubric of Germandom. Both notions would coexist into the twentieth century, as the experience of the First World War would, on the one hand, resurrect the border dispute while, on the other hand, raise new questions about the future of European nations. Taken together, these developments would not only challenge the boundaries of scientific archaeology, but also implicate the borderlands in the radical politics of the interwar era.

5 Prehistory and the Popular Imagination

In April 1909, Johanna Mestorf at last decided to retire as director of the Schleswig-Holstein Museum in Kiel.[1] The Danish newspaper *Berlingske Tidende* marked the occasion by mentioning the special commendation she received from the German government and remarking, "There is also reason to express warm thanks from the Danish side for many years of faithful work."[2] Certainly, there was much to commend. Both Germans and Scandinavians took note of a career rich in scholarly contributions and pioneering advances for women in academia. Above all, their shared admiration spoke to a broader legacy within a discipline that she had helped build through a renewal of cross-border ties. For Mestorf, its greatest reward was the museum, the once-withering antiquarian collection that she had elevated into a leading institution for archaeological research. She had contemplated writing a history of the museum following her retirement, but succumbed unexpectedly to illness just three months later.[3]

The passing of Johanna Mestorf came at an important moment of transition in regional archaeology, and coincided with a larger transformation underway in Central and northern Europe. It is tempting to see in the history of prehistoric archaeology, as with so many other social sciences, a linear trajectory of growth, perhaps even more so in light of the promising developments at the turn of the century. The spread of a standardized archaeological practice, the incredible discoveries at Haithabu, and the increasing credibility of prehistoric scholarship in the university all seemed to bear the trappings of success. From another perspective, however, the early twentieth century marked a period of crisis. The growing disciplinary split that heralded a more völkisch orientation in the first decade of the century was followed in the second by the First World War, which robbed the discipline of young talent, deprived it of financial resources, and brought much fieldwork to a standstill. The weakness of the Kiel Museum during these years is evident from the poor quality of its records

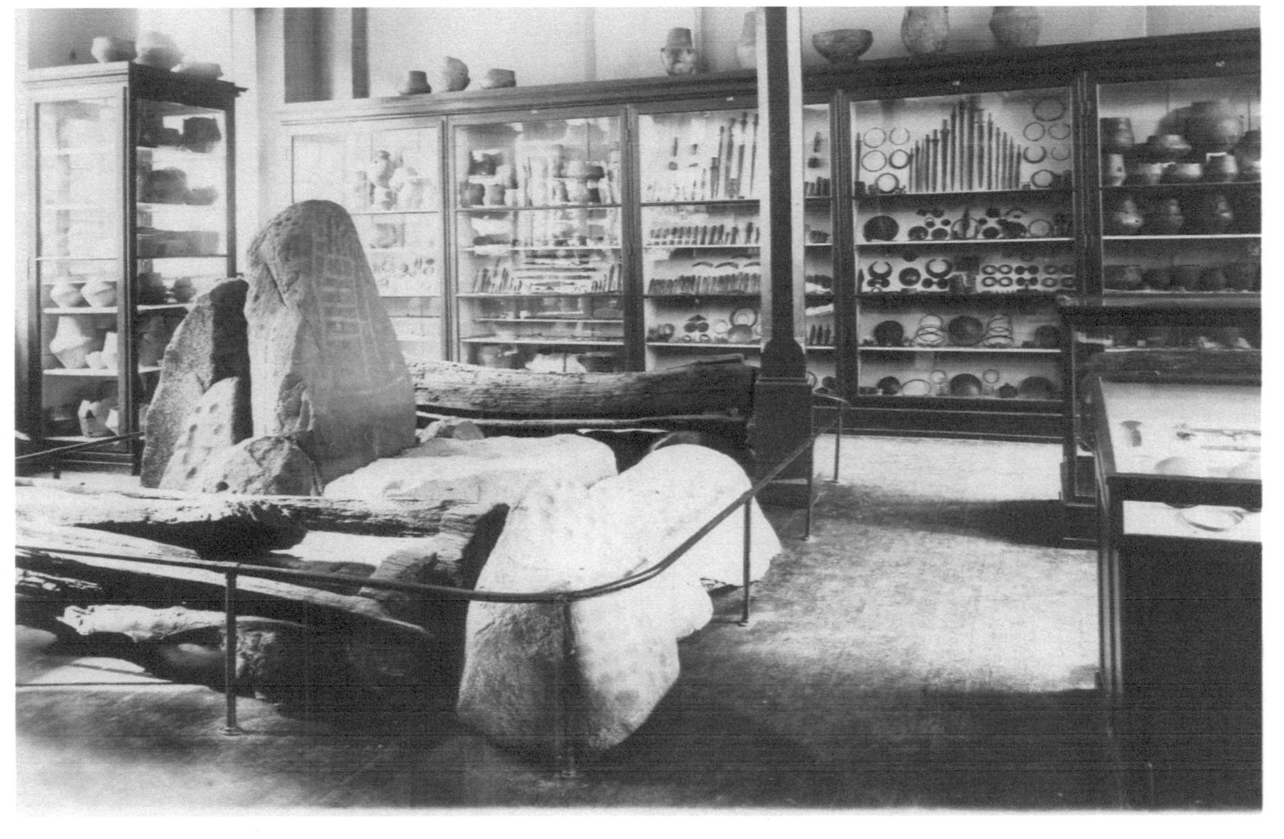

Bronze age exhibit at the Kiel Museum of antiquities in the early 1900s. Photograph courtesy Stiftung Schleswig-Holsteinische Landesmuseen Schloss Gottorf.

after the First World War. The careful system of cataloguing and preserving correspondence before 1914 broke down during this period, and much of the material dating from 1911 to 1945 has since been lost.

The museum's declining fortunes shifted the initiative for interpreting the distant past into the public sphere. Newspapers and popular books and magazines, which had always carried archaeological finds to an eager public, became critical sources of information about the past in the early 1920s, as notions of objectivity and scholarly credibility became much more fluid. A similar trend characterized the study of the past in Denmark, where Danes adapted ancient symbols to the new political opportunities arising after the First World War, especially the revisions to the German-Danish border that followed the Allied victory. The public discussions that followed the war mixed long-standing practices and beliefs about prehistory with a new symbolic lexicon for prehistoric material and emerging scientific theories about Germanic and Nordic origins, religion, and race. While these developments were tied to pre-war conceptions of the past, they grew increasingly more radical in the turbulent climate of the interwar period, as the distant past informed a search for solace from the war and alternatives to pre-war politics. In Germany, this period of crisis in the borderlands furthered the national-conservative and illiberal turn begun in the early twentieth century.

In the context of mounting pressures from the war and the changes to the map at its conclusion, the power of legitimate scholars, and indeed that sense of legitimacy itself, became question marks in Schleswig-Holstein. What, then, was the impact of the Kiel Museum's decline in the interwar period? How did scholars react to the rising popularity of the Nordic and racist thought in Weimar Germany? In what ways did such thinking influence popular thinking about the past in the region? And finally, to what degree did borderlands scholars manage to shape these emerging popular ideas? As we will see in the following chapters, the ideas circulating during the Weimar era later played a critical role in the relationship between professional archaeology and the Nazi regime in the borderlands. They remain, however, valuable in their own context as well, since they reveal much about scholarly activity in the interwar period and about the engagement of archaeologists with the broader public. Perhaps most importantly, the place of professional archaeologists during the interwar years sheds light in a broader sense on their relative power to shape perspectives on the past.

Archaeology and Cultural Politics in the First World War

Hints of the challenges facing the Kiel Museum first became apparent in February 1901, when Wilhelm Splieth, who had been invaluable in the discovery of Haithabu, died suddenly from a lung ailment in northern Italy.[4] His death was a terrible personal and professional loss for Johanna Mestorf. She lamented to colleagues, "Next to his parents the blow fell on me the hardest and from a certain standpoint even more palpably. I had trained Splieth myself … Now that he was ready, I hoped to be able to lay my life's work in his hands, and now he has been taken from me."[5] Soon after Splieth's death, Mestorf moved to hire two new assistants but struggled to find candidates who were suitably trained. Her first choice was Gustav Schwantes, whom she knew from correspondence to be a competent archaeologist and an experienced excavator. It was only when she offered him the post, however, that she learned he was only nineteen years old and had not completed his university degree.[6] Her next choice was Georg Sarauw (1862–1928), a Dane working in the National Museum who had been recommended by Müller. Mestorf made two offers, but Sarauw rejected both precisely because he would have to become a German citizen in order to be eligible for the post, which he felt would make him highly unpopular among the Danish minority.[7] A number of German scholars applied for the post, but Mestorf, true to her provincial outlook and commitment to the public, was opposed to considering outsiders, writing, "[He] must know and love our folk, have love and understanding for our countrymen, and to win their trust, be able to speak Danish and Plattdeutsch."[8] Ultimately, she elected to promote the museum custodian, Friedrich Knorr, who had been a student of art history at the University of Kiel.[9] The second position went to Carl Rothmann, a schoolteacher in Karl Müllenhoff's hometown of Meldorf in Dithmarschen.

Knorr and Rothmann represented something of a dying breed. They were among the last to earn an institutional position without formal training. Mestorf was clearly disappointed by their lack of experience, but took advantage of the chance to guide their introduction into the discipline and thereby preserve the museum's scholarly orientation. Between 1901 and 1909, she made sure that both spent time in the field directing excavations, and that they developed a familiarity with a broad variety of texts. Furthermore, she ensured that Knorr spent time training with Sophus Müller in Copenhagen and with Oscar Montelius in Stockholm, writing, "He should in general keep company with experts, because both of my gentlemen should not only become museum employees, but also prehistorians … There is much that he has to do, until he can take a firm position, for example, in relation to Kossinna and Reinecke, Schumacher, etc."[10]

After Mestorf's retirement, Knorr's tenure as director lasted only a few years before the outbreak of the First World War. His most notable contribution was an updated synthesis of the most recent finds of early Iron Age urn graves, which had been one of Mestorf's key research areas. As Knorr acknowledged in his text, the number of early iron artefact finds had grown dramatically in the twentieth century, including discoveries of iron artefacts in grave mounds associated with the late Bronze Age, which provided new ways to understand the transition between the Bronze and Iron Ages in northern Europe.[11] Above all, the growing number of finds led archaeologists to realize that the introduction of iron technology had occurred much earlier than Mestorf and Ingvald Undset had previously believed, occurring not during the La Tené period but rather through the influence of Halstatt cultures from southern Germany around the sixth century BCE.[12] In addition to his work with the museum's collection, Knorr also led a series of digs at the Haithabu site on an annual basis until 1915. His work included the supervision of over 360 pits within the inner walls and the exciting discovery of a Viking Age "boat chamber grave" (*Bootkammergrab*) on a hill outside the southwestern earthwork.[13]

The outbreak of the First World War brought these gains to a swift halt. As the fighting expanded in 1915, it created acute financial and labour shortages that forced Knorr to suspend ongoing projects.[14] The situation worsened in 1916, when the Allies established a naval blockade that produced near starvation in Kiel during the winters of 1916–17 and 1917–18 and raised the spectre of an attack on the city via the Kiel Fjord.[15] Such an assault would have had devastating consequences for the museum, which lay within easy range of the harbour. As a result, Knorr elected to pack away many of the museum's artefacts and move them inland. What remained, as one commentator recalled, "appeared unfit for showing to the larger public."[16]

The war also soured relations between Kiel and the Danish National Museum. In November 1914, Sophus Müller proposed an exchange of artefacts with Knorr, offering a number of Holstein pieces in the National Museum in return for some Danish pieces at Kiel.[17] Knorr's response was initially positive,[18] but the circumstances changed after Müller sent a list specifying his requested artefacts, which included eight pieces found near Haderslev and one near Tønder, both in North Schleswig. In December 1915, Knorr informed Müller that there "were few prospects" of convincing the German government to approve the exchange.[19] It is likely that Müller's specific requests for items from North Schleswig may not have been well received at a time of re-emerging tensions between Germans and Danes over the North Schleswig region. When the conflict began, Denmark declared itself neutral, but Germany feared that the Danes would eventually enter the war on the side of the Allies. In many ways, however, the Germans heightened tensions by enacting a number of tough measures designed to stamp out any potential disquiet along the border. They quickly censored the Danish-speaking press, placed a number of pro-Danish leaders in North Schleswig under arrest,[20] and fortified the border with a strong defence line and contingents of soldiers.[21] Members of the Danish minority, meanwhile, found themselves struggling with the ambiguities of serving in the German military, even as they hoped for its defeat.[22]

Danes across the border, meanwhile, contributed to the escalating tensions by producing a new set of images and texts stressing the linkages between Denmark and Sønderjylland, which included the appropriation of local prehistoric symbols. In general, nationalist sentiments were rising in Denmark just as in Germany, and in this climate the use of the ancient past as symbol was becoming increasingly popular, taking its place among a complex matrix of pastoral and historical imagery. The Danish Women's Movement, for example, in 1915 adopted images associated with the Golden Horns of Gallehus, which they memorialized on a banner during a suffrage march in Copenhagen.[23] In this case, Danish suffragettes focused on Kirsten Svendsdatter, the peasant girl who had first discovered the Golden Horns, as a peasant representation of the "Mother Denmark" symbol. Svendsdatter's name and likeness had a powerful resonance among Danes and allowed the suffragettes to exploit the rural sensibilities of Danish identity. The result, as Inge Adriansen has shown, was a twist on previous representations of "Mother Denmark," in which she was portrayed as a militant, almost Wagnerian Norse valkyrie, in that the new image allowed the women's movement to draw on the symbolic language of Danish unity while promoting an unassuming and non-threatening image of neutral Denmark.[24]

Danish historians and archaeologists, meanwhile, began taking up the issue of Sønderjylland in a series of new studies after 1915. For the most part, the trend involved a focus on historical geography, inspired in part by Peter Lauridsen's 1896 study of land usage and agricultural design in Sønderjylland.[25] In that study, Lauridsen had revealed consistencies in farm layouts stretching into the late medieval period, from which he deduced continuities in cultural settlement. Two decades later, the historian Hans Victor Clausen (1861–1937) conducted an analysis of place names with the Old Danish stems *-lev*, *-høi*, and *-løse*.[26] At the same time, Sophus Müller published a three-part study of the Stone, Bronze, and Iron Ages in Sønderjylland. In his article on "Sønderjylland's Bronze Age," Müller abandoned his earlier opposition to Oscar Montelius on the issue of cultural continuity, and identified the Eider River, which Danish nationalists had long seen as the true border with Germany, as the limit of a culturally distinct group inhabiting the Jutland Peninsula and Danish Islands. Müller argued that even in the early Bronze Age, which reached into the second millennium BCE, unique styles separated Sønderjylland from the lands south of the Eider.[27]

The musings of Danish scholars formed a small but important part of a much larger expansion of nationalist scholarship in the early twentieth century.

Much of this research appeared in reaction to a perceived threat of German expansion along its northern and eastern frontiers and, in an ironic twist, was often based on German models. In Eastern Europe, for example, leading scholars from the Prussian School of nationalist historiography, most notably Heinrich von Treitschke, had written German history in part as the story of a "Drive towards the East" (*Drang nach Osten*) during the late nineteenth century.[28] In response, Polish historians in Cracow developed their own nationalist tradition with a strong emphasis on tracing the history of western Poland to the Oder River. The pinnacle of this tradition in the interwar period would later appear in the work of Zygmunt Wojciechowski (1900–1955), who like Kossinna blended history, philology, and archaeology to craft a narrative of Poland's western territories as a struggle against German aggression.[29] As in Denmark, such scholarship took on a new urgency after 1914, as the Germans began to pursue the twin goals of revising the eastern border and achieving hegemony over Central and Eastern Europe.

The German defeat in November 1918 dramatically altered the calculus of the scholarly debate, and presented an unprecedented opportunity for neighbouring countries to seek border revisions from the victorious Allied powers. As a result, Germany lost its Posen and West Prussian territories to Poland and faced popular plebiscites to determine the fate of Upper Silesia and North Schleswig. The possibility of losing large swathes of territory prompted some German archaeologists to bring their scholarship directly into the political debate. Most notably, Gustaf Kossinna employed his Siedlungsarchäologie in an effort to justify Germany's claims to territory in the east. In 1919, he produced *The Weichselland: An Ancient Homeland of the Germanic People* (*Das Weichselland: Ein uralter Heimatboden der Germanen*), which argued against Polish and Russian scholars who claimed through linguistic study to have identified continuous Slavic cultural settlement east of the Elbe River. Kossinna used a number of artefact types, ranging from small bone hunting tools to large megalithic structures, as proof of the cultural affinities between peoples in the eastern territories and those in the original Indogermanic Urheimat north of the Elbe. With this evidence, he claimed that the region had borne a strongly Germanic presence since at least the early Neolithic Period.[30]

The debate over Schleswig was similar, even if the impetus for the plebiscite had come primarily from the minority within Germany. During the war, the Danes had cooperated with the Germans to protect their neutrality, and after the war remained wary of provoking German aggression.[31] Instead, the discussion over the border began in the German Reichstag in October, 1918, when *Hans Peter* Hanssen (1862–1936), a political moderate who edited the Danish-language newspaper *Hjemdal* and served as a representative in the German

Reichstag, spoke out in favour of a plebiscite in North Schleswig in accordance with Paragraph V of the Treaty of Vienna ending the Second German-Danish War. He convinced many of his colleagues to accept a new border following the so-called Clausen Line, which was based on the demographic work of Hans Victor Clausen in 1894 and ran across the peninsula a few kilometres north of Flensburg.[32] The result was the Åbenrå Resolution of 17 November 1918, which agreed that the Danes would request a plebiscite for the area north of the Clausen Line. A Danish advisory panel took the resolution to the Allies, who divided the region into three zones: Zone One including the northern third of Schleswig and the cities of Tønder, Sønderborg, and Haderslev; Zone Two encompassing a narrow strip of land from the island of Sylt to the city of Flensburg; and Zone Three covering the southern third and the cities of Schleswig and Husum.[33] In the borderlands, Ernst Christiansen (1891–1974), editor of the Danish-language newspaper *Flensborg Avis*, led a so-called Danevirke Movement (Danevirkebevægelsen) that hoped to align the border with the Danevirke and push for a far-reaching plebiscite in all three zones.[34] Most Danes, however, recognized that Zone Three stood almost no chance of turning away from Germany, and consequently that region was not included in the plebiscite.

The entire question of territorial revision in north Germany was set for a popular vote on 14 March 1920. Consequently, the months preceding the vote witnessed a massive campaign by both sides to persuade voters. Since Zone One included a majority Danish-speaking population and Zone Three was omitted from the plebiscite, the most intense campaigning centred on Zone Two around the city of Flensburg. Supporters of both sides debated the language of schools and the merits of the Danish or German economic systems. They also drew on a range of symbols, including national flags, landscape imagery, and, of course, heritage. In general, pro-Danish supporters attempted to use nationally recognized ancient motifs to appeal to the national consciousness of regional Danish-speakers. Placards included reprints of the 1906 painting of *The Girl Who Finds the Golden Horn* (*Pigen, der finder guldhornet*), by Harald Slot-Møller (1864–1937), while another featured an image of the Norse god Heimdal blowing a horn astride the Eider River above the slogan, "Awake and Vote for Denmark."[35] In the pages of *Flensborg Avis*, Ernst Christiansen wrote a series of articles stressing Flensburg's strong historical roots in Danish culture, including a legal tradition first written in the old Jütisch language, which he interpreted as historically Danish.

On the German side, the historian Christian Voigt countered Christiansen with articles in the rival German-language newspaper, *Flensburger Tageblatt.* Voigt fell back on the familiar distinctions between Danes and Schleswig-Holsteiners, writing, "The first settlements on our city's soil stem from a time lying far from that of the migration of the Danes."[36] To bolster his case, Voigt relied on the scholarship of Johannes Neuhaus (1869–1922), a lecturer on Scandinavian languages at the University of Berlin. In 1919, Neuhaus published *The Question of North Schleswig in Light of the Most Recent Prehistorical Investigations* (*Die Frage von Nord-Schleswig im Lichte der neuesten vorgeschichtlichen Untersuchungen*), in which he used folklore evidence to demonstrate the presence of "Eastern Germanic" tribes in the Schleswig region during the late Roman era. Yet, when he searched for proof beyond philological remains, he was disappointed by the absence of archaeological studies. Ignoring Sophus Müller's contributions, Neuhaus complained, "Up to the present day, no single work has ventured to take up the task of illuminating the periods of different northern settlements."[37] Neuhaus' book called for archaeological study of ethnic settlement in Schleswig, but it also forwarded suppositions based on linguistic evidence that the Danes, rather than representing long-term inhabitants of the borderland, were in fact distinct from the Jutes and Angles who first settled the region. "The Danes," he concluded, "not only did not have the lead in coming to the Eider, but rather are to be counted as third among the tribes that appeared there."[38]

The plebiscite took place on 10 February 1920 for Zone One and on 14 March 1920 for Zone Two. As expected, residents in Zone One voted overwhelmingly to return to Denmark. In Zone Two, prehistoric arguments proved ineffective in altering an outcome that was largely based on modern linguistic and cultural affinities and especially whether German or Danish would be used in schools, and the region opted to stay in Germany. The involvement of prehistory in the debate, however, made it a visible part of the physical transfer of territory, which occurred on 9 July 1920. The event itself, which took place over several days, turned into a momentous celebration for pro-Danish residents across North Schleswig. On 10 July, King Christian X (r. 1912–1947) marked the moment of reunification by riding across the border on a white horse. He and the royal family then toured the province by motorcar, and in each city were greeted by throngs of enthusiastic Sønderjyder. According to one report, the King's halt in Haderslev was especially jubilant, as "the city vanished in a sea of Dannebrog."[39] The crowning moment of the tour was the visit to Sønderborg, where the King attended a celebration atop the Dybbøl Redoubt, where the Danes had made a desperate but futile stand against the Prussians in 1864. During the ceremony, the Commandant of the town of Åbenrå presented the King first with a Dannebrog from the 1864 war, symbolizing the final victory of the Danes in the conflict, and then with replicas of the two Golden Horns of Gallehus, thus affirming the ancient and unbreakable bonds between Denmark and Sønderjylland.[40]

In the wake of the ceremony, Germans and Danes began the task of adjusting to the new border. Among the most complex issues were those relating to the final disposition of cultural goods. As early as January 1919, both Sophus Müller and Mourtiz Mackeprang (1869–1959), who succeeded Müller as director of the National Museum in 1922, expressed interest in using the German defeat in the war as an opportunity to recover the artefacts from the former Flensburg Collection. As with the plebiscite, the Germans and Danes opened a direct dialogue, and in November 1921, delegations from both sides met to discuss the issue. Mackeprang, who represented Denmark, had been a long-time supporter of reunification, but although he criticized the German government's treatment of the Danish minority in his 1912 work, *Nordslesvig, 1864–1911*, he also made conciliatory gestures to local Schleswig-Holsteiners, writing, "For the sake of our [German] adversary I have made every effort to avoid sharp words and have never forgotten, that the German people does not coincide with the Prussian government."[41] Such sentiments thus made him a strong candidate to represent the Danish side. His German counterpart in the negotiations was Ernst Sauermann (1880–1956), the curator of the Thaulow Museum of Art in Kiel, who was on hand to represent his institution as well as the Flensburg City Museum (Stadtmuseum) and the Kiel Museum.[42]

Among the Danes' most significant requests was the return of the former Flensburg Collection. The Danes based their claim on the fact that most of the artefacts had originated in North Schleswig and had been recovered by an archaeologist, Conrad Engelhardt, who was later affiliated with the Danish National Museum. Moreover, the Danes complained that the Nydam Boat, the centrepiece of the Flensburg Collection, was being improperly stored in an "inaccessible and dark attic" in the museum. As an alternative, Mackeprang proposed to display the artefacts in Sønderborg, which was close to the bog site where they had originally been discovered. The German report later claimed that Sauermann asked whether the Danes might be willing to accept a series of exchanges based on the new border, with objects stemming from the northern side to be turned over to Denmark and those from the south to Germany. According to the report, "This question was rejected by the Danish side on the grounds that Schleswig is ancient Danish land and antiquities from all of Schleswig must be valued as Danish antiquity."[43] Such sentiments hardened the position of German negotiators, who allegedly asked whether the region's cultural goods might not also have inherent value for Germany.

The antagonism from both sides suggests that the negotiations were somewhat premature. They took place, after all, only a few years after the armistice and a year after the acrimonious debate over the plebiscite. Because these were direct negotiations, there was no third party to compel a favourable settlement, and the German government was unwavering in its refusal to relinquish the Nydam Boat, even rejecting an offer of one million Danish Kroner. In the end, both sides left the meeting with some measure of disappointment. The Germans did agree to send a large body of church property, having been convinced that the items belonged to the Danish state church, while the Danes reluctantly returned a well-known sixteenth-century altarpiece from the church in Hütten near Rendsburg, but the archaeological relics in the Schleswig-Holstein Museum remained untouched.[44]

Though the Flensburg Collection remained in Germany, the episode was by no means a victory for the Kiel Museum. Indeed, the archaeologists in Kiel were conspicuous by their absence. Stine Wiell reports that Friedrich Knorr was in Berlin during the meetings, where he sought proof that parts of the Flensburg Collection were privately owned.[45] He was otherwise silent during the entire controversy, which underscored the museum's diminishing status during the early 1920s. Moreover, it highlighted the growing rift between German and Danish prehistorians working in the borderlands. The negotiations, which might have been an avenue for rebuilding broken ties, merely settled the issue for the moment, but did nothing to stem either the Danish longing for the artefacts or the German determination to retain them.

Race, Volk, and Popular Prehistory

If the war and peace settlements had played a role in once again politicizing prehistory, then the interwar period witnessed a rising popular enthusiasm for archaeology. In Denmark, the excitement that surrounded the recovery of North Schleswig persisted into the next decade. At the same time, the resolved border issue helped the country's leading political parties achieve a stable consensus based on the promotion of the national state. This transformation depended a great deal on a harmonization of politics and national culture. A number of Social Democrats in particular were inspired by to abandon hardline Marxist tenets in favour of a so-called Danish model based on Grundtvigian folkelig values, which eschewed narrow constituencies and focused on the cultivation of the whole nation.[46] The transformation thus reflected a harmonization of sorts between politics and national culture, which made public cultural institutions especially relevant as focal points of renewed patriotism. During this period, a new cohort of archaeologists led by Johannes Brøndsted (1890–1965) and Poul Nørlund (1888–1951) came into its own at a time of unprecedented patronage to the National Museum, which by 1935 was attracting over 200,000 visitors per year.[47]

Public interest in ancient heritage was also on the rise in Germany, but where ancient heritage became largely depoliticized in Denmark after the First World

War, it lent itself to a very different sort of völkisch resurgence in the Weimar Republic. There, the humiliation of defeat and the chaos of the revolution created a fresh desire, particularly among right-wing ideologues, to envision the Germanic past as an anchor to a nation facing a shattered present and seeking alternatives to an uncertain future. The experience changed the tenor of the völkisch nationalism evident during the Wilhelmine era. Most noticeably, it incorporated a greater emphasis on racial theory. As Andrew Evans has argued, the war was a principal catalyst for the metamorphosis of German anthropology, which shifted away from its liberal roots. "It was after World War I," he writes, "that the discipline began to transform itself into Rassenkunde, the overtly racist brand of racial science that dominated anthropological circles in the 1920s."[48] This shift seems to have hastened in particular the pre-war interest in the "Nordic" character of the German Volk. Within Rassenkunde, theorists such as the Swiss Germanist Andreas Heusler (1865–1940) drew on literary studies to proclaim Germany the true spiritual heir of Scandinavian saga and myth, while anthropologists like Hans F.K. Günther (1891–1968) defined a "Nordic" racial type in his seminal 1922 work, *Racial Study of the German People* (*Rassenkunde des deutschen Volkes*).[49]

In archaeology, the relationship with Rassenkunde meant that Nordic theories first emerging at the turn of the century became more ambitious in connecting prehistory to the contemporary German nation. In 1928, Gustaf Kossinna incorporated Günther's theories into a new book entitled *Origin and Spread of the Germans in Pre- and Early Historical Times* (*Ursprung und Verbreitung der Germanen in vor- und frühgeschichtlicher Zeit*). He drew on Günther's collection of skulls to show the links between ancient Germans and a distinct "Nordic" racial type. According to Kossinna, a Nordic skull was characterized by an exceptional length and relatively narrow breadth, and further revealed by deep and narrow nasal cavities, receding brow, and pronounced eye sockets. This particular type emerged from a mix of two early types of hominids that Kossinna called "Cro-Magnon" and "Aurignacian."[50] Interestingly, Kossinna claimed that the first distinctive Nordic skulls appeared around 4000 BCE in northern Germany and southern Scandinavia, which corresponded exactly to the time period and location he had designated for the early Indogermanic culture, thus linking racial aptitude to the emergence of technological and cultural advances. Accordingly, by examining skull specimens in outlying areas, Kossinna concluded that racial purity began to fall away in relation to the distance from the "pure" racial centre. Despite this decline, however, Kossinna maintained that the root area of the Germanic race and culture remained the pure core of the Nordic type, making his case through contemporary skull measurements, including that of the daughter of Otto von Bismarck.[51]

In addition to an enthusiasm for prehistory, a number of Kossinna's fellow Nordic enthusiasts adopted a growing appreciation for Viking culture. Leading the way in this trend were the historian Karl Theodor Strasser (1888–1936) and the philologist Bernhard Kummer (1897–1962). Strasser's 1928 work *Vikings and Northmen* (*Wikinger und Normannen*) emphasized the Vikings as exemplars of the Germanic spirit and reminders of its continuing force. "In the essence of the North lies eternity," Strasser proclaimed, "That which is unseen and introspective is its life's source." The spiritual longevity he celebrated in the legacy of the Vikings stood in contrast to the civilizations of the ancient Mediterranean, which Strasser considered to be finite and as removed from the North as "two different worlds."[52] Indeed, Strasser portrayed Viking society as the antithesis of Western civilization, and his histories emphasized its struggle against Western Europe. Meanwhile, Kummer studied Germanic myth and religious practice to defend the Vikings' historical reputation, which he claimed had been maligned by the very Christians who had destroyed the traditional Nordic way of life. His writing, beginning with his 1927 *The Doom of Midgard* (*Midgards Untergang*), emphasized the loss of the Viking homeland as a result of war and population displacement to the south, and argued that it was these pressures rather than simple bloodlust that led them to take to the sea and earn a most undeserving infamy as robbers and pirates.[53]

Not to be outdone, Kossinna responded to Strasser's claim that the Vikings were "without counterpart in world history." In his *Wikinger und Wäringer*, published in 1930, he claimed that the Vikings were especially tantalizing not as a unique example of the Nordic spirit but as the capstone of German prehistory. The Vikings were for Kossinna the carriers of old Germanic culture into the historical period. Because many of the records of their ways and deeds remained extant, the Vikings could cast off part of the shroud of mystery surrounding the ancient Germans and stand as a historical representation of the vanished lifestyle that Kossinna exalted in his writing. He referred to the Viking journeys as a "repetition of the colossal events of the Germanic migration (Völkerwanderung) of the fifth through seventh centuries."[54] Kossinna, in other words, placed the Vikings' migrations as the latest in the long series of Germanic movements that he viewed as the driving force of European history.

Attached to the adoration for Viking culture was a special fascination with the lost city of Haithabu. Not only was Haithabu an important relic of Viking history on German soil, but it also served as proof of the civilized quality of Viking society. Strasser, for example, envisioned Haithabu as the seat of a "Nordic kingdom" whose rune stones were the last reminders of the noble blood that had once dwelt there,[55] while Haithabu entered Kummer's work as the seat of the Danish "King" Göttrick, whom Kummer placed at the centre of a valiant attempt to save the pure Germanic way of life against the encroachments of Charlemagne and the Christian world. The site gained a status of sanctity as a bastion of a doomed but noble culture, since the conflict against Christendom eventually ended in the splintering of the Germanic Volk. "The Christian empire," Kummer wrote, "erected the border of religious hatred between the blood-related, in which the new brotherhood of confession united all the races of the world."[56]

Given this interest in the region, it is perhaps not surprising that northern Germany should be a locus of Nordic racist enthusiasm. As early as 1921, Lübeck became the centre of a newly established Nordic Society (Nordische Gesellschaft), which promoted scholarship on Scandinavia and sought out like-minded Scandinavian scholars.[57] The group's members included Günther, Kummer, and Strasser, as well as the German anthropologist Ludwig Ferdinand Clauß (1892–1974), who incorporated the concept of a "Nordic soul" into studies of ethnopsychology.[58] The group also attracted a few peripheral Scandinavian scholars, including the Germanophile Swedish geographer Sven Hedin (1865–1952) and the Norwegian eugenicist Jon Alfred Hansen Mjöen (1860–1939). Ultimately, the Nordic Society's rather grandiose visions met with only limited success in the crowded nationalist intellectual space of Weimar Germany. They did, however, manage to propagate a specific idea about the German Volk that was tied to an imagined Pan-Nordic past. As Geoffrey Field has since explained, "The Nordicists helped publicize a romantic, völkisch pre-industrial Scandinavia, using it as a kind of negative mirror through which Germans might be made aware of the depersonalizing effects of modernity and the extent to which they had trespassed from their true racial path."[59]

In the absence of scholarly leadership from Kiel, Nordic thought had something of an aggregate effect on the popular consciousness in Schleswig-Holstein. The years after the First World War witnessed a splintering of prehistoric studies in which the rising interest in the distant past led local non-specialists to seize the initiative from professional archaeologists in interpreting regional prehistory. The broad nationalist and racist trends common in inter-war Germany influenced much of this thinking, but local writing on archaeology also reflected the unique context of the borderlands. Here there was an interest in agrarian folk history (*Volksgeschichte*) and a renewed zeal for Heimat studies, which, as Celia Applegate has shown for the Rineland Palatinate, spoke to a desire for Germans to rediscover their provincial roots.[60] Such concerns inspired a number of popular histories of locales across Schleswig-Holstein, which amounted to something of a renaissance for the kind of parochial antiquarian studies that had flourished during the first half of the nineteenth century. The purpose of these authors was first, as Willi Oberkrome has pointed out, to use Volksgeschichte to recover core German national values as represented in the German peasant, and second, as Andrea-Katharina Hanke has shown in the case of Lower Saxony, to reach out to a younger generation to strengthen traditional values through an appreciation of the past.[61]

The scholarly value of these studies varied widely. Some attempted to adhere to the rules of good scholarship. One of the earliest, for example, was *The Prehistory of Flensburg and Environs* (*Die Vorgeschichte von Flensburg und Umgegend*), published in 1924 by Heinrich Philippsen (1858–1936), an advocate of Heimat studies in the Angeln region of eastern Schleswig.[62] Philippsen's background included a stint as a museum director in Hamburg and archaeological field training under the supervision of Johanna Mestorf, which included digs on the island of Föhr in the 1890s.[63] In his book, he opened with a sophisticated survey of three-age periodization in the district and an exploration of the debate over ancient settlement. The question was almost certainly a vestige of the plebiscite debate, but Philippsen's conclusion was strikingly non-partisan. In the end, he concluded, "Certainly the answer to this question is important enough scientifically, but it is wrong to want to derive from it the right to land and soil."[64]

Other works proved less erudite. Among these were the schoolteacher Max Kirmis' prehistory of Neumünster in Holstein and the pastor Emil Bruhn's study of Eiderstedt in Schleswig. Unlike Philippsen, neither Bruhn nor Kirmis had training in archaeology, and they relied on an eclectic mix of sources, including Roman texts, Norse myths, and an unsystematic assortment of historical and archaeological works, the sum of which was reflected in a blend of racist, nationalist, and Christian themes that coloured their work. Kirmis, for example, cited Sophus Müller's chronology for the Bronze Age in Holstein, but argued against the presence of ethnic Danes on the Jutland Peninsula, claiming instead that the area was firmly settled by "South Germans" from "the earliest historical period."[65] Kirmis was also concerned with marking the differences between the Germanic and Slavic peoples who settled the area around modern Neumünster in the late Neolithic period, focusing his attention on St Vicelinus, the patron saint of Holstein whose struggle to convert the Slavs in north Germany lent itself to an image of the Germans' civilizing influence. Emil Bruhn's prehistory, meanwhile, began with the biblical flood, whose "direst consequence" was the driving of "Aryan" Germanic peoples to the south. Bruhn also used historical sources to support claims about the late arrival of the Frisians near Eiderstedt, and drew on Tacitus to prove the "pre-Danish Germanic origins" of the tribes along the Eider River.[66]

Taken together, these writings reveal the ways in which scholarly literature seeped into the popular consciousness. Although their sources were eclectic and their conclusions amateurish, these Heimat researchers nevertheless engaged the edges of the archaeological field. They relied on scholarly work and appealed to the authority of professional archaeologists to strengthen their arguments, and their racial terminology reflected the focus of contemporary science. Along the border, of course, the need for finer distinctions meant that local writers could not fully utilize national theories of German origins. Yet, the theories remained attractive to provincial Schleswig-Holsteiners precisely because they were so malleable and because the nationalist spirit that they carried transferred so easily to alternative depictions of the past. Indeed, Kirmis and Bruhn demonstrate the degree to which völkisch archaeological and racial thought was so easily adaptable for the culturally diverse circumstances of the German-Danish borderlands. Moreover, they explain how these trends by the late 1920s could become so deeply imprinted on the local and national consciousness during the interwar period.

Public Archaeology and the Haithabu Site

Left out of the discussions of various Pan-Germanic or parochial visions of borderlands prehistory was the Kiel Museum. In 1923, Knorr and Rothmann received support to expand the collections into a facility formerly housing the university's hippodrome, but the difficult economic climate denied them the resources to resume excavations.[67] Prospects further dimmed a few years later when illness forced Friedrich Knorr to curtail his work and ultimately retire in 1928.[68] Meanwhile, the public clamours for more research and preservation steadily grew. In early 1926, Heinrich Philippsen led a push to resume work at the Danevirke under the auspices of the Union of Schleswig-Holstein History Teachers (Verband Schleswig-Holsteinischer Geschichtslehrer). He declared in the opening paragraph of his research proposal that the site was a "matter of honour for German scholarship," and complained that the Danes seemed to have a greater commitment to its preservation.[69] His plan called for a large-scale cartographic survey followed by the cross sectioning of parts of the wall. Carl Rothmann volunteered the museum's resources for the project, but the Union's leading members proved reluctant, preferring instead to rely on the archaeologist Hermann Hofmeister (1878–1936) from Hannover.[70]

The museum's outlook improved a few months later, when it re-opened to positive reviews.[71] The renovated exhibition offered five Bronze Age displays and a new space for displaying the Nydam Boat that greeted the visitor with a view of the soaring bow of the craft rising between two magnificent rune stones. To promote the opening, Rothmann wrote to regional teachers, "In the wake of the war the appreciation for the narrower Heimat has awakened as we have never before known, and the most far-flung pupils of our Schleswig-Holstein

Gustav Schwantes (1881–1960). Photograph courtesy Stiftung Schleswig-Holsteinische Landesmuseen Schloss Gottorf.

region must therefore take a peek in the national museum on their excursions."[72] The next year, poor health forced Friedrich Knorr to announce his retirement, and the museum leaders began a search for a new director.[73] From the beginning, Rothmann and Knorr were under pressure from Carl Schuchhardt to consider Gustav Schwantes, who was then teaching prehistory at the University of Hamburg, as the "only and best" candidate.[74] Knorr was reluctant to do so, since he remained somewhat bitter over a very public dispute with Schwantes in 1910 over discoveries from the late Iron Age.[75] Ultimately, Carl Rothmann persuaded his colleagues to accept Schwantes, pointing out that Johanna Mestorf had always wanted him for the museum and writing, "He also has very good relations with the North, which is so important for our borderland."[76]

By the time he accepted the post in March 1929, Schwantes had amassed an impressive reputation, with years of training in both regional and national archaeology. Beyond this experience were his years as a private collector, and his vision for the museum reflected both his scholarly and private pursuits. In his acceptance letter, Schwantes wrote to Rothmann to outline the changes he intended to make in the museum's policies. Chief among these was its relationship with private antiquarian enthusiasts. "One of the points in which I ... am very much in opposition to to the tradition of the museum," he wrote, "is the treatment of local museums and private collectors. I believe that one absolutely cannot do without them ... [and] that one should therefore support them and not hinder them."[77] By seeking to change this policy, Schwantes signalled that he was keenly interested in promoting the public's fascination with archaeology, but he was less willing than Mestorf to establish firm control over public discourse about the past.

Schwantes made further compromises in approaching his next priority, which was returning to the digs at Haithabu. In preparing for the excavations, Schwantes accepted support from Otto Scheel (1876–1954), who held the chair in Schleswig-Holstein regional history at the University of Kiel. As Eric Kurlander has shown, Scheel was a völkisch nationalist who held strongly irredentist and anti-Danish views.[78] But he had been deeply involved in the calls for resuming work at the Danevirke, and Schwantes credited him with securing the necessary funding for the excavation.[79] Just before the start of the digging season in 1930, Scheel and his student, Peter Paulsen (1902–1985), published a historical survey of extant literature on the site. "We hope," he wrote with great anticipation, "that with a final effort we will begin to understand the historical treasures beneath this ground. The literary sources cannot offer enough information."[80]

Despite his partnership with Scheel, Schwantes hoped that the planned excavations would help the museum reconnect with scholars in Scandinavia. Indeed, he had already made an important conciliatory gesture towards Copenhagen earlier in the year, when he permitted the publication of a new study of the Nydam Boat in the inaugural edition of the journal *Acta Archaeologica*. Intended as an organ for prehistory scholarship across Scandinavia, *Acta Archaeologica* was edited by, among others, Johannes Brøndsted, now co-director of the National Museum. The Nydam Boat piece, written by the Norwegian archaeologist Haakon Shetelig (1877–1955), widely regarded as an authority on Iron Age ship construction, was slated for publication by the Kiel Museum,[81] but Schwantes yielded to appeals from Brøndsted and Shetelig, who wrote, "The task of the *Acta* is at the moment so extraordinarily important for Nordic [Scandinavian] archaeology, that I am obliged to favour it."[82]

The digs at Haithabu represented an opportunity to build on this good will. But convincing colleagues across the border was not without controversy, as the involvement of Scheel and Paulsen gave the Danes pause. In July 1930, Scheel invited archaeologists at the National Museum to attend the beginning of the dig.[83] When the Danes failed to respond immediately, Schwantes sent a second invitation, writing: "Since the problem of Haithabu is in many respects also of great interest to our admirable colleagues in Denmark ... and since the experience of our Danish colleagues in the area of excavation and conservation would furthermore be of benefit to our undertaking, it would be a great pleasure for Professor Scheel and me, if many Danish colleagues would come to view and participate in this year's and of course also in the subsequent excavations."[84] Two weeks later, Mouritz Mackeprang at last announced to his colleagues that the decision to participate would be left up to individual scholars at the museum. "But I shall simply note," he added, "that it would also in general certainly be proper if at least one representative paid a visit."[85]

The long-awaited excavations began on 10 September 1930.[86] Although it is unclear who, if anyone, represented the National Museum in the first month of the dig, a number of scholars from Scandinavia did tour the site on 23 September, as did officials and scholars from Berlin.[87] The digs also aroused intense interest among local Germans, and Schwantes actively encouraged the public to visit the daily discoveries. "Not only scientists should undertake the pilgrimage to this venerable memorial of the last period of German heathendom," he wrote, "but rather each whose mind is receptive to the powerful speech of the monument."[88] Schwantes, who in his youth had worked as a teacher, encouraged school groups to take field trips to the site,[89] and in October asked his student assistants to present a public photo exhibition of the dig's progress.[90]

Visitors were not disappointed by the results. Schwantes, who had the benefit of learning from the work of Hermann Hofmeister and Carl Schuchardt on ancient fortifications, had decided to approach the site with a methodology vastly different from that of Friedrich Knorr. Where Knorr had relied on a series of test pits, Schwantes divided the land within the semi-circular earthwork into quadrants before excavating along a series of perpendicular linear trenches. He directed that the trenches be exactly one metre broad and reveal no more than 10 centimetres at a time, allowing him to create both a horizontal and vertical grid and to map the floor of the site.[91] In 1930, the trenches ran on north-south and east-west axes, stopping just short of the edge of the waters of the Schlei. Within the first few days, these trenches began to yield signs of housing foundations, which he surmised represented the earliest examples of home construction from the Viking Age in Germany. Moreover, the digs revealed a number of trade goods, including Carolingian ceramics, which led Schwantes to date the origin of the site to the early ninth century CE.[92] Scheel cautioned that Haithabu paled by Mediterranean standards but noted that the finds from the first season put to rest any doubt that the Oldenburg was the site of a complete urban settlement at the centre of an extensive trading network with "world-historical" importance. [93]

The scope of Schwantes' digs also revealed new clues about the culture of the Haithabu community. Specifically, they uncovered burial practices that demonstrated marked change over the course of the city's development. In 1930, Schwantes and his students discovered two separate burial sites, the first of which contained some of the oldest artefacts recovered at the site, including coins dating to the period between 825 and 850 CE. The team also found several wooden burial chambers of a "decidedly heathen character," lying beneath some of the housing foundations, further suggesting that it was among the earliest interment sites at Haithabu. The second and larger cemetery contained material dating to the eleventh century CE and bearing the hallmarks of Christian influence. Schwantes thus concluded that Haithabu predated the establishment of a Christian Church at Schleswig and that the two fields provided evidence for a widespread religious conversion at some point in the city's history. [94]

With these exciting discoveries, the 1930 season at Haithabu marked the firm reappearance of professional archaeological practice in Schleswig-Holstein. It was a return that enjoyed a great deal of popular interest, so much so in fact that Schwantes asked the local newspaper to print notices warning the crowds of onlookers to avoid traversing the work area.[95] For local antiquarian enthusiasts, the site brought together the most romantic elements of human history and natural beauty. On the eve of the 1931 digging season, the Husum journalist Felix Schmeißer took a stroll of the empty site, and his prose account of his experience, which appeared in *Schleswiger Nachrichten*, was strikingly reminiscent of the poetry of Ludwig Gerhard Kosegarten at Rügen over a hundred years earlier. Just as Kosegarten had done atop the grave mound, Schmeißer paused to contemplate his own presence at Haithabu, with his shadow "falling from the walls' heights to the fields below." He observed two crows chattering overhead. "And then," he concluded, "the magical white winter's night once again lies motionless and deathly silent over Haithabu, and nothing more disturbs the millennial sleep of the Northern necropolis."[96]

The digs at Haithabu led other popular writers to expound upon the legend and invent a tale for the lost city relating it to the nation's history. Among the earliest of these was Paul Leuchsenring's *Haithabu: A Nordic Play in Seven Scenes* (*Haithabu: Ein nordisches Schauspiel in Sieben Bildern*), which was first produced in September 1931 at the Nordmark-Landestheatre in Schleswig. Drawing on Schwantes' discovery of heathen and Christian burial sites, Leuchsenring scripted a quarrel between Chnuba, a Swedish chieftain and nominal King of Denmark in the early tenth century, and his son Sigtrygg, who rejected his father's conversion to Christianity. In the battle between the two, Haithabu burned to the ground and a new Christian city was built over the heathen ruins. Leuchsenring saw the story as a tragedy that lay not with the relationship between father and son, but with the sacrifice of the old ways. As one critic explained, "In Sigtrygg we see the tragic fate of the young man, whose nativeness forces him to struggle and act against the New, against subservience and servitude."[97] While Leuchsenring mourned the inevitable loss of the free, heathen spirit of the Germanic Volk, Heinar Schilling (1894–1955) memorialized Haithabu as a lost era of racial unity in the North in his 1936 work, *Haithabu: A Germanic Troy* (*Haithabu: Ein germanisches Troja*). Schilling characterized the Saxon war against Charlemagne as a collaborative effort among Nordic peoples, saying, "It was, so to speak, the last opportunity for the old Germanic or, if one prefers, the Aryan homeland to unite in a single political creation."[98] The repeated failures to preserve the integrity of the "homeland" served as the dramatic thrust of Schilling's account, with Haithabu standing at the centre of these tragic attempts. As Schilling lamented, "Had [this] heroic work [come] to victorious fruition, then there would be a single Germanic Reich, from Norway's hills, to Sweden's green pastures, to Finland's quiet seas, all the way to the Rhine and perhaps even to the Danube – an empire of unmingled blood and unmingled spirit – a land of the Nordic race."[99]

Conclusion

The writings of Nordic enthusiasts such as Schilling and Leuchsenring had by the 1930s transformed Haithabu – the nondescript, empty field – into a monument to the vision of Germanic prehistory that had emerged in the previous decades. Interestingly, they also placed the site at the epicentre of a changing relationship between professional archaeology and the popular imagination. Where Schwantes put to rest the myth of Haithabu through careful excavation, popular writers resurrected the legend and invested it with a new set of symbolic meanings. Their accounts extolled the mystery of the ancient city even as archaeology promised to unlock its oldest secrets, a curious paradox that both promoted archaeological study and enriched nationalist fantasies. As a result, the site became a tangible reminder of an uneasy coexistence of völkisch nationalism and objective scholarship that had coloured the practice of archaeology since the turn of the century.

By the time Schilling wrote his account, of course, the political situation had changed dramatically, and his portrayal carried a new significance in the ideological landscape of the Third Reich. It is critical to note, however, the degree to which Schilling's ideas about northern Europe were anticipated during the previous four decades, with antecedents stretching back to the early nineteenth century. Indeed, we should not be tempted to see such fantastic claims about the northern European past as sudden arrivals in German thought during the late 1920s. Rather, völkisch, nationalist, and racist strains of thought about prehistory had evolved relatively slowly, even if they were strongly influenced by the crises of the First World War and the Weimar era. Above all, the most tangible outcome of the years between 1914 and 1933 was the diversification and normalization of "Nordic thought" and its introduction into scholarly discourse. Such trends injected new meanings into the ancient past and reinforced the grand narratives of Germanic prehistory that had emerged in the early twentieth century.

These trends did not, however, necessarily mark a fundamental shift in the character of professional German archaeology. Throughout the period, traditional scholarly practices continued both to compete and blend with nationalist visions of northern prehistory. But there is no question that the institutions supporting objective archaeological practice had temporarily attenuated during the 1920s, which in turn allowed new ideologies to blossom. Moreover, the scholarly engagement in debates over Germany's eastern and northern frontiers made professionals complicit in the politicization of prehistory during the interwar era. With dwindling resources, researchers in the provinces found themselves obliged to treat on ever more equal terms with the layman and the dilettante. As a result, the pressures of the period forced professional archaeologists to move from their earlier ambivalence about nationalist and racist orientations into a state of cohabitation with a diverse and increasingly radical set of interpretations of northern European prehistory.

Similar events took place in Denmark, where the leaders of the National Museum also noted a spike in popular enthusiasm for the past.[100] Like their German counterparts, Danish archaeologists proved willing to participate in the political drama surrounding the border question and, like Schwantes in Kiel, tolerated the emergence of a proverbial cottage industry of popular writing about Denmark's prehistory. Indeed, both Danes and Germans continued to see the past as national heritage and national property. The difference between the two cases, however, is perhaps best seen through the ways in which the past was used in Denmark. There were, in contrast to Germany, fewer competing accounts of the past; rather, the comparatively stable political landscape encouraged much more unified and benign symbolic appropriations. Danes used these symbols for a variety of nationalist and political causes, such as the ceremony at the Dybbøl, but they shied away from rewriting the narrative of prehistory from which the symbols had come. Furthermore, the greater resilience of Danish institutions meant that the public entertained their excitement for archaeology in a more structured setting.

Despite these differences, it is important to stress the congruence between the German and Danish attitudes to prehistory in the interwar period. For both sides, prehistory became politicized in a manner reminiscent of the mid-nineteenth century. As before, conflict and political change created pressures that led scholars to compromise the objective norms of their discipline. The upshot was a new series of challenges to academic cooperation. Schwantes had done much to rebuild confidence in the cross-border relationship, but the reluctance among Danes to participate in the Haithabu digs revealed the chasm that had emerged within the cross-border network. It was a rupture that would widen following the accession of Adolf Hitler in 1933. As we will see in the final chapters, the Nazi regime would restore the power of professional archaeology, but it would also force Germans and Danes to confront the political consequences of the nationalist assumptions at work within their discipline.

6 Creating Nazi Archaeology

In the 1930s, a renewed passion for the past appeared in Schleswig-Holstein. One hundred years had passed since the first great effort to uncover the region's ancient remains, and the new decade recalled those early days with fresh fervour for the fruits of archaeology. This time, however, the trend took on a wholly different character. It did not confine itself to select private interests, but reached out to all through established institutions. It did not rest solely in the realm of local curiosity, but stood at the heart of a national trend. The enthusiasm for antiquity now responded to the radical political shifts within Germany. It was invested not only in the hope of a restored nation, but also in the expectation of a new society. In this decade, prehistoric archaeology was shaped by the ideology of the Nazi movement and harnessed to the purposes of the Third Reich.

For völkisch nationalists, the electoral victory of Adolf Hitler in 1933 marked the beginning of a shining age heralding a revitalized Germany. While Hitler was personally ambivalent about exalting Germanic antiquity, many of his followers saw the Nazi movement as a reconnection with ancient German values.[1] Karl Theodor Strasser, the scholar of Viking culture, excised the cultural pessimism that had coloured earlier editions of his *Wikinger und Normannen*, and in the 1933 edition of his book celebrated an impending spiritual rebirth. "Everywhere in Germany," he proclaimed, "the old heroic spirit is once again awakened. The new Führer has manifested the Nordic courage within himself, and his deeds are comparable with the works of the Vikings."[2] Strasser was not alone. A host of popular books appeared featuring prehistoric themes, while illustrated journals like *Germanien* and *Germanen-Erbe* brought archaeology into German living rooms,[3] and school curricula shifted to emphasize ancient Germanic history.[4] The Nazis sought to capture this energy and drew on Germanic antiquity both as a symbolic reservoir and a source of spiritual inspiration. Leading Reich officials such as Heinrich Himmler (1900–1945) and Alfred Rosenberg (1893–1946) fancied themselves aficionados of ancient Germanic culture and supported archaeological scholarship to further their own ideological interests. The Propaganda Ministry, meanwhile, ensured that images of German prehistory became part of the public consciousness. Even in Denmark, the tiny Danish Nazi movement (Danmarks National-Socialistiske Arbejderparti) associated itself with the ancient past and adopted the stone dolmen and Thor's hammer as its most visible icons.[5]

The Nazi zeal for northern European prehistory placed Schleswig-Holstein once again at the centre of interest. Steffen Werther's study of the German-Danish minorities during the Third Reich has shown that many so-called border fighters (*Grenzkämpfer*), who expected the regime to revise the 1920 plebiscite, found themselves struggling to balance vague notions of Volk and race. It was difficult, they discovered, to promote the plight of the German Volksdeutsche minority while also adjusting to dreams of a "Greater Germandom" (*Großgermanentum*) encompassing the Nordic lands. As the Grenzkämpfer learned to their disappointment, and as Danes later discovered to their horror, this latter vision grew steadily more important during the Nazi era, and excited national interest much more strongly than did the border question.[6] Moreover, it was this sort of Nordic thinking that drew Nazi ideologues to regional archaeology. In 1937, the German newspaper *Die Welt* featured a story on the ongoing digs at Ahrensburg, where the amateur archaeologist Alfred Rust (1900–1983) discovered one of the earliest paleolithic cultures in northern Europe.[7] The story also included photos of the nearby Haithabu project, where Heinrich Himmler was about to be named official patron. That same year, Himmler funded a new round of excavations at Haithabu under the direction of Herbert Jankuhn (1905–1990). What was remarkable about Ahrensburg and Haithabu was first the scale of the excavations, which was made possible through Nazi support, and second their national celebrity. The Propaganda Ministry even considered staging a political rally at Haithabu, with plans to dress the site in the guise of Thingstätten, the councils of the early medieval Scandinavians.[8] In the Ahrensburg report from *Die Welt*, large photographs of the ongoing excavation were accompanied by a quote from Adolf Hitler, "It is my decision to preserve and promote the great cultural works of our people from prehistory and the past. The German Volk should acknowledge these creations of a truly noble culture with joyful pride."[9]

Such changes amounted to an unprecedented politicization of prehistoric archaeology. For the first time, a major political party courted archaeologists and presented regional scholars with opportunities to serve the state on the national stage. The Nazis, after all, recognized that their propaganda claims about ancient Germans demanded a certain legitimacy that only organized scholarship could provide. They thus promoted the growth of archaeology by increasing funding for research and supporting the development of doctoral programs.[10] As a result, archaeologists regained their public role in interpreting the past after a decade of funding shortages and competition from enthusiastic amateurs. In return, Nazi patrons presumed that their support would produce scholarship favourable to the Party's ideological goals. This left German prehistorians balancing the traditional norms of their profession with the ideological demands of the state. As in many other parts of the Reich, many German archaeologists in the borderlands collaborated with the Party and the state, and Kiel archaeologists in particular became leading figures on the national stage both in academic and political circles. Most notable was Herbert Jankuhn, who in the 1930s succeeded Gustav Schwantes first as chief excavator at Haithabu and then as director of the Kiel Museum. Jankuhn's high-ranking membership in the Ancestral Heritage Branch (Ahnenerbe) of Himmler's SS organization later made him among the most controversial figures in the postwar memory of the discipline.[11]

How and why these scholars collaborated with Nazi leaders has proved a difficult question, given the reluctance of many wartime archaeologists to discuss their engagement with the regime. It has been only since their retirement and passing that a serious discussion of this topic has become possible. Since that time, a number of scholars have grimly recounted the close relationship between Nazi ideologues and archaeologists like Herbert Jankuhn.[12] Other historians have moved beyond simple ascriptions of pro-Nazi sentiment among archaeologists to include studies of larger structural causes. Among these has been the youth of prehistoric archaeology as a discipline, which made it more susceptible to Nazi manipulation than, for instance, Classical studies.[13] Because their field was a relative latecomer to academia, prehistoric archaeologists were more willing to trade their objectivity for career opportunities, leading to what Bettina Arnold and Henning Haßmann have called a "Faustian bargain" with the Reich.[14] Reinhard Bollmus as well as Uta Halle, meanwhile, have focused on the role of the state, revealing how prehistorians took advantage of competing interests within the regime.[15] Finally, Hermann Beck has argued for a broader understanding of collaboration among the educated *Bildungsbürgertum*, who broadly supported Hitler after 1933. For Beck, "Opportunism alone did not seem to explain the wholehearted (and often unsolicited) enthusiasm with which the 'National Revolution' was welcomed."[16] As a result, archaeologists would have contended not only with career benefits and political perils, but also with pressure from within their social milieu. Taken together, these contextual factors yielded what Geoffrey Cocks has called, "a morally and intellectually ambiguous accommodation to the established powers of Nazi Germany, on both the individual and collective level, in pursuit of professional and institutional status."[17]

These sorts of accounts of negotiated complicity make important contributions to our broader understanding, but leave at least two major issues unexplored. First, they tend to elide the ideological congruity between archaeologists and Nazi politicians that might have affirmed a working relationship. In other words, while archaeologists need not have been political adherents of National Socialism (though some, like Jankuhn, undoubtedly were), the fact that they ascribed national value to their work facilitated their cooperation with the state. Second, the current studies generally overlook the role of the international domain in the process of collaboration. As we have seen in the case of the borderlands, the norms that defined archaeology often extended beyond Germany's borders and implicated international networks. Consequently, no study of professional engagement during the Nazi period can be complete without a consideration of the broader archaeological community. Such an oversight relates to the general tendency in German historiography to neglect transnational factors and players, which has sparked Kiran Klaus Patel's recent plea for a "transnational historicization" that brings a broader perspective into the history of National Socialism. As he writes, "The new frontier when studying Nazism … is to overcome the dominating isolationist premise. In our practical work, we should stop seeing Nazism exclusively as a part of the German past."[18]

How, then, did the old tensions between the field's nationalist underpinnings and its cross-border practices influence local engagement with the Nazis in Schleswig-Holstein? Moreover, how and why did archaeologists in Kiel become so central to the creation of "Nazi archaeology" in the 1930s? And, finally, how did the Third Reich and Second World War transform the ways in which Germans and Danes in the borderland saw the ancient past – and each other?

Prehistorical Archaeology and Nazism

The community of professional German archaeologists in Kiel first engaged the new regime only months after Hitler's installation as chancellor in January 1933. In March of that year, the Prussian Ministry of Education issued a call for a stronger emphasis on German prehistory in primary and secondary schools. Schwantes and his colleagues responded with a collection of articles published in a special issue of the *Schleswig-Holstein School Gazette* (*Schleswig-Holsteinische Schulzeitung*). The next month, they participated in a series of lectures in Schleswig designed to promote the benefits of archaeology, racial studies, and historical preservation in the school curriculum.[19] The journal and the lectures were organized by Alfred Rosenberg's Fighting League for German Culture (Kampfbund für deutsche Kultur).

Even before the publication appeared in September, Nazism had developed a strong following among Germans in the borderlands.[20] The effects of the Great Depression had been felt especially keenly in Kiel, where the Treaty of Versailles hampered the city's shipbuilding and military-oriented industries.[21] In the countryside, the agricultural crisis that preceded the 1929 financial collapse had sparked powerful rural opposition to the Weimar Republic.[22] The state of the border also remained a key political issue, and the bitter memory of the 1920 plebiscite helped cast the period of crisis as a threat to the national community. Steffen Werther has shown that the German-Danish border lacked the resonance of the eastern frontiers, but the issue nevertheless drew both Schleswig-Holsteiners and members of the German Volksdeutsche minority in North Schleswig into either the NSDAP or to the eventual NSDAP-Nordschleswig branch headed by Jens Möller (1894–1951).[23] In Germany, these conditions laid the groundwork for a strong showing for the NSDAP in regional polls.[24] In the July and November 1932 elections, the Nazis captured around half the vote in Schleswig-Holstein.[25] Within months of Hitler's accession in January 1933, the process of "synchronization" (*Gleichschaltung*) was already underway, consolidating Party control at the local level. A rapid series of plebiscites installed National Socialist supporters in the offices of the provincial administrator, the district administrator, and the mayors of Kiel, Flensburg, and Neumünster.[26] The conformist impulse also extended to cultural and educational institutions. In May, Ernst Sauermann, who had represented the Germans during the negotiations over the Flensburg Collection in 1922, joined the Nazi Party and enjoyed the support of the Reich as director of the Provincial Institute for the Preservation of Historical Monuments (Provinzielles Institut für Denkmalpflege).[27]

There was consequently a strong context of support for Nazi goals at the time of the *Schulzeitung* articles. Yet, regional prehistory studies did not undergo the sorts of rapid changes that marked other German provinces. While cities like Trier and Bonn, where museums had only been established during the late nineteenth century, began shifting their institutional planning towards Nazi goals early in 1933,[28] the more established Kiel Museum remained structurally unchanged. The *Schulzeitung* was thus significant because it marked a more indirect form of collaboration with the state. It brought together for the first time the scholars who would become leading figures in the ensuing years. As such, it reveals much about the confluence of Nazi ideology and nationalism that coloured regional archaeology during the previous decades.

Among the contributors was Gustav Schwantes, whose piece on the northern European paleolithic joined articles from two of his students at the University of Kiel: Peter Paulsen (1902–1985) and Karl Kersten (1909–1992). Paulsen, who edited the collection on behalf of the Kampfbund, hailed from the small community of Klixbüll a few kilometres south of the post-1920 border. He had recently finished a doctoral dissertation under Schwantes on the archaeology of the early medieval Viking period in northern Germany, and had worked with Johannes Brøndsted in Copenhagen.[29] Though his work was clearly connected to archaeology, Paulsen trained as an art historian, and his principal experience came through work in the Thaulow Museum of Art in Kiel. In this capacity, he had assisted Otto Scheel in compiling the historical sources used in the 1930 Haithabu project.[30] By 1933, Paulsen was provincial head of the German Prehistory Section (Fachgruppe für deutsche Vorgeschichte) of the Kampfbund für Deutsche Kultur.[31] Kersten, meanwhile, was making a name for himself through his expertise on the northern European Bronze Age. Like Paulsen, Kersten had studied alongside Scandinavian colleagues in the 1920s, and had become acquainted with Brøndsted. Kersten's emphasis, however, lay much more clearly with field archaeology, and his contribution to the *Schulzeitung* was a report on his excavations at the Bronze Age grave hill at Grünhof-Tesperhude in Lauenburg in 1932.

Another article concerned the "Germanic Migration Period." Its author, Herbert Jankuhn, was already establishing himself as a leading archaeologist of the late prehistoric and early medieval period. Unlike many of his colleagues, Jankuhn was not a native of the region, but grew up in the region between East Prussia and Lithuania, which was also the homeland of Gustaf Kossinna. Like Kossinna, Jankuhn's background was strongly conservative. During the 1920s, he trained in the so-called black German army (Schwarze Reichswehr), and in 1934 he applied for membership in the Nazi SA paramilitary organization.[32] But his training as an archaeologist brought him outside the Kossinna circle. He completed his doctoral training at the University of Berlin in 1931 under Carl Schuchhardt with a dissertation that was critical of Kossinna's methods.[33] Through Schuchhardt's influence, Jankuhn joined Schwantes' excavations at Haithabu in 1930, and then participated in a study tour of Egypt and the Near East with the German Archaeological Institute (Deutsches Archäologisches Institut) in 1932.[34] Upon his return in 1933, he was named the director of the Haithabu project.

The *Schulzeitung* article was Jankuhn's first published work following his return to Kiel. It joined a collection of articles designed to bring the latest archaeological research to the attention of schoolteachers across the province.[35] To accomplish this, Paulsen stressed the scholarly rigour that characterized the contributions. Indeed, there was a great deal of continuity between the articles in the *Schulzeitung* and previous scholarship. Kersten's Bronze Age study, for example, was strikingly similar to a report he had published a year earlier in the journal *Die Heimat*.[36] At the same time, there was no mistaking the nationalist overtones framing the collection. The very title of the issue, "German Prehistory – A National Science," clearly evoked the work of the Gustaf Kossinna, who had passed away two years earlier. The sentiments of his research echoed in the words of Paulsen, who declared: "As far as we have knowledge of the prehistory of our people, so should it be conveyed to today's generation not only to acquire a proper appreciation of the unique and sophisticated culture of its forbears, but also to build anew and recreate a German way of life (Lebensordnung)."[37] The task of using prehistory to inculcate "a German way of life" fit well with the mission of the Kampfbund für Deutsche Kultur, which Alan Steinweis has described as one of "völkisch consciousness-raising."[38]

The contributors could thus be under no illusions about the implications of the Nazi movement for their research. In fact, as the archaeologist Peter Zylmann wrote in his article, "With the state revolution (Staatsumwälzung) the study of prehistory has received a joyful boost."[39] At the same time, there was no mistaking the process of radicalization affecting not just the political scene, but also the climate of the University of Kiel. On 10 May 1933, students of the University, with the support of members of the faculty and the Kampfbund, staged a public book burning of socialist and Jewish works in Kiel's Wilhelmplatz.[40] It was an event that also corresponded to the goals of the Kampfbund, in this case by assaulting elements at the University considered "ungermanic."[41] In short, by the summer of 1933 the moral dilemma that would confront archaeologists throughout the Nazi period had already become manifest.

Was this, then, the beginning of the "Faustian Bargain" to which Bettina Arnold and Henning Haßmann have alluded in their histories of Third Reich archaeology? There was, on the one hand, no immediate financial gain for most archaeologists in 1933. In October, Schwantes was denied a raise in his salary,[42] while Herbert Jankuhn's pay remained more or less unchanged from 1931 until 1936.[43] On the other hand, some scholars seem to have anticipated future benefits attached to the "joyful boost" of Nazi support. Schwantes, for example, made an unquestionably Germanophile claim in a 1933 issue of the journal *Forschungen und Fortschritte* when he stressed the Bronze Age collection in Kiel as the best in Germany for patrons to experience the remains of their "Germanic ancestors."[44] But his intention, as the article revealed, was to call on the government to finance the expansion of his institution. His younger colleagues, meanwhile, made even more radical accommodations in the hopes of using Nazi influence to secure their professional aspirations. Perhaps the most prominent example was Peter Paulsen, who found himself elevated to director of the Kampfbund's prehistory group only a year after completing his dissertation. Therefore, for young professionals coming of age at the beginning of the Nazi period, engagement with the regime already seemed a sure path to success.[45]

Careerist motives alone, however, could not account for the relationship between the new state and the archaeological community, even at this early stage. There were, in fact, a number of other factors stemming from both the political revolution in 1933 and the previous history of archaeology that fostered the engagement of regional prehistorians with the Reich. At times, the overlap between professional archaeology and Nazi propaganda was not a conscious accommodation. For instance, the cult status that attached to Gustaf Kossinna after his death in 1931 already emphasized the nationalist significance that he had attached to the discipline at the turn of the century. Even if his research remained controversial, the nationalist message embedded within had outlived Kossinna to inform the work of a new generation of archaeologists. It was an issue that Jankuhn himself addressed in October 1933, when he gave a public lecture in Schleswig on behalf of the Kampfbund on the topic of "Prehistory as National Scholarship," where he argued: "For centuries a foundational historical view has been drawn of the pre- and early historical period solely on the basis of written sources that has distanced it considerably from [recent history]. Since, however, the Germanic Peoples (*Germanen*) formed the most decisive element of our national body (*Volkskörper*), this sort of portrayal has misrepresented the oldest part of our national history and obscured the way to true understanding."[46] This view reiterated Kossinna's arguments from three decades earlier about the use of archaeology as a historical tool and the linkages between the prehistoric and historic narratives of national history. But the similarities did not end there. In the same lecture, Jankuhn adopted the tenets of the Nordic origin theory, telling his audience, "The origins of Germandom lie here in Schleswig-Holstein and on the Danish Islands, and from 1500 BC we can speak for the first time of German Peoples."[47] These arguments, which courted controversy in Kossinna's day, had become more commonplace by 1933. What had once sparked ambivalence in Schwantes seemed conventional to Jankuhn, and, even if he remained critical of the ways in which Kossinna had connected artefacts and ethnic groups, Jankuhn nevertheless accepted the same underlying assumptions about archaeology's capacity to produce an ethnohistorical account of the nation. At the same time, such thinking appealed to Nazi leaders because it conformed to what Claudia Koonz terms "ethnic fundamentalism," which stressed affirmations of Germanic culture and history as a contrast to the antisemitic and anti-modernist elements of Nazi ideology.[48]

Another way to understand such work is to see it as more than a conscious manipulation of data for National Socialist propaganda. Rather, it continued a long-standing tradition of presenting the past differently for professional and public consumption. As we have seen, Schwantes, Mestorf, and even Jens Worsaae had written in a similar style (if not to a similar degree) in the nineteenth and early twentieth centuries. The nationalist tradition of the discipline made it possible for German prehistorians to cooperate with the Nazi state without necessarily bending towards Nazi ideology. It also insulated them in the first year from the pressures facing scholars in other fields. They did not, for instance, feel obliged to join the Nazi Party in 1933, as Ernst Sauermann had done in order to protect cultural projects he feared would be labelled "degenerate" by the Nazis.[49] Rather, archaeologists in Schleswig-Holstein soon found themselves courted by Nazi officials, who wanted representations of Germanic antiquity that would be, as Paulsen described, "strictly scientific yet accessible."[50]

Organizational Rivalries and the International Sphere

Three years later, the Kiel Museum celebrated its hundredth anniversary.[51] By this time, the renewed interest in professional prehistoric archaeology had reversed the fortunes of the once-flagging institution. Spirits were high in October 1936, as supporters gathered at the nearby Kiel Palace to hear an anniversary address from Gustav Schwantes. There, with an enthusiasm reminiscent of Friedrich Warnstedt's address a century earlier, Schwantes marked the occasion with reflections on the museum's past, present, and future.[52] He reminded his eager listeners that the museum's task in 1936 remained the same as in 1836: to house, preserve, and study what he called "the rich treasures of the early history of our region, whose place as a bridge between Germany and Scandinavia was already clearly evident in prehistoric times."[53] Schwantes' speech thus highlighted the museum's success in very familiar terms. He stressed its regional, international, and cross-border significance without mentioning the sweeping changes in national attitudes towards archaeology.

Also left unstated was the fact that the institution's academic independence was shrinking. Even before Schwantes's address, the relatively free rein that its scholars had enjoyed in 1933 had begun to diminish as all corners of German civil society faced pressure to orient themselves to Nazi leadership and become part of a unified national community (*Volksgemeinschaft*). In practice, many organizations pursued "self-synchronization" (*Selbstgleichschaltung*) by voluntarily adopting new titles and symbols suggesting their alignment with the regime, and in some cases by installing new leaders more favourably disposed to Nazi ideology. Archaeology was no different. Although the process was by no means uniform and in some ways never completed, the discipline, both for classical archaeologists and prehistorians, had changed dramatically by the mid-1930s.

The professional ranks were quickly purged of their Jewish members, while opportunistic young archaeologists sought to unite the field under the rubric of new professional associations.

Such changes were common across academia.[54] What was unique was the Nazis' special interest in prehistoric archaeology, which created uncommon opportunities for specialists in Germanic antiquity. Above all, because the Nazi state consisted of compartmentalized and nebulous centres of power, it was possible for a number of high-level officials to pursue their personal interests in archaeology independently. The result was what Uta Halle has called the "double chance" for archaeologists to benefit from state support. Halle has shown that state offices often jockeyed for the loyalty of scholars, which allowed archaeologists to reap additional rewards and protection by accepting the patronage of one over another. In Schleswig-Holstein, the office of Alfred Rosenberg (Amt Rosenberg) and the affiliated Kampfbund für Deutsche Kultur promoted archaeological scholarship in the schools, while Heinrich Himmler's SS-Ahnenerbe began supporting the Haithabu excavations in 1934.[55] Kiel archaeologists ultimately cooperated with both groups, a fact that undermines any notion that they found themselves helplessly forced to choose between rival Nazi institutions. Instead, it supports the idea that multiple motives were at work in the first phase of the regime, and that only the path to engagement was influenced by the cultural politics of the rivalry between Heinrich Himmler and Alfred Rosenberg.

Diverse incentives and rival patrons meant that the process was rarely a smooth one. For prehistoric archaeology, Gleichschaltung entailed a long-running internal struggle closely tied to the rivalry between Himmler and Rosenberg. At its centre was Hans Reinerth (1900–1990), an archaeologist at Berlin who spent much of the 1930s trying to unite the discipline under a single institution in accordance with Nazi principles. Reinerth was an adherent of the Kossinna School and a Nazi Party member with ties to Alfred Rosenberg going back to 1928. As an archaeologist, he had a poor reputation, which included accusations of misappropriation against his mentor, R.R. Schmidt, in 1930. The Nazis offered him a second chance to advance his career. By April 1932, Reinerth had become the national director of the prehistory section of the Kampfbund für deutsche Kultur, where he was an enthusiastic advocate for blending radical ideology with mainstream scholarship.[56] "Just as racial science," he declared in 1933, "and especially the awareness of the importance and uniqueness of the Nordic race is the basis of the National Socialist world view, so it must become the foundation of all science."[57]

Reinerth's wish to create a centralized Reich Institute for German Prehistory (Reichsinstitut für deutsche Vorgeschichte) quickly brought him into conflict with such long-established institutions as the German Archaeological Institute and Roman-Germanic Commission (Römisch-Germanisch Kommission), whose focus on the Classical world did not neatly fit the new racial world view of National Socialism. Reinerth never succeeded in creating a new dominating institution, but his efforts may have contributed to the decline of classical archaeology during a time when its ranks diminished by 25 per cent. A more successful takeover occurred at the Roman Germanic Central Museum in Mainz, which was renamed the Central Museum for German Pre- and Early History (Zentralmuseum für deutsche Vor- und Frühgeschichte).[58] Eventually, a number of noted classical scholars like Werner Jaeger (1888–1961) responded by entering self-imposed exile, while others, like the German-Jewish archaeologist Gerhard Bersu (1889–1964), were forced to retire. The German Archaeological Institute, meanwhile, weathered scrutiny by emphasizing prehistoric projects in its budget reports.[59] At the same time, Reinerth's drive to consolidate the discipline worsened the lingering antagonism from the Kossinna-Schuchhardt debates of the early twentieth century. In May 1934, Reinerth brought Kossinna's prehistorical society, now renamed the Reich League for German Prehistory (Reichsbund für deutsche Vorgeschichte), under the control of the Kampfbund. He struggled, however, to convince most of his colleagues to recognize his authority as director.[60] He faced especially stiff opposition from Carl Schuchhardt and Wilhelm Unverzagt (1892–1971), who remained sympathetic to the plight of the German Archaeological Institute and Roman-Germanic Commission. By 1935, the ensuing power struggle created space for Heinrich Himmler to bring his SS organization into the fray.

The struggle underway at the national level had a distinct local corollary in Kiel. Both Peter Paulsen and Otto Scheel were committed adherents of Reinerth and Rosenberg, while Schwantes, Jankuhn, and Kersten proved more ambivalent. Viewed more closely, the lines dividing the two sides were not always clear, and the differences at times came down to personal loyalties and rivalries. Initially, Schwantes and Jankuhn expressed interest in the Reichsbund, even going so far as to lead a tour of the Haithabu site on behalf of the group in September 1935.[61] Later, they withdrew their support after Reinerth asked them to speak out against Carl Schuchhardt and Wilhelm Unverzagt. Two key developments finally led to an irreparable split by 1936. The first stemmed from personal conflicts at the University of Kiel that gripped the campus during the spring. At issue was a long-standing competition between Peter Paulsen and Herbert Jankuhn for the directorship of the Haithabu project. Years before, when Jankuhn was away on his study tour in Egypt, museum custodian Carl Rothmann wrote to the Education Ministry to ask that Paulsen be named to the position.[62] Schwantes, however, favoured bringing Jankuhn back to Haithabu, arguing that he had excavated at the site previously and had much more field experience. Paulsen took his mentor's rejection as a personal insult, and when Schwantes and Jankuhn later refused to join the Reichsbund, Paulsen began to raise questions about their political loyalty. He based his accusations on their relationship to Gerhard Bersu, and for good measure suggested that Schwantes was a socialist and freemason.[63]

In March 1936, Jankuhn reported to the rector of the University that Paulsen had been spreading accusations among the student body, and he requested a meeting to confront Paulsen about the rumours.[64] In April, Paulsen, Jankuhn, and Schwantes met with the rector to address the charges. Paulsen, faced with written testimony from students, acknowledged his role in a whisper campaign against not only Schwantes and Jankuhn, but also Karl Kersten, who had been accused of harbouring communist sympathies. Jankuhn later recorded that when the rector asked Paulsen to sum up his view of the three men, "Herr Dr Paulsen explained, that in his opinion neither Prof. Schwantes nor Dr Jankuhn or Dr Kersten were opponents of National Socialism and that his stated suspicions were baseless."[65] Paulsen claimed that the accusations had come originally from Hans Reinerth and the leadership of the Reichsbund, though he expected that they would deny making any charges. In response, the rector reprimanded Paulsen and threatened him with dismissal in the event of further defamations.[66] The meeting settled the issue, if only for the moment, but Jankuhn had been prepared to fight fire with fire. Among the documents he had prepared in rebuttal were copies of correspondence between Bersu and Hans Reinerth, suggesting that it was he, rather than Jankuhn, who had close ties to the Jewish scholar.[67]

In many ways, a conflict of this nature was inevitable. The new paths for advancement offered by Nazi organizations such as the Reichsbund could succeed only insofar as they surmounted the established practices and expectations of the discipline. In this way, an orientation towards Nazism did not go uncontested within the supposedly "young" discipline of archaeology. Yet, Schwantes, Jankuhn, and Kersten could scarcely ignore the political risks involved in ignoring state-sponsored groups. Thus, while they may have first flirted with the regime on their own volition, their deepening commitment reflected a strategic adaptation to internal pressure not only from high-level Nazi functionaries, but also from ambitious colleagues.

Nazism and Cross-Border Scholarship

The second series of events that polarized prehistoric archaeology surrounded efforts to preserve old relations and forge new ones with scholars in Scandinavia. In 1936, Jankuhn travelled to Copenhagen to visit the Viking collection of the National Museum and meet with Johannes Brøndsted. The visit led to an exchange of artefacts for comparative analysis and raised again possibilities for future German-Danish cooperative projects.[68] But these hopes were tempered by the shifting political climate in Germany. For Brøndsted and his colleagues, many of whom were politically liberal or leftist, the rise of the Third Reich presented a number of challenges to any potential cross-border work. One was the fear that the Nazis would demand the return of North Schleswig, which coloured Danish relations with the Reich through 1940.[69] In reality, though the hopes of reannexation were strong among many members of the German minority in Denmark,[70] Hitler harboured no such ambitions, and in fact looked to the German minority to foster closer ties between the two countries.[71] The gap between the perception in Berlin and along the border was nevertheless wide enough to invite fears of a new border struggle.

Another factor was the pervasive influence of völkisch thinking in Germany during the 1930s and the close ties of Nordic racist groups with the Reich. While National Socialist ideology was hazy on the cultural value of Scandinavia, many Nazi leaders were in fact fascinated with the racial and cultural connections between Germany and the Nordic countries. Himmler and Rosenberg, though bitterly divided by personal enmity, were actually not very far apart ideologically on this issue. Both adhered to a belief in the superiority of a specifically "Nordic race," which led each of them to look to Scandinavia as the source of pure racial blood. Both were drawn to the "Blood and Soil" ideology of Walther Darré, whose work, *The Rural Community as the Life Source of the Nordic Race* (*Das Bauerntum als Lebensquell der Nordischen Rasse*), characterized Scandinavia as the home of the "rural ideal" for Nordic racist thinkers and used it as an example in his celebration of the themes of hearth and home.[72] Finally, both Rosenberg and Himmler felt a need for a new elite in Germany composed of the purest examples of the "Nordic" type. It was a need that drew each of them to the study of the ancient Germanic past as crucial to delineating the qualities of the future elite and the creation of a new racial order.[73]

If the coddling of irredentist sentiment stirred fears of a renewed border conflict, the Nazi endorsement of "Nordic thought" inspired contrasting overtures to Scandinavia. Both complicated the relationship between Kiel and Copenhagen.[74] For this reason, the years 1936 and 1937 were especially critical in the creation of Nazi archaeology, since they witnessed at least three major controversies that brought together the domestic pressures facing German prehistorians with concerns about the discipline's international commitments. The first of these involved the participation of Scandinavian scholars in German academic conferences. In 1936, Hans Reinerth worked with the Nordic Society in Lübeck to organize a series of international conferences on topics of Germanic and Nordic archaeology. Reinerth clearly hoped to take the lead from archeologists in Kiel in linking German and Scandinavian prehistoric scholarship. The first of these conferences, "House and Home in the Nordic Region" (Haus und Hof im nordischen Raum), took place in July 1936 in Lübeck. Among the participants were Johannes Brøndsted of Denmark and Holger Arbman (1904–1968) of Sweden. Both men attended in a spirit of shared academic interest, but they quickly faced criticism at home over the meeting's potential for politicization.[75] Indeed, Reinerth made no secret about how he wished to frame the conference. In the introduction to the published proceedings, he compared the prehistoric mingling of Germanic peoples to the scholarly cooperation of the present day: "We know that we have not only arisen from the same blood, but rather that the culture of our lands experienced its growth on the same foundation and from reciprocal fertilization. We believe that scholarly research of the past and present legacy of our people must always be borne by the thought of unified cooperation."[76]

The gathering was a great success for Reinerth in that it attracted a mixed participation of Germans and Scandinavians. But it also brought Reinerth into further conflict with Herbert Jankuhn, whose Haithabu project provided a wealth of information about house construction in the Viking Age. Reinerth seems to have recognized the need to include Haithabu in the conference, but he neglected to invite Jankuhn or his colleagues in Kiel to participate. Instead, he arranged a private tour of the site for the conference participants led not by current museum staff, but by Alfred Tode, who was a former staff member allegedly fired in 1933 for theft.[77] The current directors of the Haithabu project learned about the tour only after the conference had ended. Later that year, Reinerth invited Jankuhn to present on the Haithabu project at a second planned conference.[78] Jankuhn used the invitation as an opportunity to express his dismay:

> To your request of the 20th of November of this year regarding a slideshow presentation on Haithabu, allow me to inform you that I am not in a position to hold this lecture. The incidents that occurred immediately following the Lübeck conference Haus und Hof make it impossible ... First it has had an alienating effect in Scandinavia that both of the German institutes that have laid their chief focus on researching Nordic house construction, namely the Stettin Museum through its excavations in Wollin and our museum through the investigations in Haithabu, Stellerburg, and Hodorf, were omitted [from the conference]. A very unfortunate situation arose however through the excursion to Haithabu itself ... The numerous Scandinavian experts, who through personal experience are much better oriented with the state of our work than many German colleagues, were simply not able to understand that a man was speaking here who clearly had no information about

> the results of our investigations, while they themselves had a much more exact knowledge of them.[79]

It is likely that Jankuhn felt his academic position threatened by Reinerth's actions, but his letter stayed focused on the potential damage to the reputation of German archaeology in Scandinavia. By framing his arguments in this way, he was able to express a legitimate concern for German scholars while undermining one of Reinerth's principal objectives.

The conference had a noticeable impact on German-Scandinavian academic relations. Even before the publication of the "Haus und Hof" volume, the Danish National Museum rejected an application from Reinerth and Otto Scheel to attend the Sixth Nordic Archaeology Congress being planned for the summer of 1937. According to the Kiel archaeology student Erich Pieper, who was studying in Copenhagen, the Danes had decided that their German colleagues simply did not have enough connections to Nordic research.[80] But Pieper later learned from Brøndsted that the real reason stemmed from suspicions about Reinerth and Scheel. "It would be desirable," Pieper wrote to Jankuhn, "not to mention essential, if we could put a stop to such incidents, since otherwise the ... excellent ties of some German researchers to the North would be endangered."[81]

The distrust also affected the practice of archaeology in the field. The controversy over the Nordic Congress coincided with negotiations between Kiel and Copenhagen for a new collaborative project at Haithabu. Johannes Brøndsted, like Sophus Müller before him, had long followed the research at the Oldenburg, and had expressed interest in cross-border work at the site since 1935.[82] As the two sides began to arrange the project in early 1937, however, the academic and political climate gave the Danes pause. Brøndsted shared his countrymen's reservations with a Swedish colleague: "I spoke today with Dr Mackeprang about the question of German-Swedish-Danish collaborative work at Haithabu. Dr Mackeprang had his concerns with reference to [the possibilty] that Schwantes is indeed not independent and that one cannot know what, for example, Alfred Rosenberg would undertake or order undertaken."[83] What is interesting in this letter is that Mouritz Mackeprang, while choosing not to distrust Schwantes on account of his Nazi connections, feared that his German counterpart would be unable to prevent the Nazi Party from misusing any collaborative scholarship. For his part, Brøndsted shared Mackeprang's concerns, but was nevertheless mindful of the long history of cooperation with the Kiel Museum, adding, "I find it ill advised to say no to an outstretched hand from Kiel, precisely when the Swedes also come along."[84]

The Swedish and Danish representatives discussed the issue in Copenhagen the next month, concluding that a cooperative project was desirable, but that, as one participant observed, "the respective institutions must not be implicated."[85] What the Scandinavians needed, therefore, was reassurance from Schwantes, and for that reason they called a second meeting with the Germans to be held in Copenhagen in October 1937.[86] At Schwantes' insistence, they also invited Jankuhn, but Mackeprang voiced reluctance about his participation, writing to Brøndsted, "That Jankuhn as the only director of the excavations comes along, is nothing to which we have any say."[87] Despite the initial hesitation, the meeting reached an agreement on plans for a collaborative excavation. The Danes and Swedes received a written promise from the German side guaranteeing the political safety of the project. For the final agreement, the Danes wrote, "There is consensus that the German invitation to shared and collegial cooperation at Haithabu will follow in the understanding that it does not involve institutional participation, rather purely factual, through experts who can stand both inside and outside of scholarly institutions."[88] The project, the group decided, would begin in the late fall of 1937, with a visiting team of younger scholars without strong institutional ties. Ultimately, this included Holger Arbman (1904–1968), Roar Skovmand (1908–1987) from Denmark, and Helmer Salmo (1903–1973) from Finland. To the relief of the Danes, the Norwegian delegation elected not to participate. As Mackeprang explained, "I am personally against it, both because their connections to Haithabu are even less than those of the Finns, and also because the entire enterprise can be viewed as a link in the Germans' ongoing fraternal tendency (Verbrüderungstendenz)."[89] By contrast, he argued, a project with just Danes, Swedes, and Finns, who had long worked on the Haithabu question, could present itself as a genuine undertaking "of general archaeological interest."[90]

As the Haithabu meeting reaffirmed the scholarly ties between Copenhagen and Kiel, a final dilemma brought fresh government pressure to the practice of international scholarship. During the summer of 1937, Jankuhn applied to attend a Baltic Historical Congress scheduled to take place in Riga in August.[91] His hopes were dashed, however, when he got word from Paulsen that Rosenberg's office was forbidding German scholars from participating due to "the well-known measures taken by the Latvian government against Germandom in the Baltic."[92] Jankuhn later learned that an exception was being made for Otto Scheel, who had close ties to the Reichsbund. In response, Jankuhn complained to the Ministry of Education that it should have been their prerogative to authorize international academic travel.[93] He also sent a letter to Bolko von Richthofen (1903–1971), president of the Professional League of German Prehistorians (Berufsverein deutscher Vorgeschichtsforscher) to reiterate his concerns over the pernicious influence of Reichsbund scholars abroad.[94] Such pressure ultimately worked to convince the Education Ministry to find a solution. The Ministry reversed the prohibition in July and asked Jankuhn to join Paulsen in Riga, but with the caveat that Scheel would lead the delegation.[95]

Compromise helped settle the controversies of 1937, but the consequences continued to plague the discipline during the following year. On a 1938 study tour in Sweden, Jankuhn met with Holger Arbman, who complained about the translation of his contribution to the "Haus und Hof" volume. Reinerth had allegedly denied Arbman a chance to review the proofs, and when he finally presented the German translation, the result was a poor misrepresentation of the original.[96] That same year, the Dane Poul Nørlund accused Reinerth of interfering with the German edition of his book, *Viking Settlements in Greenland: Their Origins and Fate* (*Wikingersiedlungen in Grönland: Ihre Entstehung und Schicksal*). In this case, Reinerth had done more than tamper with the translation; he had attempted to add an unauthorized introduction, which Nørlund had only been able to excise after a protracted struggle with the German publisher.[97]

In a private letter to Richthofen, Jankuhn bemoaned German archaeology's diminished standing abroad. He began by noting that Nørlund had discouraged Arbman from authorizing further German translations of his work, where they might be subjected to manipulation. Then he conveyed his fears about the cumulative toll of such controversies, offering along the way a rare glimpse into his personal world view:

> To you these things may be trivial; they gain meaning, when one places them in the context of the power struggle of the European North ... On the one side, the West European countries ... have attempted to exploit the voice [in Scandinavia] against Germany in the interest of spreading the ideals of the great democracies ... In our field the consequence has been that Scandinavian works begin to be translated more often into English or French rather than the previously predominant German ... [W]ith the strong infusion of the Western European languages into scholarly life comes a displacement of interest from Germany to Western Europe, that France and England will very skillfuly exploit for cultural propaganda.[98]

Jankuhn's case for opposing the Reichsbund thus blended scholarly and national interests. His assessment tied Germany's international academic standing to questions of its political survival as a great power. He did not blame Nazism for the precarious status of German academia abroad, but instead painted a picture of Germany's embattled place in the world not unfamiliar to Nazi ideologues. For Jankuhn, the real threat came not from the German regime, but from colleagues like Reinerth, whose ambitions endangered the normal practices of scholarship.

The international controversies of 1936 and 1937 overlapped with a growing relationship between the archaeologists at Kiel and the Nazi state. The struggle over the discipline's international ties served as a key incentive for Jankuhn and his colleagues to bring their work under the authority of Himmler's SS-Ahnenerbe. Before the "Haus und Hof" debate, Himmler enjoyed a nominal role as "patron" (*Schirmherr*) and had provided some financial support.[99] A few months later, however, the relationship began to become more official. In March 1937, Jankuhn welcomed Himmler on a personal tour of the Haithabu site, where the two allegedly discussed the SS acquisition.[100] Two months later, Jankuhn and Karl Kersten joined the Nazi Party.[101] In the spring of 1938, Schwantes received a chair in prehistoric studies at the University of Kiel, and Jankuhn, through Himmler's intercession, became director of the Kiel Museum.[102]

At the time, Jankuhn maintained that the collaboration with the SS-Ahnenerbe was purely for funding reasons. As he explained in the preface to his 1938 site report: "With the adoption of the excavation by the Reichsführer SS and Chief of the German Police Heinrich Himmler and the transfer to the Ahnenerbe, the excavations and their handling have removed [the site] from a condition of uncertainty caused by many factors and have placed it on a more secure foundation permitting grander planning."[103] After the war, however, both Jankuhn and Schwantes insisted that the goal had been to protect the site from a takeover by Alfred Rosenberg and Hans Reinerth.[104] In truth, both motives were important. Long-standing shortages of funding for archaeological projects and power struggles within the discipline certainly helped drive Kiel prehistorians into the arms of the Reich. But there had always been a level of enthusiasm, or what Jankuhn had called a "positive attitude," about Nazism that made the relationship an easy one.[105] Thus, the argument that Jankuhn resisted the SS takeover, which was common among his colleagues after the war, is unconvincing.[106] It is probably more accurate to say, as the archaeologist Günther Haselhoff recalled after 1945, that Jankuhn pursued other alternatives for dealing with the Reichsbund controversy. Before joining the SS, he had turned to the university administration and to the Berufsverein to create counterweights to Reinerth's Reichsbund. Such efforts had helped him manage the Paulsen and Riga controversies, but they occurred alongside the negotiations with the SS. Indeed, the success of these alternatives raises the question of why he decided in 1938 to turn the Haithabu project completely over to Himmler.

Jankuhn's motives, in fact, lay in part beyond the scope of Haithabu, his research, and his career. They rested on concerns about the fate of Germany's place in international scholarship. His decision stemmed from a desire to defend traditional scholarly practice and to preserve long-standing relations with Scandinavia. In short, Jankuhn's outlook on his discipline's world standing flowed from the same nationalist orientation that informed his research and that encouraged his casual adoption of Kossinna's rhetoric in his writing. It supported a view of

German archaeology as poised between international cooperation and competition. In this context, membership in the SS-Ahnenerbe was a matter not only of protection but also of power, both at home and abroad.

Once Jankuhn and Kersten joined the SS-Ahnenerbe in early 1938 and served the Reich as archaeologists, the boundaries between their politics and their research became increasingly blurred. Thus, it is significant that this final step in the creation of Nazi archaeology was not complete until after the Haithabu project meeting in Copenhagen.[107] It was at this gathering that the Kiel archaeologists confronted the last potential obstacle to their increasing union with the Nazi state. Certainly, Jankuhn's Scandinavian colleagues did not ask him to join the SS. Instead, they simply implied that they would continue working with the Germans, despite the political risks. It was an accommodation intended to preserve academic cooperation. For the Germans, however, it amounted to tacit approval that allowed Jankuhn and his colleagues to balance the traditional norms of their discipline with the new demands of the Third Reich.

Conclusion

By 1938, the archaeologists at the Schleswig-Holstein Museum had completed a journey down a long road to Nazism. Even if it seems in hindsight to have been fairly straight and narrow, the process remained unfinished and the results uneven, and the archaeologists working under the patronage of Heinrich Himmler retained a great deal of independence. Their academic freedom showed in their writing. Nils Vollertsen has argued that Jankuhn wrote differently for specific audiences. In his addresses to the National Socialist Association of University Teachers (NS-Dozentenbund), for instance, he offered a colonialist interpretation of late Germanic prehistory, arguing for a "northern Germanic" conquest of Eastern Europe. In a separate publication for the Kiel journal *Offa*, he implied that Haithabu's greatest historical significance came from its role in spreading Germanic power eastwards. In his international presentations, however, he tempered his expansionist claims, arguing instead for the significance of Haithabu in Christianizing northern Europe.[108] Clearly, affiliation with Nazism did not fully politicize mainstream archaeological research, but it compelled scholars to juggle two identities and required audiences to see past conflicting interpretations.

In light of such halting commitments, it is worth asking how Himmler and his scholars benefited from their relationship. For the SS-Ahnenerbe, the costs were enormous. The discipline of archaeology grew dramatically under Nazi support, with state funds creating new university chairs and minting dozens of new PhDs. In return, the official visits to excavation sites, the minor alterations to academic publications, and the short passages recognizing the role of government patrons may have seemed a small yield for so much investment. Yet, on closer inspection, the benefits were not so meagre as they appeared. Tens of thousands of Reichsmarks had restored the place of professional scholarship after a lost decade, but they also bought legitimacy and power. By forging ties to scholars like Jankuhn, the SS-Ahnenerbe managed to gain control of the most important prehistoric cultural sites in western Germany, including the Haithabu site.[109] The organization also acquired the indirect endorsement of the very scholars it fostered. Jankuhn and his colleagues may have eschewed the outlandish claims of the amateurs within the SS-Ahnenerbe, but there remained an unspoken alignment of popular and scholarly discourses about the past. In this case, the fusion of the two served to support the Nazi vision of Volksgemeinschaft.

For Jankuhn and his colleagues, the rewards were more immediate and more tangible. In the late summer of 1937, Schwantes accepted a newly created chair in prehistory at the University of Kiel created by special order of Prussian Minister-President Hermann Göring.[110] A few months later, Heinrich Himmler helped secure Jankuhn's promotion to the now-vacant position of director of the Kiel Museum, which confounded an attempt by Reinerth to apply for the post.[111] Himmler's Ahnenerbe also made the Haithabu project its top priority, devoting over 65,000 RM per year to expanded excavations there and offering another substantial sum for exhibitions and aerial photography along the Danewerk and surrounding sites.[112]

On the eve of the Second World War, Herbert Jankuhn had become, in the words of Michael Kater, a "parade horse" for Himmler.[113] He was a reputable scholar who brought credibility to SS research. But, as Henning Haßmann and Detlef Jantzen have shown, he was also "one of the most influential prehistorians of the Third Reich."[114] Perhaps more importantly, he and his colleagues at Kiel had found a new balance between the demands of rigorous, international scholarship and the ideological goals of the National Socialist regime. Any impression of stability, however, was illusory. The engagement with the regime had been a process in which the roles and motives of archaeologists changed much between 1933 and 1938. There was no reason now for the relationship to become any less dynamic in 1939. Indeed, the outbreak of war, the occupation of Denmark and Norway, and the shifting fortunes of the Wehrmacht would challenge the difficult equilibrium of the previous years and thereby alter the future of archaeology in the borderlands.

7 The Fate of Archaeology in the Borderlands

Borderlands archaeology changed dramatically in 1944. In that year, the city of Kiel endured tremendous air attacks that threatened the region's principal academic institutions. The naval bases and wartime industries dotting the Kiel Fjord were tempting targets for Allied bombers, and the nearby city centre was often not spared. This strategic geography proved devastating for the Kiel Museum, which had the misfortune of standing so close to the city's harbour. A series of assaults on 4 and 5 January destroyed the Kiel Palace but just missed the museum. And then, after a few months of relative calm, a second attack on 22 May targeted the waterfront and the shipyards.[1] This time, incendiary bombs reached the museum, burning the structure to the ground along with numerous volumes of scholarship and archival records. Its prized artefacts had been moved to safety, but even they barely escaped harm.

The bombing was only the beginning. Well before the final German surrender, the effects of the war had already shattered the foundations of the discipline of archaeology in Germany. Along with widespread damage to the University of Kiel, the loss of so many young students at the front, and diminishing control over scattered artefacts, the destruction of the museum signalled a looming transformation at the end of the Second World War. At the same time, a much more subtle but no less powerful transition was underway within the practice of archaeology. During the war, the Germans' embrace of nationalist theories reached their radical apogee and became politicized as never before. By 1944, they had begun to follow the fortunes of the Third Reich. For German scholars, their complicity with the regime, the realities of occupation, and the experience of defeat reshaped the intellectual field.

At first glance, such dramatic change suggests that the "Zero Hour" (Stunde Null) tolled early for German archaeology in the borderlands. After 1945, the notion of a sharp break between the Nazi and postwar eras became a popular way of understanding all aspects of Germany's breathtaking political, economic, and cultural transformation. Recently, however, belief in the Stunde Null phenomenon has fallen into doubt as historians have uncovered the various continuities that survived the Nazi state.[2] The borderlands were no different, and the seismic shifts underway at war's end were not as complete as they had seemed. There were a number of overlapping elements that complicated the transition in German archaeology. Many of the most prominent scholars from the Nazi years, including Jankuhn, Schwantes, Kersten, and Rust, remained active leaders in regional research as they revived their careers and refashioned their personal histories after the war. At the same time, many of their practices and conclusions remained untouched in their published writings.

The account of the Kiel Museum's final days in 1944 reminds us of perhaps the most salient continuity. When many of its artefacts faced certain annihilation, it was not a German who came to their rescue. It was Søren Telling (1895–1968), a Dane, who came to Kiel to salvage heritage sites from the depredations of the war. Only days before the Allied raid, Telling hastily organized a rescue of the two massive Haithabu rune stones from the main hall.[3] Without his timely intervention, ancient remains treasured by both sides would certainly have been lost. Telling's example is but one of the ways in which cross-border cooperation remained essential to archaeology and museum work during the war. Even as engagement with the regime deepened, archaeologists in the region continued to let their long-standing international commitments guide their choices. Moreover, the occupation of Denmark and Norway further strained cross-border relations while altering the ways Germans and Scandinavians worked together. After the war, the relationship would prove crucial, as the past became embroiled in the final stages of the German-Danish border dispute and as scholars on both sides confronted the consequences of the nationalist assumptions within their discipline.

The experience in the borderlands during and after the Second World War thus reflected the friction between the sense of rupture at the end of the war and the potent vestiges of the foregoing years. This does not mean, however, that we should dismiss entirely the notion of a Stunde Null. Certainly, the suddenness of the trauma and the overwhelming need to come to terms with defeat through reinvention lent themselves to a convenient fiction. As Mary Fulbrook has explained, "The notion of a 'Zero Hour' may have little to recommend it … but it certainly summarizes a widely prevalent sense that an entirely fresh start had to be made."[4] Myth making aside, it is impossible to ignore the many rapid changes that began in the last years of the war. In assessing these less convenient realities of the period, a number of key questions emerge. First, how did the relationship between German archaeologists and the state change during the Second World War? What role did international scholars, particularly in Scandinavia, play in a war involving far-ranging conquest and long-term occupation? And when the fighting ended, how did German specialists remake themselves and rebuild their institutions? This last question is one not limited to the processes of denazification and restoration; rather, it demands a glimpse beyond the immediate postwar horizon, where memories lingered long after 1950.

(Battle)Field Work: Borderlands Archaeologists in the Second World War

The Reich's need for archaeologists did not end with the invasion of Poland in September 1939. As was the case for a number of fields, including geography, anthropology, and sociology, archaeology was essential to a nation fighting an ideological war. From 1939 to 1943, the mounting conquests of the German war effort were closely tied to the territorial imperialism inherent in Nazi ideology.[5] Thus, even as Herbert Jankuhn recalled, "being of the firm opinion with almost all good Germans that World War II was imposed upon Hitler,"[6] he and his colleagues nevertheless seem to have supported the expansive ambitions of the Nazi state. Moreover, each, with the exception of the aging Schwantes, expressed a willingness to serve the Reich in the conflict. After the Polish invasion, Jankuhn requested that he be allowed to join the aerial photography unit of the Luftwaffe,[7] while Alfred Rust, who was too old for front-line units, asked to be allowed to serve from Ahrensburg, but offered up his experience from travels in the Near East.[8] Peter Paulsen, meanwhile, travelled to Warsaw with a group of colleagues from Rosenberg's office in the late autumn of 1939 and began systematically looting the museums and cultural institutions in the captured city.[9]

Schleswig-Holstein archaeologists offered their skills to the war effort wherever it was needed. At first, it was most needed close to home. During the Polish campaign, Jankuhn delivered a series of lectures on "The Origin of the Polish State," in which he argued against the Polish nationalist historiography of Zygmunt Wojciechowski by asserting that the Poles were occupying "the settlement zone of Germanic tribes."[10] He also maintained that many of Poland's historical leaders were descended from Germanic stock. While his claims were outlandish in their generalizations, Jankuhn nevertheless attempted to ground them with historical research and the results of his own archaeological studies into early medieval fortifications, whose styles he linked to specific ethnic groups. By undermining the Poles' historical claims to their own country, the lectures represented an important step in the evolution of archaeology as propaganda. Where scholars had previously written to affirm a Nazi program of national pride and renewal, they were now employing their research to justify a policy of foreign conquest.

As the war expanded westwards in 1940, this sort of collaboration intensified. Like Peter Paulsen in 1939, Karl Kersten and Herbert Jankuhn journeyed to the occupied zones after the successful invasion of Western Europe, where they conducted research projects on critical heritage sites. Shortly after the Germans landed in Denmark and Norway in April 1940, the two were dispatched to the region, with Jankuhn working in Norway and Kersten in Denmark to survey and preserve grave hills in potential military operation zones. Jankuhn later journeyed to France to study megalithic graves in Brittany and join a team of German scholars studying the famed Bayeux Tapestry, which recounted the Norman conquest of England in 1066 CE. His research ostensibly concerned the use of textile imagery to illuminate material culture in early medieval Europe,[11] but it was likely no coincidence that the project occurred against the backdrop of a planned German invasion of Great Britain.[12]

The Bayeux project ultimately remained unfinished, as the invasion of the Soviet Union in 1941 made the eastern occupation zone a top priority. Indeed, it was on the Eastern Front where the collaboration between archaeologists and the Nazis reached its most radical point. For Himmler, SS-Ahnenerbe activities in Russia marked an important step in the long-standing tradition of "Eastern Research" (*Ostforschung*), which in this case represented an incoherent set of academic practices that reinforced German territorial ambitions in Eastern Europe.[13] Just as Nazi propagandists began to place more stress upon a "war of annihilation" (*Vernichtungskrieg*) against the Bolsheviks, so the rhetoric of archaeological writing changed and began casting the narrative of prehistory in terms of a great struggle between East and West. The classical archaeologist Joseph Wiesner (1913–1975) used this interpretation to explain what was at stake in the battle with the Soviet Union, writing, "The decisive struggle in the East, in spite of its uniqueness, does not stand alone, but is the climax of millennia of opposition between the Indogermanic peoples of the Nordic race and the foreign strength of the Eastern steppes."[14] Archaeology could thus do what politics and history alone could not: it provided a unique sense of depth to a narrative of conflict and conquest in the East. It awarded continuity and hence legitimacy to massive invasions, and it could claim to be acting as part of an almost sacred patriotic duty of reading the past and aligning its message with the needs of a nation at war.

Affirming this message were "discoveries" of Germanic remains in the occupied territories of Russia and Ukraine. For this reason, Himmler was eager to secure artefacts in the recently captured territories. In the summer of 1942, he dispatched Jankuhn and Kersten to the Crimea, where the two undertook a survey of sites belonging to the ancient Goths. Though Jankuhn minimized his involvement during his interviews with Michael Kater in the 1960s,[15] there is no question that he and Kersten took part in seizing artefacts from institutions in southern Ukraine in 1942 and 1943. Anja Heuss' review of the records indicates that the two shipped nearly two dozen crates of artefacts back to Germany.[16] While they later implied that the effort was aimed at saving the material from the battle zone, their reports from the time suggest that they wished, on the one hand, to keep artefacts out of the hands of the Rosenberg scholars and, on the other, to explore the links between Gothic and Germanic peoples.[17] In fact, Kersten's work included a study of the Crimea's so-called Gothic cave cities (*Höhlenstädte*) in order to compare them with his own studies of settlement sites in Europe.[18] Jankuhn went one step further, expressing interest in the racial legacy of an ancient Germanic presence in southern Ukraine. One of the photos from his Ukrainian travels, which are now among his papers at the Schleswig-Holstein Museum, presumably depicts a Ukrainian child with a note on the back written in Jankuhn's handwriting, "Nina, blonde-haired, blue-eyed girl." Along the way, Jankuhn and his colleagues can scarcely have missed the signs of mass killing taking place at the hands of Einsatzgruppe D, which was operating in the area alongside the SS Division Wiking.[19] At the same time, these scholars, by seizing artefacts in the occupied zones, participated directly in the war crimes of the regime.

After the end of the Ukrainian expedition in 1943, the turning tide of the war offered fewer opportunities for fieldwork abroad. By this time, Peter Paulsen had already been transferred to an SS training facility.[20] Karl Kersten returned to Kiel to assume the duties of director of the Kiel Museum, where he remained until the end of the war. Jankuhn, meanwhile, briefly assumed his professorship at the University of Rostock. After 1944, he was recalled and sent first to the SS Division Wiking and later to the IVth SS Panzer Corps, where he served as a military intelligence officer.[21] Along with his unit, he surrendered to the Allies in May 1945 and entered an American POW camp.

In assessing the four years in which these scholars served the German war machine as archaeologists, two defining characteristics are immediately clear. The first is a trend of increasing cooperation with the Reich. The delicate balance between scientific objectives and political concerns tipped decisively. Even if field missions had scientific goals, their outcomes primarily served German war aims. The second feature of the period is the often-observed distinction between the western and eastern occupation zones. As Heuss has shown, the archaeologists who operated on both fronts generally took a more exploitative approach to ancient sites and remains in Eastern Europe. They were far more likely to loot sites and institutions in Poland and Ukraine and less likely to encounter resistance there from local officials or occupation authorities. In these cases, the acts of German prehistorians matched the diverse attitudes and policies that the Reich applied to its enemies. When looking solely at the acts of borderland prehistorians in France and the Soviet Union, it is tempting to see a simple progression of increasing engagement with the regime, and to interpret the activities of prehistorians through the lens of ideology. Yet, it is important to note that in these instances, scholars whose careers had been built researching within the relatively narrow confines of northern Europe were working outside their usual networks and therefore faced less pressure from the normal practices of their field. How then, would their attitudes and behaviour in these settings compare with their wartime work in the borderlands, and in occupied Denmark and Norway?

Between Complicity and Cooperation: Cross-Border Archaeology, 1940–1943

In early 1942, most Germans expected victory. The Wehrmacht held most of Western Europe and stood deep in Soviet territory, while at home Nazi planners prepared for the postwar order. Their visions included an important role for archaeology to anchor German hegemony. This was the case in Kiel, where in February 1942 the mayor shared his plans for the city's future in a letter to the staff of the antiquities museum. He promised to support a new facility in the city centre. "In this location, it would form in connection with the Kiel Palace an expanded Museum Quarter facing the Fjord," he wrote, "This 'Museum Island' would lie in the heart of the city traffic and thereby be accessible in the most convenient manner for locals and foreigners alike."[22]

Such ambitions, however, most likely offered little comfort to local scholars, who could only see the pledges of the mayor as a belated attempt at consolation. In reality, the mayor had written even as the growing threat of air attack forced museum staff to move artefacts to safe locations throughout the region. Transport companies had been hired to demolish one of the museum's walls in order to hoist the Nydam Boat onto a waiting truck. Once removed, it was driven slowly through the winding streets amid a crowd of onlookers and carried away to Schierensee Manor in western Holstein. Crates of smaller artefacts followed and were distributed at locations throughout the province.[23] At the same time, the region's great archaeological monuments stood in danger of damage from military operations. Most notably, Schwantes protested plans to install new fortifications at the Danevirke, but failed to prevent the military from constructing deep anti-tank trenches and artillery emplacements along the fragile earthworks.[24]

Evacuation of the Nydam Boat, 1941. Photograph courtest Stiftung Schleswig-Holsteinische Landesmuseen Schloss Gottorf.

With his younger colleagues serving in the field, Schwantes would have faced even greater difficulties had it not been for the intervention of Søren Telling. Telling had little training as an archaeologist, but his father had been a museum director in the Jutland town of Randers, and Telling's own interest in antiquities had led him to develop ties to the Danish National Museum. Telling was also politically active, and became a significant figure within Frits Clausen's DNSAP. In 1938, however, he mysteriously decided to immigrate to Germany, and apply for German citizenship, which was an unorthodox move for a Danish patriot. In his memoirs, Telling claims that he wished to work with the scholars at the Kiel Museum, although it is possible that his decision was motivated by his radical politics. In either case, Telling managed to secure a position as technical assistant at the museum just as he was moving away from his former Nazi commitments. When the Germans invaded his home country in 1940, Telling became deeply disillusioned with the Nazi regime. He ultimately chose to remain in Kiel, but made it his mission to protect what he saw as his country's cultural heritage in Schleswig-Holstein.[25]

It was thus as a Dane that Telling made common cause with Gustav Schwantes in opposing threats to regional monuments. When he and Schwantes failed to persuade Wehrmacht officials to halt construction, Telling conducted impromptu digs along the Danevirke. In May 1941, he oversaw the evacuation of the Nydam Boat and much of the Kiel Museum's collection. Finally, after the January 1944 raid that nearly destroyed the museum, he took it upon himself to remove the Haithabu rune stones from the main exhibit hall. In his memoirs, Telling recalled wrangling with local officials to arrange transport for the stones. He claimed that local authorities denied him access to a truck, admonishing him to "just let the old junk burn up."[26] Undaunted, Telling went to Admiral Hans Bütow, chief of staff of the Baltic Sea Command, who lent him both a vehicle and a team of Russian labourers. What followed was a harrowing operation to move the stones under the piercing screams of air raid sirens only days before the museum was destroyed.

The friction between scholars and the regime extended beyond the home front. In northern Europe, Jankuhn and his colleagues found the Nazis' imperialist ambitions difficult to reconcile with their professional goals. Unlike France and Ukraine, the threat posed to antiquities in Scandinavia not only affected the materials with which borderlands archaeologists worked, but also jeopardized their relationships with Scandinavian colleagues. With this in mind, Herbert Jankuhn requested permission to conduct a tour of archaeological monuments in Norway shortly after the end of the Scandinavian campaign. In response, SS-Ahnenerbe chief secretary Wolfram Sievers (1905–1947) arranged to have Jankuhn's military training cancelled before dispatching him to Oslo and Kersten to Copenhagen.[27]

During the summer and fall of 1940, Kersten and Jankuhn struggled with the military and with occupation authorities to prevent damage to sensitive sites. In making their case, they appealed to the Nazis' desire to preserve racial and cultural harmony between Germans and Scandinavians. In Denmark, for example, Kersten, who was opposing Luftwaffe plans to construct airfields near ancient burial sites in Jutland, referenced the poor morale of the populace in his report: "There is no mistaking at the moment the strong resentment against Germany. I could not find among any of the numerous people of all classes with whom I spoke in Jutland an understanding for Germany's situation and the necessity of the German invasion."[28]

In Norway, Jankuhn faced a tough battle with the SS and SD over plans to ensure site preservation in the country and in particular to continue the

Norwegian excavation at the massive Raknehaugen grave hill outside Oslo.[29] Jankuhn entered into a heated argument with Franz Walter Stahlecker (1900–1942), who was then overseeing the SS in Norway, over the need and usefulness of the project. He not only wanted the site to be preserved, but made clear that it was important for the Germans to adopt a policy of supporting Norwegian scholars, which was a low priority for Stahlecker but for Jankuhn was a critical step for improved relations. "With it," he agued, "one would best be able to dispel the animosity or at least the reserve of the Norwegians towards the Germans."[30] Ultimately, Jankuhn convinced Himmler to intercede in favour of the Norwegian Antiquities Museum (Oldsaksamling) in Oslo. In a letter to Sievers in May 1940, Himmler wrote: "Securing Norwegian monuments is a matter of honour for the SS and Police ... I am making the 12,000 RM available for the excavation. I ask, however, that Jankuhn not take the dig away from the Norwegians, rather that the Ahnenerbe simply appear to be protective and supportive. Jankuhn can function as expert friend and adviser. The matter calls for a great deal of tact. We must naturally be mindful of the feelings of the Norwegians, because it is understandable that they do not see us Germans as friends."[31] In his letter, Himmler clearly saw the project as an opportunity to foster goodwill with Scandinavian scholars and enlist their aid in advancing Nazi goals.

Such gestures, however, did not improve Scandinavian attitudes towards the Germans. The majority of researchers at the Oldsaksamling had voiced opposition to Nazism long before the occupation. Even as Jankuhn worked to build good ties to his colleagues in Oslo, the director of the Oldsaksamling, Anton Wilhelm Brøgger (1884–1951) was speaking out against the occupation.[32] Indeed, accounts of Jankuhn's activities in Norway have placed him at the centre of this narrative, in which he appears as a figure whose pro-Nazi sentiments precluded his erstwhile loyalties to colleagues abroad. He is often blamed for denouncing Brøgger in the autumn of 1940 and contributing to his subsequent arrest.[33] After the war, Jankuhn adamantly denied the charges, and in a 1949 letter Brøgger affirmed that he had never accused Jankuhn of the act. In fact, Brøgger reported that he had been arrested twice in 1941, the first time by Norwegian "Quislingers," and the second time by occupation authorities.[34] In any case, it was clear that Brøgger's colleagues saw little need in making distinctions between Jankuhn and other agents of German occupation, and relations remained icy both during and after the war.

In Denmark, cooperation was challenged not only by staunch opposition to the occupation, but also by the Danes' greater autonomy under German rule. Only a handful of Danish scholars chose to collaborate with the Germans, and even fewer of these had connections to the National Museum. One of those who did was the geographer Gudmund Hatt (1884–1960), who had worked at the National Museum in the 1920s. Hatt was prosecuted after the war for his role in founding a Danish-German Association (Dansk-Tysk Forening) in 1940 and later for radio broadcasts in which he portrayed Germany and Japan as victims of the Western democracies and expressed pro-Axis sympathies.[35] The broadcasts fit Hatt's research, which understood the expansion of great powers as a natural force of geopolitics.[36] But Hatt's sympathies did not amount to an endorsement of the occupation. As Henrik Larsen has argued, Hatt was never involved with Nazism, and his radio work had the support of the Danish government, who saw him as a moderate alternative to a more pro-Nazi commentator.[37] A more overtly pro-Nazi orientation characterized the young archaeologist Mogens Mackeprang (1905–1986), who was finishing his doctoral studies during the war. Mackeprang was a member the right-wing National Student Action (National Studenter-Aktion). Although he never joined the Danish Nazi Party, his pro-German sympathies stemmed in part from his anti-democratic political views. During the war, Mackeprang contributed political articles to the NSA journal, *Akademisk Aktion*, and also published archaeological essays for the Nordic Society in Lübeck on the Germanic roots of the ancient Jütisch tribes.[38] Steffen Werther has attempted to explain this behaviour by pointing out that among many of the active members of the Danish Nazi Party, collaboration was a means not to affirm political affinity but to use the notion of a "Greater Germandom" (*Großgermanentum*) to enhance their own authority and preserve Danish autonomy within the Nazi's wartime empire.[39]

As in Norway, the vast majority of Danes resisted the Germans. A handful of scholars, such as the prehistoric archaeologist and explorer of Greenland Eigil Knuth (1903–1996), were active in the resistance movement, and provided intelligence to the Allies.[40] Most voiced their protests through more subtle non-cooperation. Danes by and large rejected German attempts at cultural propaganda, including the so-called German Scientific Institute, which was established in Copenhagen and administered by Otto Scheel. As Manfred Jakubowski-Tiessen has explained, "The German scholars remained ostracized from academic circles in Denmark, and this isolation worsened with the growing tension between the domestic populace and the occupation authority."[41]

At other times, Danish prehistorians turned to their work to restore hope in a nation facing an uncertain future with Germany. Just as in the nineteenth century, Danes looked to the country's past to provide a sense of distinction at a moment of national threat. Poul Nørlund observed this phenomenon in the staggering number of visitors to the National Museum, which grew by almost 25,000 per year between 1940 and 1942. He attributed the increase to "the powerful awakening of national feeling brought about by the German yoke."[42] Brøndsted carefully cultivated this yearning with a series of public addresses on Danish history and prehistory, and in his 1942 book, *Rest along the Way* (*Rast Undervejs*), he integrated lessons on Danish antiquity with musings on the beauty of Denmark's landscape. Similar works aimed at a popular audience included S.A. Andersen's 1945 study, *The Golden Horns of Gallehus*, which accompanied an attempt by two craftsmen, Aksel Theilmann and Rolf Schütze, to create new replicas of the lost artefacts. Finally, Danish prehistorians worked with the public to rescue endangered sites. Radio and press announcements appealed to Danish citizens to be vigilant against the damage to bogs that came from using peat as fuel and the potential harm from German military construction, which threatened an estimated three hundred grave hills and monuments across the country. The museum called on willing volunteers to join them in the field, and cast the excavations not only as an act of preservation, but also as one of patriotism.

The Danes wanted to act independently, but found that they had to turn to Karl Kersten for help. The National Museum had no shortage of volunteers willing to dig, but they faced the problem of obtaining timely notification and authorization from the Germans. Kersten thus served as a liaison between the Danes and the German military. He contested construction wherever possible and advocated for emergency digs where necessary. Although he complained about the obstinance of both sides, Kersten nevertheless managed to negotiate deals in which Danes were able to conduct their own excavations.[43] Even after he left the country in the fall of 1940, Kersten maintained contact with Nørlund and Brøndsted through 1943, and helped pave the way for a series of digs across the country. In southern Denmark, this included eight Bronze Age hills at Skrydstrup on the outskirts of Haderslev and another sixteen at Esbjerg on the west coast. After the war, Nørlund mentioned Kersten's contributions in his war memoir, writing, "I will gladly here express my appreciation for the tactful manner in which he tended his task, all the more so as I was not at all effusively friendly towards him in the time that he worked [in Denmark]."[44]

There were thus moments in which scholarship and professional ties challenged commitments to the regime. In Germany, Nazi policies led German and Danish prehistorians to foster old bonds to protect regional interests, while in Denmark and Norway, German prehistorians from the borderlands sought to preserve academic ties even if that meant opposing war objectives. At the same time, the Danes found themselves relying on their former cross-border network to support symbolic acts of resistance against the occupation. Of course, it is worth pointing out that even in Eastern Europe, scholars did not blindly support Nazi goals. SS-Ahnenerbe archaeologists were not willing to embrace Himmler's dreams of creating a Großgermanentum if it meant destroying archaeological treasures. While in Ukraine, for example, Jankuhn wrote to Himmler's personal staff office in August 1943 to complain about the German destruction of the prehistory museum in Kharkov, writing, "And thus one of the most important museums in Russia, with invaluable scientific finds, is surrendered to destruction through the actions of the German civil administration."[45] Yet, the level of respect for those treasures, and of deference to the foreign scholars who worked with them, was markedly different in Scandinavia. To some extent, it is likely that personal relationships played a role, such as those between Kersten and the Danes. It was less the case in Norway, where Jankuhn's support for the Oldsaksamling earned him few friends. Ultimately, what made Scandinavia unique was first that the artefacts there fell more directly into the orbit of Kiel archaeologists, and second that Nordic scholars were an important part of their field, perhaps even more so than colleagues in other parts of Germany. It was thus for these reasons that Jankuhn and Kersten expended much of their political capital in Denmark and Norway. They did so not simply to exploit the opportunities presented by conquest, but to rescue antiquities, protect their valuable ties to Nordic scholars, and thereby preserve the traditional practices of their field.

Such examples, of course, do not warrant an absolution of Kiel archaeologists during the Nazi conquest. Regardless of their professional and scientific motives, the fact remained that they travelled abroad as agents of military conquest and occupation. They appropriated the heritages of their neighbours not only through physical looting, but also by subjecting them to their own research agendas. They imposed upon their neighbours an academic regime that converged with the Nazis' plans for a new European order. We must be mindful, of course, of the level of ambiguity that coloured this project. Conflicting commitments to academic networks and scientific norms, on the one hand, and the needs of the war effort, on the other, created moments in which German prehistorians questioned Nazi goals. At times, it led them to work against the interests of the Reich. But no amount of prevarication prevented the scarred professional relationships that followed the end of the war. By the time the bombs fell on Kiel in May 1944, the full consequences of the Nazi years had already shaken the foundations upon which German prehistory work had rested for over a century.

Ruin and Recovery

Six months after the destruction of the museum in Kiel, the crisis for borderlands archaeology worsened. On a cold November morning, Søren Telling received a request to remove the contents of two railway cars parked near the tiny hamlet of Owschlag. When Telling arrived at the station and peeked inside the carriages, he was astonished to find crates of artefacts from the Kiel Museum. The German Navy had decided to evict the collection from the Schierensee Manor in order to use the building for military purposes. They had neglected to notify the museum staff in advance, leaving Telling to contend with dented and battered crates. Some had completely shattered, spilling artefacts, including at least one Bronze Age sword, about the carriage floor.[46] War regulations at the time afforded him only twenty-four hours to move the contents, so Telling scrambled to unload the crates and store them temporarily in a nearby garage. Schwantes and Kersten ultimately managed to convince the Navy to transport the artefacts to a guesthouse near Owschlag, but even these new quarters failed to provide a proper environment for the delicate material.[47]

Schwantes complained that the mistreatment of the collection was "perhaps singular in the history of German museums."[48] He might have recognized that he was living through a singular epoch. As the war drew to its tumultuous close, air raids, shortages, and the threats of invasion diminished concerns for archaeology. The shrinking boundaries of the Nazi empire forced scholars abroad either to return home to pick through the ruins of their institutions, or otherwise to find another way to contribute to the war effort. Such was the case for Jankuhn, who served as an intelligence officer first in the so-called Wiking Division of the SS and later in the IVth SS-Panzerkorps as it battled the Soviets in Austria.[49] Gustav Schwantes, meanwhile, relocated with his wife for health and safety reasons to the village of Twedt, where he struggled to coordinate preservation efforts without a telephone connection.[50] This left the management of regional archaeology to Karl Kersten, who had returned to Kiel in 1943,[51] and to Søren Telling, who managed to escape conscription in the civilian Volkssturm militia and continue his archaeological salvage operations until the final surrender in May 1945.[52]

Only at the end of the war was it possible to think about restoring the institution, and even then the challenges were daunting. Schwantes and Kersten quickly realized that they could not rebuild in Kiel. "You could scarcely conjure an image of today's Kiel in your wildest dreams," Schwantes wrote to a friend. "It is unfortunately no longer a small city, but rather an erstwhile metropolis of widely scattered rubble."[53] The devastation left few spaces available, and Schwantes learned that the British military was considering shipping the Schleswig-Holstein collection to the Hamburg Ethnological Museum. At the same time, Schwantes complained that the city leadership "lays greater weight on the accommodations for a factory than on ten museums."[54] Added to these pressures were the collection's ties to a resurgent Danish nationalism in Denmark and southern Schleswig. Such attitudes were, of course, inseparable from the broader response to the liberation of Denmark, but they also represented a local reaction to the influx of displaced persons. An estimated 300,000 refugees streamed into Schleswig-Holstein at the end of the war, increasing the region's population by as much as 20 per cent.[55] The Danish minority in Schleswig-Holstein feared that such a demographic shift would threaten its already precarious status.

The combination of cultural fears, population pressure, and political opportunity created by the occupation raised for a final time the border question between Germany and Denmark. For its part, the Danish government declared that it had no territorial interests in the borderlands, and its official policy was to work for the interests of the Danish minority in Germany.[56] Many Danes on both sides of the border, however, joined a "Free South Schleswig" movement that advocated annexing the rest of the former duchy. A number of Danish archaeologists shared this sentiment, including Johannes Brøndsted, who in a public address in 1947 declared, "May Denmark as a healthy and vital state recognize its national obligation and hear this: don't leave South Schleswig (Sydslesvig) in the lurch."[57] The involvement of prominent archaeologists accompanied renewed discussions about the return of the Nydam and Thorsberg collections. The calls for repatriation got a boost after the Danes managed to reclaim two critical heritage items: the contentious *Lion of Idstedt* (*Idstedsløven*), a monument commemorating the victory at the Battle of Idstedt in 1851, and a related set of Idsted-Løven medallions, which Søren Telling had discovered resting in the Kiel Palace.[58] With the return of these items to Copenhagen, there was every reason for borderlands residents to believe that the British might also return the Nydam Boat. Poul Nørlund approached the British government directly after the war and asked that they oversee the transfer of the Nydam and Thorsberg Collections to the safety of the Sønderborg Palace (Sønderborg Slot), which had become Sønderjylland's largest provincial museum.[59] In public circles, the debate once again fostered claims of ancient ownership to territory. Activists circulated petitions in Flensburg for a new plebiscite for South Schleswig, which, in their words, "has since time immemorial belonged to Denmark."[60] At the same time, prominent scholars from Copenhagen expressed both sympathy for the Free South Schleswig movement and concern about the protection of the artefacts.

These hopes proved ephemeral, though they lent greater urgency to restoring regional archaeology. On the border question, there was little support outside the region for reannexation, and none of the Western Allies were willing to alter a border that had been set by a popular plebiscite in 1920. In the interests of peace, the British occupation authorities joined the Danish Parliament in ordering activists in Flensburg to stop circulating their petitions.[61] The persistent calls for repatriation nevertheless placed extraordinary pressure on Schwantes and Kersten not only to safeguard their artefacts, but also to rebuild their former institutional standing in order to convince the British occupation and their Danish colleagues that Germany should retain possession. Schwantes worried that the British might see the artefacts as a reparations issue, writing to a colleague, "The museum is in the possession of the Prussian state, whose property falls subject to reparations owed the occupying powers ... This legally affords Denmark the possibility of collectively demanding as reparations all finds stemming from North Schleswig, including the Nydam finds."[62] For Schwantes, any solution would have to alter the perception that the collections were German national property. On the one hand, this was a legal imperative. "This danger can only be faced," he wrote, "with an immediate transfer of the antiquities museum [from the Prussian state] to the possession of the province."[63] On the other hand, it would also have to take Danish opinion into account.

With these considerations in mind, Schwantes and Kersten developed a plan. The first step was to secure an appropriate location. The looming controversy over the border was yet another reason why a site in Kiel or Holstein would be unsuitable. They thus rejected both the British government's proposal to house the collections in Hamburg, and later an offer from the University of Kiel to spare some space in the university library. Instead, they looked for a site in one of the smaller cities in the region. The most obvious choice was Flensburg, which rested directly on the border and had been home to Conrad Engelhardt's museum in the 1850s. But the British disapproved. Major G.F. Wilmot, the head of the British Monuments, Fine Arts, and Archives branch, declined their proposal on the grounds that a new museum in Flensburg might inflame separatist tensions.[64] The next two choices were the towns of Schleswig and Husum. Schleswig ultimately won out, in part because Husum would place the museum on the less populated western coast. Moreover, the government in Schleswig welcomed the move as fitting with its plans to revitalize the town through tourism.[65] To cement the deal, regional leaders offered to install the collection in the Gottorf Palace (Schloss Gottorf), which provided a magnificent exhibition space and a series of outside structures for housing prized pieces such as the Nydam Boat.

Relocating the Kiel Museum to Schleswig was ultimately a wise choice, because it had meaning to both Germans and Danes. For Germans, the Gottorf Palace, which had been the residence of the former dukes of Schleswig, offered an opportunity to bring together the region's antiquity with the more recent history of Schleswig-Holstein. For Danes, the site had significance for both regional and national history. As the journalist Niels Friss pointed out to his readers, the palace was the birthplace of two Danish kings, while one of the barracks on the grounds had once housed Denmark's Fourth Dragoons. Both sides could appreciate that the museum would now stand only a few kilometres from the Haithabu and Danevirke sites, which would encourage archaeological tourism and support future research. To preserve the long-standing ties to Kiel, Schwantes secured an arrangement that would allow the director of the museum to hold a chair at the university and also supervise the activities of the Provincial Office for the Preservation of Historic Monuments.[66]

The second part of the plan was to secure support for needed renovations to the palace. When Gottorf came under the control of local German officials in March 1947, it was serving as a temporary home to eight hundred war refugees and was in dire need of restoration.[67] When conditions had not improved two years later,[68] Kersten pressed the German government to help him house the Nydam Boat, writing:

> In light of such a great meaning of the Nydam Boat it is understandable that the Danish state in 1920 and more recently has demanded the transfer of the Nydam finds. The current situation therefore demands the prompt completion and opening of the Nydam Hall ... Also in view of the extraordinarily frequent visits to our year-old special exhibit and the completely unfitting present condition of the displayed Nydam Boat, which above all can no longer be represented to the large numbers of Scandinavian visitors, we ask in consideration of these circumstances for the immediate preparation of the requested … funding from the 1949 budget.[69]

A few months later, Schwantes gave specific figures to the Education Ministry, claiming that over 15,000 visitors had viewed the museum in August of 1949 alone. In echoing Kersten's request for funding for a special Nydam Hall, he added, "This [request] is all the more urgent in light of the international danger that exists for the Nydam Boat."[70] With these arguments, Schwantes and Kersten each emphasized the international importance of the museum's antiquities, but their appeals reflected the unique character of Schleswig-Holstein. In other words, they no longer claimed the collections as artefacts of a single national past; rather, they portrayed them as part of a shared heritage.

Such pressure seems to have been effective, since it appealed to a West German government eager to integrate the country into the European community of nations. In the spring of 1950, the renovated Schleswig-Holstein State Archaeology Museum (Archäologisches Landesmuseum) opened to the public. The institution included a separate Nydam exhibit in the former Fourth Dragoon barracks. Karl Kersten, whom Schwantes publicly called "one of my greatest discoveries," succeeded his retiring mentor as director of both the museum and the Provincial Preservation Office.[71] Kersten's reputation and history of friendly ties with Scandinavia lent the museum a level of credibility, but the question remained how cross-border visitors, and more importantly Danish scholars, would respond. Søren Telling, who had risked his own safety to preserve the collection, promoted the museum in the Danish press while praising the "congenial tone" of the city of Schleswig towards its Danish visitors.[72] Over the next year, Swedish and Danish archaeologists toured the museum, and began reporting positively on the product of Kersten's labours. After his first visit in 1950, Poul Nørlund recognized Gottorf as one of the most significant museums in all of Europe, declaring, "All northern scholars must come to Schleswig."[73] Brøndsted offered even more praise, saying, "It seems magical to me that such a museum could be built with such little money! I have in all my wide travels never seen a museum that can measure with this one in beauty and quality."[74] Seven years later, the Danes, in what amounted to the most powerful sign of reconciliation, named Kersten a Knight of the Order of the Dannebrog for his service to archaeology and to Denmark.[75]

The endorsements from Nørlund and Brøndsted helped ease popular demands for repatriating the artefacts. In the meantime, the Danish Social Democratic Party, whose interests in cooperating with the German Social Democrats led it to oppose the agitation on the border, had won a convincing victory in national elections, and had laid to rest the possibility of a new plebiscite.[76] Gradually, border Danes came to terms with the fact that the artefacts so critical to their national heritage would never return to Danish soil. Niels Friss captured the ambivalence of the moment, recalling the long history of the struggle over antiquities in the borderlands and arguing that their current fate was somewhat fitting: "The Flensburg Collection's treasures, the Thorsberg and Nydam finds with the great boat … have returned to the disputed land from whose earth they emerged: Slesvig. Perhaps that would have pleased its finder, Conrad Engelhardt, when he could now no longer take them back to Flensburg or Copenhagen, to see them so beautifully displayed in the Danish Dragoon's drilling house at the historic Gottorf Castle – and to know that they will never again return to Kiel."[77] Friss best expressed what was emerging as a new equilibrium between Germans and Danes and their shared claims to the remains of their pasts. With calls for reannexation fading and hopes of recovering regional artefacts beginning to diminish, Friss encouraged his readers to see the collection as an affirmation of Denmark's historical ties to the region. In this way, the new museum, which protected and displayed Schleswig-Holstein's past in a setting removed from the sites of conflict in Flensburg and Kiel, at last reflected the cross-border space that had proved so vital to the discovery of prehistory in the borderlands.

Narratives of Past and Present after 1945

The restoration of its principal institutions in 1950 was a crucial step, but did not complete regional archaeology's postwar transformation. In the ensuing decade, archaeologists would rebuild their networks, develop new theories and practices, and, perhaps most importantly, refashion themselves. As was the case in other fields, rehabilitating scholars with ties to the Nazis was part of restoring the discipline of archaeology. Prehistorians with strong Nazi ties and without strong connections in the discipline, such as Hans Reinerth, had little chance of returning to the profession. Scholars like Herbert Jankuhn, however, regained academic positions because their colleagues valued their academic contributions and were willing to publicly defend them and because so many fellow professionals had retired, fled into exile, or been killed in the fighting.[78] All that was required for these scholars to thrive in postwar West Germany was some clever reinvention.

Herbert Jankuhn's case is especially illustrative. In May 1945, Jankuhn entered an American prisoner of war camp and was required to report his previous activities to denazification authorities. He submitted a questionnaire in which he confirmed his membership in the Waffen SS and the University Instructors League (NS-Dozentenbund). He even mentioned his one-time status as candidate (Anwärter) for admission into the SA and his brief stint with the National Socialist Teachers League (NS-Lehrerbund) in 1934. He did not, however, report his role in the SS-Ahnenerbe, and in his account of his foreign travels omitted his 1942 trip to the Crimea. With these small modifications, Jankuhn had begun altering his image. He could scarcely deny his affiliation with the Nazis, but by omitting his role as a scholar working in an official capacity for the regime, he distanced himself not only from the activities most closely associated with war crimes but also from those engagements that might prove most harmful to his career.

After being cleared by the denazification board in 1949,[79] Jankuhn was free to manipulate his account further. Within seven years of his release, Jankuhn's curriculum vitae appeared in a volume detailing the biographies of present and former professors at the University of Kiel. Jankuhn's entry recounted his many institutional positions, including his former directorship in Kiel, his professorship in Rostock, his lecture series at Hamburg, his visiting professorship at the University of Kiel, and his new chair at the University of Göttingen.[80] But his prominent role in state archaeology during the 1930s and 1940s had completely fallen away. Instead, the biography represented the new professional face of Herbert Jankuhn. Though his role in cultural politics had been extensive during the Third Reich, and his power within his profession almost unparalleled, the traces of those years had vanished. Indeed, the silence within German academia was so complete that even former students like Heinrich Härke and Michael Gebühr reported that they had not learned the extent of their mentor's Nazi ties until almost fifty years later.[81]

It was much more difficult for Jankuhn to hide his past from his colleagues abroad. In 1963, the East German journal *Das Hochschulwesen* accused Jankuhn of looting museums in Warsaw during the war.[82] Five years later, Norwegian colleagues still bitter over his alleged treatment of Anton Wilhelm Brøgger denied him the opportunity to speak at the University of Oslo.[83] At the same time, he faced questions from the Canadian historian Michael Kater about his involvement with the SS-Ahnenerbe. In these moments where silence failed, Jankuhn, as did so many other Germans, turned to justification. For this, he needed the help of his colleagues. Indeed, he had already done this during his years as a prisoner of war, when he asked a number of prominent colleagues, including Gustav Schwantes, Günther Haselhoff, and Peter Zylmann, to write letters supporting his return to his academic position. Their apologies centred on the need to protect the integrity of archaeological research. In his letter, Peter Zylmann explained, "Jankuhn found himself between the Scylla Rosenberg and the Charybdis Himmler; had he not nominally chosen one side or the other, the great work at Haithabu would have come to nothing or been given over to a less capable man."[84] Years later, Jankuhn pushed this point further in an exchange with the historian Rolf Seeliger when he explained that German archaeologists had not been alone in worrying about the threat to scholarship. As he explained, "My entry into the SS occurred among other things on the direct request of Swedish colleagues, who said that only through such a step could the scholarly integrity of [my] excavations be assured."[85]

It is easy to dismiss these letters as fiction. Yet, their efforts to rationalize choices made during the Second World War were not simple fabrications, but often bore at least a passing resemblance to the crises that archaeologists perceived during the 1930s. When Peter Zylmann wrote of the urgent imperative to preserve the integrity of the Haithabu site, he implicitly blamed the SS but, in fact, may have been thinking of Jankuhn's struggles with Hans Reinerth and Peter Paulsen. Moreover, there is no evidence that Scandinavians actively supported Jankuhn's SS connections, but it is possible that Jankuhn simply blended the complaints he heard from Holger Arbman and other Scandinavian scholars in the 1930s and his own concerns about German standing abroad into an account that foisted responsibility for his choices onto the Swedes. In this way, the tales Jankuhn and his colleagues told after the war wove together a complex array of disparate pressures to portray a far simpler dilemma: whether to cooperate with the Nazis or to compromise their scholarship. In other words, the letters that ultimately salvaged Jankuhn's career, and that no doubt rescued the professional lives of many others, took what had once been professional opportunity and depicted it instead as insidious coercion. There were, to be sure, no claims to full moral vindication, but there were pleas for understanding and assurances of academic integrity. For the rehabilitated scholar, this seems to have been enough to warrant a return to the profession.

The discipline to which these scholars returned also faced a difficult process of rehabilitation. The changes were evident in German publications during the 1950s and 1960s. As Jankuhn continued to research the Haithabu site, he altered his postwar reports so that they no longer sought to integrate the site into an ethnohistorical narrative, but focused instead on its value as a critical juncture of trading networks.[86] Moreover, as Heiko Steuer has shown, Jankuhn made major revisions to his 1938 popular work, *Haithabu: An Early German City* (*Haithabu: Eine germanische Stadt der Frühzeit*), and in 1956 published it as *Haithabu: A Trading Centre of the Viking Age* (*Haithabu: Ein Handelsplatz der Wikingerzeit*). The new edition omitted, of course, the site's former SS sponsors in the history of the digs, and posited a new view of Slavic contributions to regional trade while removing loaded terms such as "*Germanentum*," and "*Deutschtum*."[87]

At first glance, these sorts of changes may seem superficial. Altering labels and moving away from typologies appear as simple adjustments aimed at preserving the core of the discipline. The scientific methods that had revolutionized the understanding of the distant past were unaffected by the shift in interpretation. But something important had changed. By turning its back on its Nazi past, German archaeology was likewise forced to abandon the nationalist assumptions that had lain at the foundation of the field since the nineteenth century. The shift altered three important aspects of archaeological practice. The first concerned the place of theory. After decades of practising their discipline under the guidance of ethnic settlement theories, archaeologists suddenly found themselves grappling with what Günter Smolla has dubbed the "Kossinna Syndrome," in which method became divorced from theory.[88] Rather than confront the implications of old theories and sort out valuable insights from potentially negative elements, German prehistorians became allergic to theory altogether, and confined themselves to a cultivation of practice that isolated them internationally. Thus, as Heinrich Härke has complained, German fieldwork became an exercise in precise excavation techniques and thick description at a time when Scandinavians were engaging the structuralist and neo-Marxist theories of British and American scholars such as Louis Binford, Colin Renfrew, and David Clarke.[89]

The second dimension was the relationship between archaeologists and the public. Despite the perceived distance between the specialist and layman, archaeology had always been a shared enterprise. The public had a clear role to play in the discovery and preservation of ancient remains, and major finds invariably held both scientific and cultural value. In Ahrensburg, for example, Alfred Rust's paleolithic discovery had been a key source of pride for the tiny community. But the intertwining of the public and professional domains often meant that the moral choices of one impacted the views of the other. This became especially clear in 2000, when the town expressed interest in honouring Rust's 100th birthday with an honorary citizenship and a walking trail in his name leading to the site he had made famous. Only later did the town leaders learn of Rust's connections to the SS, which complicated the commemoration. That year, the mayor convened a town hall meeting with historians, archaeologists, and residents to debate the issue. As one angry participant explained, "I am ashamed of what is happening here … It is a political and moral question and not one of whether a great archaeologist should be honoured."[90] In the end, the town compromised by denying Rust his honorary citizenship but by pressing ahead with the trail project, which quietly opened as the Alfred-Rust-Wanderweg in 2005. Clearly, the significance of Rust's discovery, like those of many of his colleagues, had been marred by the moral implications of his scholarship.

The shift away from nationalism has, finally, affected the broader meaning of archaeology. For over a century, the enthusiasm for prehistoric study had rested in large part on its promise of discovering a national past, but its adherence to pure scholarship in the postwar era left its practitioners struggling to reignite popular interest. The chasm became clear in 2003 with the debut of the national exhibition "People, Periods, Places: Archaeology in Germany" (Menschen, Zeiten, Räume: Archäologie in Deutschland) in Bonn and Berlin. The event showcased a spectacular collection of artefacts from three decades of research across Germany. Visitors crowded around stone carvings, bronze amulets, and iron swords. Impressive displays drew casual observers into the professional's craft of grid coordinates, ground-penetrating radar, and the latest tools of the laboratory. It was the first nationwide exhibit in over thirty years and was deemed by the Cultural Ministry to be a matter "of national importance,"[91] yet the nation was strikingly absent. There was no effort to distinguish German archaeology from its neighbours, no overarching presentation of the German past, and, above all, little explanation why archaeology matters to Germans today.

The contrast with Denmark is noteworthy. There, museums seem more at ease discussing their collections as part of a national enterprise. In Roskilde, visitors to the Viking Ship Museum (Vikingeskibsmuseet) view films reminding them of "our Viking ancestors," while the National Museum in Copenhagen devotes an entire wing to "Danish Prehistory." Such appellations are hardly surprising, given the very different wartime history of Danish archaeology. After 1945, the Danes very publicly punished Nazi collaborators. Mogen Mackeprang's youth earned him a strong admonition, while Gudmund Hatt was forced into retirement.[92] At the same time, Danish prehistorians celebrated the role their discipline had played in wartime resistance. Even so, they did not shy away from confronting their own ties to nationalism. In the National Museum's Danish wing, for instance, an exhibit accompanying replicas of the lost Golden Horns of Gallehus now mentions their political use in the 1920 plebiscite.

Threading this delicate needle has been more challenging in Germany. The discipline's close ties to Nazism have rendered even casual national appeals suspect, while the reluctance of German scholars to confront their Nazi past meant that little conversation was possible before the passing of the wartime generation. Yet, the popularity of the 2003 Bonn and Berlin exhibitions testifies to the ways that archaeology is still of tremendous interest to Germans. Amateur enthusiasts continue to consume information about prehistory not only through state museums, but also through history magazines such as *Damals* and through websites like Archäologie-Online. Professional archaeologists remain important in teaching the public about the past through these types of media, but they have struggled to establish a lasting connection even as they continue to depend on public assistance in preserving finds and funding research.

In response, a number of new strategies have appeared linking past and present by appealing to different levels of identity. At the Schleswig-Holstein Landesmuseum, Michael Gebühr heightened interest in bog bodies during the 1970s by stressing their personal connections to museum patrons. In both his popular writing on the subject and his museum exhibit design, he invited readers and museum visitors to use a mathematical formula and calculate for themselves the possibility that the bodies might be (very) distant relatives. "Seen from this perspective," he wrote, "the human remains in the bog body display lose some of their horror, and certainly some of their exoticism, while the graves of those vanished periods lose part of their remoteness and possibly acquire something of a personal relationship."[93] At the Bonn and Berlin exhibitions, the organizers aligned their presentation with the German federal states. Whether learning about the latest advances in Romano-German relations in Baden-Württemberg or Viking trade networks in Schleswig-Holstein, visitors were encouraged to make a connection with the foremost relics of their home states. While such approaches were at least as artificial as former nationalist appeals, they nevertheless complemented what the public might see in a state museum. They also better fit the localized contexts in which archaeologists work. And they recalled the earliest days of Central and northern European archaeology, when amateurs banded together to preserve the cultural heritage of their own communities.

Conclusion

In the summer of 1947, the director of the Borderland Museum in Flensburg (Grenzlandmuseum) sent Gustav Schwantes a letter in which he declared, "I am adamantly convinced that our children, if we ourselves do not live to experience it, will see a united Europe. This rage of nationalism that we [have seen] is but the last bacchanal before the collapse."[94] Only two years before, Flensburg had been the final bastion of the Third Reich and the Grenzlandmuseum had been a temporary redoubt for die-hard Nazis preparing a last stand.[95] Now its director questioned not only the Nazism for which they fought, but also the nationalism that lay underneath. His words expressed the palpable sense of rupture that followed the Second World War. It was plain that many Germans at the "Zero Hour" perceived a very different future ahead. Historians have tended to portray this concept as a belief in a new beginning, free from the short-lived Nazi era. But the letter on Schwantes' desk spoke of a sharp break with a past much older than Hitler. The "bacchanal" to which the letter alluded was the crescendo of a long path whose course was destined to bend in a new direction for the next generation. Schwantes' reply is not extant, but he could hardly have disagreed as he sat only miles from his ruined university and destroyed museum.

Six decades later, the break proved less complete than the two men might have imagined. Writing and theory about prehistory changed in the intervening years, and the practice of archaeology rested, much like its institutions, on wholly new foundations. But years of silence and omission failed to mask the marks of its past. From the accusations that followed Jankuhn in 1968 to the controversy over Alfred Rust in Ahrensburg in 2000, borderlands archaeology remained clouded by doubts that outlived the war generation. Salvaging the discipline meant keeping moral consequences at bay, but it proved impossible in the end to forestall them indefinitely. As a result, it was up to the next generation to confront an unsettled legacy while seeking new ways to reconnect with colleagues abroad and with the public at home.

The Nazi era marked, if not a "bacchanal," then certainly a radical apogee of nationalism within German archaeology. The ties to nationalism, though by no means the same across the discipline, nonetheless paved a path to Nazism in the 1930s and informed a more intense and morally dubious politicization in the 1940s. War made demands on scholars that went beyond simple pedagogy and propaganda. It endangered their work and strained their networks.

And, ultimately, it rendered untenable the tensions between their scientific and nationalist projects. Even before its cataclysmic end, the conflict intellectually bankrupted theories of ethnic settlement and placed into question older notions about the value of prehistory.

The Nazi era was also a high point for the national significance of the borderlands. Because of the importance of Nordic racism for both archaeological theory and Nazi ideology, scholars in Schleswig-Holstein were in great demand. This is why they became leaders in the major organizations, and why the state promoted their work across the country. Yet, celebrity came at a price. Despite the best efforts of Schwantes, Kersten, and Jankuhn to protect sites in Denmark or fund digs in Norway, the distance between them and their Scandinavian peers was never greater than during these years. For their Danish counterparts, the borderlands grew in importance to a country in the grip of foreign occupation. Prehistory became both a means of rallying the public and of showing resistance. At the moment of liberation, the patriotic sentiments engendered by the war resurrected once again the Danish national question, whose answer was as ever to be found at the place where Danes would draw their southern border.

It is therefore surprising that only five years later Danes could celebrate the opening of the new Landesmuseum and forego their long-held claims on prized artefacts. To make sense of this final turn, it is necessary to recognize the things that did not change after the war. When Jankuhn clashed with occupation authorities in Oslo, when Kersten assisted emergency digs in Denmark, and when Telling risked his safety to rescue the Haithabu rune stones, they each made clear their belief in the importance of cooperation between Germans and Scandinavians. After the war, this principle guided the process of restoration. In Schleswig, Schwantes and Kersten advocated an institution that would appeal not to national significance but to regional identity, and it was in this spirit that their Danish colleagues offered praise. The two sides thus broke with the recent past, but they also expressed sentiments about their local homeland that would have been familiar to the founders of the museum in the nineteenth century. Above all, they affirmed once again the cross-border relationships that had defined the preservation of antiquity in the borderlands for over a century.

In 2003, at the same moment that the organizers of the Bonn and Berlin exhibition were promoting a regional, "federal character" in their display, the Nydam exhibit stood empty outside the Gottorf Palace in Schleswig. Just as in the days of Conrad Engelhardt and the Flensburg Museum, the Nydam Boat had travelled across the sea to Denmark. This time, however, the boat had not been stolen. It was on loan to the National Museum in Copenhagen.

Conclusion

A simple stroll through the centre of present-day Copenhagen invariably leads to contact with reminders of northern European antiquity. In the shadow of the Parliament building (Rådshuset), two sculpted Bronze Age "lure-blowers" (*Lurblæserne*) look down from a high pedestal. On the surrounding streets, souvenir shops greet passersby with displays of plastic horned helmets and Viking dolls with fuzzy beards. In a similar way, the past is a popular attraction in Schleswig-Holstein. Visitors leaving the train station in Schleswig are greeted by a sign bedecked with the image of a long ship commemorating twelve hundred years of the town's history. It is only a short distance to the Haithabu site, where patrons can tour the walls and munch on "Viking burgers" at a nearby café before heading out to visit the Danevirke or travelling to the Gottorf Palace to view mummified bog bodies behind glass.

Such has become the norm in Europe. The distant past remains a part of life, but after two centuries amid the struggles of modern nations, it has been largely relegated to the realm of heritage tourism. The fuzzy-bearded Viking still represents Denmark, but it does so now as part of a kitschy consumer experience.[1] Meanwhile, the artefacts that Germans and Danes once banded together to discover, struggled to preserve, and fought one another to possess now stand on display for visitors from around the world and, as with the Nydam Boat, once again cross borders in academic exchange. At the Danevirke, the walls testifying to early medieval strife and the more recent German-Danish Wars now attract tourists with a collection of German and Danish flags fluttering in the breeze. It is an interesting fate for these relics of acrimony. It suggests that the relationship between the distant past and modern national frontiers has changed dramatically from the period between the 1830s and the 1950s, when archaeology and antiquities museums stood astride a tense dynamic of conflict and cooperation. Clearly, sites and artefacts have retained a certain symbolic power, but the period in which they were most embattled appears to have passed. As a result, we can now look back and draw some conclusions about antiquity and identity in the German-Danish borderlands.

In many ways, the Schleswig-Holstein region exemplifies the ways in which the modern uses of the past have been challenged in the nebulous spaces between identity groups. The phenomenon is by no means limited to Europe or even the West. Philip Kohl, Mara Kozelsky, and Nachman Ben-Yehuda have showcased similar episodes from archaeological traditions from other places around the world, where specialists also drew on material remains to establish temporal and spatial boundaries for their constituent groups, seek their primordial origins, supplement nationalist or ethnic interpretations of language and myth, cast an image of unity, promote desires for renewal or restoration, or exalt present-day cultures through appeals to the past.[2] Just as in Schleswig-Holstein, conflicting claims often confounded appropriations in regions where ethnic or cultural groups overlap. But none of these similarities should lead us to understand the case of the German-Danish borderlands solely as an exemplar. In fact, we have seen how this particular region was critical to the making of modern Germany and Denmark. At the same time, its own history tells us something new about how archaeology and museums informed the complex relationships in the frontier zone.

As a starting point, we must first recognize what Tara Zahra has called the "world of national ambiguity" that characterizes border regions.[3] In this case, the uses of the past went beyond simple pronouncements of German or Danish identity. Rather, this study has discussed four principal self-conceptions that attached to archaeology: individual, provincial, national, and scientific. Together, they acted as interdependent variables to shape the discipline and its impact on the border question. Beginning in the early nineteenth century, the sense of alienation between past and present sparked a new personal interest in antiquity that, through the work of antiquarian associations, informed an emerging spirit of patriotism. The pressures of the border dispute pushed antiquarians in the borderlands to translate their private curiosity about antiquity into a more precise local identity in the duchies. Typically, their goal was to integrate the region into a burgeoning national imagination. Whether it was a German vision of a united Schleswig-Holstein belonging to the German Volk, or a Danish conception of Sønderjylland bound to Denmark and circumscribed at the Eider, the image that resulted became, in Alon Confino's words, "a symbolic depiction of the locality, the territorial state, and the nation at one and the same time."[4] Finally, the investigation of prehistoric remains led to an emerging scholarly orientation that bred confidence in the power to reconstruct the past objectively while affirming notions of its relevance to the present.

Private and public cultural identities converged in the museum. Here, the small world of private collectors gave way to a dialogue between experts and the public and gave rise to professional prehistoric archaeology. When the Kiel, Copenhagen, and Flensburg museums were founded, there was little distinction between curator and discoverer, and it was under the auspices of museums that the first antiquities associations sought the remains of the past and maintained contact with collectors. As collections grew, they lent themselves to a second, didactic function. Each artefact on display could on its own conjure the spirit of antiquity, but when placed together in sequence, they could reconstruct the story of the past. It was thus in the creation of the museum exhibit that antiquarians like Christian Jürgensen Thomsen, Heinrich Handelmann, and Johanna Mestorf wrestled with the questions that shaped the first theories of archaeology. At the same time, the search for more relics to fill empty display cases drove Jens Worsaae, Conrad Engelhardt, Wilhelm Splieth, and Friedrich Knorr to dig in the field, where emerging theories informed new discoveries. Theory and experience in turn engendered a set of practices, which crystallized within an intellectual field separating amateurs from professionals. While the university remained important in the development of the discipline, and in Germany especially was often the sine qua non for scholarly credibility, the earliest innovations and later the guiding norms and practices of archaeology in this region developed primarily in the museum.

Studies in the past two decades have made it clear that museums were key arbiters of cultural memory, as they organized and presented the past in a public space.[5] Moreover, as Peter McIsaac has argued, they exercised a powerful pull that reached beyond the exhibition to a "notional" space in the Western mind, which came to comprehend the world within the bounds of an "inventoried consciousness."[6] From the museums featured in this study, we have seen that the power to shape collective memory developed over time and in a specific historical context. The emergence of regional institutions was part of a process that aimed to rejoin aspects of prehistory to living memory. Its origins lay with a sense of stewardship born of a common liberal and patriotic sentiment and reflecting a shared commitment to saving the past for the present. Later, with the outbreak of the German-Danish Wars, questions over preservation gave way to debates over ownership, as antiquarians linked artefact provenance and national territory, and equated possession of prized symbols like the Nydam Boat with a claim on the things they symbolized.

The historical trajectory of antiquarian study consequently appeared as one of increasing politicization and engagement with nationalist causes. Yet, there remained a strong tendency towards cross-border cooperation. No museum functioned in isolation. Relationships were key, and curators found themselves struggling to align their institutions with national traditions of remembering while preserving an orientation towards international academic norms. The incongruities manifested themselves in debates about the arrangement of exhibitions, beneath which lay more fundamental disagreements about sources of authority: on whose systems of classification to rely and whose models to follow. Christian Flor, for example, believed his collection of "Nordic" antiquities in Kiel should correspond to C.J. Thomsen's museum in Copenhagen, while Heinrich Handelmann sought to render his exhibit compatible with that of Ludwig Lindenschmit in Mainz. At times, the connections among museums developed into hierarchies, as between Copenhagen and Kiel or between Kiel and the local Kreismuseen, or as rivalries, as between Kiel and Flensburg. At other times, they formed important mechanisms for shifting ways of ordering the past within countries. Johanna Mestorf, for example, followed Worsaae's thinking on the Three Age system against Handelmann's wishes because the Danish method seemed a better scientific model and was more widely accepted in northern Europe.

Because the status of a "national" museum hinged on its connections at home and abroad, scholarly networks were also essential. Indeed, one of the main objectives of this book has been to trace the history of a distinct academic field, which developed throughout the years of the border dispute. Academic degrees and institutional affiliations assured some level of participation in the discipline, but acceptance within the field also hinged on relationships extending beyond traditional academic structures. In many cases, personal friendships preceded collegial ties and proved instrumental in stretching the boundaries of the field across the border. Together, such points help us understand how Mestorf could weigh theories and effect change in the Kiel Museum despite her status as an academic outsider. They also help account for the expansion of museums during the nineteenth and twentieth centuries, the discovery of major finds like the Haithabu site, and ultimately the limits of collaboration between regional archaeologists and the Nazi regime.

From their affiliation with institutions and their membership in a community of scholars, archaeologists derived a scholarly identity that shaped their corresponding attachment to the nation and afforded them a role in nationalist movements. At the same time, however, the norms and practices of their scientific personae made them imperfect agents of nationalism. Such a conclusion should remind us to exercise care in our understanding of, to borrow Peter Judson's term, "national activists,"[7] and may even lead us to question under which circumstances the term should apply. In this case, archaeologists sometimes seemed to fit the bill. Their discoveries, writings, and exhibitions made artefacts available for appropriation as symbols. Moreover, their scholarly authority was valuable for promoting a vision of national belonging, while their participation was often assured through a perceived duty to use their work to educate the public. Finally, they often characterized the image of the past in national terms. There were, however, limits to their engagement with the public. First, there were moments of ebb and flow in regional institutions, which created periods of institutional weakness in which antiquarians and archaeologists found themselves unable to control the production or reception of knowledge about prehistory. In the years following the Second German-Danish War, the Kiel Museum was unable to act against outside looting, as in the case of Gustav Freytag, while in the 1920s the museum languished while popular writers mixed scientific and romanticized views of regional prehistory.

Even in their peak years, archaeologists and curators betrayed their own conflicted allegiances in the presentation of the past. In their museum exhibits, for example, they attempted to convey a meaningful image of antiquity, but the absence of the past inevitably counterpoised its presence in the artefacts. Through a combination of artefact and artifice, they were obliged to negotiate the space between antiquity and modernity. It was a mission that exposed the lingering tensions between a need to maintain objective distance from the past and an impulse to integrate it with the present, which characterized the representation of the past throughout the period under study. The push and pull of objectification and alienation meant that archaeology struggled to preserve a balance between its role as a scholarly discipline of a fixed past and its place in shaping a fluid and contested cultural memory.

Before the post–Second World War era, prehistorians largely failed to acknowledge the paradox, because they saw no reason to question its inherent value to the present. In other words, they believed that even if they objectively learned about ancient cultures, they would reach conclusions directly relevant to their modern communities. Methodological training and theoretical interpretation fell within the orbit of the expert, but the notion of a higher purpose, itself a legacy of the discipline's roots in antiquarianism and history, was something that the specialist and the layman could share. It might compel scholars to connect their research to questions of national belonging, but it also allowed them to pursue an inverse objective: to use appeals to modern identity to support scholarly research. Thus, Kossinna and Jankuhn in Germany and Worsaae and Brøndsted in Denmark actively used their work to endorse nationalist causes. Mestorf and Schwantes, meanwhile, used similar language, but did so to solicit the help of non-specialists to promote scholarship or to encourage them to report finds. For this reason, we might conclude that while prehistorians in the borderlands generally served as mobilizers of modern consciousness, they were not always "nationalist activists."

The strategies employed in such exhibitions as Berlin and Bonn's Archäologie in Deutschland or the Golden Horn special exhibit in the National Museum suggest that archaeology, when accompanied by self-critical reflection, can profitably encourage public support by appealing to a perceived present-day value. The problem in previous years was that archaeologists worked uncritically, and adopted an approach beset with two logical flaws. The first was that it posited an unwarranted correlation between past and present cultures by equating ancient peoples with modern communities. The second was that notions of provincial or national identity were based on false assumptions of consensus. In fact, there were significant disagreements among regional antiquarians about what it meant to be a German or Dane, or a Schleswig-Holsteiner or Sønderjyder. Furthermore, colleagues outside the region often held very different views about the relationship between the borderlands and the nation. Perhaps most significantly, German scholars such as Jacob Grimm and Karl Müllenhoff used the past to seek German heritage far north of the provincial borders of the Kaiserreich. At the turn of the century, Gustaf Kossinna used scientific methods to place the borderlands at the centre of a much more expansive notion of Germandom. His conclusions extolled the borderlands as a bridge between erstwhile components of a racialized Volk, but along the way effaced the tidy distinctions erected by Schleswig-Holstein specialists between Germans and Danes.

To understand how this occurred, we must consider more closely the search for prehistoric origins in the borderlands. We have seen how this was a principal question for both antiquarians and archaeologists, but that not everyone approached it in the same way. All might agree that tracing the roots of ancestors promised to reveal the prospective new nation-state in Germany, or the transforming nation-state in Denmark, as the natural embodiment of a long-standing community. As in Peter Thaler's example of the Schleswig historians, provincial antiquarians also wished to delineate the settlement patterns of ancient tribes in order to justify claims through the presumed ties between national communities and the natural landscape.[8] In other words, the thinking ran that *where we once were is where we now belong*. Outside the province, however, German scholars such as Grimm, Müllenhoff, and Kossinna followed threads of texts and artefacts in search of a more definite terminal point at which prehistory might reveal something elemental about the German people. In contrast to their colleagues in the borderlands, they believed to a greater degree that *where we came from tells us who we are*. Generations of scholars employed different forms of evidence, whether they were runes, texts, or artefacts, and redefined the criteria of the search, so that a hunt for the essence of a spiritual Volk gave way to a search for a pure exemplar of the Germanic race. In each instance, however, eager scholars found themselves following familiar trails ever northward.

By the early twentieth century, this broader, völkisch view of the German-Danish borderlands gained acceptance in academic circles, as in the case of Oscar Montelius in Sweden. Fewer scholars were willing to go as far as Kossinna's Nordic theory, and archaeologists in Kiel and Copenhagen expressed reluctance to accept sweeping national narratives. Yet, the provincial orientation of regional institutions in Kiel precluded a more focused debate, while the museum's weakness in the interwar era promoted the growth of radical interpretations among popular writers. Finally, in the 1930s, the rise of the Third Reich altered the relationship between scholars and the state, leading young archaeologists like Herbert Jankuhn to adopt more explicitly the underlying tenets of Nordic theory and thereby exploit points of congruence between National Socialist thinking and nationalist archaeological interpretation.

The distinctions between Germany and Denmark in this instance are striking. The borderlands had been a central issue in Danish national politics, and, just as Germans were inspired by the writings of J.G. Fichte and J.G. Herder to seek their national character in the past, so too did the Danes similarly turn to the folkish thinking of N.F.S. Grundtvig. Yet, the Danes consistently sought their uniqueness in a narrower context. Even though some of the country's most treasured relics, like the Nydam Boat, the Golden Horns, or the Danevirke, had been found in in Schleswig, Danes nevertheless reconciled themselves in the twentieth century to what Knud Jespersen has called a historical "process of reduction," with a border far from the Eider.[9] In 1920, Danes cast new copies of the Golden Horns to celebrate the return of North Schleswig and negotiated urgently for the return of the Nydam Boat, but most ultimately resisted calls for the annexation of South Schleswig after the Second World War and left the area's artefacts to the Landesmuseum. Meanwhile, Poul Nørlund charted the spectacular growth of the National Museum, which suggested that, in contrast to Kiel, state institutions in Denmark succeeded in dominating the dialogue on national prehistory.

In a study of the two nationalist traditions, Leni Yahil has explained the differences by comparing what she understood as the Germans' expansionist and more aggressive nationalist thought with the Danes' more introspective and passive self-conception.[10] To refine the distinctions, we might add George Mosse's view that the German intellectual tradition viewed the distant past as a window to an unadulterated vision of the Volk free of the detritus of modern life,[11] which led scholars to reject historical influences and value the borderlands for its potential as an Urheimat. The Grundtvigian view, however, stressed the uniqueness of Danish character over time, which encouraged scholars to seek distinction in both history and prehistory, to include Nordic pagan and Christian influences, and to cultivate Danishness in areas of Schleswig where it was most likely to flower. Second, the centrality of Sønderjylland in Danish politics and culture coupled with the country's small size diminished the cleavages between nation and province that prevailed in German Schleswig-Holstein. Regional artefacts like the Golden Horns were thus much less ambiguous national symbols. Certainly, Danes continue to stress minor differences between residents of Copenhagen and Haderslev or Sønderborg, but the fact that they have so easily shared the same past explains why, as Norman Berdichevsky concluded, "After 1920 … the theme of 'danskheden' in South Jutland exercised little appeal as most Danes were convinced that the national struggle had been culminated with success."[12]

The moment of Danish "success," of course, coincided with defeat and collapse in Germany. Progressive engagement with the Third Reich drove German prehistoric archaeology, particularly in the borderlands, to a radical nationalist perspective that seriously challenged scholarly reputations. Bitter years of war and occupation strained the international field and revealed unequivocally how nationalist paradigms had become incompatible with academic norms. With their museum destroyed, their artefacts scattered, and their careers in jeopardy, German prehistorians in Schleswig-Holstein fell back on their provincial roots to rebuild their institutions, and in the ensuing years recast the significance of their research by appealing to the regional and, as Michael Gebühr's bog body exhibit showed, the personal identities of their readers and patrons. Fully restoring the field, however, demanded renewed ties to colleagues abroad, whose assent could temper demands for repatriating artefacts and lend credibility to new institutions and research.

The opening of the Landesmuseum in the Gottorf Palace in 1950 marked an important turning point in the history of border relations. The new institution conveyed one final historical lesson about regional museums, which was that alongside exhibit styles and artefact arrangements was the essential role of place. This was important at moments throughout the last two centuries. The founders of the first museum knew that they could best draw a desired audience of educated middle-class patrons in Kiel. Engelhardt calculated that a museum in Flensburg might promote pro-Danish sentiment across Schleswig. And Schwantes and Kersten believed that the Gottorf Palace might ease tensions after the Second World War. Over fifty years later, my own work in the archives at Gottorf was briefly interrupted when the museum received a joint visit from Denmark's Queen Margrethe II and German Federal President Horst Köhler, who came to celebrate the 1,200th anniversary of the founding of Schleswig. Their visit symbolized the ways in which the threads of history and prehistory had come together in this place. Before them were the relics of an ancient past once claimed by both Germans and Danes housed in a structure that evoked, on the one hand, the close ties between Denmark and the old duchies of Schleswig and Holstein and, on the other, centuries of conflict between dukes and kings and later between national armies. The tour showed how this museum had become part of another "successful culmination," in which embattled heritages could rest comfortably within a site whose own history facilitated mutual claims. The visit, though seemingly narrow in purpose, nevertheless exemplified the point made by Norman Berdichevsky that Schleswig-Holstein is important because it affirms the possibility of peace for border conflicts around the globe.[13]

Renewed cooperation returned the history of archaeology in the borderlands to their starting point, where it had once made possible the discovery of the ancient past in a contested frontier region. Indeed, one of the most significant conclusions of this study is that cross-border relationships remained indispensable throughout the history of the border dispute, which teaches us a valuable lesson about the creation of national identities. We learn that they not only depend on the interaction of a complex matrix of smaller attachments, but also that they invariably unfold in a transnational space. In part, this dynamic yielded volatility, and as Charles Bright and Michael Geyer have argued in the American context or as Sebastian Conrad discovered in the history of German colonization, led to a delimiting impulse,[14] such as occurred in Worsaae's and Müller's quest for the singularity of ancient Danes. At the same moment, the cross-border dimension tantalized with the promise of something beyond the nation's horizons. It yielded a corresponding push to incorporate myths, symbols, and traditions from abroad to invoke an even grander destiny. Such was inherent in the lure of "Germanic" or "Nordic" ascriptions. Deriving broader corollaries, however, demanded access to elements abroad. While borderlands scholars by no means acted alone, their transnational experience afforded them a unique power to mediate this pursuit. Finally, the reconciliation after the German-Danish Wars, the disastrous engagement with Nazism, and the successful restoration of institutions in the post–Second World War era revealed that cross-border ties were needed to negotiate the limits imposed not only by neighbouring national identities, but also by the regional and scientific self-conceptions upon which these identities were founded.

Memorial stone at the Danevirke commemorating joint restoration efforts in 2001. Photograph courtesy J. Laurence Hare.

To draw together the threads of this book, we might return to our starting point at the Danevirke in Schleswig and consider one final "artefact." There, alongside the ancient walls, visitors encounter a simple marker carved in the shape of a rune stone. This is no ancient relic, but a new memorial that evokes both the ancient site and its modern context. Etched upon its face is a tribute to a joint restoration project at the site carried out in 2001 by Pioneer Battalion 620 of Germany and the Second Engineer Battalion of Denmark. The monument reminds us of the enduring lure of prehistory in the modern era, while its words assure us that the history of the German-Danish borderlands is not simply an account of struggle, but is also one of reconciliation. Just as archaeology once participated in the long border dispute, so too has it taken part in its resolution. Neither Germans nor Danes have abandoned their links to the past, but the stone indicates that both have made space for the claims of their neighbours. They have seized the imperative to protect ancient remains and used it as an opportunity to strengthen the ties between their respective countries. Finally, the stone represents an ongoing process of appropriation, in which archaeology steps outside its objective frame to teach us about our modern selves. Only now the lesson is one of shared commitment. In centuries past, rune stones were erected as lasting signs of great deeds. Perhaps the same might be said of this memorial. Given the decades of bitterness, such a gesture is worthy of commemoration.

Notes

Introduction

1 Eric Hobsbawm and Terence Ranger, eds., *The Invention of Tradition* (Cambridge: Cambridge University Press, 1983); Susan A. Crane, *Collecting and Historical Consciousness in Early Nineteenth-Century Germany* (Ithaca: Cornell University Press, 2000).

2 Suzanne L. Marchand, *Down from Olympus: Archaeology and Philhellenism in Germany, 1750–1970* (Princeton: Princeton University Press, 1996).

3 Yannis Hamilakis, *The Nation and Its Ruins: Antiquity, Archaeology, and the National Imagination in Greece* (Oxford: Oxford University Press, 2007), 14.

4 On Ayodhya, see Reinhard Bernbeck and Susan Pollock, "Ayodhya, Archaeology, and Identity," *Current Anthropology* 39, no. 1 (1996): 138–42; On Philip II, see Phyllis Williams Lehmann, "The So-called Tomb of Philip II: A Different Interpretation," *American Journal of Archaeology* 82, no. 3 (1980): 339–53.

5 Stine Wiell, *Flensborgsamlingen 1852–1864 og dens skæbne* (Flensburg: Studieafdeling ved Dansk Centralbibliotek for Sydslesvig, 1997).

6 Robin Ostow, ed., *(Re)Visualizing National History: Museums and National Identities in Europe in the New Millennium* (Toronto: University of Toronto Press, 2008).

7 See Heinz-Gerhard Haupt and Jürgen Kocka, "Comparative History: Methods, Aims, Problems," in Deborah Cohen and Maura O'Connor, eds., *Comparison and History: Europe in Cross-National Perspective* (New York: Routledge, 2004), 31; Hartmut Kaeble, "Between Comparisons and Transfers – and What Now?" in Heinz-Gerhard Haupt and Jürgen Kocka, eds., *Comparative and Transnational History: Central European Approaches and New Perspectives* (New York: Berghahn, 2009), 33–5.

8 Knud J.V. Jespersen, *A History of Denmark*, 2nd ed. (New York: Palgrave, 2011), 22.

9 Anthony D. Smith, *The Nation in History: Historiographical Debates about Ethnicity and Nationalism* (Hanover, NH: University Press of New England, 2000), 6–20.

10 Benedict Anderson, *Imagined Communities: Reflections on the Origins and Spread of Nationalism* (London: Verso, 1991); Hobsbawm and Ranger, *Invention of Tradition*, 6.
11 John A. Armstrong, *Nations before Nationalism* (Chapel Hill: University of North Carolina Press, 1982).
12 Anthony D. Smith, *The Ethnic Origins of Nations* (Oxford: Blackwell, 1986), 25.
13 Anderson, *Imagined Communities*, 80.
14 Anthony D. Smith, *The Cultural Foundations of Nations: Hierarchy, Covenant, and Republic* (Oxford: Blackwell, 2008), 19–22.
15 John Hutchinson, "Cultural Nationalism and Moral Regeneration," in John Hutchinson and Anthony D. Smith, eds., *Nationalism* (Oxford: Oxford University Press, 1994), 123. See also John Hutchinson, *The Dynamics of Cultural Nationalism* (London: Allen and Unwin, 1987).
16 Bruce Trigger, "Alternative Archaeologies: Nationalist, Colonialist, Imperialist," *Man* 19, no. 3 (1984): 355–70.
17 Philip L. Kohl, "Nationalism and Archaeology: On the Construction of Nations and the Reconstruction of the Remote Past," *Annual Review of Anthropology* 27 (1998): 226.
18 Philip L. Kohl, "National and International Influences in Archaeology, 19th-Century Beginnings to Post-Processual Ponderings," paper presented at the International Colloquium, "National Scholarship and Transnational Experience: Politics, Identity, and Objectivity in the Humanities and Social Sciences," Chapel Hill, NC, 2006.
19 See, e.g., Philip L. Kohl and Clare Fawcett, eds., *Nationalism, Politics, and the Practice of Archaeology* (Cambridge: Cambridge University Press, 1995).
20 Peter Sahlins, *Boundaries: The Making of France and Spain in the Pyrenees* (Berkeley: University of California Press, 1989), 8.
21 Jens J.A. Worsaae, *Dänemarks Vorzeit durch Alterthümer und Grabhügel beleuchtet*, translated by N. Bertelsen (Copenhagen: Reitzel, 1844), iv. Here and elsewhere throughout, the translations are my own, unless indicated otherwise.
22 Pierre Bordieu, " Intellectual Field and Creative Project," *Social Science Information* 8 (Apr. 1969): 89–119.
23 Fritz Ringer, "Intellectual History, the Intellectual Field, and the Sociology of Knowledge," *Theory and Society* 19, no. 3 (1990): 269–94; Neil Fligstein and Doug McAdam, *A Theory of Fields* (Oxford: Oxford University Press, 2012), 3.
24 In a critique of the work of Fritz Ringer, Martin Jay first questioned the degree to which current intellectual fields can exist diachronically as well as synchronically. See Martin Jay, "Fieldwork and Theorizing in Intellectual History: A Reply to Fritz Ringer," *Theory and Society* 19, no. 3 (June 1990): 311–21.
25 Pierre Bourdieu, *Homo Academicus*, translated by Peter Collier (Stanford: Stanford University Press, 1984), 149–51.

26 Fligstein and McAdam, *Theory of Fields*, 24–6.
27 Many regions and towns within the borderlands share a variety of names reflecting the changing state affiliations and language groups in the area. For the sake of clarity, this study will employ the current spellings related to a given area's position in present-day Germany and Denmark.
28 Birgit Sawyer and Peter Sawyer, *Medieval Scandinavia: From Conversion to Reformation circa 800–1500* (Minneapolis: University of Minnesota Press, 1993), 51–2.
29 Manfred Jessen-Klingenberg, *Standpunkte zur neueren Geschichte Schleswig-Holsteins* (Malente: Schleswig-Holsteischer Geschichtsverlag, 1998), 24–5.
30 Peter Thaler, *Of Mind and Matter: The Duality of National Identity in the German-Danish Borderlands* (West Lafayette, IN: Purdue University Press, 2009), 47.
31 Inge Adriansen, *Denkmal und Dynamit: Denkmälerstreit im deutsch-dänischen Grenzland* (Neumünster: Wachholtz, 2011).
32 Peter Thaler, "The Discourse of Historical Legitimization: A Comparative Examination of Southern Jutland and the Slovenian Language Area," *Nationalities Papers* 40, no. 1 (2012): 19.
33 Malcolm Anderson, "European Frontiers at the End of the Twentieth Century," in Malcolm Anderson and Eberhart Bort, eds., *The Frontiers of Europe* (London: Continuum, 1998), 1.
34 Thomas M. Wilson and Hastings Donnan, "Nation, State, and Identity at International Borders," in Thomas M. Wilson and Hastings Donnan, eds., *Border Identitites: Nation and State at International Frontiers* (Cambridge: Cambridge University Press, 1998), 10.
35 Sahlins, *Boundaries*, 270–1.
36 James Björk, *Neither German nor Pole: Catholicism and National Indifference in a Central European Borderland* (Ann Arbor: University of Michigan Press, 2008); Tara Zahra, *Kidnapped Souls: National Indifference and the Battle for Children in the Bohemian Lands, 1900–1948* (Ithaca: Cornell University Press, 2008).
37 Peter Judson, *Guardians of the Nation: Activists on the Language Frontiers of Imperial Austria* (Cambridge, MA: Harvard University Press, 2006), 3.

1. Antiquarians and Patriots

1 Jürgen Habermas, *The Structural Transformation of the Public Sphere: An Inquiry into a Category of Bourgeois Society*, translated by Thomas Burger and Frederick Lawrence (Cambridge, MA: MIT Press, 2000), 72–3.
2 Crane, *Collecting and Historical Consciousness*, 19–21.
3 Peter Blickle, *Heimat: A Critical Theory of the German Idea of Homeland* (Rochester: Camden House, 2002), 5.
4 Alon Confino, *The Nation as a Local Metaphor: Württemberg, Imperial Germany, and*

National Memory, 1871–1918 (Chapel Hill: University of North Carolina Press, 1997), 241.

5 Franz Georg Kaltwasser, "The Common Roots of Library and Museum in the Sixteenth Century: The Example of Munich," *Library History* 20, no. 3 (2004): 164.

6 H.D. Schepelern, "Natural Philosophers and Princely Collectors: Worm, Pauldanus, and the Gottorp and Copenhagen Collections," in Oliver Impey and Arthur MacGregor, eds., *The Origins of Museums: The Cabinet of Curiosities in Sixteenth- and Seventeenth-Century Europe* (Oxford: Oxford University Press, 1985), 122–3. Worm's cabinet was catalogued in Ole Worm, *Museum Wormianum: Seu historia rerum rariorum, quam artificialium, tam domesticarum, quam exoticarum, quae Hafniae Danorum in oedibus authoris servantur* (Lugduni Batavorum: Apud Iohannem Elsevirium, 1655).

7 François-Xavier Dillmann, "Frankrig og den nordiske fortid – de første etaper af genopdagelsen," in Else Roesdahl and Preben Meulengracht Sørensen, eds., *The Waking of Angantyr: The Scandinavian Past in European Culture* (Aarhus: Aarhus University Press, 1996), 16.

8 Inge Adriansen, *Nationale symboler i det danske rige, 1830–2000*, vol. 2, *Fra undersåtter til nation* (Copenhagen: Museum Tuscalanums Forlag, 2003), 142.

9 Schepelern, "Natural Philosophers and Princely Collectors," 125; Ole Klindt-Jensen, *A History of Scandinavian Archaeology* (London: Thames & Hudson, 1975), 18–20.

10 The title is sometimes spelled, "Gottorp."

11 Schepelern, "Natural Philosophers and Princely Collectors," 124–5.

12 Wilhelm Heß, "Major, Johann Daniel," in *Allgemeine Deutsche Biographie* 20 (1884): 112; Georg Kossak, "Zur Geschichte der Urgeschichtsforschung in Schleswig-Holstein," *Christiana Albertina* 2 (1966): 53.

13 Johann Daniel Major, *Bevölckertes Cimbrien, oder die zwischen der Ost- und West-See gelegene Halb-insel Deutschlandes nebst dero Ersten Einwohnern und ihr eigendlichen durch viel und grosse Umwege geschehenen Ankunfft summarischer weise vorgestellt* (Plön: Schmied, 2006), 61–75.

14 Erich Hoffmann, "Nikolaus Falck und die Schleswig-Holsteinische Frage," *Zeitschrift der Gesellschaft für Schleswig-Holsteinische Geschichte* 111 (1986): 145.

15 The title "heathen altar" was used in an eighteenth-century illustration by an unknown artist depicting a dolmen in Oldenburg. A reprint is located in ALM Nachlass Gustav Schwantes.

16 Jan Albert Bakker, *Megalithic Research in the Netherlands: From "Giants' Beds" and "Pillars of Hercules" to Accurate Investigations* (Leiden: Sidestone, 2010), 13, 48.

17 Rosemary Sweet, *Antiquaries: The Discovery of the Past in Eighteenth-Century Britain* (London: Continuum, 2004), 277.

18 Adriansen, *National symboler*, vol. 2, 142–4.

19 John L. Greenway, *The Golden Horns: Mythic Imagination and the Nordic Past* (Athens: University of Georgia Press, 1977), 2.

20 Adam Gottlob Oehlenschläger, "Guldhornene," translated by George Borrow; reprinted in Edmund Gosse, ed., *The Gold Horns* (London: Thomas J. Wise, 1913), 12–14.

21 N.F.S. Grundtvig, "Introduction to Norse Mythology," in Niels Lyhne Jensen, ed., *A Grundtvig Anthology* (Cambridge: James Clarke, 1984), 47.

22 Leni Yahil, "National Pride and Defeat: A Comparison of Danish and German Nationalism," *Journal of Contemporary History* 26 (1991): 459–60.

23 Otto Brandt, *Geschichte Schleswig-Holsteins: Ein Grundriss*, 8th ed. (Kiel: Mühlau, 1981), 231.

24 Vagn Skovgaard-Petersen, *Danmarks Historie* (Copenhagen: Gyldendal, 1985), vol. 5, 159–61; Uffe Østergård, "Statehood, Ethnicity, and Nationalism: The Case of Denmark," in Preben Kaarsholm and Jan Hultin, eds., *Inventions and Boundaries: Historical and Anthropological Approaches to the Study of Ethnicity and Nationalism* (Roskilde: International Development Studies, Roskilde University, 1994), 261–303.

25 Johann Gottlieb Fichte, *Addresses to the German Nation*, translated by R.F. Jones and G.H. Turnbull (Chicago: Open Court, 1922), 104–5.

26 Eda Sagarra and Peter Skrine, *A Companion to German Literature* (Oxford: Blackwell, 1999), 44; Peter Watson, *The German Genius: Europe's Third Renaissance, the Second Scientific Revolution, and the Twentieth Century* (New York: Harper, 2011), 293.

27 Tina Grütter, *Melancholie und Abgrund: Die Bedeutung des Gesteins bei Caspar David Friedrich; Ein Beitrag zum Symboldenken der Frühromantik* (Berlin: Reimer, 1986), 185.

28 Ludwig Gotthard Kosegarten, "Das Hünengrab"; reprinted in Grütter, *Melancholie und Abgrund*, 217.

29 Ibid., translated by and reprinted in Lewis Holmes, *Kosegarten's Cultural Legacy: Aesthetics, Religion, Literature, Art, and Music* (New York: Peter Lang, 2005), 46.

30 Grütter, *Melancholie und Abgrund*, 35.

31 Wieland Schmied, *Caspar David Friedrich*, translated by Russell Stockman (New York: Abrams, 1995), 56.

32 Helmut Börsch-Supan, *Caspar David Friedrich*, translated by Sarah Twohig and John William Gabriel (Munich: Prestel, 1990), 162.

33 Jacob Burckhardt, *The Civilization of the Renaissance in Italy*, translated by S.G.C. Middlemore (New York: Barnes & Noble, 1999), 81.

34 Charles Taylor, *Sources of the Self: The Making of Modern Identity* (Cambridge, MA: Harvard University Press, 1989), 176.

35 Jerrold Seigel, *The Idea of the Self: Thought and Experience in Western Europe since the Seventeenth Century* (Cambridge: Cambridge University Press, 2005), 43. For his part, Seigel rejects Taylor's assertion that modern individuals sought to resolve

this problem by drawing solely from within themselves. "To regard people as partial agents of their self-existence," he explains, "is not at all the same as to assert that they need only themselves in order to effect it."

36 Kaspar Monrad, *The Golden Age of Danish Painting* (New York: Hudson Hills, 1993), 177–8.

37 Börsch-Supan, *Caspar David Friedrich*, 9.

38 Klindt-Jensen, *History of Scandinavian Archaeology*, 46–9.

39 Christine Davenne, *Cabinets of Wonder*, translated by Nicholas Elliot (New York: Abrams, 2012), 16–24.

40 Peter Rowley-Conwy, *From Genesis to Prehistory: The Archaeological Three Age System and Its Contested Reception in Denmark, Britain, and Ireland* (Oxford: Oxford University Press, 2007), 37–9.

41 Jørgen Jensen, *The Prehistory of Denmark* (London: Methuen, 1982), 2.

42 Kristian Kristiansen, "A Short History of Danish Archaeology: An Analytical Perspective," in Kristian Kristiansen, ed., *Archaeological Formation Processes: The Representativity of Archaeological Remains from Danish Prehistory* (Copenhagen: Nationalmuseets Forlag, 1985), 13.

43 C. Stephen Briggs, "C.C. Rafn, J.J.A. Worsaae, Archaeology, History and Danish National Identity in the Schleswig-Holstein Question," *Bulletin of the History of Archaeology* 15, no. 2 (2005): 5.

44 Jørgen Jensen, *Thomsens Museum: Historien om Nationalmuseet* (Copenhagen: Glydendal, 1992), 17–21.

45 Wolfgang Prange, "Die Siegefeier der Kieler Universität 1815: Nachlese zur Dahlmanns Waterloo-Rede," in Wolfgang Prange, Henning Unverhau, Angela Lange, and Carsten Jahnke, *Beiträge zur Schleswig-holsteinischen Geschichte: Ausgewählte Aufsätze* (Neumünster: Wachholtz, 2002), 553–4.

46 Warnstedt to Thomsen, 14 Oct. 1827; quoted in Jensen, *Thomsens Museum*, 119–20.

47 Uwe Jens Lornsen, *Über das Verfassungswerk in Schleswigholstein* (Kiel: Mohr, 1830), 3–4.

48 Thomsen to Hildebrand, 17 Mar. 1831; quoted in Jensen, *Thomsens Museum*, 119.

49 Falck to Thomsen, 28 May 1831, NM 2/4, no. 141.

50 A.J. Michelsen, "Nikolaus Falck," *Deutsche Allgemeine Biographie*, vol. 6 (Leipzig: Duncker & Humboldt, 1877), 539–43.

51 Thaler, *Of Mind and Matter*, 111.

52 Hoffmann, "Nikolaus Falck," 146–9.

53 Kristian Kristiansen, "Dansk arkæologi – fortid og fremtid," *Fortid og Nutid* 26, no. 2 (1975), 279–80.

54 Stewart Oakley, *The Story of Denmark* (London: Faber & Faber, 1972), 157–9; Kristian Kristiansen, "Economic Development in Denmark since Agrarian Reform," in Kristiansen, *Archaeological Formation Processes*, 43–4.

55 Carl von Kindt to the directors of the Schleswig-Holstein Antiquities Society, 13 Apr. 1835, ALM AA 1835/039; reprinted in Dagmar Unverhau, *Das Danewerk 1842: Beschreibung und Aufmass* (Neumünster: Wachholtz, 1988), 105–6.
56 Skovgaard-Petersen, *Danmarks Historie*, vol. 5, 192.
57 Jürgen Brockstedt, *Frühindustrialisierung in Schleswig-Holstein, anderen norddeutschen Ländern und Dänemark* (Neumünster: Wachholtz, 1983), 20–50.
58 Nikolaus Falck, "Schreiben des Herrn Etatsraths Jochims an den Herausgeber über einen dem ersten gehörigen Runenstein," *NSM* 3 (1835): 815.
59 Crane, *Collecting and Historical Consciousness*, 6.
60 Nikolaus Falck, "Ueber die Sammlung nordischer Alterthümer in Kopenhagen," *NSM* 2 (1834): 858.
61 Mouritz Mackeprang, "Oldsagskommissionen i København og Oldsagssamlingen i Kiel: Et stykke Dansk-Tysk museumshistorie," *SJAB* (1932): 94.
62 Carl von Kindt to the directors of the Schleswig-Holstein Antiquities Society, 13 Apr. 1835, in Unverhau, *Danewerk 1842*, 105.
63 Directors of the Royal Commission for the Preservation of Antiquities in Copenhagen to Nikolaus Falck, 20 Sept. 1831, ALM AA 1834/001b.
64 Mackeprang, "Oldsagskommissionen," 95.
65 See Thomsen to Falck, 27 Mar. 1832, ALM AA 1834/002.
66 Christian Paulsen diary entry, 9 Sept. 1820; reprinted in Knud Fabricius and Johannes Lomholt-Thomsen, eds., *Flensborgeren, Christian Paulsens Dagbøger* (Copenhagen: Gyldendal, 1946), 24–5.
67 Unverhau, *Danewerk 1842*, 35–6.
68 Stig Juul, "Christian Detlef Paulsen," in Povl Engelstoft, ed., *Dansk Biografisk Leksikon* (Copenhagen: Schultz, 1940), vol. 27, 51–4.
69 Thaler, *Of Mind and Matter*, 116–17.
70 Jens Peter Ædigus, *Christian Flor: Pædagogen, politikeren, folkeoplyseren* (Odense: Odense Universitetsforlag, 1994), 69–71. Outzen and Wertauff had co-written *Assessments of the Danish Language in the Duchy of Schleswig* (*Priisskrifter angaaende det danske Sprog i Hertugdømmet Slesvig*) in 1819, which sounded a warning call for the future of Danish in the region.
71 "Christian Flor," *Illustreret Tidende* (Apr. 1875): 291–3.
72 Ædigus, *Christian Flor*, 70–1.
73 Paulsen, diary entry, 26 Dec. 1834, in *Flensborgeren*, 211.
74 Ibid.
75 Werner Buchholz, "Andreas Ludwig Jacob Michelsen," *Neue Deutsche Biographie* (Berlin: Duncker und Humboldt, 1993), vol. 17, 453–4; Friedrich Schmidt-Sibeth, "Georg Ludwig Balemann," *Schleswig-Holstein Biographisches Lexikon* (Neumünster: Wachholtz, 1974), vol. 3, 25–8.
76 Kossak, "Zur Geschichte der Urgeschichtsforschung," 56–7.

77 Provisorisch genehmigte Statuten der Schleswig-Holstein-Lauenburgische Gesellschaft für die Sammlung und Erhaltung vaterländische Alterthümer, ALM AA 1834/001.

78 Manfred Jessen-Klingenberg, *Standpunkte zur neueren Geschichte Schleswig-Holsteins*, 48–50.

79 Thomsen to Flor, 17 June 1834, ALM AA 1834/016.

80 Thomsen to Falck, 27 Mar. 1832, ALM AA 1834/002.

81 Ibid.

82 Directors of the Royal Commission for Antiquities to Falck, 27 Mar. 1832, ALM AA 1834/002.

83 Proclomation from Frederik VI, 27 May 1834, ALM AA 1834/001.

84 Vorstand der Gesellschaft für die Sammlung und Erhaltung vaterländischer Alterthümer, "Einladungsschreiben," Protokoll des Vorstandes, ALM KM 3.

85 "Verzeichnis sämtlicher Mitglieder der Gesellschaft bis August 1836," *BGSH* (1836): 64–78.

86 Thomsen to Falck, 16 Nov. 1833, ALM AA 1834/005.

87 Mackeprang, "Oldsagskommissionen," 94.

88 Warnstedt to Falck, 24 Dec. 1833, ALM AA 1834/006.

89 Falck, "Vermischte Nachrichten und Bemerkungen vaterländische Alterthümer betreffend," *NSM* 3 (1835): 555.

90 Directors of the Royal Commission to Falck, 27 Mar. 1832, ALM AA 1834/002.

91 *BGSH* (1837): 32.

92 Henning Ratjen, *Geschichte der Universität zu Kiel* (Kiel: Schwers'schen, 1870), 110.

93 Friedrich von Warnstedt, *Ueber Alterthums-Gegenstände: Eine Ansprache an das Publicum* (Kiel: Mohr, 1835), 4.

94 Ibid.

95 Die Schleswig-Holstein-Lauenburgische Kanzlei to the Schleswig-Holstein Administration at Gottorf, 15 Sept. 1840; reprinted in Unverhau, *Danewerk 1842*, 156.

96 Christian Paulsen and Henning Ratjen to the Royal Government in Schleswig-Holstein, 25 Nov. 1844, ALM AA 1844/043.

97 *BGSH* (1837): 22–3.

98 Warnstedt, *Ueber Alterthums-Gegenstände*, 6–7.

99 Thomsen to Flor, 23 Jan. 1836, ALM AA 1836/009.

100 Thomsen to Flor, 6 May 1834, ALM AA 1834/014; 23 Oct. 1834, ALM AA 1834/021; 21 Oct. 1837, ALM AA 1837/083; 9 Mar. 1838, ALM AA 1838/006; Flor to Thomsen, 19 Nov. 1843 and 17 Apr. 1844, NM 2/4, 141.

101 Kossack, "Urgeschichtsforschung in Schleswig-Holstein," 56.

102 Directors of the Royal Commission to the directors of the Schleswig-Holstein

Antiquities Society, 24 Dec. 1836, ALM AA 1836/030; Steering Committee meeting minutes, undated, ALM AA 1845/unnumbered.

103 "Mittheilungen aus der Correspondenz des Vorstandes," *BGSH* (1836): 7–8.

104 D.F. Eschricht, "Ueber die Schädel und Gerippe in unsern Grabhügeln," *NSM* 6 (1837): 691.

105 Warnstedt, *Ueber Alterthums-Gegenstände*, 7–8.

106 Unverhau, *Danewerk 1842*, 40–3.

107 Hoffmann, "Nikolaus Falck," 150–1.

108 Nikolaus Falck, "Miscellen," *ASHL* 1 (1842): 366–8.

2. National Prehistories in the German-Danish Wars

1 Conrad Engelhardt, "Udgravningerne i Sønderbrarup Mose," *Dagbladet* (17 Aug. 1860), excerpted in ALM AFS/F17–18.

2 Fritz Graef, *Geschichte des Flensburger Museums nordischer Altertümer* (Neumünster: Wachholtz, 1929).

3 Wiell, *Flensborgsamlingen*, 3, 15.

4 Worsaae to his mother, 7 June 1846; reprinted in J.J.A. Worsaae, *En Oldgranskers Erindringer*, edited by Victor Hermansen (Copenhagen: Gyldendalske, 1934), vol. 1, 282–3.

5 Ibid.

6 Worsaae, *Erindringer*, 93.

7 Worsaae, "J.J.A. Worsaae's Erindringer om Frederik VII," in Worsaae, *Af en Oldgranskers Breve*, vol. 2, *1848–1885*, edited by Victor Hermansen (Copenhagen: Gyldendalske, 1938), 14.

8 Briggs, "C.C. Rafn, J.J.A. Worsaae, Archaeology, History and Danish National Identity," 6–7.

9 Worsaae, "Erindringer om Frederik VII," 14.

10 Worsaae, "Undersögelser af Gravhöie i Danmark," *ANO* (1840–41): 137–66.

11 Ibid., 76.

12 Ibid.

13 J.J.A. Worsaae, *Viking Ireland: Jens Worsaae's Accounts of His Visit to Ireland, 1846–47*, edited by David Henry (Balgavies, Angus: Pinkfoot Press, 1995), ix.

14 Briggs, "C.C. Rafn, J.J.A. Worsaae," 9–12.

15 Rowley-Conwy, *From Genesis to Prehistory*, 77.

16 See Flor to Worsaae, 19 Nov. 1843 and 15 May 1844, NM 2/3, no. 81.

17 Worsaae, *Erindringer*, 115.

18 Worsaae, "Den nationale Oldkydighed i Tyskland," ANO (1846): 119–20.

19 Ibid., 118.

20 Worsaae, *Erindringer*, 130.

21 Jost Hermand, *Old Dreams of a New Reich: Volkish Utopias and National Socialism*, translated by Paul Levesque and Stefan Soldovieri (Bloomington: Indiana University Press, 1992), 5–6.

22 Jost Hermand, "Back to the Roots: The Teutonic Revival from Klopstock to the Wars of Liberation," in Reinhold Grimm and Jost Hermand, eds., *From the Greeks to the Greens: Images of the Simple Life* (Madison: University of Wisconsin Press, 1989), 52.

23 Quoted in Jörg Jochen Müller, *Germanistik und deutsche Nation, 1806–1848* (Stuttgart: Metzler, 2000), 143.

24 George S. Williamson, *The Longing for Myth in Germany: Religion and Aesthetic Culture from Romanticism to Nietzsche* (Chicago: University of Chicago Press, 2004), 84–7.

25 Jacob Grimm, *Deutsche Mythologie*, 4th ed. (Götersloh: Bertelsmann, 1876), vol. 1, 10–12.

26 Nyerup to Wilhelm Grimm, 17 Mar. 1810; reprinted in Ernst Schmidt, ed., *Briefwechsel der Gebrüder Grimm mit nordischen Gelehrten* (Berlin: Dümmler, 1885), 7–8.

27 Nyerup to Wilhelm Grimm, 24 July 1816, in ibid., 68.

28 Wilhelm Grimm to Nyerup, 26 Mar. 1810, in ibid., 13.

29 Wilhelm Grimm to Nyerup, 28 Aug. 1818, in ibid., 77.

30 Rafn to Jacob Grimm, 25 June 1828, in ibid., 152.

31 Åke Holmberg, "On the Practicability of Scandinavianism: Mid-nineteenth-Century Debate and Aspirations," *Scandinavian Journal of History* 9, no. 3 (1984): 178.

32 Inger Jensen and Jørgen Steen Jensen, "Det Kongelige Nordiske Oldskriftselskabs breve 1825–1864: Dansk kulturformidling på verdensplan," *Aarbøger for nordisk Oldkyndighed og Historie* (1987): 211–75.

33 Rafn to Jacob Grimm, 1 June 1833, in Schmidt, *Briefwechsel*, 154.

34 Wolfram Siemann, *The German Revolution of 1848–49*, translated by Christiane Banerji (Houndmills: Macmillan, 1998), 66–7.

35 Brandt, *Geschichte Schleswig-Holsteins*, 252–4.

36 Jespersen, *History of Denmark*, 65.

37 Grundtvig in Jensen, *A Grundtvig Anthology*, 100.

38 Grundtvig, "Niels Ebbesen," translated by Charles Wharton Stork, in Jensen, *A Grundvig Anthology*, 193–5.

39 Henneberg Antiquities Association to the Schleswig-Holstein Antiquities Society, undated, ALM AA 1848/042.

40 Brian Vick, *Defining Germany: The 1848 Parliamentarians and National Identity* (Cambridge, MA: Harvard University Press, 2002), 140.

41 Jacob Grimm to Rafn, 15 Dec. 1848, in Schmidt, *Briefwechsel*, 158–61.

42 Klaus von See, *Freiheit und Gemeinschaft: Völkish-nationales Denken in Deutschland zwischen Französischer Revolution und Erstem Weltkrieg* (Heidelberg: Winter, 2001), 46–7.

43 Adriansen, *Nationale symboler*, vol. 2, 39.
44 Rafn to Grimm, 4 Dec. 1848, in Schmidt, *Briefwechsel*, 157.
45 Rafn to Grimm, 13 Feb. 1849, in ibid., 161–7.
46 Grimm to Rafn, 15 Dec. 1848, in ibid., 158–61.
47 Otto Vaupell, *Kampen for Sønderjylland: Krigene 1848–1850 og 1864* (Copenhagen: Reitzel, 1888), 16–20.
48 J.J.A. Worsaae, *Danevirke: Danskhedens gamle Grændsevold mod Syden* (Copenhagen: Reitzel, 1848), 2–3.
49 Ibid., 6.
50 Ibid., 8.
51 J.J.A. Worsaae, *Om en forhistorisk, saakaldet "tydsk" Befolkning i Danmark, med Hensyn til Nutidens politiske Bevægelser* (Copenhagen: Reitzel, 1849), 3.
52 Ibid., 7, 27.
53 P.A. Munch, "Om Indskriften paa det i Sönder-jylland 1734 fundne Guldhorn," *ANO* (1847): 327–52.
54 Munch, "Undersögelser angaaende Danmarks ethnografiske Forhold i det ældste Tider, og om Eensartetheden i Danmarks Befolkning," *ANO* (1848): 216–27.
55 Rowley-Conwy, *From Genesis to Prehistory*, 80.
56 Worsaae, "Jernalderens Begyndelse i Danmark, oplyst gennem Gravfund," *ANO* (1848): 376–89.
57 Worsaae, Om en forhistorisk, saakaldet "tydsk Befolkning," 12.
58 Brandt, *Geschichte Schleswig-Holsteins*, 260–2.
59 Jensen, *Thomsens Museum*, 148.
60 Wilhelm Scherer, *Karl Müllenhoff: Ein Lebensbild* (Heide: Westholsteinische Verlagsanstalt, 1991), 60–1.
61 *BGSH* (1850): 68.
62 Universität Kiel to Karl Müllenhoff, 13 Mar. 1851, ALM AA 1851/057.
63 Heinrich Handelmann, "Die Schleswig-Holstein-Lauenburgische Gesellschaft für die Sammlung und Erhaltung vaterländischer Althertümer in Kiel in den Jahren 1850–1860," *BGSH* (1861): 2–3.
64 Sophie Jaspersen to Conrad Engelhardt, 16 Dec. 1851, ALM AFS/1.
65 L. Clausen to Conrad Engelhardt, 5 May 1854, ALM AFS/11.
66 Wiell, *Flensborgsamlingen*, 32–4.
67 Ibid., 49.
68 Ibid., 54–5.
69 Engelhardt to Worsaae, undated, ALM AFS/10–11. In the letter Engelhardt mentions the recent report from the Schleswig-Holstein Antiquities Society, which was published in 1852. He also misspells the name of the pharmacist Mechlenburg, who later became an important contributor to Flensburg, but not until 1853. It is thus likely that this letter was written in the late summer or autumn of 1852.

70 Ibid.
71 W.H. Kolster to Ludwig Pelt, 17 July 1851, ALM AA 1851/061.
72 See, e.g., Henningsen to Engelhardt, 6 June 1856, ALM AFS/16.
73 Conrad Engelhardt, *Thorsbjerg Mosefund* (Copenhagen: G.E.C. Gad, 1863), 10–11.
74 Piepgras to Engelhardt, 29 Nov. 1855, ALM AFS/14.
75 Wiell, *Flensborgsamlingen*, 89.
76 Engelhardt to Thomsen, 2 June 1858, ALM AFS/F5–F7; Hansen to Engelhardt, ALM AFS/62.
77 Engelhardt to Thomsen, 24 July 1858, ALM AFS/F8–F10.
78 Engelhardt, *Thorsbjerg Mosefund*, 17.
79 Conrad Engelhardt, "Om Sønder-Brarup Funder," *SP* 1 (1860): 169–86.
80 Conrad Engelhardt, *Nydam Mosefund, 1859–1863* (Copenhagen: G.E.C. Gad, 1865), 2–3.
81 Wiell, *Flensborgsamlingen*, 105, 159.
82 Engelhardt, *Nydam Mosefund*, 5–6.
83 Hansen to Engelhardt, 4 July 1858, ALM AFS/62; Engelhardt to the Royal Ministry for the Duchy of Schleswig, 18 Aug. 1861, ALM AFS/108.
84 A. Regenberg to Engelhardt, 24 Mar. 1859, ALM AFS/80.
85 Wiell, *Flensborgsamlingen*, 79, 85.
86 Engelhardt to Thomsen, 10 Jan. 1858, ALM AFS/F1–F2.
87 Brandt, *Geschichte Schleswig-Holsteins*, 265–6.
88 Thaler, *Of Mind and Matter*, 36.
89 Brandt, *Geschichte Schleswig-Holsteins*, 269.
90 Theodor Fontane, *Der Schleswig-Holsteinische Krieg im Jahre 1864* (Berlin: Decker, 1866).
91 David Blackbourn, *History of Germany, 1780–1918: The Long Nineteenth Century*, 2nd ed. (Malden, MA: Blackwell, 2003), 192.
92 Briggs, "C.C. Rafn, J.J.A. Worsaae, Archaeology, History and Danish National Identity," 15–18.
93 Stine Wiell, *Kampen om oldtiden: Nationale oldsager siden 1864* (Aabenraa: Jellings Bogtrykkeri, 2000), 25.
94 Wiell, *Flensborgsamlingen*, 177–80.
95 Engelhardt, *Nydam Mosefund*, 10.
96 Graef, *Geschichte des Flensburger Museums*, 7.
97 Wiell, *Flensborgsamling*, 183–5.
98 "Slesvigske Oldsagsamling," *Berlingske Tidende* (28 Nov. 1864), excerpted in ALM AFS/G15.
99 Editorial, *Berlingske Tidende (*28 Nov. 1864), excerpted in ALM AFS/G15. The writer was responding to Christian Jessen's call for the return of the collection on behalf of the Schleswig-Holstein Antiquities Society.

100 Worsaae to Udenrigsministeriet, 18 June 1865, ALM AFS/G6a.

101 Editorial, *Berlingske Tidende* (9 Aug. 1865), excerpted in ALM AFS/G14.

102 "Museet i Flensborg," *Dagbladet* (29 Aug. 1864), excerpted in ALM AFS/G14.

103 "Friedens Tractat zwischen Oesterreich, Preußen und Dänemark von 30. Oktober 1864," *Reichs-Gesetz-Blatt für das Kaiserthum Oesterreich* 38 (1864): 278–98.

104 Editorial, *Berlingske Tidende* (9 Aug. 1865), excerpted in ALM AFS/G14.

3. Discovery and Rediscovery at Haithabu

1 Celia Applegate, *A Nation of Provincials: The German Idea of Heimat* (Berkeley: University of California Press, 1990).

2 Confino, *Nation as a Local Metaphor*, 149.

3 Verordnungsblatt für das Herzogthum Schleswig 7 (1864), vii.

4 Christian Jessen, quoted in *Berlingske Tidende* (28 Nov. 1864), excerpted in ALM AFS/G15.

5 Graef, *Geschichte des Flensburger Museums*, 9–13.

6 Gustav Freytag, "Das Museum für vaterländische Alterthümer in Kiel," *Die Grenzboten* 27 (1868): 154.

7 Ibid., 159.

8 "Der Wirtschaftsfreund. Schleswig-Holsteinische Schiffsalterthümer," *IN* (14 July 1866), excerpted in ALM AA 1869/140a.

9 This exchange was mentioned in a letter from Johanna Mestorf to Heinrich Handelmann, 24 Nov. 1868, ALM AA 1868/093.

10 Johanna Mestorf to Heinrich Handelmann, 8 Feb. 1867, ALM AA 1867/047.

11 Mestorf to Handelmann, 8 Feb. 1867, ALM AA 1867/047.

12 Ibid.

13 Carl Theodor Scheel-Plessen to Klaus Groth, 15 January 1866, ALM AA 1866/037.

14 Johanna Mestorf, "Nachruf: Gottfried Heinrich Handelmann," ALM BA1904/139.

15 Karl Weinhold, "Bericht des Vorstandes," *BGSH* (1864): vii.

16 Graef, *Geschichte des Flensburger Museums*, 14–15.

17 Heinrich Handelmann, "Bericht des Vorstandes," *BGSH* (1869): 4.

18 Johanna Mestorf, *Führer durch das Schleswig-holsteinische Museum vaterländischer Alterthümer* (Kiel: Schmidt & Klaunig, 1895), 3.

19 Heinrich Handelmann, *Die amtlichen Ausgrabungen auf Sylt: 1870, 1871 und 1873* (Kiel: Mohr, 1873), v.

20 Mestorf, *Führer*, 3.

21 Wilhelm Seelig, "Zum Schutze der vaterländischer Alterthümer," *KZ* (24 Apr. 1882), excerpted in ALM AA 1882/380a.

22 The most notable work on Mestorf to date is Julia K. Koch and Eva-Maria Martens, eds., *Eine Dame zwischen 500 Herren: Johanna Mestorf – Werk und Wirkung* (Münster: Waxmann, 2002).

23 See esp. Kristine von Soden and Gaby Zipfel, eds., *70 Jahre Frauenstudium* (Cologne: Paul Rugenstein, 1979); Patricia Mazon, *Gender and the Modern Research University: The Admission of Women to German Higher Education, 1865–1914* (Stanford: Stanford University Press, 2003). For the history of women in archaeology, see Margarita Diaz-Andreu and Marie Louise Stig Sørensen, eds., *Excavating Women: A History of Women in European Archaeology* (London: Routledge, 1998).

24 Eva-Maria Mertens, "Johanna Mestorf: Lebensdaten," in Koch and Mertens, *Eine Dame zwischen 500 Herren*, 32; Friedrich Knorr, "Johanna Mestorf 1909," *Mittheilungen des anthropologischen Vereins in Schleswig-Holstein* (1911): 3–4.

25 Knorr, "Johanna Mestorf 1909," 4.

26 Mestorf Diary, 19 Nov. 1874.

27 Mestorf to Sven Nilsson, 25 Nov. 1861, ALM Nachlass Mestorf; Mestorf to Worsaae, 9 Sept. 1869, NM 2/3, no. 83.

28 Ann-Sofie Ohlander, "En utmordenlig balansakt: Kvinliga forskarpionjärer i Norden," *Historisk Tidskrift* 1 (1987): 2–22.

29 Ida Blom, "Nation-Class-Gender: Scandinavia at the Turn of the Century," *Scandinavian Journal of History* 21, no. 1 (1996): 8.

30 Mestorf to Nilsson, July 1865, ALM Nachlass Mestorf.

31 Johanna Mestorf, *Der archäologische Congreß in Bologna: Aufzeichnungen* (Hamburg: Meißner, 1871).

32 Mestorf to Handelmann, 8 Feb. 1867, ALM AA 1867/047.

33 Mestorf to Handelmann 24 Nov. 1868, ALM AA 1868/093.

34 Mestorf to Hildebrand, 26 Sept. 1873, ALM Nachlass Mestorf.

35 Mestorf to Hildebrand, 18 Nov. 1873, ALM Nachlass Mestorf.

36 Mestorf Diary, 7 June 1877. She mentions that this description came to her in a letter from Handelmann. The letter itself is not extant.

37 Mestorf Diary 19 Dec. 1873.

38 Mestorf Diary, 8 Dec. 1874.

39 Mestorf to Heinrich Handelmann, 8 Feb. 1867, ALM AA 1867/047.

40 See Heinrich Handelmann, *Schleswig-Holsteinisches Museum vaterländischer Alterthümer* (Kiel: Schwers'sche, 1879).

41 Worsaae had levelled this complaint more generally against the entire German archaeological community. See J.J.A. Worssae, *Om Sønderjyllands Oldtidsminder* (Copenhagen: Gyldendalske, 1865), 6.

42 Kurt Böhner, "Ludwig Lindenschmit and the Three Age System," in Glyn Daniel, ed., *Towards a History of Archaeology: Being the Papers Read at the First Conference*

on the History of Archaeology in Aarhus, 29 Aug. – 2 Sept. 1978 (London: Thames & Hudson, 1981), 120–6.

43 Lindenschmit to Handelmann, 30 Nov. 1874, ALM AA 1874/049.

44 Mestorf Diary, 18 Feb. 1876.

45 Engelhardt to Handelmann, 27 Nov. 1879, ALM AA 1879/130. In this letter, Engelhardt suggested he was either unable or unwilling to provide assistance with certain portions of the former Flensburg Collection.

46 Mestorf to Worsaae, 17 Nov. 1881, ALM Nachlass Mestorf.

47 Mestorf to Worsaae, 28 Aug. 1875, NM Afd. 2, 3/83.

48 Mestorf to Worsaae, 9. Feb. 1876, NM Afd. 2, 3/83.

49 Mestorf to Minister Dr Falk, Ministerium der geistlichen, Unterrichts- und Medicinalangelegenheiten, 3 Aug. 1877, ALM Nachlass Mestorf.

50 Mestorf to Handelmann, 20 Sept. 1867, ALM AA 1867/061.

51 Johanna Mestorf, *Die vaterländischen Alterthümer Schleswig-Holsteins: Ansprache an unsere Landesleute* (Hamburg: Meißner, 1877), 5.

52 Ibid., 3–5.

53 See among others C.H. Fuhlendorf to Mestorf, 20 Jan. 1891, ALM OA Hamburg-Sülldorf 1891/003, Mestorf Diary, 30 Jan. 1891.

54 Handelmann to Königliche Regierung Abteilung für Kirchen- und Schulwesen, 7 Jan. 1882, ALM AA 1882/unnumbered.

55 "Das Dithmarscher Alterthumsmuseum," *KZ* (11 Dec. 1882), excerpted in ALM AA 1882/380d.

56 Mestorf, "Public Address to the Schleswig-Holsteinischer Antropologischer Verein," 20 Dec. 1882, ALM AA 1882/unnumbered; emphasis in original text read on behalf of Mestorf by Adolph Pansch.

57 Mestorf Diary, 16 Nov. 1889.

58 Mestorf, "Public Address." Mestorf was criticizing Ingvald Undset, *Jernalderens Begyndelse i Nord-Europa: En Studie in sammenlignede arkæologi* (Kristiania: Cammermeyer, 1881).

59 Mestorf Diary, 26 May 1877.

60 Ibid., 3 and 6 July, 1877.

61 Handelmann to Oberpräsident und Universitäts-Kurator, 9 June 1875, ALM AA 1876/203a.

62 Mestorf Diary, 17 June 1877.

63 Ibid., 16 Aug. 1877.

64 Ibid., 1 May 1878.

65 See, e.g., Handelmann to Mestorf, 4 July 1881, ALM AA 1881/274.

66 Mestorf Diary, 3 June 1891.

67 Mestorf to Worsaae, 17 Nov. 1881, ALM Nachlass Mestorf.

68 Johanna Mestorf Diary, 27 Apr. – 1 May, 1875.

69 Klindt-Jensen, *History of Scandinavian Archaeology*, 86.

70 Stine Wiell, "Johanna Mestorf und einige dänische Archäologen ihres Zeitalters," in Koch and Mertens, *Eine Dame zwischen 500 Herren*, 152.

71 Sophus Müller, *Die nordische Bronzezeit und deren Periodentheilung*, translated by Johanna Mestorf (Jena: Hermann Costenoble, 1878), 312–16.

72 Ibid. On Worsaae's view, see *Sønderjyllands Oldtidsminder*, 25–8.

73 Sophus Müller, *Nordische Altertumskunde nach Funde und Denkmäler aus Dänemark und Schleswig Gemeinfasslich dargestellt von Dr Sophus Müller*, translated by Otto Jiriczek (Strassburg: Trübner, 1897), vol. 1, vi–vii.

74 See Stine Wiell, "The Story of the Nydam II Find," in Anna-Carin Andersson et al., eds., *"The Kaleidoscopic Past": Proceedings of the 5th Nordic TAG Conference Göteborg, 2–5 Apr. 1997* (Göteborg: Göteborg University, Department of Archaeology, 1998), 333–46.

75 Povl Bagge, "Nationalismus und Antinationalismus in Dänemark um 1900," *Geschichte in Wissenschaft und Unterricht* 15, no. 5 (1964): 291–303.

76 Heinrich Handelmann, *38. Bericht zur Alterthumskunde Schleswig-Holsteins: Zum 50 jährigen Gedächtniss der Eröffnung des Schleswig-Holsteinischen Museums vaterländischer Alterthümer zu Kiel* (Kiel: Mohr, 1882).

77 L. Pedersen to Wilhelm Splieth, 8 Feb. 1891, ALM OA Haithabu/Danewerk 1891/9a. Pedersen also sent the Museum a section of the wall with intact artifacts. See Mestorf Diary, 7 Mar. 1891.

78 Mestorf Diary, 9 Apr. 1888.

79 Wilhelm Splieth, Report on the Danevirke delivered to the General Meeting of the German Anthropology Society in Lübeck, Apr. 1897, SHLA Abt. 309/21070; reprinted in Dagmar Unverhau, "Möchte nun unser Hedeby vor unsern Blicken erstehen," in Klaus Brandt and Michael Müller-Wille, eds., *Haithabu und die frühe Stadtentwicklung im nördlichen Europa* (Neumünster: Wachholtz, 2002), 37–8.

80 Ibid. See also Regierungspräsident to Schleswig-Holstein Museum, 24 Feb. 1898, ALM OA Haithabu 1898/33a.

81 Mestorf to the Oberpräsident in Schleswig, Staatsminister von Köller, 25 Feb. 1898, ALM OA Haithabu 1898/33a. The "*Limes*" Mestorf mentioned were the *Limes Germanicus*, which were fortifications marking the boundaries of the Roman Empire in Central Europe.

82 See, e.g., Müller to Splieth, 5 Nov. 1900, ALM OA Haithabu, 1900/136.

83 Müller, *Nordische Altertumskunde*, vol. 2, 234–8.

84 The Arab trader al-Tartûshi reportedly visited the town in 965 CE; reported in Hildegard Elsner, *Haithabu: Schaufenster einer frühen Stadt* (Schleswig: Archäologisches Landesmuseum, 1989).

85 *Annales regni Francorum, inde ab a. 741. usque ad. a 829* (Hannover: Impensis bibliopoli Hahniani, 1895).

86 Heinrich Handelmann and Wilhelm Splieth, *Neue Mittheilungen von den Runesteinen bei Schleswig* (Kiel: Paul Toeche, 1889), 10.
87 See Friedrich Knorr, "Schleswig und Haithabu," *Schleswig-Holsteinisches Heimatbuch* (1924): 24–31.
88 "Zur Sicherung der Oldenburg," *SN*, 18 Feb. 1901, excerpted in ALM OA Haithabu, 1901/unnumbered.
89 Mestorf to Müller, 1 Jan. 1901, NM 2 KA, unnumbered.
90 Mestorf to Müller, 27 June 1900 and 1 June 1901, NM Afd. 2, KA 319/00 and 285/01.
91 Mestorf to Müller, 6 and 18 June 1901, NM Afd. 2, KA 323/01.
92 Mestorf to the Oberpräsidium in Schleswig, 16 Feb. 1903, ALM Nachlass Mestorf, unnumbered.
93 Volker Hilberg, personal communication, 4 Feb. 2004. Hilberg is one of the current directors of the Haithabu project at the Schleswig-Holstein Archäologisches Landesmuseum in Schleswig, Germany.
94 "Nachrichten," *KZ*, 18 Sept. 1903, excerpted in ALM OA Haithabu, 1903/unnumbered.
95 Christian Jensen, in ALM OA Haithabu, 1908/194.
96 Eilean Hooper-Greenhill, *Museums and the Shaping of Knowledge* (London: Routledge, 1992), 167–89.

4. Nationalism, Science, and the Search for Origins

1 Mitglieder-Verzeichniss der deutschen anthropologischen Gesellschaft zu Kiel, 14 Aug. 1878, ALM AA 1878/unnumbered.
2 Statuten der Deutsche anthropologische Gesellschaft, in ALM AA 1878/025.
3 Heinrich Handelmann, Announcement of the Ninth General Convention of the German Society for Anthropology, Ethnology, and Prehistory in Kiel, Nov. 1877, ALM AA 1877/unnumbered.
4 Richard Holmes, *The Age of Wonder: How the Romantic Generation Discovered the Beauty and Terror of Science* (New York: Vintage, 2010), xvi.
5 Woodruff D. Smith, *Politics and the Sciences of Culture in Germany, 1840–1920* (New York: Oxford University Press, 1991), 234–40.
6 Konrad Jarausch, *Students, Society, and Politics in Imperial Germany: The Rise of Academic Illiberalism* (Princeton: Princeton University Press, 1982), 49–72.
7 Alfred Kelly, *The Descent of Darwin: The Popularization of Darwinism in Germany, 1860–1914* (Chapel Hill: North Carolina University Press, 1981), 106–7; Richard Weikart, "The Origins of Social Darwinism in Germany, 1859–1895," *Journal of the History of Ideas* 54, no. 3 (1993): 469–88.

8 Andrew Zimmerman, *Anthropology and Antihumanism in Imperial Germany* (Chicago: University of Chicago Press, 2001).

9 Dr Freese to Handelmann, 4 June 1871, ALM OA Rendswühren 1871/181A; reprinted in Michael Gebühr, *Moorleichen in Schleswig-Holstein* (Neumünster: Wachholtz, 2002), 22.

10 Handelmann, Forensic Certificate, 6 June 1871, ALM OA Rendswühren 1871/181L; reprinted in Gebühr, *Moorleichen*, 23. This incident was also described in *BGSH* (1872): 8–9.

11 Heinrich Handelmann and Adolf Pansch, *Moorleichenfunde in Schleswig-Holstein* (Kiel: Schwer'sche, 1873), 35.

12 Johanna Mestorf, "Moorleichen," *Die Heimat* (Aug. 1900): 166–8.

13 Handelmann and Pansch, *Moorleichenfunde*, 6–11.

14 Heinrich Handelmann, "Der Leichenfund in Rendswührener Moor (Kreis Kiel)," *BGSH* (1872): 74–83. Handelmann mentions ten prominent bog body finds up to that point, including one in Ireland and nine in the duchies and Denmark.

15 Karin Sanders, *Bodies in the Bog: The Archaeological Imagination* (Chicago: University of Chicago Press, 2009), 92–3.

16 P.V. Glob, *The Bog People: Iron Age Man Preserved*, translated by Rupert Bruce-Mitford (Ithaca: Cornell University Press, 1969), 68–82.

17 Handelmann and Pansch, *Moorleichenfunde*, 8.

18 Mestorf to F. Wibel, undated, ALM MuG 5b.

19 Karel Sklenar, *Archaeology in Central Europe: The First 500 Years*, translated by Iris Lewitova (New York: Leicester University Press, 1983), 102–4.

20 Bruce Trigger, *A History of Archaeological Thought* (Cambridge: Cambridge University Press, 1989), 87–98.

21 Klindt-Jensen, *History of Scandinavian Archaeology*, 82–3.

22 See Undset, *Jernalderens begyndelse.*

23 Johanna Mestorf, *Urnenfriedhöfe in Schleswig-Holstein* (Hamburg: Meissner, 1886).

24 Gustav Schwantes, "Rückblick auf Johanna Mestorf aus dem Jahren 1940"; reprinted in Dagmar Unverhau, *"Hochachtungsvoll Ihrer Autorität ergebenster Gustav Schwantes": Der Briefwechsel zwischen Gustav Schwantes und Johanna Mestorf 1899 bis 1909 und seine Verwendung im Prioritätsstreit mit Friedrich Knorr* (Neumünster: Wachholtz, 2000), 176–8.

25 Müller, *Nordische Altertumskunde*, vol. 1, 115.

26 Ibid., 314.

27 Klindt-Jensen, *History of Scandinavian Archaeology*, 88–94.

28 Rudolf Virchow, "Die altnordischen Schädel zu Kopenhagen," *Archiv für Anthropologie* 4 (1871): 55.

29 Handelmann and Pansch's report, *Moorleichenfunde*, was divided into two sections

detailing both the archaeological and anthropological analyses of regional bog bodies.

30 Edith Feiner, "Adolf Pansch," in *Neue Deutsche Biographie*, edited by Olaf Klose and Eva Rudolph (Neumünster: Wachholtz, 1976), vol. 4, 180–2.

31 K. Koldewey, *Die erste Deutsche Nordpolar-Expedition im Jahre 1868* (Gotha: Justus Perthes, 1871).

32 H. Glenn Penny and Matti Bunzl, "Introduction," in H. Glenn Penny and Matti Bunzl, eds., *Worldly Provincialism: German Anthropology in the Age of Empire* (Ann Arbor: University of Michigan Press, 2003), 14–15.

33 Adolf Pansch, "Der anthropologische Verein in Schleswig-Holstein." *FNN*, 28 Feb. 1878, excerpted in ALM AA 1878/020.

34 Schleswig-Holstein Oberpräsident Carl Theodor Scheel-Plessen to Handelmann, 17 Apr. 1877, ALM AA 1877/unnumbered.

35 Zimmerman, *Anthropology and Antihumanism*, 48–54.

36 Pansch, "Der anthropologische Verein."

37 Mestorf to Wibel, undated; Hermann Schaafhausen to Johanna Mestorf, 11 Apr. 1871, ALM MuG 5b.

38 Benoit Massin, "From Virchow to Fischer: Physical Anthropology and 'Modern Race Theories' in Wilhelmine Germany," in George W. Stocking, Jr., ed., Volksgeist *as Method and Ethic: Essays on Boasian Ethnography and the German Anthropological Tradition* (Madison: University of Wisconsin Press 1996), 79–154, 86–7.

39 Johanna Mestorf, "Der anthropologische Verein," *LN* (20 Dec. 1877), excerpted in ALM AA 1878/022.

40 Mestorf to Gustav Schwantes, 15 Dec. 1906, ALM Nachlass Schwantes; reprinted in Unverhau, "*Hochachtungsvoll Ihrer Autorität*," 91.

41 George Mosse, *The Crisis of German Ideology: The Intellectual Origins of the Third Reich* (New York: Fertig, 1998), 15.

42 Hermand, *Old Dreams of a New Reich*, 47–64.

43 Vagn Dybahl, *Danmarks Historie*, edited by John Danstrup and Hal Koch (Copenhagen: Politikens Forlag, 1965), vol. 12, 51.

44 Adriansen, *National symboler*, vol. 2, 109. The Valkyrie statue now rests in Churchill Park in Copenhagen.

45 Manfred Jessen-Klingenberg, *Standpunkte zur neueren Geschichte Schleswig-Holsteins*, 129.

46 Dybahl, *Danmarks Historie*, vol. 12, 257–66.

47 Carl S. Petersen, "Peter Lauridsen," in Povl Engestoft, ed., *Dansk Biografisk Leksikon* (Copenhagen: J.H. Schultz, 1938), vol. 14, 153–4.

48 Mestorf to the Oberpräsident in Schleswig, Staatsminister von Köller, 25 Feb. 1898, ALM OA Haithabu 1898/033a.

49 Ludwig Andresen,"Die goldenen Hörner von Gallehus," *Die Heimat* (Sept. 1906): 221–3.

50 Ludwig Andresen, "Die Fundstelle der goldenen Hörner von Gallehus," *Die Heimat* (May 1911): 115–18.

51 Konrad H. Jarausch and Michael Geyer, *Shattered Past: Reconstructing German Histories* (Princeton: Princeton University Press, 2003), 40–2.

52 Andreas Dörner, "Der Mythos der nationalen Einheit: Symbolpolitik und Deutungskämpfe bei der Einweihung der Herrmannsdenkmal im Jahre 1875," *Archiv für Kulturgeschichte* 79, no. 2 (1997): 396–402.

53 Hermand, *Old Dreams of a New Reich*, 26–30.

54 Williamson, *Longing for Myth*, 250–9.

55 Stewart Spencer, "The 'Romantic Operas' and the Turn to Myth," in Thomas S. Grey, ed., *The Cambridge Companion to Wagner* (Cambridge: Cambridge University Press, 2008), 72.

56 Hannu Salmi, *Imagined Germany: Richard Wagner's National Utopia* (New York: Peter Lang, 1999), 32.

57 Friedrich Nietzsche, *Beyond Good and Evil: A Prelude to a Philosophy of the Future*, translated by Walter Kaufmann (New York: Vintage, 1966), 197.

58 Karl Müllenhoff, *Deutsche Altertumskunde*, 5 vols. (Berlin: Weidmannsche Buchhandlung, 1883). Müllenhoff especially argued against the writings of the Nrowegian philologist Christian Bang, who had traced similarities between the motifs in the Eddas and established Greek and Roman mythology.

59 According to Alexander Häusler, the designation for the original bearers of the European parent language was the subject of controversy. In 1823, the German philologist Julius von Klaproth (1783–1835) used the term "Indogerman," while his colleagues in England were already using the term "Indoeuropean." The two words nevertheless referred to the same group. See Alexander Häusler, "Zum Ursprung der Indogermanen: Archäologische, anthropologische und sprachwissenschaftlicher Gesichtspunkte," *Ethnographisch-archäologische Zeitschrift* 39 (1998): 3. More recently, Robert Cowan has traced the term "Indogerman" back to the writings of Conrad Malte-Brunn in 1810. See Robert Cowan, *The Indo-German Identification: Reconciling South Asian Origins and European Destinies* (Rochester: Camden House, 2010), 3.

60 Heinz Grünert, *Gustaf Kossinna (1858–1931): Vom Germanisten zum Prähistoriker; Ein Wissenschaftler im Kaiserreich und in der Weimarer Republik* (Rahden: Marie Leidorf, 2002), 47–9. Gustaf Kossinna openly admitted his debt to Müllenhoff in *Die Herkunft der Germanen: Zur Methode der Siedlungsarchäologie*, 2nd ed. (Leipzig: Kabitzsch, 1920), 1.

61 Gustaf Kossinna, *Die deutsche Vorgeschichte: Eine hervorragend nationale Wissenschaft* (Leipzig: Kabitzsch, 1911), 237.

62 Kossinna, Museum Diary, Kiel, Sept. 1900, HU Nachlass Kossinna A-VII-1, 1.

63 Müllenhoff, *Deutsche Altertumskunde*, vol. 4, x–xi; Kossinna, *Die Herkunft der Germanen*, 18–19.

64 Marchand, *Down from Olympus*, 182–3.

65 Gustaf Kossinna, *Ursprung und Verbreitung der Germanen in Vor- und Frühgeschichtlicher Zeit* (Leipzig: Kabitzsch, 1928), 2.

66 Grünert, *Kossinna*, 57–8.

67 Kossinna, *Die Herkunft der Germanen*, 18–19.

68 Kossinna, Museum Diary, 1900–1901, HU Nachlass Kossinna A-VIII-1, 3, 5.

69 Müllenhoff, *Deutsche Altertumskunde*, vol. 5, 1.

70 Bernard Mees, "Völkische Altnordistik: The Politics of Nordic Studies in German-Speaking Countries, 1926–1945," in Geraldine Barnes and Margaret Clunies Ross, eds., *Old Norse Myths, Literature, and Society: Proceedings of the 11th International Saga Conference*, University of Sydney, 2–7 July 2000 (Sydney: Centre for Medieval Studies, University of Sydney, 2000), 319.

71 Gustaf Kossinna, "Die indogermanisch Frage archäologisch beantwortet," *Zeitschrift für Ethnologie* 34 (1902): 161–2.

72 Kossinna, *Herkunft der Germanen*, 3–4.

73 Ibid., 28–9.

74 Kossinna, *Ursprung*, 180–2.

75 Kossinna, *Deutsche Vorgeschichte*, 108–22.

76 Kossinna was specifically attacking two of Montelius' key works: *Brooches from the Bronze Age* (1880) and *On the Dating of the Bronze Age, Particularly in Relation to Scandinavia* (1885).

77 Marchand, *Down from Olympus*, 184–5.

78 Massin, "Virchow to Fischer," 115–17.

79 Kaethe Riecken to Friedrich Knorr, 17 July 1909, ALM AA 1909/unnumbered.

80 Müller to Kossinna, 9 Feb. 1903, HU Nachlass Kossinna, reprinted in Hildegard Gräfin Schwerin von Krosigk, *Gustaf Kossinna: Der Nachlaß; Versuch einer Analyse* (Neumünster: Wachholtz, 1982), 176.

81 Kristiansen, "Dansk arkaeologi," 292.

82 See, e.g., Montelius to Kossinna, 1 May 1900, HU Nachlass Kossinna; reprinted in von Krosigk, *Gustaf Kossinna,* 170–1.

83 Otto von Friesen, "Emigration from Sweden in Ancient Times," in H. Lundborg and J. Runnstrom, eds., *The Swedish Nation in Word and Picture* (Stockholm: Tullberg, 1921), 13.

84 Montelius, "The Immigration of Our Forefathers to the North," in ibid., 11.

85 Heinz Grünert, "Von Pergamon bis Garz: Carl Schuchhardt – Begründer der prähistorischen Burgenarchäologie in Mitteleuropa," *Das Altertum* 33, no. 2 (1987): 104–5; Ulrich Veit, "Gustaf Kossinna and His Concept of National

Archaeology," in Heinrich Härke, ed., *Archaeology, Ideology, and Society: The German Experience* (New York: Peter Lang, 2000), 51.

86 Carl Schuchhardt, *Alteuropa: Eine Vorgeschichte unseres Erdteils*, 2nd ed. (Berlin: de Gruyter, 1926), 284.

87 Protokoll der Konferenz von Vertretern vorgeschichtlichen Museen Berlin, 9 June 1906, ALM AA 1906/117b.

88 Georg Thilenius to the Schleswig-Holstein anthropologischer Verein, 1 Mar. 1909, ALM AA 1909/unnumbered; Thilenius had been director of the Hamburg Museum since 1904.

89 Schuchhardt to Kossinna, 28 Nov. 1908; reprinted in von Krosigk, *Gustaf Kossinna*, 189.

90 Hermann Schneider, "Rassereinheit und Kultur," *Mannus* 1 (1909): 247.

91 Gustaf Kossinna, "Zum Dreiperiodensystem," *Mannus* 2 (1910): 309–12.

92 Michael Gebühr, "Gustav Schwantes und die Ethnogenese der Germanen," paper presented at "'Eine hervorragend nationale Wissenschaft': Arbeitsgespräch im Rahmen des Sonderforschungsbereichs 541," Freiburg, 2–3 July 1999, 37.

93 Gustav Schwantes, *Frühe Jahre eines Urgeschichtsforschers (1881–1914)* (Kiel: Wachholtz, 1983), 89–95.

94 See Gustav Schwantes, "Der Urnenfriedhof bei Jastorf im Kreise Uelzen," *Jahrbuch für das Provinzialmuseum Hannover* (1904): 13–26.

95 Schwantes to Mestorf, 4 Dec. 1907, ALM AA 1907/216; reprinted in Unverhau, "*Hochachtungsvoll Ihrer Autorität*," 95–6.

96 Mestorf to Schwantes, 7 Dec. 1907, ALM Nachlass Schwantes; reprinted in Unverhau, "*Hochachtungsvoll Ihrer Autorität*," 98.

97 Allan A. Lund, *Germanenideologie im Nationalsozialismus: Zur Rezeption der 'Germania' des Tacitus im Dritten Reich* (Heidelberg: Winter, 1995), 79; Wiebke Künnemann, "Jastorf, Geschichte und Inhalt eines archäologischen Kulturbegriffs," *Die Kunde* NF 46 (1995): 71.

98 Gustav Schwantes, *Aus Deutschlands Urgeschichte*, 2nd ed. (Leipzig: Quelle & Meyer, 1913), 104–7.

99 Gebühr, "Gustav Schwantes," 5, 19. The first citation Schwantes gives to Kossinna was in the 6th ed. of *Aus Deutschlands Urgeschichte* in 1935, and even here he misspells the title of Kossinna's work, *Die deutsche Vorgeschichte.*

100 Gustav Schwantes, "Die Germanen," *Volk und Rasse: Vierteljahrsschrift für Deutsches Volkstum* 1 (1926): 73.

101 John Lewis Gaddis, *The Landscape of History: How Historians Map the Past* (Oxford: Oxford University Press, 2002), 38; emphasis in original.

102 Zimmerman, *Anthropology and Antihumanism*, 214.

103 Ibid, 86.

5. Prehistory and the Popular Imagination

1 Mestorf to Müller, 9 Mar. 1909, NM 1 200/09.
2 "Professor Johanna Mestorf," *Berlingske Tidende* (19 Apr. 1909), excerpted in NM Afd. 1, KA 203/09.
3 Knorr, "Johanna Mestorf 1909," 3.
4 Funeral Announcement for Wilhelm Splieth, 10 Feb. 1901, ALM BioA.
5 Mestorf to Georg Sarauw, 8 Mar. 1901, ALM AA 1901/030b.
6 Mestorf to Schwantes, 20 Feb. 1901; Schwantes to Mestorf, 23 Feb. and 6 Mar. 1901, SHLB Nachlass Schwantes.
7 Sarauw to Mestorf, 13 and 20 Mar. 1901, ALM AA 1901/030c and 030e.
8 Mestorf to Sarauw, 8 Mar. 1901, ALM AA 1901/030b.
9 Unverhau, "Möchte nun unser Hedeby," 34.
10 Müller to Mestorf, 13 Mar. 1902, ALM Nachlass Mestorf 1902/23b; Mestorf to Montelius, 25 Mar. 1901; quoted in Unverhau, "Möchte nun unser Hedeby," 35. The references are to Gustaf Kossinna; Paul Reinecke (1842–1958), Chief Conservator of the Bavarian State Office for the Preservation of Ancient Monuments; and Karl Schumacher (1860–1934), a classical archaeologist known for his work on the *Limes Germanicus* fortifications.
11 Friedrich Knorr, *Friedhöfe der älteren Eisenzeit in Schleswig-Holstein* (Kiel: Lipsius & Fischer, 1910), 5–7.
12 Schwantes, "Rückblick auf Johanna Mestorf aus dem Jahre 1940"; reprinted in Unverhau, "*Hochachtungsvoll Ihrer Autorität,*" 176.
13 Joachim Stark, *Haithabu-Schleswig-Danewerk: Aspekte einer Forschungsgeschichte mittelalterlicher Anlagen in Schleswig-Holstein* (Oxford: B.A.R., 1988), 16–17, 69. In this type of burial, the bodies were interred in an underground chamber with the boat placed on top as grave goods.
14 Friedrich Knorr, "Bericht über Sicherung und Ausgrabung des Museums vaterländischer Altertümer an der Oldenburg und Danewerk," unpublished report, 20 Feb. 1926, ALM Nachlass Heinrich Philippsen.
15 Ulrich Lange, *Geschichte Schleswig-Holsteins: Von den Anfängen bis zur Gegenwart*, 2nd ed. (Neumünster: Wachholtz, 2003), 514.
16 "Das Museum vaterländischer Altertümer in Kiel," newspaper clipping labelled as "*Sonntagsbeilage der Kieler Zeitung* 1921," (excerpted in ALM MuG 15.
17 Müller to Knorr, 2 Nov. 1914, NM Afd. 2 735/14.
18 Knorr to Müller, 20 Nov. 1914, ALM OA Haithabu-Danewerk 1914/unnumbered.
19 Knorr to Müller, 14 Dec. 1915, NM Afd. 2 115/15.
20 Terry Hunt Tooley, "Fighting without Arms: The Defense of German Interests in Schleswig, East and West Prussia, and Upper Silesia, 1918–1921," PhD dissertation, University of Virginia, 1986, 15.

21 Mogens Scott Hansen, *Sikringstilling Nord: En tysk befæstningslinie i Sønderjylland* (Hørsholm: Miljøministeriet, Skov- og Naturstylrelsen, 1992).
22 See Inge Adriansen, *Første verdenskrig i mikroperspektive: Maria Gørrigsens åbenbaringer* (Sønderborg: Historisk Samfund for Als og Sundeved, 2003).
23 "Historical Odyssey behind Golden Horns," *Copenhagen Post* (24 Aug. 2004).
24 Inge Adriansen, "Danish and German National Symbols," *Ethnologia Scandinavica: A Journal for Nordic Ethnology* 21 (1991): 36–8.
25 Peter Lauridsen, "Om de gamle danske Landsbyformer," *AOH* (1896): 97–110.
26 H.V. Clausen, "Studier over Danmarks Oldtidsbebyggelse," *AOH* (1916): 1–226.
27 Sophus Müller, "Sønderjyllands Bronzealder," *AOH* (1914): 245–6.
28 Vejas Gabriel Liulevicius, *The German Myth of the East: 1800 to the Present* (Oxford: Oxford University Press, 2009), 90–1.
29 Markus Krzoska, *Für ein Polen on Oder und Ostsee: Zygmunt Wojciechowski (1900–1955) als Historiker und Publizist* (Osnabrück: Fibre, 2003), 27–33, 65–70.
30 Gustaf Kossinna, *Das Weichselland: Ein uralter Heimatboden der Germanen*, 3rd ed. (Leipzig: Kabitzsch, 1940), 2–14.
31 Jespersen, *History of Denmark*, 27.
32 H.V. Clausen, *Nordslesvig, 1863–1893: Den nationale stilling på landet* (Flensburg: Möller & Rasmussen, 1894).
33 Henrik Becker-Christensen, "Den nye Grænse," in Henrik Becker-Christensen, ed., *Grænsen i 75 Aar, 1920–1995* (Åbenrå: Institut for Grænseregionsforskning, 1995), 36.
34 Hans Lund, "Ernst Christiansen," *Dansk Biografi* (Copenhagen: Schultz Forlag, 1934), vol. 5, 206–7. On the Danevirke Movement, see Axel Johnson, *Danevirkemænd og Ejderfolk: Den grænsepolitiske opposition i Danmark, 1920–1940* (Flensburg: Studieafdelingen ved Dansk Centralbibliothek for Sydslesvig, 2005).
35 Inge Adriansen and Immo Doege, *Deutsch oder Dänisch?: Bilder zum nationalen Selbstverständnis aus dem Jahre 1920* (Flensburg: Gesellschaft für Flensburger Stadtgeschichte, 1992), 12–15.
36 Christian Voigt, "Die alte dänische Stadt Flensburg!" *Flensburger Tageblatt* (29 Jan. 1920), 1.
37 Johannes Neuhaus, *Die Frage von Nordschleswig im Lichte der neuesten vorgeschichtlichen Untersuchungen* (Jena: Diederichs, 1919), 8.
38 Ibid., 36.
39 "Die 'Wieder'vereinigung," *KZ* (14 July, 1920): 1.
40 "Die Uebernahme der ersten Zone," *KNN* (14 July, 1920): 1.
41 Mouritz Mackeprang, *Nord-Schleswig von 1864–1911* (Jena: Diederichs, 1912), 1.
42 "Die Verteidigung des Nydamer Bootes," ALM OA Nydam 60. The archive retains a copy of the reports from the German delegation prepared on 27 Nov. 1966. The reports are unsigned and undated, but were certainly prepared after

1924, which is the date mentioned for the transfer of the Nydam Boat to its new facility in Kiel.

43 Ibid.

44 Wiell, *Flensborgsamlingen*, 230–2.

45 Ibid., 228. The report in the ALM archive does not mention Knorr's involvement.

46 Jespersen, *History of Denmark*, 80–2, 118–20.

47 Poul Nørlund, "Nationalmuseet i de Onde Aar," *Nationalmuseets Arbejdsmark* (1946): 6–7.

48 Andrew Evans, *Anthropology at War: World War I and the Science of Race in Germany* (Chicago: University of Chicago Press, 2010), 190–1.

49 Mees, "Völkische Altnordistik," 319–21; Jürg Glauser and Julia Zernack, eds., *Germanentum im* Fin de Siècle*: Wissenschaftsgeschichtliche Studien zum Werk Andreas Heusler* (Basel: Schwabe, 2005); Hans F.K. Günther, *Rassenkunde des deutschen Volkes* (Munich: Lehmann, 1922).

50 Kossinna, *Ursprung*, 58–68.

51 Ibid., 84–5.

52 Karl Theodor Strasser, *Wikinger und Normannen* (Hamburg: Hanseatische Verlagsanstalt, 1928), 9–14.

53 Bernhard Kummer, *Der nordische Mensch der Wikingerzeit* (Leipzig: A. Klein, 1937), 11–17.

54 Gustaf Kossinna, *Wikinger und Wäringer* (Bonn: Mannus, 1930), 39–41.

55 Strasser, *Wikinger und Normannen*, 74–6.

56 Kummer, *Nordische Mensch*, 6.

57 Hans-Jürgen Lützhoft, *Der nordische Gedanke in Deutschland, 1920–1940* (Stuttgart: Klett, 1971), 55.

58 Ludwig Ferdinand Clauß, *Die nordische Seele: Artung, Prägung, Ausdruck* (Halle: Niemeyer, 1923).

59 Geoffrey G. Field, "Nordic Racism," *Journal of the History of Ideas* 38, no. 3 (1977): 532.

60 Celia Applegate, "Localism and the German Bourgeoisie: The 'Heimat' Movement in the Rhenish Palatinate before 1914," in David Blackbourn and Richard J. Evans, eds., *The German Bourgeoisie: Essays on the Social History of the German Middle Class from the Late Eighteenth to the Early Twentieth Century* (London: Routledge, 1991), 225–6.

61 Willi Oberkrome, "Entwicklungen und Varianten der deutschen Volksgeschichte, 1900–1960," in Manfred Hettling, ed., *Volksgeschichten im Europa der Zwischenkriegszeit* (Göttingen: Vandenhoeck & Ruprecht, 2003), 73–5; Andrea-Katharina Hanke, *Die niedersächsische Heimatbewegung im ideologisch-politischen Kräftespiel zwischen 1920 und 1945* (Hannover: Hahnsche, 2004), 99.

62 Helgo Klatt, "Heinrich Philippsen," in *Schleswig-Holstein Biographisches Lexikon* (Neumünster: Wachholtz, 1970), vol. 1, 222–3.

63 See ALM OA Untersum/Föhr 1893/71, 1899/90b and 1901/18.

64 Heinrich Philippsen, *Die Vorgeschichte von Flensburg und Umgegend: Funde aus der Stein-, Bronze- und Eisenzeit von Flensburg und der weiteren Umgebung, besonders Angeln* (Flensburg: Flensburger Nachrichten, 1924), 48–9.

65 Max Kirmis, *Die Urgeschichte von Neumünster: Ein Beitrag zur Kulturgeschichte Holsteins* (Neumünster: Dittmann, 1921).

66 Emil Bruhn, *Zur Heimatgeschichte Eiderstedts: Heft 1, Aus der Urgeschichte; Zur Geschichte der Besiedlung und der Bevölkerung* (Garding: Lühr & Dircks, 1926), 4.

67 "Erweiterung des Museums vaterländischer Altertümer," *KZ* (22 Sept. 1923), excerpted in ALM MuG 15.

68 Rothmann to Knorr, 2 May 1928, ALM MuG 19. Knorr was forced to resign due to complications from an "incurable, excruciating" illness, which was reported in "Friedrich-Knorr-Ausstellung im Eutiner Kreisheimatmuseum," *Ostholstein Anzeiger* (18 Nov. 1972), excerpted in ALM MuG 72.

69 Philippsen, "Forderungen des Verbandes Schleswig-Holsteinischer Geschichtslehrer zur Förderung der Danewerkforschung," unpublished manuscript, 20 Feb. 1926, ALM Nachlass Heinrich Philippsen.

70 "Wiederaufnahme der Dannewerkforschung," *SN* (22 Feb. 1926), 2–3.

71 "Vor 2000 Jahren," *Schleswig-Holsteinische Volkszeitung* (9 Sept. 1927); "Die Neugestaltung des Museums vaterländischer Altertümer: Ein Rundgang," *KNN* (23 Nov. 1926); "Das Museum Vaterländischer Altertümer in Kiel," *Eutiner Zeitung* (29 June 1927), excerpted in ALM MuG 18.

72 Carl Rothmann, "Schleswig-Holsteinishes Museum vaterländischer Altertümer," *Schleswig-Holsteinische Schulzeitung* (18 Dec. 1926), excerpted in ALM MuG 18.

73 Rothmann to Knorr, 2 May 1928, ALM MuG 19.

74 Wilhelm Unverzagt to Rothmann, 17 Feb. 1928, ALM MuG 19.

75 Unverzagt, "*Hochachtungsvoll Ihrer Autorität*," 141–56.

76 Rothmann to Unverzagt, 20 Feb. 1928, ALM MuG 19.

77 Schwantes to Rothmann, 28 Mar. 1929, ALM MuG 19.

78 Eric Kurlander, "National Liberal, Nordic Prophet," in Ingo Haar and Michael Fahlbusch, eds., *German Scholars and Ethnic Cleansing, 1919–1945* (New York: Berghahn, 2004), 204.

79 Schwantes to Mackeprang, 2 Aug. 1930, ALM OA Haithabu-Danewerk.

80 Otto Scheel and Peter Paulsen, *Quellen zur Frage Schleswig-Haithabu im Rahmen der fränkischen, sächsischen und nordischen Beziehungen* (Kiel: Mühlau, 1930), v.

81 Shetelig to Schwantes, 16 Jan. 1929; Rothmann to Shetelig, 19 Jan. 1929, ALM OA Nydam 47.

82 Shetelig to Schwantes, 14 Mar. 1930, ALM OA Nydam 47.

83 Scheel to Mackeprang, 30 July 1930, ALM OA Haithabu-Danewerk.
84 Schwantes to the directors of the National Museum, 2 Aug. 1930, ALM OA Haithabu-Danewerk.
85 Mackeprang to the First Department of the National Museum, 16 Aug. 1930, NM Afd. 1 KA 583/30.
86 "Haithabu–Hollingstedt: Zum Beginn der Ausgrabungen in der Oldenburg," *SN* (10 Sept. 1930): 1.
87 "Die Weltgeschichtliche Bedeutung Haithabus," *SN* (25 Sept. 1930): 2.
88 Schwantes, "Die Ausgrabungen in Haithabu," *Zeitschrift für Ethnographie* 63 (1931): 240.
89 "Neue Funde in der Oldenburg," *SN* (14 Sept. 1930): 3.
90 "Die Ausgrabungen in der Oldenburg: Lichtbildervortrag im Kunstverein," *SN* (27 Oct. 1930): 1.
91 Schwantes, "Ausgrabungen in Haithabu," 239.
92 Schwantes, "Die Schleswig-Haithabu Frage im neuen Licht," *Nachrichtenblatt für deutsche Vorzeit* 7, no. 12 (1931): 1.
93 Otto Scheel, "Haithabu als Problem des Ostseeraums," *Die Heimat* (Apr. 1931), 81–4.
94 Schwantes, "Die Schleswig-Haithabu Frage," 1–2.
95 "Neue Funde in der Oldenburg," *SN* (14 Sept. 1930): 3.
96 Felix Schmeißer, "Romantische Haithabu- und Dannewirke-Wanderungen," *SN* (8 July 1931): 2.
97 "Uraufführung im Nordmark-Landestheater Paul Leuchsenrings 'Haithabu,'" *SN* (14 Sept. 1931): 3.
98 Heinar Schilling, *Haithabu: Ein germanisches Troja* (Leipzig: Koehler & Amelang, 1936), 134.
99 Ibid., 248.
100 Kristiansen, "Dansk arkaeologi," 292.

6. Creating Nazi Archaeology

1 Bernard Mees, "Hitler and Germanentum," *Journal of Contemporary History* 39, no. 2 (Apr. 2004): 266–7.
2 Strasser, *Wikinger und Normannen*, 5.
3 Bettina Arnold, "The Past as Propaganda," *Archaeology* (July/Aug. 1992): 30–7.
4 G. Asmus and N. Franck, *Heil Hitler, Herr Lehrer: Volksschule, 1933–1945; Das Beispiel Berlin* (Reinbek: Rowohlt, 1983), 107–11; Henning Haßmann, "Archäologie und Jugend im 'Dritten Reich': Ur- und Frühgeschichte als Mittel der politisch-ideologischen Indoktrination von Kindern und Jugendlichen," in Achim Leube and Morten Hegewisch, eds., *Prähistorie und Nationalsozialismus: Die mittel- und*

osteuropäische Ur- und Frühgeschichtsforschung in den Jahren 1933–1945 (Heidelberg: Synchron, 2002), 110–16.

5 Adriansen, *National symboler*, vol. 1, 113, 133–5.

6 Steffen Werther, *SS Vision und Grenzland Realität: Vom Umgang dänischer und "volksdeutscher" Nationalsozialisten in Sønderjylland mit der "großgermanischen" Ideologie der SS* (Stockholm: Acta Universitatis Stockholmiensis, 2012).

7 Alfred Rust, *Vor 20.000 Jahren: Eiszeitliche Rentierjäger in Holstein* (Neumünster: Wachholtz, 1937).

8 See Rainer Stommer, *Die inszenierte Volksgemeinschaft: Die "Thing-Bewegung" im Dritten Reich* (Marburg: Jonas Verlag, 1985). The Propaganda Ministry had envisioned such a Thingplatz for the Haithabu site. See Henning Haßmann and Detlef Jantzen, "'Die deutsche Vorgeschchte – eine nationale Wissenschaft': Das Kieler Museum vorgeschichtlicher Altertümer im Dritten Reich," *Offa-Zeitschrift* 51 (1994): 20.

9 J. Weyh, "Vorgeschichtliche Stätten in Schleswig-Holstein," *Die Welt: Sonntagsbeilage der Nordische Rundschau* (27 Mar. 1937): 1.

10 Haßmann, "Archaeology in the 'Third Reich,'" in Härke, *Archaeology, Ideology, and Society*, 86–9.

11 Michael Kater, *Das Ahnenerbe der SS, 1935–1945: Ein Beitrag zur Kulturpolitik des Dritten Reiches*, 2nd ed. (Munich: Oldenbourg, 1997); Heiko Steuer, "Herbert Jankuhn und seine Darstellungen zur Germanen- und Wikingerzeit," in Heiko Steuer, ed., *Eine hervorragend nationale Wissenschaft: Deutsche Prähistoriker zwischen 1900 und 1995* (Berlin: de Gruyter, 2001), 417–73; Heather Pringle, *The Master Plan: Himmler's Scholars and the Holocaust* (London: Fourth Estate, 2006), esp. 221–6.

12 See esp. Dirk Mahsarski, *Herbert Jankuhn (1905–1990): Ein deutscher Prähistoriker zwischen nationalsozialistischer Ideologie und wissenschaftlicher Objektivität* (Rahden: Marie Leidorf, 2011).

13 Arnold, "Past as Propaganda," 30.

14 Arnold and Haßmann, "Archaeology in Nazi Germany: The Legacy of the Faustian Bargain," in Kohl and Fawcett, *Nationalism, Politics, and the Practice of Archaeology*, 70.

15 Reinhard Bollmus, *Das Amt Rosenberg und seine Gegner: Studien zum Machtkampf im nationalsozialistischen Herrschaftssystem* (Stuttgart: Deutsche Verlags-Anstalt, 1970); Uta Halle, *"Die Externsteine sind bis auf weiteres germanisch!" Prähistorische Archäologie im Dritten Reich* (Bielefeld: Verlag für Regionalgeschichte, 2002), 509.

16 Hermann Beck, *The Fateful Alliance: German Conservatives and Nazis in 1933; The* Machtergreifung *in a New Light* (New York: Berghahn, 2008), xiii.

17 Geoffrey Cocks, *Psychotherapy in the Third Reich* (New York: Oxford University Press, 1985), 4.

18 Kiran Klaus Patel, "In Search of a Transnational Historicization: National Socialism and Its Place in History," in Konrad H. Jarausch and Thomas Lindenberger, eds., *Conflicted Memories: Europeanizing Contemporary Histories* (New York: Berghahn, 2007), 110.

19 "Der erste Kursus im Kreise Schleswig für deutsche Vorgeschichte," SN (3–4 Oct. 1933), 1-4, excerpted in ALM MuG 222.

20 Manfred Jessen-Klingenberg, *Standpunkte zur neueren Geschichte Schleswig-Holsteins*, 134.

21 Lange, *Geschichte Schleswig-Holsteins*, 536.

22 Ibid., 544. See also Rudolf Heberle, *Landbevölkerung und Nationalsozialismus: Eine soziologische Untersuchung der politischen Willensbildung in Schleswig-Holstein 1918 bis 1932* (Stuttgart: Deutsche Verlags-Anstalt, 1963).

23 Werther, *SS Vision und Grenzland Realität*, 17.

24 Jessen-Klingenberg, *Standpunkte zur neueren Geschichte Schleswig-Holsteins*, 134; Norman Berdichevsky, *The Danish-German Border Dispute, 1815–2001: Aspects of Cultural and Demographic Politics* (Bethesda, MD: Academica, 2002), 85.

25 Geoffrey Pridham and Jeremy Noakes, *Documents on Nazism* (New York: Viking, 1974), 116. In July 1932, 51% of voters in the provinces cast ballots for the National Socialists, while the proportion dropped to 45.7% in November.

26 Lange, *Geschichte Schleswig-Holsteins*, 553–5.

27 Thomas Scheck, *Denkmalpflege und Diktatur: Die Erhaltung von Bau- und Kunstdenkmälern in Schleswig-Holstein und im Deutschen Reich zur Zeit des Nationalsozialismus* (Berlin: Verlag für Bauwesen, 1995).

28 Mathias Wiegert, "Ur- und Frühgeschichtsforschung in der westlichen Rheinprovinz von 1933–1942," in Beat Naef, ed., *Antike und Altertumswissenschaft in der Zeit von Faschismus und Nationalsozialismus* (Cambridge: Cambridge University Press, 1998), 495.

29 Peter Paulsen, *Studien zur Wikinger Kultur: Inaugural-Dissertation zur Erlangung der Doktorwürde der Hohen Philosophischen Fakultät der CAU zu Kiel* (Kiel: Buddenbrook Dekan, 1932), 108.

30 Scheel and Paulsen, *Quellen zur Frage Schleswig-Haithabu*.

31 "Die Organisation der Fachgruppe für deutsche Vorgeschichte (im K.f.D.K.) im Schleswig-Holstein, Lauenburg, und Landesteil Lübeck," *Schleswig-Holsteinische Schulzeitung* (23 Sept. 1933): 579.

32 Mahsarski, *Herbert Jankuhn*, 36; Jankuhn, Allied Fragebogen, Military Government of Germany, ALM Nachlass Jankuhn, unnumbered.

33 Herbert Jankuhn, *Gürtelgarnituren der älteren römischen Kaiserzeit im Samland* (Königsberg: Leupold, 1932). On Jankuhn's criticism of Kossinna, see also Mahsarski, *Herbert Jankuhn*, 91–100.

34 Ibid., 420–1. Jankuhn is first mentioned as a member of the excavation team at Haithabu in a newspaper article, "Die Ausgrabung in der Oldenburg: Lichtbildervortrag im Kunstverein," *SN* (27 Oct. 1930): 1.

35 Peter Zylmann, "Der Lehrer und die Urgeschichte," *Schleswig-Holsteinische Schulzeitung* (23 Sept. 1933): 590.

36 Karl Kersten, "Die Untersuchung eines bronzezeitlichen Grabhügels in der Gemarkung Grünhof-Tesperhude," *Die Heimat* 43 (1932): 62–7.

37 Peter Paulsen, "Aufgaben und Richtlinien der Fachgruppe für die deutsche Vorgeschichte (im K.f.D.K.) in den Herzogtümern Schleswig-Holstein, Lauenburg, und in dem Landesteil Lübeck," *Schleswig-Holsteinische Schulzeitung* (23 Sept. 1933): 578.

38 Alan E. Steinweis, "Weimar Culture and National Socialism: The Kampfbund für deutsche Kultur," *Central European History* 24, no. 4 (1991): 405.

39 Zylmann, "Die Lehrer und die Urgeschichte," 590.

40 Jessen-Klingenberg, *Standpunkte zur neueren Geschichte Schleswig-Holsteins*, 133.

41 Steinweis, "Weimar Culture," 405.

42 Kurator der Universität Kiel und Preußische Ministerium für Wissenschaft to Gustav Schwantes, 20 Oct. 1933, SHLB Nachlass Schwantes Cb47/680.

43 Jankuhn, Allied Fragebogen. Jankuhn's reported income was 2,400 RM for 1931, 1934, and 1935. He reported 2,000 RM for 1932 and 1,000 RM for 1933, but he was away from his post travelling in connection with his German Archaeological Institute study tour during this time.

44 Schwantes, "Welches europäische Volk kann seine Ahnenreihe in die älteste Zeit zurückführen?" *Forschungen und Fortschritte* 9 (1933): 407.

45 This stress on opportunism forms the thesis of Jörn Jacobs brief treatment of the career of Peter Paulsen during the Nazi Period. See Jorn Jacobs, "Peter Paulsen: Ein Wanderer zwischen zwei Welten," in Leube and Hegewisch, *Prähistorie und Nationalsozialismus*, 451–9.

46 Herbert Jankuhn, "Die Vorgeschichte als nationale Wissenschaft," *SN* (3–4 Oct. 1933): 1–2, excerpted in ALM MuG 222.

47 Ibid.

48 Claudia Koonz, *The Nazi Conscience* (Cambridge, MA: Harvard University Press, 2003), 13.

49 Scheck, *Denkmalpflege und Diktatur*, 152–3. Specifically, Scheck mentions Sauermann's work to protect the *Geisteskämpfer* sculpture at the St Nikolai Church in Kiel, which was sculpted by Ernst Barlach in 1928.

50 Paulsen, "Aufgaben und Richtlinien," 579.

51 The museum had by now dropped the term "vaterländisch" from its title in order to reflect the museum's emphasis on local prehistory. Schwantes explained that many patrons had been confused by the term, which had led them to expect exhibits from the recent historical period. See Schwantes, "Vorwort," in Gustav Schwantes, ed., *Festschrift zur Hunderjahrfeier des Museums vorgeschichtlicher Altertümer in Kiel* (Neumünster: Wachholtz, 1936), i.

52 "Die Hundertjahrfeier des Kieler Museums," *SN* (11 Oct. 1936), 1–2.
53 Schwantes, "Vorwort," i.
54 Robert P. Ericksen, *Complicity in the Holocaust: Churches and Universities in Nazi Germany* (Cambridge: Cambridge University Press, 2012), 145–53.
55 Kater, *Ahnenerbe*, 81.
56 Gunter Schöbel, "Hans Reinerth: Forscher-NS Funktionär-Museumsleiter," in Leube and Hegewisch, *Prähistorie und Nationalsozialismus*, 334–7.
57 Quoted in Bollmus, *Amt Rosenberg*, 154.
58 Haßmann, "Archaeology in the 'Third Reich,'" 90; Arnold, "Past as Propaganda," 32.
59 Marchand, *Down from Olympus*, 349–50.
60 Bollmus, *Amt Rosenberg*, 171–5.
61 Reinerth to Jankuhn, 5 Sept. 1935, and Jankuhn to Reinerth, 10 Sept. 1935, ALM Nachlass Jankuhn GB 21.
62 Rothmann to the Ministerium für Wissenschaft, Kunst und Volksbildung 4 July 1933, ALM Nachlass Rothmann.
63 Jankuhn to the rector of the Christian-Albrechts-Universität, 30 Mar. 1936, ALM Nachlass Jankuhn GB 21.
64 Ibid.
65 Jankuhn, Akten-Notiz Besprechung zwischen CAU Rektor, Dahm, Ritterbusch, Schwantes, Paulsen, und Jankuhn, undated, ALM Nachlass Jankuhn GB 21.
66 Ibid.
67 Jankuhn included a copy of two letters from Reinerth to Bersu, dated 4 Sept. 1931 and 4 Feb. 1932, in which Reinerth asked for assistance in securing a teaching position; in ALM Nachlass Jankuhn GB 21.
68 Jankuhn to Brøndsted, 18 Mar., 31 Mar., and 4 Apr. 1936; Brøndsted to Jankuhn, 20 Feb. and16 Apr. 1936, NM Afd. 1 470/36.
69 Karen Gram-Skjoldager, "Herre i eget hus? Den danske regerings politik i Sønderjylland, 1933–1940," *Historie* 2 (2003): 299–336.
70 Ingrid Riese, "Det tyske mindretals valgkamp 1939," *Historie* 20, no. 2 (1994): 177–219.
71 Valdis O. Lumans, "The Nordic Destiny: The Peculiar Role of the German Minority in Hitler's Plans and Policies for Denmark," *Scandinavian Journal of History* 15, no. 2 (1990): 101–23.
72 Anna Bramwell, *Blood and Soil: Richard Walther Darré and Hitlers' "Green Party"* (Bourne End, Buckinghamshire: Kendal Press, 1985), 41, 50–3; Seppo Kuusisto, *Alfred Rosenberg in der nationalsozialistische Aussenpolitik, 1933–39* (Helsinki: SHS, 1984), 38.
73 Robert Cecil, *The Myth of the Master Race: Alfred Rosenberg and Nazi Ideology* (New York: Dodd Mean, 1972), 154–6.

74 Lutzhöft, *Nordische Gedanke*, 303–11.

75 Steffen Stumann Hansen, "The Wandering Congress: The Sixth Nordic Archaeological Meeting in Denmark 1937," *Acta Archaeologica* 74, no. 1 (2003): 294–95.

76 Hans Reinerth, "Haus und Hof im vorgeschichtlichen Norden: Weg, Stand und Aufgabe der Forschung," in Hans Reinerth, ed., *Haus und Hof im Nordischen* Raum, vol. 1 (Hamburg: Lippert, 1937), 1.

77 Jankuhn, "Gutachten über Dr Tode" undated, ALM Nachlass Jankuhn GB 21. According to Jankuhn, Alfred Tode's dismissal had resulted in court proceedings between Tode and Schwantes.

78 Reinerth to Jankuhn, 20 Nov. 1936, ALM Nachlass Jankuhn GB 21.

79 Jankuhn to Reinerth, 3 Dec. 1936, ALM Nachlass Jankuhn GB 21.

80 Hansen, "Wandering Congress," 296.

81 Pieper to Jankuhn, 8 June 1937, ALM Nachlass Jankuhn GB 21.

82 Brøndsted to Schwantes, 19 Jan., 5 Feb., 6 Mar., and 6 Sept. 1935; Schwantes to Brøndsted, 11 Feb. 1935, NM Afd. 1 73/35.

83 Brøndsted to C.A. Nordmann, 1 May 1937, NM Afd. 1 426/37.

84 Ibid.

85 "Møde paa Nationalmuseet den 19/6 1937," NM Afd. 1 426/37.

86 Schwantes to Mackeprang, 5 Oct. 1937, NM Afd. 1 426/37.

87 Mackprang to Brøndsted, 8 Oct. 1937, NM Afd. 1 426/37.

88 Report on the meeting of 26 Oct. 1937 in the National Museum, Copenhagen, NM Afd. 1 426/37.

89 Mackeprang to Brøndsted, 8 Oct. 1937.

90 Ibid.

91 Plans for the conference had been discussed as early as 1935. See Schwantes to Brøndsted, 11 Feb. 1935, NM Afd. 1 73/35.

92 Der Beauftragte des Führers für die gesamte geistige und weltanschauliche Erziehung der NSDAP to Gaubeauftragten für Vorgeschichte und Landesleiter des Reichbundes für Deutsche Vorgeschichte, 9 June 1937, ALM Nachlass Jankuhn GB 21.

93 Jankuhn to Buttler, Ministerium für Wissenschaft, Erziehung und Volksbildung, 16 June 1937, ALM Nachlass Jankuhn GB 21.

94 Jankuhn to Richthofen, 16 June 1937, ALM Nachlass Jankuhn GB 21.

95 Ministerium für Wissenschaft, Erziehung und Volksbildung to Jankuhn, 14 July 1937, ALM Nachlass Jankuhn GB 21.

96 Jankuhn to Richthofen, 18 Mar. 1938, ALM Nachlass Jankuhn GB 21.

97 Jankuhn, "Mein Verhältnis zu Reinerth," undated, ALM Nachlass Jankuhn GB 21.

98 Jankuhn to Richthofen, 18 Mar. 1938, ALM Nachlass Jankuhn GB 21. The letter was marked "persönlich" in the header.

99 Kater, *Ahnenerbe*, 89.

100 Haßmann and Jantzen, "'Die deutsche Vorgeschichte,'" 15.
101 "Beurteilung von SS Sturmbannführer Prof. Dr Herbert Jankuhn," 12 Feb. 1945, BA NS 21/51.
102 Wolfram Sievers to Heinrich Himmler, 11 Apr. 1938, BA NS 21/346.
103 Herbert Jankuhn, *Haithabu: Eine germanische Stadt der Frühzeit* (Neumünster: Wachholtz, 1938), viii.
104 This argument became a key factor in Jankuhn's defence during his trial in 1949. See the proceedings of Jankuhn's denazification hearing, 6 June 1949, ALM Nachlass Jankuhn GB 15.
105 Jankuhn to the Rector of the Christian-Albrechts-Universität, 30 Mar. 1936, ALM Nachlass Jankuhn GB 21.
106 Günther Haselhoff, "Eidesstattliche Erklärung," 12 June 1947, and Schwantes, "Eidesstattliche Erklärung," 16 Apr. 1947, ALM Nachlass Jankuhn GB 15.
107 The timing of the Ahnenerbe project was discussed in a letter from Wolfram Sievers, secretary of the Ahnenerbe, and Jankuhn, 2 Feb. 1938, BA NS 21/346. It was later recalled in Schwantes' "Gutachten" on behalf of Jankuhn, written 16 Apr. 1947, in ALM Nachlass Jankuhn GB 15.
108 Nils Vollertsen, "Herbert Jankuhn, hedeby-forskningen og det tyske samfund 1934–1976," *Fortid og Nutid* 36, no. 4 (1989): 238–39.
109 Halle, *Externsteine*, 429–30.
110 Account from Alfred Haffner in "Alfred Rust und die Rahmenbedingungen für die Archäologie im Dritten Reich," Public Forum, Ahrensburg, 24 Nov. 2000, 13–14, transcript in ALM Nachlass Alfred Rust.
111 Heinrich Himmler to Martin Bormann, 18 Jan. 1938, BA NS 21/346. On Reinerth's bid, see Sievers to Himmler, 11 Apr. 1938, BA NS 21/346.
112 Kater, *Ahnenerbe*, 82; Herbert Jankuhn, "Die Ausstellungen," in Herbert Jankuhn, ed., *Jahrestagungen: Bericht über die Kieler Tagung* (Neumünster: Wachholtz, 1944), 241–6.
113 Kater, *Ahnenerbe*, 81
114 Haßmann and Jantzen, ""'Die deutsche Vorgeschchte,'" 20.

7. The Fate of Archaeology in the Borderlands

1 The attack included bombers from the US 303rd Bombardment Group (H), whose log from the mission is reprinted in Harry D. Gobrecht, *Might in Flight: A Daily Diary of the Eighth Air Force's Hell's Angels 303rd Bombardment Group (H)* (San Clemente, CA: 303rd Bombardment Group (H) Association, 1993), 423–4.
2 Konrad Jarausch, *After Hitler: Recivilizing Germans, 1945–1995*, translated by Brandon Hunziker (Oxford: Oxford University Press, 2006), 12.
3 Søren Telling, *25 Aar paa Danevirke* (Holbaek: Nordan, 1965), 26–30.

4 Mary Fulbrook, *Dissonant Lives: Generations and Violence through the German Dictatorships* (Oxford: Oxford University Press, 2011), 260.

5 On the connections between Nazism and territorial expansion, see Aristotle Kallis, *Fascist Ideology: Territory and Expansionism in Italy and Germany, 1922–1945* (London: Routledge, 2000), esp. 160–4.

6 Gedächtnisprotokoll Michael Kater-Herbert Jankuhn, Göttingen, 14 May 1963 ALM Nachlass Jankuhn GB 27.

7 Jankuhn to Sievers, 8 Oct. 1939, BA NS 21/51. Jankuhn had made a similar request in Jankuhn to Luftfahrtsministerium, 22 Apr. 1939, ALM Nachlass Jankuhn GB 15.

8 Rust to Sievers, 18 Dec. 1940, ALM Nachlass Alfred Rust.

9 Pringle, *Master Plan*, 197.

10 Herbert Jankuhn, "Zur Entstehung des polnischen Staates," *KB* (1940): 73.

11 Anja Heuss, *Kunst- und Kulturgutraub: Eine vergleichende Studie zur Besatzungspolitik der Nationalsozialisten in Frankreich und der Sowjetunion* (Heidelberg: Winter, 2000), 221–4.

12 Carola Hicks, *The Bayeux Tapestry: The Life Story of a Masterpiece* (London: Chatto & Windus, 2006), 213–20. Ultimately the war prevented the completion of a planned multivolume study of the Tapestry.

13 Michael Burleigh, *Germany Turns Eastwards: A Study of Ostforschung in the Third Reich* (Cambridge: Cambridge University Press, 1988), 25.

14 Joseph Wiesner, "Der Osten als Schicksalsraum Europas und des Indogermanentums," *Germanien* 6 (June 1942): 220.

15 Gedächtnisprotokoll Michael Kater-Herbert Jankuhn, ALM Nachlass Jankuhn GB 27.

16 Heuss, *Kunst- und Kulturgutraub*, 235.

17 Heather Pringle reports that Jankuhn's interest in the Goths stemmed from his encounter with the Gothic artefacts from the Kerch region of the Crimea that were housed in the Berlin Museum. See Pringle, *Master Plan*, 221.

18 Ibid., 233–6; Heuss, *Kunst- und Kulturgutraub*, 235–6.

19 Pringle, *Master Plan*, 222–3. Allegedly, Jankuhn met in Sept. 1942 with one of the commanders of Einsatzgruppe D, which was carrying out massacres in the region; the two discussed the locations of museum collections.

20 Ibid., 207.

21 Jankuhn, Allied Fragebogen, undated, in ALM Nachlass Jankuhn, unnumbered.

22 Office of the Oberbürgermeister to Schleswig-Holstein Museum, 10 Feb. 1942, ALM MuG 30.

23 Karl Kersten, "Aktenvermerk," 8 Dec. 1944, ALM Reg. Akt. 1.1.1.

24 Jørgen Kühl, "Heinrich Himmler, Søren Telling og Danevirke," *Sønderjyske Årbøger* (1999): 157–9.

25 Telling, *25 Aar paa Danevirke*, 8–9.

26 Ibid., 26–7.
27 Sievers to Franz Walter Stahlecker, 24 Apr. 1940, BA NS 21/59. Jankuhn at the time was enrolled in the Police School in Prietzsh/Elbe.
28 Kersten, "Bericht über eine Reise durch Dänemark zum Schutz der vorgeschichtlichen Denkmäler im Auftrage des Reichsführers SS in der Zeit vom 23. Oktober bis zum 5. Nov. 1940," BA NS 21/86.
29 Jankuhn to the Commandant of the SD Einsatzkommando Oslo, 4 May 1940, BA NS 21/59.
30 Quoted in Mahsarski, *Herbert Jankuhn*, 207.
31 Himmler to Sievers, 29 May 1940, BA NS 21/59.
32 Charlotte Blindheim, "De fem lange år på Universitets Oldsaksamling," *Viking: Tidsskrift for norøn arkeologi* 48 (1980): 32.
33 These allegations first appeared in Anders Hagen, "Arkeologi og politikk," *Viking* 49 (1986): 270. Since then, they have been repeated in Arnold and Haßmann, "Archaeology in Nazi Germany," 76; Barbara Scott, "Archaeology and National Identity: The Norwegian Example," *Scandinavian Studies* 68, no. 3 (1996): 1053–75; Pringle, *Master Plan*, 311–13; and Jorunn Sem Fure, "Heinrich Himmler som humanistisk prosjektleder," *Fortid* 2 (2007): 79.
34 A.W. Brøgger to Jankuhn, 24 Mar. 1949, ALM Nachlass Jankuhn, unnumbered.
35 Jes Martens, "Die nordische Archäologie und das 'Dritte Reich,'" in Leube and Hegewisch, *Prähistorie und Nationalsozialismus*, 611–13.
36 Joachim Lund, "'At opretholde Sindets Neutralitet' – Geografen Gudmund Hatt, det ny Europa og det store verdensdrama," in John T. Lauridsen, ed., *Over stregen – Under besættelsen* (Copenhagen: Gyldendal, 2007), 252–64.
37 Henrik Gutzon Larsen, "Gudmund Hatt (1884–1960)," *Geographers: Bibliographic Studies* 28 (2009): 20–2.
38 Lars Schreiber Pedersen, "Arkæolog på afveje – Mogens B. Mackeprang," in Lauridsen, *Over stregen – Under besættelsen*, 543–49.
39 Werther, *SS Vision und Grenzland Realität*, 254–83.
40 Bjarne Grønnow and Jens Fog Jensen, *The Northernmost Ruins of the Globe: Eigil Knuth's Archaeological Investigations in Peary Land and Adjacent Areas of High Arctic Greenland* (Copenhagen: Museum Tusculanum, 2009), 18.
41 Manfred Jakubowski-Tiessen, "Kulturpolitik im besetzten Land: Das Deutsche Wissenschaftliche Institut in Kopenhagen 1941 bis 1945," *Zeitschrift für Geschichtswissenschaft* 42, no. 2 (1994): 129–37.
42 Nørlund, "Nationalmuseet i de Onde Aar," 8.
43 Kersten, "Bericht über eine Reise durch Dänemark."
44 Nørlund, "Nationalmuseet," 9–10.
45 Jankuhn to the Amt Ahnenerbe 13 Aug. 1943, BA NS 15/620.
46 Kersten, Aktenvermerk, 8 Dec. 1944.

47 Schwantes to Apotheker Sonder, 3 Jan. 1945, ALM Reg. Akt. 1.1.1.

48 Ibid.

49 Jankuhn, Allied Fragebogen, 4–6.

50 Schwantes to Schleswig-Holstein Oberpräsident, 2 Nov. 1944, ALM Reg. Akt. 1.1.1.

51 See, e.g., Werner Best to Sievers, 24 July 1944, BA NS 21/52.

52 Supplement to Personal Identification for Søren Telling from the Office of the Reichsminister für Wissenschaft, Erziehung und Volksbildung, 2 May 1945, ALM Reg. Akt. 1.1.2.

53 Schwantes to Reinecke, 24 Sept. 1946, SHLB Nachlass Schwantes Cb 47/681.

54 Schwantes, "Denkschrift über die Sicherstellung und Rückführung der Sammlungen des Schleswig-holsteinischen Museums vorgeschichtlicher Alertümer in Kiel während und nach dem Kriege," 10 Sept. 1946, ALM Reg. Akt. 1.1.1.

55 Hannes Harding, *Displaced Persons in Schleswig-Holstein, 1945–1953* (Frankfurt: Peter Lang, 1997), 48.

56 Berdichevsky, *German-Danish Border Dispute*, 113; Thaler, *Of Mind and Matter*, 42.

57 Johannes Brøndsted and Lis Jacobsen, *Sydslesvig Frit: To Taler holdt i København* (Copenhagen: Roesenkilde og Bagger, 1947), 8.

58 "Neue Bestrebungen, das Nydam-Boat ins Schloss zu Sonderburg zu schaffen," translation from the Danish article in *Sønderjyden*, 23 Sept. 1949, in ALM OA Nydam 60; On the history of the monument, see Bjørn Poulson and Ulrich Schulte-Wülwer, *Idstedløven: Et national monument og dets skæbne* (Herning: Poul Kristensens, 1993). "Paa Jagt efter Isted-Løvens Medaillioner," *Flensborg Avis* (17 Nov. 1945), excerpted in ALM Reg. Akt. 1.1.2; Adriansen, *Denkmal und Dynamit*, 112–14.

59 "Neue Bestrebungen."

60 Quoted in Berdichevsky, *German-Danish Border Dispute*, 112.

61 Ibid., 112–22.

62 Schwantes to Prof. Dr Burck, 6 Aug. 1946, SHLB Nachlass Schwantes Cb 47/683.

63 Ibid.

64 Schwantes, "Denkschrift über die Sicherstellung und Rückführung."

65 "Slesvig, Slesvig: Omstridte Land – og Byen med," *Flensborg Avis* (12 May 1951), excerpted in ALM MuG 37.

66 Niels Friss, "Omstridte Fortidsminder atter paa slesvigske Grund," *Berlingske Tidende* (28 Apr. 1950), excerpted in ALM MuG 34. The two kings were Frederik I (1471–1533) and Christian III (1503–1559).

67 Captain Ewan Phillips to the Landesverwaltung, 17 Jan. 1947, ALM MuG 32.

68 Ref. Ohrenschall, Landesregierung, to Landesminister Dr Schenk, Ministerium für Volksbildung, 14 Feb. 1949, ALM MuG 32a.

69 Kersten to the Landesministerium für Volksbildung, 2 June 1949, ALM OA Nydam 60.
70 Schwantes to the Landesministerium für Volksbildung, 12 Aug. 1949, ALM OA Nydam 60.
71 Quoted in "Schloß Gottorf: Erfüllung meines Lebenstraumes," *KN* (22 Sept. 1950), excerpted in ALM MuG 35.
72 Telling, "Gottorp som Museet," *Jyllands Posten* (24 Aug. 1950), excerpted in ALM MuG 35.
73 "Schloß Gottorf: Erfüllung meines Lebenstraumes."
74 "Prof. Bröndsted in Schleswig Anerkennung für Gottorp-Museum," *SN* (12 Apr. 1951), excerpted in ALM MuG 35.
75 Jørgen Kühl, "Søren Telling und das Danewerk," *Demokratische Geschichte* 19 (2008): 34.
76 Berdichevsky, *German-Danish Border Dispute*, 113.
77 Friss, "Omstridte Fortidsminder," excerpted in ALM MuG 34.
78 Arnold and Haßmann, "Archaeology in Nazi Germany," 73–4.
79 Denazification Judgment against Herbert Jankuhn, Oberster Spruchgerichtshof, Hamm, 6 June 1949, ALM Nachlass Jankuhn, GB 15.
80 Friedrich Volbehr and Richard Weyl, *Professoren und Dozenten der Christian-Albrechts-Universität zu Kiel* (Kiel: Ferdinand Hirt, 1956), 49.
81 Härke, "*Archaeology, Ideology, and Society*," 23; Michael Gebühr, personal communication, 16 Feb. 2004.
82 G. Heidorn et al., "Zur Hochschulpolitik der Sozialistischen Einheitspartei Deutschlands, 1946–1949/50: Unter besonderer Berücksichtigung der Entwicklung in Rostock," *Das Hochschulwesen* 11, nos. 9 and 11 (1963): 647–48.
83 Pringle, *Master Plan*, 311–13.
84 Zylmann, Gutachten für Herbert Jankuhn, 19 Sept. 1946, SHLB Nachlass Schwantes Cb 47/681.
85 Jankuhn to Rolf Seeliger, 27 May 1968, ALM Nachlass Jankuhn GB 15.
86 This focus on trade had even coloured Jankuhn's site reports in the propaganda journal, *Germanien*. See, e.g., Herbert Jankuhn, "Haithabu und Birka," *Germanien* 5 (May, 1941): 175–80; here Jankuhn had differentiated between the function of Haithabu as an intermediary trading centre and Birka as a regional market for goods from Western Europe.
87 Steuer, "Herbert Jankuhn," 451–4.
88 Günter Smolla, "Das Kossinna-Syndrome," *Fundberichte aus Hessen* 80, no. 19 (1979/80): 1–9.
89 Heinrich Härke, "All Quiet on the Western Front?: Paradigms, Methods, and Approaches in West German Archaeology," in Ian Hodder, ed., *Archaeological*

Theory in Europe: The Last Three Decades (London: Routledge, 1991), 187–222; Björn Myhre, "Theory in Scandinavian Archaeology since 1960: A View from Norway," in ibid., 164–73. On the Anglo-American approach, see Stephan Shennan, "Trends in the Study of Later European Prehistory," *Annual Review of Anthropology* 16 (1987): 365–7.

90 Heinrich Jaenecke, quoted in "Alfred Rust und die Rahmenbedingungen," 35.

91 Quoted in Wolfgang Menghin and Dieter Planck, eds., *Menschen, Zeiten, Räume: Archäologie in Deutschland* (Stuttgart: Theiss, 2003), 14.

92 Larsen, "Gudmund Hatt," 17.

93 Michael Gebühr, "Sind die Moorleichen 'unsere Ururgroßeltern'?" *Die Heimat* 85 (1978): 324–5.

94 Grenzlandmuseum Flensburg to Schwantes, 16 July 1947, ALM Reg. Akt. 1.1.2.

95 Gerhard Paul, *Der Untergang 1945 in Flensburg* (Kiel: Schleswig-Holstein Landeszentrale für politische Bildung, 2012), 12.

Conclusion

1 Adriansen, *National symboler*, vol. 2, 149. Adriansen reports that this process was already partly underway during the 1930s, when copies of the Golden Horns of Gallehus were produced for commercial purposes.

2 Philip L. Kohl, Mara Kozelsky, Nachman Ben-Yehuda, eds., *Selective Remembrances: Archaeology in the Construction, Commemoration, and Consecration of National Pasts* (Chicago: University of Chicago Press, 2007). Within this volume, see esp. Victor Shnirelman, "Russian Response: Archaeology, Russian Nationalism, and the 'Arctic Homeland,'" 51–2; and Gheorghe Alexandru Niculescu, "Archaeology and Nationalism in the History of the Romanians," 127–8.

3 Zahra, *Kidnapped Souls*, 4.

4 Confino, *Nation as a Local Metaphor*, 189.

5 See most notably Susan A. Crane, ed. *Museums and Memory* (Stanford: Stanford University Press, 2000).

6 Peter McIsaac, *Museums of the Mind: Germany Modernity and the Dynamics of Collecting* (University Park: Pennsylvania State University Press, 2007), 11–12.

7 Judson, *Guardians of the Nation.*

8 Thaler, "Discourse of Historical Legitimization."

9 Jespersen, *History of Denmark*, 3.

10 Yahil, "National Pride and Defeat."

11 Mosse, *Crisis of German Ideology*.

12 Berdichevsky, *German-Danish Border Dispute*, 138.

13 Norman Berdichevsky, Rachel Bradley, Clive H. Schofield, and Andrew Harris,

The German-Danish Border: The Successful Resolution of an Age-Old Conflict or Its Redefinition? (Durham, UK: International Boundaries Research Unit, 1999).

14 Charles Bright and Michael Geyer, "Where in the World Is America? The History of the United States in the Global Age," in Thomas Bender, ed., *Rethinking American History in a Global Age* (Berkeley: University of California Press, 2002), 66–7; Sebastian Conrad, *Globalisation and the Nation in Imperial Germany*, translated by Sorcha O'Hagan (Cambridge: Cambridge University Press, 2010).

Bibliography

Adriansen, Inge. "Danish and German National Symbols." *Ethnologia Scandinavica* 21 (1991): 34–52.

– *Første verdenskrig i mikroperspektive: Maria Gørrigsens åbenbaringer*. Sønderborg: Historisk Samfund for Als og Sundeved, 2003.

– *Nationale symboler i det danske rige, 1830–2000*. 2 vols. Copenhagen: Museum Tuscalanums Forlag Københavns Universitet, 2003.

– *Denkmal und Dynamit: Denkmälerstreit im deutsch-dänischen Grenzland*. Neumünster: Wachholtz, 2011.

Adriansen, Inge, and Immo Doege. *Deutsch oder Dänisch?: Bilder zum nationalen Selbstverständnis aus dem Jahre 1920*. Flensburg: Gesellschaft für Flensburger Stadtgeschichte, 1992.

Ædigus, Jens Peter. *Christian Flor: Pædagogen, politikeren, folkeoplyseren*. Odense: Odense Universitetsforlag, 1994.

Andersen, Svend Aage. *Guldhornene fra Gallehus: et par nye rekonstruktioner og deres forudsætninger*. Copenhagen: Populær-Videnskabeligt-forlag, 1945.

Anderson, Benedict. *Imagined Communities: Reflections on the Origins and Spread of Nationalism*. London: Verso, 1991.

Anderson, Malcolm, and Eberhart Bort, eds. *The Frontiers of Europe*. London: Continuum, 1998.

Anna-Carin Andersson, et al. *"The Kaleidoscopic Past": Proceedings of the 5th Nordic TAG Conference Göteborg, 2–5 April 1997*, 333–46. Göteborg: Göteborg University, Department of Archaeology, 1998.

Applegate, Celia. *A Nation of Provincials: The German Idea of Heimat*. Berkeley: University of California Press, 1990.

Armstrong, John A. *Nations before Nationalism*. Chapel Hill: University of North Carolina Press, 1982.

Arnold, Bettina. "The Past as Propaganda." *Archaeology* (July/Aug. 1992): 30–7.

Asmus, G., and N. Frank. *Heil Hitler, Herr Lehrer: Volksschule 1933–1945; Das Beispiel Berlin*. Reinbek: Rowholt, 1983.

Bagge, Povl. "Nationalismus und Antinationalismus in Dänemark um 1900." *Geschichte in Wissenschaft und Unterricht* 15, no. 5 (1964): 291–303.

Bakker, Jan Albert. *Megalithic Research in the Netherlands: From "Giants' Beds" and "Pillars of Hercules" to Accurate Investigations*. Leiden: Sidestone, 2010.

Barnes, Geraldine, and Margaret Clunies Ross, eds. *Old Norse Myths, Literature, and Society: Proceedings of the 11th Annual International Saga Conference*, University of Sydney, 2–7 July 2000. Sydney: Centre for Medieval Studies, University of Sydney, 2000.

Beck, Hermann. *The Fateful Alliance: German Conservatives and Nazis in 1933; The* Machtergreifung *in a New Light*. New York: Berghahn, 2008.

Becker-Christensen, Henrik, ed. *Grænsen i 75 Aar, 1920–1995*. Aabenraa: Institut for Grænseregionsforskning, 1995.

Bender, Thomas, ed. *Rethinking American History in a Global Age*. Berkeley: University of California Press, 2002.

Berdichevsky, Norman. *The Danish-German Border Dispute, 1815–2001: Aspects of Cultural and Demographic Politics*. Bethesda, MD: Academica, 2002.

Berdichevsky, Norman, Rachel Bradley, Clive H., Schofield, and Andrew Harris. *The German-Danish Border: The Successful Resolution of an Age-Old Conflict or Its Redefinition?* Durham, UK: International Boundaries Research Unit, 1999.

Bernbeck, Reinhard, and Susan Pollock: "Ayodhya, Archaeology, and Identity." *Current Anthropology* 37, no. 1 (1996): 138–42.

Björk, James. *Neither German nor Pole: Catholicism and National Indifference in a Central European Borderland*. Ann Arbor: University of Michigan Press, 2008.

Blackbourn, David. *History of Germany, 1780–1918: The Long Nineteenth Century*. 2nd ed. Malden, MA: Blackwell, 2003.

Blackbourn, David, and Richard J. Evans, eds. *The German Bourgeoisie: Essays on the Social History of the German Middle Class from the Late Eighteenth to the Early Twentieth Century*. London: Routledge, 1991.

Blickle, Peter. *Heimat: A Critical Theory of the German Idea of Homeland*. Rochester: Camden House, 2002.

Blindheim, Charlotte. "De fem lange år på Universitets Oldsaksamling." *Viking: tidsskrift for norøn arkeologi* 48 (1980): 38–48.

Blom, Ida. "Nation-Class-Gender: Scandinavia at the Turn of the Century." *Scandinavian Journal of History* 21, no. 1 (1996): 1–16.

Bollmus, Reinhard. *Das Amt Rosenberg und seine Gegner: Zum Machtkampf im nationalsozialistischen Herrschaftssystem*. Stuttgart: Deutsche Verlags-Anstalt, 1970.

Börsch-Supan, Helmut. *Caspar David Friedrich*. Translated by Sarah Twohig and John William Gabriel. Munich: Prestel, 1990.

Bourdieu, Pierre. "Intellectual Field and Creative Project." *Social Science Information* 8 (Apr. 1969): 89–119.

– *Homo Academicus*. Translated by Peter Collier. Stanford: Stanford University Press, 1984.

Bramwell, Anna. *Blood and Soil: Richard Walther Darré and Hitler's "Green Party."* Bourne End, Buckinghamshire: Kendal Press, 1985.

Brandt, Klaus, and Michael Müller-Wille, eds. *Haithabu und die frühe Stadtentwicklung im nördlichen Europa*. Neumünster: Wachholtz, 2002.

Brandt, Otto. *Geschichte Schleswig-Holsteins: Ein Grundriss*. 8th ed. Kiel: Mühlau, 1981.

Briggs, C. Stephen. "C.C. Rafn, J.J.A. Worsaae, Archaeology, History and Danish National Identity in the Schleswig-Holstein Question." *Bulletin of the History of Archaeology* 15, no. 2 (2005): 4–25.

Brockstedt, Jürgen. *Frühindustrialisierung in Schleswig-Holstein, anderen norddeutschen Ländern und Dänemark*. Neumünster: Wachholtz, 1983.

Brøndsted, Johannes, and Lis Jacobsen. *Sydslesvig Frit: To Taler holdt i København*. Copenhagen: Roesenkilde og Bagger, 1947.

Bruhn, Emil. *Zur Heimatgeschichte Eiderstedts: Heft 1, Aus der Urgeschichte; Zur Geschichte der Besiedlung und der Bevölkerung*. Garding: Lühr & Dircks, 1926.

Buchholz, Werner. "Andreas Ludwig Jacob Michelsen." *Neue Deutsche Biographie*, vol. 17, 453–4. Berlin: Duncker & Humboldt, 1993.

Burckhardt, Jacob. *The Civilization of the Renaissance in Italy*. Translated by S.G.C. Middlemore. New York: Barnes & Noble, 1999.

Burleigh, Michael. *Germany Turns Eastwards: A Study of Ostforschung in the Third Reich*. Cambridge: Cambridge University Press, 1988.

Carr, William. *Schleswig-Holstein: A Study in National Conflict*. Manchester: Manchester University Press, 1963.

Cecil, Robert. *The Myth of the Master Race: Alfred Rosenberg and Nazi Ideology*. New York: Dodd Mead, 1972.

Christiansen, Niels Finn, et al. *Danmarks Historie*, vol. 7. Edited by Søren Mørch. Copenhagen: Gyldendal, 1988.

Clausen, H.V. *Nordslesvig, 1863–1893: Den nationale stilling på landet*. Flensburg: Möller & Rasmussen, 1894.

Clauß, Ludwig Ferdinand. *Die nordische Seele: Artung, Prägung, Ausdruck*. Halle: Niemeyer, 1923.

Cocks, Geoffrey. *Psychotherapy in the Third Reich*. New York: Oxford University Press, 1985.

Cohen, Deborah, and Maura O'Connor, eds. *Comparison and History: Europe in Cross-National Perspective*. New York: Routledge, 2004.

Confino, Alon. *The Nation as a Local Metaphor: Württemberg, Imperial Germany, and National Memory, 1871–1918*. Chapel Hill: University of North Carolina Press, 1997.

Conrad, Sebastian. *Globalisation and the Nation in Imperial Germany*. Translated by Sorcha O'Hagan. Cambridge: Cambridge University Press, 2010.

Cowan, Robert. *The Indo-German Identification: Reconciling South Asian Origins and European Destinies*. Rochester: Camden House, 2010.

Crane, Susan A. *Collecting and Historical Consciousness in Early Nineteenth-Century Germany*. Ithaca: Cornell University Press, 2000.

Crane, Susan A., ed. *Museums and Memory*. Stanford: Stanford University Press, 2000.

Daniel, Glyn, ed. *Towards a History of Archaeology: Being the Papers Read at the First Conference on the History of Archaeology in Aarhus, 29 Aug – 2 Sept. 1978*. London: Thames & Hudson, 1981.

Davenne, Christine. *Cabinets of Wonder*. Translated by Nicholas Elliot. New York: Abrams, 2012.

Diaz-Andreu, Margarita, and Marie Louise Stig Sørensen, eds. *Excavating Women: A History of Women in European Archaeology*. London: Routledge, 1998.

Dörner, Andreas. "Der Mythos der nationalen Einheit: Symbolpolitik und Deutungskämpfe bei der Einweihung der Hermannsdenkmal im Jahre 1875." *Archiv für Kulturgeschichte* 79, no. 2 (1997): 396–410.

Dybahl, Vagn. *Danmarks Historie*, vol. 12. Copenhagen: Politikens Forlag, 1965.

Engelhardt, Conrad. *Thorsbjerg Mosefund*. Copenhagen: G.E.C. Gad, 1863.

– *Nydam Mosefund, 1859–1863*. Copenhagen: G.E.C. Gad, 1865.

Engelstoft, Povl. *Dansk Biografisk Leksikon*. Copenhagen: Schultz, 1940.

Elsner, Hildegard. *Haithabu: Schaufenster einer frühen Stadt*. Schleswig: Archäologisches Landesmuseum, 1989.

Ericksen, Robert P. *Complicity in the Holocaust: Churches and Universities in Nazi Germany*. Cambridge: Cambridge University Press, 2012.

Evans, Andrew. *Anthropology at War: World War I and the Science of Race in Germany*. Chicago: University of Chicago Press, 2010.

Fabricius, Knud, and Johannes Lomholt-Thomsen, eds. *Flensborgeren, Christian Paulsens Dagbøger*. Copenhagen: Gyldenal, 1946.

Feiner, Edith. "Adolph Pansch." *Neue Deutsche Biographie*, vol. 4, 180–2. Edited by Olaf Klose and Eva Rudolph. Neumünster: Wachholtz, 1976.

Fichte, Johann Gottlieb. *Addresses to the German Nation*. Translated by R.F. Jones and G.H. Turnbull. Chicago: Open Court, 1922.

Field, Geoffrey G. "Nordic Racism." *Journal of the History of Ideas* 38, no. 3 (1977): 523–40.

Fligstein, Neil, and Doug McAdam. *A Theory of Fields*. Oxford: Oxford University Press, 2012.

Fontane, Theodor. *Der Schleswig-Holsteinische Krieg im Jahre 1864*. Berlin: Decker, 1866.

Fulbrook, Mary. *Dissonant Lives: Generations and Violence through the German Dictatorships*. Oxford: Oxford University Press, 2011.

Fure, Jorunn Sem. "Heinrich Himmler som humanistisk prosjektleder." *Fortid* 2 (2007): 76–81.

Freytag, Gustav. "Das Museum für vaterländische Alterthümer in Kiel." *Die Grenzboten* 27 (1868): 158–60.

Gaddis, John Lewis. *The Landscape of History: How Historians Map the Past.* Oxford: Oxford University Press, 2002.

Gebühr, Michael. "Sind die Moorleichen 'unsere Ururgrosseltern'?" *Die Heimat* 85 (1978): 321–6.

– "Gustav Schwantes und die Ethnogenese der Germanen." Paper presented at "'Eine hervorragend nationale Wissenschaft': Arbeitsgespräch im Rahmen des Sonderforschungsbereichs 541." Freiburg, 2–3 July 1999.

– *Moorleichen in Schleswig-Holstein.* Neumünster: Wachholtz, 2002.

Glauser, Jürg, and Julia Zernack, eds. *Germanentum im* Fin de Siècle*: Wissenschaftsgeschichtliche Studien zum Werk Andreas Heuslers.* Basel: Schwabe, 2005.

Glob, P.V. *The Bog People: Iron Age Man Preserved.* Translated by Rupert Bruce-Mitford. Ithaca: Cornell University Press, 1969.

Gobrecht, Harry D. *Might in Flight: A Daily Diary of the Eighth Air Force's Hell's Angels 303rd Bombardment Group (H).* San Clemente, CA: 303rd Bombardment Group (H) Association, 1993.

Graef, Fritz. *Geschichte des Flensburger Museums nordischer Altertümer.* Neumünster: Wachholtz, 1929.

Gram-Skjoldager, Karen. "Herre i eget hus? Den danske regerings politik i Sønderjylland, 1933–1940." *Historie* 2 (2003): 299–336.

Greenway, John L. *The Golden Horns: Mythic Imagination and the Nordic Past.* Athens: University of Georgia Press, 1977.

Grey, Thomas S., ed. *The Cambridge Companion to Wagner.* Cambridge: Cambridge University Press, 2008.

Grimm, Jacob. *Deutsche Mythologie*, vol. 1. 4th ed. Göttersloh: Bertelsmann, 1876.

Grimm, Reinhold, and Jost Hermand, eds. *From the Greeks to the Greens: Images of the Simple Life*, 48–62. Madison: University of Wisconsin Press, 1989.

Grosse, Edmund. *The Golden Horns.* London: Thomas J. Wise, 1913.

Grundtvig, N.F.S. *A Grundtvig Anthology.* Edited by Niels Lyhne Jensen. Cambridge: James Clark, 1984.

Grünert, Heinz. "Von Pergamon bis Garz: Carl Schuchhardt – Begründer der prähistorischen Burgenarchäologie in Mitteleuropa." *Das Altertum* 33, no. 2 (1987): 104–13.

– *Gustaf Kossinna (1858–1931): Vom Germanisten zum Prähistoriker; Ein Wissenschaftler im Kaiserreich und in der Weimarer Republik.* Rahden: Marie Lehdorf, 2002.

Grütter, Tina. *Melancholie und Abgrund: Die Bedeutung des Gesteins bei Caspar David Friedrich; Ein Beitrag zum Symboldenken der Frühromantik.* Berlin: Dietrich Reimer, 1986.

Grønnow, Bjarne, and Jens Fog Jensen. *The Northernmost Ruins of the Globe: Eigil Knuth's Archaeological Investigations in Peary Land and Adjacent Areas of High Arctic Greenland.* Copenhagen: Museum Tusculanum, 2009.

Günther, Hans F.K. *Rassenkunde des deutschen Volkes.* Munich: Lehmann, 1922.

Haar, Ingo, and Michael Fahlbusch, eds. *German Scholars and Ethnic Cleansing, 1919–1945.* New York: Berghahn, 2004.

Habermas, Jürgen. *The Structural Transformation of the Public Sphere: An Inquiry into a Category of Bourgeois Society.* Translated by Thomas Burger and Frederick Lawrence. Cambridge, MA: MIT Press, 2000.

Hagen, Anders. "Arkeologi og politikk." *Viking* (1986): 269–78.

Halle, Uta. *"Die Externsteine sind bis auf weiteres germanisch!" Prähistorische Archäologie im Dritten Reich.* Bielefeld: Verlag für Regionalgeschichte, 2002.

Hamilakis, Yannis. *The Nation and Its Ruins: Antiquity, Archaeology, and National Imagination in Greece.* Oxford: Oxford University Press, 2007.

Handelmann, Heinrich. *Die amtlichen Ausgrabungen auf Sylt: 1870, 1871 und 1873.* Kiel: Mohr, 1873.

– *Schleswig-Holsteinisches Museum vaterländischer Alterthümer.* Kiel: Schwers'sche, 1879.

– *38. Bericht zur Alterthumskunde Schleswig-Holsteins: Zum 50 jährigen Gedächtniss der Eröffnung des Schleswig-Holsteinischen Museums vaterländischer Alterthümer zu Kiel.* Kiel: Mohr, 1882.

Handelmann, Heinrich, and Adolf Pansch. *Moorleichenfunde in Schlewsig-Holstein.* Kiel: Schwers'sche, 1873.

Handelmann, Heinrich, and Wilhelm Splieth. *Neue Mittheilungen von den Runensteinen bei Schleswig.* Kiel: Paul Toeche, 1889.

Hanke, Andrea-Katharina. *Die niedersächsische Heimatbewegung im ideologisch-politischen Kräftespiel zwischen 1920 und 1945.* Hannover: Hahnsche, 2004.

Hansen, Mogens Scott. *Sikringsstilling Nord: En tysk befæstningslinie i Sønderjylland.* Hørsholm: Miljøministeriet, Skov- og Naturstyrelsen, 1992.

Hansen, Steffen Stumann. "The Wandering Congress: The Sixth Nordic Archaeological Meeting in Denmark, 1937." *Acta Archaeologica* 74 (2003): 293–305.

Harding, Hannes. *Displaced Persons in Schleswig-Holstein, 1945–1953.* Frankfurt: Peter Lang, 1997.

Härke, Heinrich, ed. *Archaeology, Ideology, and Society: The German Experience.* Frankfurt: Peter Lang, 2000.

Haßmann, Henning, and Detlef Jantzen. "'Die deutsche Vorgeschichte – eine nationale Wissenschaft': Das Kieler Museum vorgeschichtlicher Altertümer im Dritten Reich." *Offa-Zeitschrift* 51 (1994): 9–23.

Haupt, Heinz-Gerhard, and Jürgen Kocka, eds. *Comparative and Transnational History: Central European Approaches and New Perspectives.* New York: Berghahn, 2009.

Häusler, Alexander. "Zum Ursprung der Indogermanen: Archäologische, anthropologische und sprachwissenschaftliche Gesichtspunkte." *Ethnographisch-archäologische Zeitschrift* 39 (1998): 1–46.

Heberle, Rudolf. *Landbevölkerung und Nationalsozialismus: Eine soziologische Untersuchung der politischen Willensbildung in Schleswig-Holstein 1918 bis 1932*. Stuttgart: Deutsche Verlags-Anstalt, 1963.

Heidorn, G., et al. "Zur Hochschulpolitik der Sozialistischen Einheitspartei Deutschlands, 1946–1949/50: Unter besonderer Berücksichtigung der Entwicklung in Rostock." *Das Hochschulwesen* 11, nos. 9 and 11 (1963): 645–57, 803–16.

Hermand, Jost. *Old Dreams of a New Reich: Volkish Utopias and National Socialism.* Translated by Paul Levesque and Stefan Soldovieri. Bloomington: Indiana University Press, 1992.

Hettling, Manfred, ed. *Volksgeschichten im Europa der Zwischenkriegszeit.* Göttingen: Vandenhoek & Ruprecht, 2003.

Heuss, Anja. *Kunst- und Kulturgutraub: Eine vergleichende Studie zur Besatzungspolitik der Nationalsozialisten in Frankreich und der Sowjetunion.* Heidelberg: Winter, 2000.

Hicks, Carola. *The Bayeux Tapestry: The Life Story of a Masterpiece.* Londong: Chatto & Windus, 2006.

Hobsbawm, Eric, and Terence Ranger, eds. *The Invention of Tradition.* Cambridge: Cambridge University Press, 1983.

Hodder, Ian, ed. *Archaeological Theory in Europe: The Last Three Decades.* London: Routledge, 1991.

Hoffmann, Erich. "Nikolaus Falck und die Schleswig-Holsteinische Frage." *Zeitschrift der Gesellschaft für Schleswig-Holsteinische Geschichte* 111 (1986): 143–56.

Holmberg, Åke. "On the Practicability of Scandinavianism: Mid-Nineteenth-Century Debate and Aspirations." *Scandinavian Journal of History* 9, no. 3 (1984): 171–82.

Holmes, Lewis. *Kosegarten's Cultural Legacy: Aesthetics, Religion, Literature, Art, and Music.* New York: Peter Lang, 2005.

Holmes, Richard. *The Age of Wonder: How the Romantic Generation Discovered the Beauty and Terror of Science.* New York: Vintage, 2010.

Hooper-Greenhill, Eilean. *Museums and the Shaping of Knowledge.* London: Routledge, 1992.

Hutchinson, John. *The Dynamics of Cultural Nationalism.* London: Allen and Unwin, 1987.

Hutchinson, John, and Anthony D. Smith, eds. *Nationalism.* Oxford: Oxford University Press, 1994.

Impey, Oliver, and Arthur MacGregor, eds. *The Origins of Museums: The Cabinet of Curiosities in Sixteenth- and Seventeenth-Century Europe.* London: House of Stratus, 2001.

Jakubowski-Tiessen, Manfred. "Kulturpolitik im besetzten Land: Das Deutsche Wissenschaftliche Institut in Kopenhagen 1941 bis 1945." *Zeitschrift für Geschichtswissenschaft* 42 (1994): 129–37.

Jankuhn, Herbert. *Haithabu: Eine germanische Stadt der Frühzeit.* Neumünster: Wachholtz, 1938.

Jankuhn, Herbert, ed. *Jahrestagungen: Bericht über die Kieler Tagung*. Neumünster: Wachholtz, 1944.

Jarausch, Konrad H. *Students, Society, and Politics in Imperial Germany: The Rise of Academic Illiberalism*. Princeton: Princeton University Press, 1982.

– *After Hitler: Recivilizing Germans, 1945–1995*. Translated by Brandon Hunziker. Oxford: Oxford University Press, 2006.

Jarausch, Konrad H., and Michael Geyer. *Shattered Past: Reconstructing German Histories*. Princeton: Princeton University Press, 2003.

Jarausch, Konrad H., and Thomas Lindenberger, eds. *Conflicted Memories: Europeanizing Contemporary Histories*. New York: Berghahn, 2007.

Jay, Martin. "Fieldwork and Theorizing in Intellectual History: A Reply to Fritz Ringer." *Theory and Society* 19, no. 3 (1990): 311–21.

Jensen, Inger, and Jørgen Steen Jensen. "Det kongelige Nordiske Oldskriftselskabs breve 1825–1864: Dansk kulturformidling på verdensplan." *Aarbøger for nordisk Oldkyndighed og Historie* (1987): 211–75.

Jensen, Jørgen. *The Prehistory of Denmark*. London: Methuen, 1982.

– *Thomsens Museum: Historien om Nationalmuseet*. Copenhagen: Gyldendal, 1992.

Jespersen, Knud J.V. *A History of Denmark*. 2nd ed. New York: Palgrave, 2011.

Jessen-Klingenberg, Manfred. *Standpunkte zur neueren Geschichte Schleswig-Holsteins*. Malente: Schleswig-Holsteinischer Geschichtsverlag, 1998.

Johnson, Axel. *Danevirkmænd og Ejderfolk: Den grænsepolitiske opposition i Danmark, 1920–1940*. Flensburg: Studieafdeling ved Dansk Centralbibliothek for Sydslesvig, 2005.

Judson, Peter. *Guardians of the Nation: Activists on the Language Frontiers of Imperial Austria*. Cambridge, MA: Harvard University Press, 2006.

Juul, Stig. "Christian Detlef Paulsen." In Povl Engelstoft, ed., *Dansk Biografisk Leksikon*, vol. 27, 51–4. Copenhagen: J.H. Schultz, 1940.

Kaarsholm, Preben, and Jan Hultin, eds. *Inventions and Boundaries: Historical and Anthropological Approaches to the Study of Ethnicity and Nationalism*. Roskilde: International Development Studies, Roskilde University, 1994.

Kallis, Aristotle. *Fascist Ideology: Territory and Expansionism in Italy and Germany, 1922–1945*. London: Routledge, 2000.

Kaltwasser, Franz Georg. "The Common Roots of Library and Museum in the Sixteenth Century: The Example of Munich." *Library History* 20, no. 3 (2004): 163–81.

Kater, Michael. *Das Ahnenerbe der SS, 1935–1945: Ein Beitrag zur Kulturpolitik des Dritten Reiches*. 2nd ed. Munich: Oldenbourg, 1997.

Kelly, Alfred. *The Descent of Darwin: The Popularization of Darwinism in Germany, 1860–1914*. Chapel Hill: University of North Carolina Press, 1981.

Kirmis, Max. *Die Urgeschichte von Neumünster: Ein Beitrag zur Kulturgeschichte Holsteins*. Neumünster: Dittmann, 1921.

Klatt, Helgo. "Heinrich Philippsen." In *Schleswig-Holstein Biographisches Lexicon*, vol. 1, 222–3. Neumünster: Wachholtz, 1970.

Klindt-Jensen, Ole. *A History of Scandinavian Archaeology*. London: Thames & Hudson, 1975.

Klose, Olaf, and Eva Rudolph, eds. *Neue Deutsche Biographie*. Neumünster: Wachholtz, 1976.

Knorr, Friedrich. *Friedhöfe der älteren Eisenzeit in Schleswig-Holstein*. Kiel: Lipsius & Fischer, 1910.

– "Schleswig und Haithabu." *Schleswig-Holsteinisches Heimatbuch* (1924): 24–31.

Koch, Julia K., and Eva-Maria Martens, eds. *Eine Dame zwischen 500 Herren: Johanna Mestorf – Werk und Wirkung*. Münster: Waxmann, 2002.

Kohl, Philip L. "Nationalism and Archaeology: On the Construction of Nations and the Reconstruction of the Remote Past." *Annual Review of Anthropology* 27 (1998): 233–46.

– "National and International Influences in Archaeology, 19th-Century Beginnings to Post-Processual Ponderings." Paper presented at the International Colloquium, "National Scholarship and Transnational Experience: Politics, Identity, and Objectivity in the Humanities and Social Sciences." Chapel Hill, NC, 2006.

Kohl, Philip L., and Clare Fawcett, eds. *Nationalism, Politics, and the Practice of Archaeology*. Cambridge: Cambridge University Press, 1995.

Kohl, Philip L., Mara Kozelsky, and Machman Ben-Yehuda, eds. *Selective Remembrances: Archaeology in the Construction, Commemoration, and Consecration of National Pasts*. Chicago: University of Chicago Press, 2007.

Koldewey, K. *Die erste Deutsche Nordpolar-Expedition im Jahre 1868*. Gotha: Justus Perthes, 1871.

Koonz, Claudia. *The Nazi Conscience*. Cambridge, MA: Harvard University Press, 2003.

Kossak, Georg. "Zur Geschichte der Urgeschichtsforschung in Schleswig-Holstein." *Christiana Albertina* 2 (1966): 51–62.

Kossinna, Gustaf. "Die indogermanisch Frage archäologisch beantwortet." *Zeitschrift für Ethnologie* 34 (1902): 161–222.

– *Die deutsche Vorgeschichte: Eine hervorragend nationale Wissenschaft*. Leipzig: Kabitzsch, 1911.

– *Die Herkunft der Germanen: Zur Methode der Siedlungsarchäologie*. 2nd ed. Leipzig: Kabitzsch, 1920 [1911].

– "Die vorgeschichtliche Ausbreitung der Germanen in Deutschland." *Zeitschrift des Vereins für Volkskunde* 6 (1896): 1–14.

– *Ursprung und Verbreitung der Germanen in Vor- und Frühgeschichtlicher Zeit*. Leipzig: Kabitzsch, 1928.

– *Wikinger und Wäringer*. Bonn: Mannus, 1930.

– *Das Weichselland: Ein Uralter Heimatboden der Germanen*. Danzig: Kafemann, 1919.

Kristiansen, Kristian. *Archaeological Formation Processes: The Representativity of Archaeological Remains from Danish Prehistory*. Copenhagen: Nationalmuseets Forlag, 1985.

– "Dansk arkæologi – fortid og fremtid." *Fortid og Nutid* 26, no. 2 (1975): 279–319.

Krzoska, Markus. *Für ein Polen on Oder und Ostsee: Zygmunt Wojciechowski (1900–1955) als Historiker und Publizist.* Osnabrück: Fibre, 2003.

Kühl, Jørgen. "Heinrich Himmler, Søren Telling, og Danevirke." *Sønderjyske Årbøger* (1999): 153–78.

– "Søren Telling und das Danewerk." *Demokratische Geschichte* 19 (2008): 23–40.

Kummer, Bernhard, *Midgards Untergang: germanische Kult und Glaube in den letzten heidnischen Jahrhunderten*. Leipzig: Pfeiffer, 1927.

– *Der nordische Mensch der Wikingerzeit.* Leipzig: A. Klein, 1937.

Künnemann, Wiebke. "Jastorf, Geschichte und Inhalt eines archäologischen Kulturbegriffs." *Die Kunde* NF 46 (1995): 61–122.

Kuusisto, Seppo. *Alfred Rosenberg in der nationalsozialistische Aussenpolitik, 1933–39*. Helsinki: SHS, 1984.

Lange, Ulrich. *Geschichte Schleswig-Holsteins: Von den Anfängen bis zur Gegenwart.* 2nd ed. Neumünster; Wachholtz, 2003.

Larsen, Henrik Gutzon. "Gudmund Hatt (1884–1960)." *Geographers: Bibliographic Studies* 28 (2009): 17–37.

Lauridsen, John T., ed. *Over stregen – Under besættelsen*. Copenhagen: Gyldendal, 2007.

Lauridsen, Peter. *Da Sønderjylland vaagnede*. 8 vols. Copenhagen: Lehmann & Stages, 1909–22.

Lehmann, Phyllis Williams, "The So-called Tomb of Philip II: A Different Interpretation." *American Journal of Archaeology* 82, no. 3 (1980): 339–53.

Leube, Achim, and Morten Hegewisch, eds. *Prähistorie und Nationalsozialismus: Die mittel- und osteuropäische Ur- und Frühgeschichtsforschung in den Jahren 1933–1945*. Heidelberg: Synchron, 2002.

Liulevicius, Vejas Gabriel. *The German Myth of the East: 1800 to the Present*. Oxford: Oxford University Press, 2009.

Lornsen, Uwe Jens. *Über das Verfassungswerk in Schleswigholstein*. Kiel: Mohr, 1830.

Lumans, Valdis O. "The Nordic Destiny: The Peculiar Role of the German Minority in Hitler's Plans and Policies for Denmark." *Scandinavian Journal of History* 15, no. 2 (1990): 101–23.

Lund, Allan A. *Germanenideologie und Nationalsozialismus: Zur Rezeption der "Germania" des Tacitus im Dritten Reich*. Heidelberg: Winter, 1995.

Lund, Hans. "Ernst Christiansen." *Dansk Biografi*, vol. 5, 206–7. Copenhagen: Schultz Forlag, 1934.

Lundborg, H., and J. Runnstrom, eds. *The Swedish Nation in Word and Picture*. Stockholm: Tullberg, 1921.

Lützhoft, Hans-Jürgen. *Der nordische Gedanke in Deutschland, 1920–1940*. Stuttgart: Klett, 1971.

Mackeprang, Mouritz. *Nord-Schleswig von 1864–1911*. Jena: Diederichs, 1912.

Mahsarski, Dirk. *Herbert Jankuhn (1905–1990): Ein deutscher Prähistoriker zwischen nationalsozialistischer Ideologie und wissenschaftlicher Objektivität*. Rahden: Verlag Marie Leidorf, 2011.

Major, Daniel. *Bevölkertes Cimbrien oder die zwischen der Ost- und Westsee gelegene Halbinsel Deutschlandes, nebst dero ersten Einwohnern und ihrer eigentlichen durch viel und grossen Umwege geschehene Ankunft*. Plön, Schmied, 1692.

Marchand, Suzanne L. *Down from Olympus: Archaeology and Philhellenism in Germany, 1750–1970*. Princeton: Princeton University Press, 1996.

Mazon, Patricia. *Gender and the Modern Research University: The Admission of Women to German Higher Education, 1865–1914*. Stanford: Stanford University Press, 2003.

Mees, Bernard. "Hitler and Germanentum." *Journal of Contemporary History* 39, no. 2 (2004): 255–70.

McIsaac, Peter. *Museums of the Mind: Germany Modernity and the Dynamics of Collecting*. University Park: Pennsylvania State University Press, 2007.

Menghin, Wilfried, and Dieter Planck, eds. *Menschen, Zeiten, Räume: Archäologie in Deutschland*. Stuttgart: Theiss, 2003.

Mestorf, Johanna. *Der archäologische Congreß in Bologna: Aufzeichnungen*. Hamburg: Meißner, 1871.

– *Die vaterländischen Alterthümer Schleswig-Holsteins: Ansprache an unsere Landesleute*. Hamburg: Meißner, 1877.

– *Urnenfriedhöfe in Schleswig-Holstein*. Hamburg: Meißner, 1886.

– *Führer durch das schleswig-holsteinische Museum vaterländischer Alterthümer*. Kiel: Schmidt & Klaunig, 1895.

Michelsen, A.J. "Nikolaus Falck." *Deutsche Allgemeine Biographie*, vol. 6, 539–43. Leipzig: Duncker & Humboldt, 1877.

Monrad, Kaspar. *The Golden Age of Danish Painting*. New York: Hudson Hills, 1993.

Mosse, George. *The Crisis of German Ideology: The Intellectual Origins of the Third Reich*. New York: Howard Fertig, 1998.

Müllenhoff, Karl. *Deutsche Altertumskunde*. 5 vols. Berlin: Weidmannsche Buchhandlung, 1883.

Müller, Jörg Jochen. *Germanistik und deutsche Nation, 1806–1848*. Stuttgart: Metzler, 2000.

Müller, Sophus. *Die nordische Bronzezeit und deren Periodentheilung*. Translated by Johanna Mestorf. Jena: Hermann Costenoble, 1878.

– *Nordische Altertumskunde nach Funde und Denkmäler aus Dänemark und Schleswig Gemeinfasslich dargestellt von Dr Sophus Müller*. Translated by Otto Jiriczek. 2 vols. Strassburg: Trübner, 1897.

Naef, Beat, ed. *Antike und Altertumswissenschaft in der Zeit von Faschismus und Nationalsozialismus*. Berlin: Verlag für Bauwesen, 1995.

Neuhaus, Johannes. *Die Frage von Nordschleswig im Lichte der neuesten vorgeschichtlichen Untersuchungen*. Jena: Diederichs, 1919.

Nietzsche, Friedrich. *Beyond Good and Evil: A Prelude to a Philosophy of the Future*. Translated by Walter Kaufmann. New York: Vintage, 1966.

Nørlund, Poul. "Nationalmuseet i de onde aar." *Nationalmuseets Arbejdsmark* (1946): 5–14.

Oakley, Stewart. *The Story of Denmark*. London: Faber & Faber, 1972.

Ohlander, Ann-Sofie. "En utmordentlig balansakt: Kvinliga forskarpionjärer i Norden." *Historisk Tidskrift* 1 (1987): 2–22.

Ostow, Robin, ed. *(Re)Visualizing National History: Museums and National Identities in Europe in the New Millennium*. Toronto: University of Toronto Press, 2008.

Paul, Gerhard. *Der Untergang 1945 in Flensburg*. Kiel: Schleswig-Holstein Landeszentrale für politische Bildung, 2012.

Paulsen, Peter. *Studien zur Wikinger Kultur: Inaugural-Dissertation zur Erlangung der Doktorwürde der Hohen Philosophischen Fakultät der CAU zu Kiel*. Kiel: Buddenbrook Dekan, 1932.

Penny, H. Glenn, and Matti Bunzl, eds. *Wordly Provincialism: German Anthropology in the Age of Empire*. Ann Arbor: University of Michigan Press, 2003.

Petersen, Carl S. "Peter Lauridsen." In Povl Engestoft, ed., *Dansk Biografisk Leksikon*, vol. 14, 153–4. Copenhagen: J.H. Schultz, 1938.

Philippsen, Heinrich. *Die Vorgeschichte von Flensburg und Umgegend: Funde aus der Stein-Bronze- und Eisenzeit von Flensburg und der weiteren Umgebung, besonders Angeln*. Flensburg: Flensburger Nachrichten, 1924.

Poulson, Bjørn, and Ulrich Schulte-Wülwer. *Idstedløven: Et national monument og dets skæbne*. Herning: Poul Kristensens, 1993.

Prange, Wolfgang, Henning Unverhau, Angela Lange, and Carsten Jahnke. *Beiträge zur schleswig-holsteinischen Geschichte: Ausgewählte Aufsätze*. Neumünster: Wachholtz. 2002.

Pridham, Geoffrey, and Jeremy Noakes. *Documents on Nazism*. New York: Viking, 1974.

Pringle, Heather. *The Master Plan: Himmler's Scholars and the Holocaust*. London: Fourth Estate, 2006.

Ratjen, Henning. *Geschichte der Universität zu Kiel*. Kiel: Schwers'schen, 1870.

Reinerth, Hans, ed. *Haus und Hof im Nordischen Raum*. 2 vols. Hamburg: Lippert, 1937.

Riese, Ingrid. "Det tyske mindretals valgkamp 1939." *Historie* 20, no. 2 (1994): 177–219.

Ringer, Fritz. "Intellectual History, the Intellectual Field, and the Sociology of Knowledge." *Theory and Society* 19, no. 3 (1990): 269–94.

Roesdahl, Else, and Preben Meulengracht Sørensen, eds. *The Waking of Agantyr: The Scandinavian Past in European Culture*. Aarhus: Aarhus University Press, 1996.

Rowley-Conwy, Peter. *From Genesis to Prehistory: The Archaeological Three Age System and Its Contested Reception in Denmark, Britain, and Ireland.* Oxford: Oxford University Press, 2007.

Runge, Johann. *Sønderjyden Christian Paulsen: Et slevigsk levendsløb.* Flensburg: Studieafdeling ved Dansk Centralbibliothek for Sydslesvig, 1981.

Rust, Alfred. *Vor 20.000 Jahren: Eiszeitliche Rentierjäger in Holstein.* Neumünster: Wachholtz, 1937.

Sagarra, Eda, and Peter Skrine. *A Companion to German Literature.* Oxford: Blackwell, 1999.

Sahlins, Peter. *Boundaries: The Making of France and Spain in the Pyrenees.* Berkeley: University of California Press, 1989.

Salmi, Hannu. *Imagined Germany: Richard Wagner's National Utopia.* New York: Peter Lang, 1999.

Sanders, Karin. *Bodies in the Bog: The Archaeological Imagination.* Chicago: University of Chicago Press, 2009.

Sawyer, Birgit, and Peter Sawyer. *Medieval Scandinavia: From Conversion to Reformation circa 800–1500.* Minneapolis: University of Minnesota Press, 1993.

Scheck, Thomas. *Denkmalpflege und Diktatur: Die Erhaltung von Bau- und Kunstdenkmälern in Schleswig-Holstein und im Deutschen Reich zur Zeit des Nationalsozialismus.* Berlin: Verlag für Bauwesen, 1995.

Scheel, Otto, and Peter Paulsen. *Quellen zur Frage Schleswig-Haithabu im Rahmen der fränkischen, sächsischen und nordischen Beziehungen.* Kiel: Mühlau, 1930.

Scherer, Wilhelm. *Karl Müllenhoff: Ein Lebensbild.* Heide: Westholsteinische Verlagsanstalt, 1991.

Schilling, Heinar. *Haithabu: Ein germanisches Troja.* Leipzig: Koehler & Amelang, 1936.

Schmidt, Ernst, ed. *Briefwechsel der Gebrüder Grimm mit nordischen Gelehrten.* Berlin: Dümmler, 1885.

Schmied, Wieland. *Caspar David Friedrich.* Translated by Russell Stockman. New York: Abrams, 1995.

Schuchhardt, Carl. *Alteuropa: Eine Vorgeschichte unseres Erdteils.* 2nd ed. Berlin: de Gruyter, 1926.

Schwantes, Gustav. "Der Urnenfriedhof bei Jastorf im Kreise Uelzen." *Jahrbuch für das Provinzialmuseum Hannover* (1904): 13–26.

– *Aus Deutschlands Urgeschichte.* 2nd ed. Leipzig: Quelle & Meyer, 1913 [1908].

– "Die Germanen." *Volk und Rasse: Vierteljahrsschrift für Deutsches Volkstum* 1 (1926): 69–84, 153–70.

– "Welches europäische Volk kann seine Ahnenreihe in die älteste Zeit zurückführen?" *Forschungen und Fortschritte* 9 (1933): 407ff.

– *Frühe Jahre eines Urgeschichtsforschers (1881–1914).* Kiel: Wachholtz, 1983.

Schwantes, Gustav, ed. *Festschrift zur Hundertjahrfeier des Museums vorgeschichtlicher Altertümer in Kiel.* Neumünster: Wachholtz, 1936.

Scott, Barbara. "Archaeology and National Identity: The Norwegian Example." *Scandinavian Studies* 68, no. 3 (1996): 321–42.

Seidilin, A. *Digte*. Copenhagen: Gyldendal, 1803.

Seigel, Jerrold. *The Idea of the Self: Thought and Experience in Western Europe since the Seventeenth Century*. Cambridge: Cambridge University Press, 2005.

Shennan, Stephan. "Trends in the Study of Later European Prehistory." *Annual Review of Anthropology* 16 (1987): 365–82.

Shennan, Stephan, ed. *Archaeological Approaches to Cultural Identity*. London: Unwin Hyman, 1989.

Siemann, Wolfram. *The German Revolution of 1848–9*. Translated by Christiane Banerji. Houndmills: Macmillan, 1998.

Sklenar, Karel. *Archaeology in Central Europe: The First 500 Years*. Translated by Iris Lewitova. New York: Leicester University Press, 1983.

Skovgaard-Petersen, Vagn. *Danmarks Historie*, vol. 5. Copenhagen: Gyldendal, 1985.

Smith, Anthony D. *The Ethnic Origins of Nations*. Oxford: Blackwell, 1986.

– *The Nation in History: Historiographical Debates about Ethnicity and Nationalism*. Hanover, NH: University Press of New England, 2000.

– *The Cultural Foundations of Nations: Hierarchy, Covenant, and Republic*. Oxford: Blackwell, 2008.

Smith, Woodruff D. *Politics and the Sciences of Culture in Germany, 1840–1920*. New York: Oxford University Press, 1991.

Smolla, Günter. "Das Kossinna-Syndrome." *Fundberichte aus Hessen* 80, no. 19 (1979/80): 1–9.

Stark, Joachim. *Haithabu-Schleswig-Danewerk: Aspekte einer Forschungsgeschichte mittelalterlicher Anlagen in Schleswig-Holstein*. Oxford: B.A.R., 1988.

Steinweis, Alan E. "Weimar Culture and the Rise of National Socialism: The Kampfbund für deutsche Kultur." *Central European History* 24, no. 4 (1991): 402–23.

Steuer, Heiko, ed. *Eine hervorragend nationale Wissenschaft: Deutsche Prähistoriker zwischen 1900 und 1995*. Berlin: de Gruyter, 2001.

Stocking, George W., Jr., ed. Volksgeist *as Method and Ethic: Essays on Boasian Ethnography and the German Anthropological Tradition*. Madison: University of Wisconsin Press, 1996.

Stommer, Rainer. *Die inszenierte Volksgemeinschaft: Die 'Thing Bewegung' im Dritten Reich*. Marburg: Jonas, 1985.

Strasser, Karl Theodor. *Wikinger und Normannen*. Hamburg: Hanseatische Verlaganstalt, 1928.

Sweet, Rosemary. *Antiquaries: The Discovery of the Past in Eighteenth-Century Britain*. London: Continuum, 2004.

Taylor, Charles. *Sources of the Self: The Making of Modern Identity*. Cambridge, MA: Harvard University Press, 1989.

Telling, Søren. *25 Aar paa Danevirke*. Holbæk: Forlaget Norden, 1965.

Thaler, Peter. *Of Mind and Matter: The Duality of National Identity in the German-Danish Borderlands*. West Lafayette, IN: Purdue University Press, 2009.

– "The Discourse of Historical Legitimization: A Comparative Examination of Southern Jutland and the Slovenian Language Area." *Nationalities Papers* 40, no. 1 (2012): 1–22.

Tooley, Terry Hunt. "Fighting without Arms: The Defense of German Interests in Schleswig, East and West Prussia, and Upper Silesia, 1918–1921." PhD dissertation, University of Virginia, 1986.

Trigger, Bruce. "Alternative Archaeologies: Nationalist, Colonialist, Imperialist." *Man* 19, no. 3 (1984): 355–70.

– *A History of Archaeological Thought*. New York: Cambridge University Press, 1989.

Undset, Ingvald. *Jernalderens Begyndelse i Nord-Europa: En Studie in sammenlignede arkæologi*. Kristiania: Cammermeyer, 1881.

Unverhau, Dagmar. *Das Danewerk 1842: Beschreibung und Aufmass*. Neumünster: Wachholtz, 1988.

– *"Hochachtungsvoll Ihrer Autorität ergebenster Gustav Schwantes": Der Briefwechsel zwischen Gustav Schwantes und Johanna Mestorf 1899 bis 1909 und seine Verwendung im Prioritätsstreit mit Friedrich Knorr*. Neumünster: Wachholtz, 2000.

Vaupell, Otto. *Kampen for Sønderjylland: Krigene 1848–1850 og 1864*. Copenhagen: Reitzel, 1888.

Vick, Brian: *Defining Germany: The 1848 Parliamentarians and National Identity*. Cambridge, MA: Harvard University Press, 2002.

Virchow, Rudolf. "Die altnordischen Schädel zu Kopenhagen." *Archiv für Anthropologie* 4 (1871): 55–91.

Volbehr, Friedrich, and Richard Weyl. *Professoren und Dozenten der Christian-Albrechts-Universität zu Kiel*. Kiel: Ferdinand Hirt, 1956.

Vollertsen, Nils. "Herbert Jankuhn, hedeby-forskningen og det tyske samfund 1934–1976." *Fortid og Nutid* 36, no. 4 (1989): 235–51.

Von Krosigk, Hildegard Gräfin Schwerin. *Gustaf Kossinna: Der Nachlaß; Versuch einer Analyse*. Neumünster: Wachholtz, 1982.

Von See, Klaus. *Freiheit und Gemeinschaft: Völkisch nationales Denken in Deutschland zwischen Französischer Revolution und Erstem Weltkrieg*. Heidelberg: Winter, 2001.

Von Soden, Kristine, and Gaby Zipfel, eds. *70 Jahre Frauenstudium*. Cologne: Paul Rugenstein, 1979.

Von Warnstedt, Friedrich. *Ueber Alterthums-Gegenstände: Eine Ansprache an das Publicum*. Kiel: Mohr, 1835.

Watson, Peter. *The German Genius: Europe's Third Renaissance, the Second Scientific Revolution, and the Twentieth Century*. New York: Harper, 2011.

Weikart, Richard. "The Origins of Social Darwinism in Germany, 1859–1895." *Journal of the History of Ideas* 54, no. 3 (1993): 469–88.

Werther, Steffen. *SS Vision und Grenzland Realität: Vom Umgang dänischer und "volksdeutscher" Nationalsozialisten in Sønderjylland mit der "großgermanischen" Ideologie der SS.* Stockholm: Acta Universitatis Stockholmiensis, 2012.

Wiell, Stine. *Flensborgsamlingen 1852–1864 og dens skæbne.* Flensburg: Studieafdeling ved Dansk Centralbibliothek for Sydslesvig, 1997.

– *Kampen om oldtiden: Nationale oldsager siden 1864.* Aabenraa: Jellings Bogtrykkeri, 2000.

Williamson, George S. *The Longing for Myth in Germany: Religion and Aesthetic Culture from Romanticism to Nietzsche.* Chicago: University of Chicago Press, 2004.

Wilson, Thomas M., and Hastings Donnan. *Border Identities: Nation and State at International Frontiers.* Cambridge: Cambridge University Press, 1998.

Worm, Ole. *Danicorum Monumentorum libri sex.* Hafniae: Moltkenius, 1643.

– *Museum Wormianum: Seu historia rerum rariorum, quam artificialium, tam domesticarum, quam exoticarum, quae Hafniae Danorum in oedibus authoris servantur.* Lugduni Batavorum: Apud Iohannem Elsevirium, 1655.

Worsaae, J.J.A. *Dänemarks Vorzeit durch Alterthümer und Grabhügel beleuchtet.* Translated by N. Bertelsen. Copenhagen: Reitzel, 1844.

– *The Primeval Antiquities of Denmark.* Translated by William J. Thoms. London: John Henry Parker, 1844.

– *Danevirke: Danskhedens gamle Grænsevold mod Syden.* Copenhagen: Reitzel, 1848.

– *Om en forhistorisk, saakaldet "tydsk" Befolkning i Danmark, med Hensyn til Nutidens politiske Bevægelser.* Copenhagen: Reitzel, 1849.

– *Om Slesvigs eller Sønderjyllands Oldtidsminder.* Copenhagen: Gyldendalske, 1865.

– *En Oldgranskers Erindringer.* Edited by Victor Hermansen. 2 vols. Copenhagen: Gyldenalske, 1934.

– *Af en Oldgranskers Breve.* Edited by Victor Hermansen. 2 vols. Copenhagen: Gyldendalske, 1938.

– *Viking Ireland: Jens Worsaae's Accounts of His Visit to Ireland, 1846–47.* Edited by David Henry. Balgavies, Angus: Pinkfoot Press, 1995.

Yahil, Leni. "National Pride and Defeat: A Comparison of Danish and German Nationalism." *Journal of Contemporary History* 26 (1991): 453–78.

Zahra, Tara. *Kidnapped Souls: National Indifference and the Battle for Children in the Bohemian Lands, 1900–1948.* Ithaca: Cornell University Press, 2008.

Zimmerman, Andrew. *Anthropology and Antihumanism in Imperial Germany.* Chicago: University of Chicago Press, 2001.

Index

German and European Studies

General Editor: Rebecca Wittmann

1. Emanuel Adler, Beverly Crawford, Federica Bicchi, and Rafaella Del Sarto, *The Convergence of Civilizations: Constructing a Mediterranean Region*
2. James Retallack, *The German Right, 1860–1920: Political Limits of the Authoritarian Imagination*
3. Silvija Jestrovic, *Theatre of Estrangement: Theory, Practice, Ideology*
4. Susan Gross Solomon, ed., *Doing Medicine Together: Germany and Russia between the Wars*
5. Laurence McFalls, ed., *Max Weber's "Objectivity" Revisited*
6. Robin Ostow, ed., *(Re)Visualizing National History: Museums and National Identities in Europe in the New Millennium*
7. David Blackbourn and James Retallack, eds., *Localism, Landscape, and the Ambiguities of Place: German-Speaking Central Europe, 1860–1930*
8. John Zilcosky, ed., *Writing Travel: The Poetics and Politics of the Modern Journey*
9. Angelica Fenner, *Race under Reconstruction in German Cinema: Robert Stemmle's Toxi*
10. Martina Kessel and Patrick Merziger, eds., *The Politics of Humour in the Twentieth Century: Inclusion, Exclusion, and Communities of Laughter*
11. Jeffrey K. Wilson, *The German Forest: Nature, Identity, and the Contestation of a National Symbol, 1871–1914*
12. David G. John, *Bennewitz, Goethe,* Faust: *German and Intercultural Stagings*
13. Jennifer Ruth Hosek, *Sun, Sex, and Socialism: Cuba in the German Imaginary*
14. Steven M. Schroeder, *To Forget All and Begin Again: Reconciliation in Occupied Germany, 1944–1954*
15. Kenneth S. Calhoon, *Affecting Grace: Theatre, Subject, and the Shakespearean Paradox in German Literature from Lessing to Kleist*
16. Martina Kolb, *Nietzsche, Freud, Benn, and the Azure Spell of Liguria*
17. Hoi-eun Kim, *Doctors of Empire: Medical and Cultural Encounters between Imperial Germany and Meiji Japan*
18. J. Laurence Hare, *Excavating Nations: Archaeology, Museums, and the German-Danish Borderlands*

www.ingramcontent.com/pod-product-compliance
Lightning Source LLC
LaVergne TN
LVHW090154080826
844660LV00013B/806/J
9781442648432